Tracing Your Ancestors
The A-Z Guide

Pauline Saul, FSG

Published by
COUNTRYSIDE BOOKS
in association with
FEDERATION OF FAMILY
HISTORY SOCIETIES (PUBLICATIONS) LTD

First published 1985
Fifth edition 1995
© Pauline Saul 1995

COUNTRYSIDE BOOKS
3 Catherine Road
Newbury, Berkshire
and
FEDERATION OF FAMILY
HISTORY SOCIETIES (PUBLICATIONS) LTD
The Benson Room,
Birmingham and Midland Institute,
Margaret Street, Birmingham B3 3BS

INTRODUCTION

No one book could possibly give the answers to all the questions which arise in family history research. It should be helpful, however, to know where to find specialist advice.

Hence the emphasis in the pages which follow is on sources of information in book form or indexes to which you can refer, and to articles in journals, many of which you should find in reference libraries. If you belong to a family history society it may have copies in its library of the journals mentioned, as most Societies have been exchanging these on a regular basis for a number of years.

You will find this a very practical reference book – its aim is to point you in the right direction in which to find help in connection with your research. As with any book of this type the problem is more to know what to omit than what to include. A number of words which are still in current usage with the same meaning e.g. common law, have been omitted and can be found in any standard dictionary. Medieval terms, and the more obscure occupations, have also been omitted as the Federation of Family History Societies has published separate books covering these subjects. I hope the omissions do not mar its usefulness. A general bibliography will be found in the alphabetical sequence of the text.

The idea for this book originated with the late F. C. Markwell and myself but its subsequent development represents the efforts of a team of people over a period of some years. It has not always been practicable or possible to include the many items or suggestions submitted by readers but nevertheless their interest is appreciated. Contributions for consideration are always welcome as are amendments and updates.

I gratefully acknowledge the many contributions, practical help and advice given by Pauline Litton especially, Susan Lumas, Brian Christmas, Jeremy Gibson, Derek Palgrave, the late Alan Reed and my colleagues at home and overseas with specialist knowledge of their particular subject or country's records and therefore best fitted to update the relevant sections of the book. I would also like to thank Col. Iain Swinnerton who supplied the listing of Units for the British Army; Shirley McKenna for her assistance in drawing the county maps; and all those who have written with suggestions and amendments for this new edition enabling me to add to the interest and accuracy of the text.

The names of authors of books and articles from which factual information has been taken are mentioned where appropriate in the text.

F. C. Markwell, better known as Fred to his many friends and colleagues, died suddenly in April 1993. Anyone who had any dealings with him never ceased to be amazed by his seemingly limitless drive, enthusiasm and knowledge of family history. If Fred couldn't inspire you about 'this ancestry business' then no-one could.

He is greatly missed by all who knew him, not least of all myself, but I consider it a privilege to have been his friend.

Pauline Saul FSG

1995

USEFUL ADDRESSES

Administrator of FFHS Mrs. Pauline Saul, The Benson Room, Birmingham and Midland Institute, Margaret Street, Birmingham B3 3BS.

Noel Currer-Briggs, 3 High Street, Sutton-in-the-Isle, Cambs CB6 2RB.

British Library Newspaper Library, Colindale Avenue, London NW9 5HE

Debrett Ancestry Research Ltd, PO Box 7, Alresford, Hampshire SO24 9EN.

Family Tree Magazine, 61 Great Whyte, Ramsey, Huntingdon, Cambridgeshire PE17 1HL.

Gale Research Co., Detroit, USA

The Genealogical Publishing Co. Inc., 1001 N. Calvert Street, Baltimore, MD 21202, USA.

General Register Offices
St Catherine's House, 10 Kingsway, London WC2B 6JP
New Register House, Edinburgh, Scotland EH1 3YT
49-55 Chichester Street, Belfast, NI BT1 4HL
8-11 Lombard Street East, Dublin 2, Republic of Ireland
Greffe, Royal Court House, St Peter Port, Guernsey (also Alderney, Herm and Sark)
States Office, Royal Square, St Helier, Jersey
Finch Road, Douglas, Isle of Man

Guildhall Library, Aldermanbury, London EC2P 2EJ

Her Majesty's Stationery Office (Government Book shops)
49 High Holborn, London WC1V 6HB (counter service)
33 Wine Street, Bristol BS1 2BQ
9-21 Princess Street, Manchester M60 8AS
258 Broad Street, Birmingham B1 2HE
71 Lothian Road, Edinburgh EH3 9AZ
16 Arthur Street, Belfast BT1 4GD
HMSO Publications Centre (mail, fax and telephone orders only), PO Box 276, London SW8 5DT. General enquiries: 0171 873 8200; telephone orders: 0171 873 9090; fax orders: 0171 873 8200

Institute of Heraldic & Genealogical Studies, Northgate, Canterbury, Kent CT1 1BA

Local History, Robert & Susan Howard, 3 Devonshire Promenade, Lenton, Nottingham NG7 2DS.

National Library of Wales, Aberystwyth, Dyfed SY23 3BU

National Maritime Museum, Greenwich, London SE10 9NF

Oriental and India Office Collections, 197 Blackfriars Road, London SE1 8NG

Phillimore & Co., Shopwyke Hall, Chichester, Sussex. PO20 6BQ

Pinhorns, Norman's Place, Calbourne, Isle of Wight PO30 4QR

Public Record Office, Ruskin Avenue, Kew, Richmond, Surrey TW9 4DU

Public Record Office, Chancery Lane, London, WC2A 1LR

Roberts Medals Ltd, 6 Titan House, Calleva Park, Aldermaston RG7 4QW.

Scottish Association of Family History Societies, Mr A.J.L. Macleod, 51/3 Mortonhall Road, Edinburgh EH9 2HN

Society of Genealogists, 14 Charterhouse Buildings, Goswell Road, London EC1M 7BA

Somerset House (Principal Probate Registry), Strand, London WC2R 1LP

NOTES FOR READERS

The body of the text is in strict alphabetical order and, to save space, the following abbreviations have been used.

AGRA	Association of Genealogists and Record Agents
BMSGH	Birmingham and Midland Society for Genealogy and Heraldry
CRO	County Record Office
DRO	Diocesan Record Office
FHS	Family History Society
FFHS	Federation of Family History Societies
FHN&D	Family History News & Digest
GRO	General Register Office
HMSO	Her Majesty's Stationery Office
IGI	International Genealogical Index
IHGS	Institute of Heraldic and Genealogical Studies
IRC	International Reply Coupon
LDS	Church of Jesus Christ of Latter-Day Saints
PRO	Public Record Office
SOG	Society of Genealogists
Gen.Mag	Genealogists' Magazine (magazine of the Society of Genealogists)
TMA	The Midland Ancestor (journal of Birmingham and Midland SGH)
FTM	Family Tree Magazine
Admon.	Administration
PCC	Prerogative Court of Canterbury
BTs	Bishops' Transcripts
PCY	Prerogative Court of York
PRs	Parish Registers
pp	pages
q.v.	'which see' (cross-referenced)
sae	stamped addressed envelope

At the end of the book is a map showing the locations of the various record repositories in Central London. (Reprinted by kind permission of the Public Record Office.) Note particularly that the PRO Chancery Lane will close during 1996; records will be transferred to a new extension at Kew. The Census Room will remain in London in a central microfilm Reading Room, the location of which is yet to be decided. See: Public Record Office.

Additional examples and illustrations are reprinted by kind permission of the following contributors, to whom we are extremely grateful: Birmingham and Midland Institute, Jeremy Gibson, Institute of Heraldic and Genealogical Studies, Ian Laidlow, Witney Lumas, National Library of Wales, Oriental and India Office Collections, Derek Palgrave, John Perkins, The Church of Jesus Christ of Latter-Day Saints.

You should be able to obtain copies of articles mentioned in the text by writing to the Secretary of the Society concerned (you may have to pay for a photocopy or for a copy of the journal). Otherwise, write to the FFHS Administrator, enclosing self-addressed, stamped envelope and two extra 2nd class stamps or 3 IRCs.

Where referred to SOG leaflets cost 20p plus postage.

With a few exceptions FFHS publications are priced below £5. Unless an item is specifically withdrawn it is rarely out of stock for more than three months. Therefore in many instances prices and editions are omitted and quoted only if they are non-FFHS publications. Please remember that prices may alter from those given at time of publication.

A comprehensive list of FFHS Publications and a list of all member societies of the FFHS, together with the names and addresses of their secretaries, is available from the Administrator (see Useful Addresses).

And above all before visiting any record repository **check before you go** that they currently hold the records you wish to view. Those few minutes beforehand could save a lot of wasted time and money.

APPENDIX I
Division of Record Groups between Kew and Chancery Lane (with addresses)

APPENDIX II
Public Record Office Leaflets series

APPENDIX III
Units of the British Army

APPENDIX IV
Chapman County Codes for England, Wales, Scotland, Ireland and Channel Islands

APPENDIX V
Maps showing Counties etc. of England, Wales, Scotland and Ireland before and after 1974

If you can't read all your books at any rate handle or, as it were, fondle them. Peer into them, let them fall open where they will, read from the first sentence that arrests the eye, set them back on the shelves with your own hands, arrange them on your own plan so that if you don't know what is in them you at least know where they are. Let them be your friends, let them at any rate be your acquaintances.

(From the Guide to Chartwell)

ABBREVIATIONS When you set out your family tree, you will find it convenient to use abbreviations. There is no absolute agreement on this, but one golden rule, avoid the use of 'b', it might be interpreted as born, baptised or buried! Here are some suggestions:

Born — bn.
Baptised — bapt. or C (christened).
Banns — B.
Both of this parish — b.o.t.p.
Of this parish — o.t.p.
Licence — (married by licence) lic.
Married — m (It is usual to put an = between husband and wife on a family tree).
Divorced — div.
Unmarried — unm. Died unmarried — d.unm.
Died without issue — d.s.p. (Latin — decessit sine prole); o.s.p.; obiit s.p.
Daughter — dau.
Son — s.

Abbreviations of Christian names often found in parish registers are given in the section on Christian names. However, you are advised not to use abbreviations for names in your own records.

Months are best abbreviated by using the first three letters.

For further reading on the subject see West Surrey FHS Research Aids No.10 *Abbreviations used by family historians*.

ABRAHAM MEN A class of pretended lunatics who wandered about England seeking alms after the dissolution of the religious houses, hence beggars.

ACCOMMODATION REGISTER It is the fate of many of us that our family history research has to be carried out at Record Offices far afield. Where this necessitates an overnight stay, you might consider consulting the Accommodation Register set up by the FFHS. It contains the names and addresses of family historians in many parts of the country who are willing to give hospitality to fellow enthusiasts at a very reasonable charge. The Accommodation Register is only available to members of FHSs; please give the name of your Society and membership number when ordering a copy.

Equally, write to the co-ordinator if you can offer accommodation to other family historians; address obtainable from the Administrator of the FFHS in exchange for sae.

ACHIEVEMENT An heraldic term: a full display of armorial bearings, including shield, crest, helm, torse and mantling, together with motto, supporters and compartment where permitted. A badge or badges may be included.

ACT BOOKS Records of Ecclesiastical Courts. Prior to 1733 they are usually written in Latin. (Useful for Wills references etc. when originals do not survive.)

ADMINISTRATION Letters of ADMON. See Intestacy.

ADMIRALTY see Royal Navy.

ADOPTION Adoption as a legal process was begun in England and Wales on 1st January 1927. Anyone 'adopted' before that date was most probably fostered and the following does not apply. (Tracing the natural parents of a fostered child, especially if there was a change of surname, is a very difficult and specialist exercise.)

Registers of adopted children commenced on that date and the indexes can be seen at St.Catherine's House (q.v.) where they are on open shelves. They give the adopted name of the child and date of adoption but not the real parentage.

There are formal procedures laid down by the Children's Acts (1975 and 1989) whereby an adopted person over the age of 18 years can exercise their right to obtain a copy of their original birth entry, assuming it was in this country. See pamphlet *Access to birth records*, obtainable from the Registrar-General, local Social Services Departments or an adoption society. A request for a copy of an original birth entry cannot be refused but must follow counselling for all those adopted before 12 November 1975. Counselling is designed to give available data about the adoption, and to emphasise some of the main personal problems and stresses consequent upon the application. See *Lost Children* by P. Toynbee, Hutchinson, 1985.

Adoption records have not survived evenly across the country, their whereabouts are described by Georgina Stafford in *Where to Find Adoption Records – a guide for counsellors*, British Agencies for Adoption and Fostering, 2nd ed. 1993, price £17.50. Copies available from BAAF, 11 Southwark Street, London SE1 1RQ. BAAF produces a range of leaflets and books on adoption.

The National Organisation for Counselling and Adoptees and their Parents (NORCAP), 3 New High Street, Headington, Oxford OX3 7AJ, will also provide help and advice. Please send sae or 2 IRCs with enquiry.

This access to birth records extends only to those who have themselves been adopted. For anyone else – their own children or other relatives – the 1958 Adoption Act permits an application to one of three Courts (the High Court, the Westminster Court or the court where the adoption was made). An application should be made to the Chief Clerk to the court concerned.

Further information is contained in the Factsheet *Tracing the Natural Parents of Adopted Persons* available from the Administrator of the FFHS in exchange for sae and an extra 1st class stamp or 3 IRCs.

With regard to adoption in Scotland, contact the Registrar General, New Register House, Princes Street, Edinburgh, EH1 3YT. Records are confidential and there may be very few available before 1945.

Adoption records date from July 1953 for the Republic of Ireland. Enquiries to Registrar General, Joyce House, 8-11 Lombard Street East, Dublin 2. For records in Northern Ireland write to General Register Office, Oxford House, 49-55 Chichester Street, Belfast BT1 4HL.

ADVOWSON Right of presenting a clergyman to a benefice.

AFFIDAVIT Written statement, confirmed by oath, to be used as judicial evidence. See Parish Registers.

AG. LAB. Enumerators' directions for the 1841 census advised 'time may be saved, by writing the following words, shortly thus, ... Ag. Lab. for Agricultural Labourer...'

AGRA see also Professional Researchers, Ireland and Scotland. You will see these letters in advertisements by professional researchers – though not in all. It denotes membership of the Association of Genealogists and Record Agents. The Association aims to maintain a high standard of integrity and efficiency amongst its members who agree to abide by a Code of Practice. A complaints procedure is also in operation. A list of members who offer professional service, together with their addresses, and areas of expertise, is available by post for £2.50 or 6 IRCs from the Joint Secretaries: AGRA, Badgers Close, Horsham, West Sussex RH12 5RU.

AGRICULTURE see Rural Life and Swing Riots.

AIR FORCE see Royal Air Force.

ALE ASSIZE An assessment to ensure that ale was of good quality. An ale-taster, usually chosen by the local inhabitants, had to report malpractices to the manorial court.

ALE DRAPER An Innkeeper.

ALEHOUSES Victuallers and alehouse keepers have had to be licensed by the Justices since the Alehouse Act of 1552. Lists of licences (Recognisances/ Certificates) granted are usually found in the Quarter Sessions records, most of which have been deposited in CROs.
See *Victuallers' Licences* by Jeremy Gibson and Judith Hunter, FFHS.

ALIAS The Master of the Rolls said in 1730 that he was 'satisfied that anyone may take upon him what surname and as many surnames as he pleases.' In 1822 Lord Chief Justice Abbot added 'A name assumed by the voluntary act of a man adopted by all who know him and by which he is constantly called, becomes as much and as effectively his name as if he had obtained an Act of Parliament to confer it upon him.'
Those statements are still pertinent if one considers entertainers (Frances Gumm was better known as Judy Garland) or a child who takes the surname of its step-father but nevertheless there is still a widely held view that there were other reasons for using an alias. One of them related to copyhold land and occurred when the mother of a family remarried, having had children by her first marriage. Quite often, if the children were very young, they could take the surname of their step-father, but in order not to lose their claim to their natural father's copyhold land, they would use both names as their surname.
Remember that the only place where the entitlement to copyhold land could be registered was in the manor courts, and without birth certificates etc. to prove descent from a particular person it was easier to continue the surname, so the alias would continue for generations and would be used very much as a hyphenated surname of today.

9

Aliases were also used on occasions (1) in cases of illegitimacy to indicate the father's name, (2) to distinguish between two possible spellings of a surname e.g. Shaw and Shore (3) when a foreign surname was Anglicised. It can also indicate Catholicism or Nonconformity where couples had married in their own chapels, not an Anglican church, and therefore the marriage was not valid in law.

Alias is often abbreviated to 'als' and quite often the mark used to indicate abbreviation makes it look like 'ats'.

ALIENS see also Immigration and Naturalization. From 1792 aliens were required to register with the Justices of the Peace, giving name, address, rank and occupation. Householders who provided lodgings for aliens had to give notice to the parish authorities and returns were sent to the Clerk of the Peace. Such records are likely to be in the CRO. Other sources of information are to be found in the PRO. For details see Section 12 − 'Immigrants to Britain', *Tracing Your Ancestors in the Public Record Office*, 4th ed. (see PRO). Price £6.95. Obtainable from the FFHS.

ALNAGER A sworn officer appointed to examine and attest the measurement and quality of woollen goods.

ALUMNI see also Universities. Alphabetical list of former students, often with genealogical details.

ANCIENT ORDER OF FORESTERS FRIENDLY SOCIETY Founded in 1833 membership not only gave security in time of sickness and death but participation in the running of the Brothers' court (branch) affairs long before most had a parliamentary vote, since the majority of members were labourers, shoemakers, carpenters, etc.

A booklet entitled *My Forebears Were ... Members of the Ancient Order of Foresters Friendly Society* by Audrey Fisk and Roger Logan can be purchased for £1.75 from the Foresters Heritage Trust, at its head office 12 College Place, Southampton SO9 1FP. Their museum is housed there also and on display are examples of early minute books and printed material.

Many of the Order's archives are now being published. Lists are available or in preparation for a number of Courts. Further details from 72 Frimley Grove, Frimley, Camberley, Surrey GU16 5JY.

ANGLICAN CHURCH The Church of England is commonly known as the Anglican Church; all English and Welsh PRs (q.v.) relate to this denomination.

Records of the Church of England: a practical guide for the Family Historian by Susan Bourne and Andrew H. Chicken is a useful summary of the various types of record available, extending beyond PRs, BTs and contents of the Parish Chest to include Records relating to the Clergy, Church Administration and finance, Church membership in central government records and the Church's role in Education. Obtainable from FTM price £3.55 inc. p&p.

ANGLO-FRENCH FAMILY HISTORY SOCIETY see France.

ANGLO-GERMAN FAMILY HISTORY SOCIETY see Germany.

ANGLO-IRISH FAMILY HISTORY SOCIETY see Ireland.

ANGLO-SCOTTISH FAMILY HISTORY SOCIETY see Scotland.

ANNUAL REGISTER This was first published in 1758 and continues to the present day. The earlier volumes contain a great deal of miscellaneous information to interest the family historian, not just names and dates galore but those snippets that we fondly refer to as 'putting flesh on the bones'. e.g. 24 May 1802. Lately, the wife of Alexander Ratcliffe, of Blackleach, in Saddleworth, three sons, baptised Abraham, Isaac and Jacob; all, with the mother, likely to do well. The mother is herself a twin, and has been before delivered of twins.

Volumes for the 20th century are perhaps more in keeping with its sub-title *A view of the history, politics and literature for the year*. Published by the Longman Group Ltd they should be available in the History Department of most larger libraries, though not always on open access. You may have to ask for them.

ANNUITY An *annuity* is defined as 'an investment of money entitling investor to series of equal annual sums' and *tontine* as 'annuity shared by subscribers to loan, the shares increasing as subscribers die till last survivor gets all, or till specified date when remaining survivors share the proceeds'.

The British State Tontine and Annuity records of the 17th and 18th centuries are in the PRO and the British Museum. They are said to be vast, disordered and dirty!

The records contain unique information about whole families, though these were largely of middle class origin. However, masters frequently took out annuities for their own benefit, running on the lives of young and healthy servants or employees, so more humble people figure in the records.

As with modern annuities it was essential to have accurate details of age, status and parentage, and to update the records with changes of status, e.g. marriage, changes of address and death. There are sometimes supporting documents such as baptismal, marriage and death certificates, wills and certificates of existence.

For further information, consult F.L. Leeson's *Guide to the Records of the British State Tontines and Life Annuities in the 17th and 18th centuries* published by the SOG in 1968. In 1987 a later list was found of survivors of the British State Tontines and Annuities earlier than those of 1730 and 1749 which were listed in the above Guide. A list printed in 1764 is in the Library of the Institute of Historical Research, Senate House, University of London WC1E 7HU. This covers nominees not only of the first State Tontine of 1693, but also of the Life Annuitants of 1745, 1746 and 1757 who died before 4 January 1764, giving their ages and dates of death.

A photocopy of the list has been deposited in the library of the SOG and the information is also being added to the Tontine and Annuity Card Indexes now housed in the library of Debrett Ancestry Research Ltd; details of services/charges on request.

APOTHECARIES The Society of Apothecaries was founded in 1617. The majority of the society's historical records have been deposited at the Guildhall Library (q.v.). Books to help you are *Apothecaries of London* by Dr W.S.C. Copeman published in 1967 and *A Study of the English Apothecary from 1660 to 1760* by Juanita L. Burnby, published by the Wellcome Institute for the History of Medicine, 1983.

In the library of the SOG you will find a copy of a book printed in 1840 with the title *A List of Persons who have obtained Certificates as Apothecaries from 1 Aug 1815 to 31 July 1840*. Apothecaries ranked after physicians, doctors and surgeons in status.

The Pharmaceutical Society was founded in 1841; its archives are at its offices, 1 Lambeth High Street, London SE1 7JN.

APPRENTICESHIP see also Poor Law. A stamp duty was imposed on apprenticeship indentures by an Act of 1710. The records of the tax – up to 1811 – are in a series of Apprenticeship Books in the PRO. Details are given in PRO Records Information 44 entitled *Apprenticeship Records as Sources for Genealogy in the PRO*. The books give the name of the apprentice, address, name of father (until 1750), name and trade of master. Copies of many of the books are in the Library of the SOG which also has some of the original books. They have an index for the period 1710 to 1774. An index of masters has been published.

The Overseers of the Poor in each parish were responsible for apprenticing the orphans of the parish or the children of paupers. It suited the overseers to apprentice them to a master in another parish, for they would be liable to receive parish relief, if needed, in that parish. The apprenticeship records were usually kept with other parish documents, and have found their way to the CROs, if they were not previously lost or destroyed. In the towns where Guilds were established, their records often include lists of apprentices and masters. For example, the apprenticeship books of Bristol run to 23 volumes for the period 1532 to 1849.

See *Was He Apprenticed?* by Anthony J. Camp, Vol.1 No.3 FTM (Mar-Apl 1985) and *Compell'd to weep ... The Apprenticeship System* by Jim Golland, Vol.23 No.4 Gen. Mag. (Dec 1989). Promised for 1995 is *My ancestor was apprenticed: how can I find out more about him?* by Lilian Gibbens, SOG.

Child Apprentices in America from Christ's Hospital, London 1617-1778 by Peter Wilson Coldham, lists approximately 1,000 names from the registers of Christ's Hospital scholars. Details of the child are given plus father's name and occupation, name of the Master and destination in America. Published by Genealogical Publishing Co. Inc., 1990. Indexed. Price $21.50.

ARCHAEOLOGICAL SOCIETIES see also Bibliography. Do not be misled by the title. These societies were not only concerned with the far distant past. Many have published 'Transactions' and these often contain research material on families relating to quite recent times for the area they cover. Such 'Transactions' can be located in Reference Libraries and are often indexed.

ARCHDEACON He was the Bishop's deputy with jurisdiction over incumbents in his Archdeaconry. The Archdeacon's Court dealt with probate, granting of licences etc. (see Stella Colwell's *Family History Book* p.52).

ARCHITECTS If you have an ancestor who was an architect of some note read a book by H.M.Colvin entitled *Biographical Dictionary of English Architects 1660-1840*, published by John Murray, 1978. Also *Lives of British Architects* by Beresford Chancellor, Duckworth 1909 and *Short Dictionary of British Architects* by Dora Ware, George Allen & Unwin, 1967.

An account of a specific piece of research on the subject is given in *Have you Architectural Ancestors?* FTM Vol.2 No.2 (Jan-Feb 1986).

ARCHIVES see also County Record Offices, National Trust, Public Record Office, Record Offices, Royal Archives.

'The Archives' is the term used for a repository of documents and records of all kinds relating to the past. These may be official or unofficial. The Royal Commission on Historical Manuscripts, Quality House, Quality Court, Chancery Lane, London WC2A 1HP holds the National Register of Archives, which is available for public use in its search rooms; the object is to list the whereabouts of all archive material which may be of historical value. These include private collections of deeds of large or small estates, records of charity institutions, public bodies, journals, diaries, family photographs, marriage settlements, manorial records and many others.

Scotland has its own National Register of Archives (NRA(S)) based at West Register House, Charlotte Square, Edinburgh EH2 4DF. Guides to records in Scotland are produced by The Scottish Records Association.

There is a book by David Iredale entitled *Enjoying Archives* first published in 1973 by David and Charles and re-issued in 1980 by Phillimore. It is packed with information, yet is a pleasure to read. Another excellent guide is by F.G. Emmison entitled *Archives and Local History* published by Phillimore. *A Guide To English Historical Records* by Alan Macfarlane, Cambridge University Press, 1983, describes the nature of many of the records which have become our archives. *An archive is not a library* says Althea Douglas, FTM Vol.9 No.11 (Sep 1993).

British Archives ed. Janet Foster and Julia Sheppard, Macmillan, 2nd ed 1989, price £65. The price may prohibit the majority from owning one but libraries should have a copy of this comprehensive reference book. Over 1300 institutions are listed – from national and local libraries to the specialist and lesser known institutions. Indexed and cross-referenced.

ARMIGER Person entitled to bear heraldic arms.

ARMORIAL BEARINGS see also Heraldry. This is a synonym for an Achievement of Arms, or what is commonly called today a Coat of Arms, though originally this term meant just the arms borne on the coat worn over the armour itself. Armorial bearings include the arms, crest, supporters, motto etc.

Between 1793 and 1882 a tax of two guineas had to be paid for displaying arms on a carriage and one guinea if displayed in some other way. The tax was not formally abolished until 1945.

ARMOURERS AND BRAZIERS There was a London Livery Company for these trades. A brazier was a worker in brass. *An introduction to the Worshipful Company of Armourers and Braziers* by R.S. Foster-Brown gives the history of the company.

ARMY see also Chelsea Royal Hospital, Commonwealth War Graves Commission, Household Cavalry, Light Brigade, Medals, Medical Profession, Militia and Royal

Marines, Servicemen's Wills, and Oriental and India Office Collections for those who served in India.

It is a popular fallacy that it is only possible to trace a soldier ancestor if he was an Officer — this is not so. It is perfectly possible to trace an ordinary soldier but for any measure of success you must know his regiment or a campaign in which he fought. As with everything, there are exceptions to this!

Most military records are in the PRO. Only the records of men whose engagements ended before 1914 may be researched there. Next-of-kin or descendants seeking information of men who served after 1913 should write to The Ministry of Defence (CS(R)2b), Bourne Avenue, Hayes, Middlesex UB3 1RF.

The PRO has published *Army Records for Family Historians* by Simon Fowler, 2nd ed. 1993, PRO Publications, price £4.75 counter price at PRO shops, or £5.40 inc. p&p from the FFHS.

See also PRO Family Fact Sheets 2 and 3: *Tracing an Ancestor in the Army: Soldiers*, and *Tracing an Ancestor in the Army: Officers* and PRO Records Information leaflets:

(59) *British Army Records as sources for Biography and Genealogy*
(6) *Operational Records of the British Army in the First World War*
(7) *Operational Records of the British Army during the Second World War*
(61) *Operational Records of the British Army, 1660-1914*
(101) *Service Medal and Award Rolls: War of 1914-1918, WO 329*
(105) *First World War: Indexes to Medal Entitlement*
(108) *Records of Medals*
(115) *Military Maps of World War I*
(123) *Army Pension Records*

A useful descriptive index for those wishing to trace records relating to a particular campaign or action, or to do with general administration of the Army, is the *Alphabetical Guide to certain War Office and other Military Records preserved in the Public Record Office*. Most entries are to places or subjects but some relate to particularly eminent soldiers. The index for regiments may include entries of interest for family and social history.

See Civil Registration for notes on relevant indexes at St.Catherine's House for servicemen and their families. At the PRO, there are French and Belgian certificates of deaths for British soldiers who died in hospitals or elsewhere outside the immediate war zone, 1914-20, arranged by first letter of surname. For the Second World War, there are retrospective registers of deaths from enemy action in the Far East 1941-1945.

Muster Rolls and Pay Lists: these refer to soldiers on the strength: on detachment: on leave etc. They often give details of a man's pay and enable you to ascertain when a man was taken on the strength or was discharged or if he served in a particular regiment at all.

Description Books give names of recruits, age, trade, physical features, place of birth and where enlisted. They are exceedingly patchy especially for earlier years. A check list by F.L. Leeson appeared in Gen. Mag. Vol. 20 nos 5 and 6 (March and June 1981). See also SOG Leaflet No.12 *Army Muster and Description Books: a Finding Aid*.

Casualty Lists are in existence for 1809 to 1857 and give name, rank, trade, birthplace, next of kin and a copy of a will if one was made.

Records of Courts Martial 1684 to 1847 are available (see Records Information leaflet 84) as are Records of Pensioners (1735 on); the latter are at the PRO (see also Chelsea Royal Hospital).

War Office District Pension Returns, 1842-83 Class WO22. (The majority end in 1862. 1862-1882 are nearly all colonial ones; some Irish and New Zealand returns and a volume relating to pensioners who were prisoners on convict ships during the period 1862-67). These returns are arranged by the district where the pension was paid. Therefore, if you have a soldier ancestor whose regiment is unknown, but whose place of residence after discharge to pension is known, it is possible to locate him in these returns. They give details of regiment, which will lead to other War Office sources. The returns occasionally include pensions paid to the widows and children of men of the Mercantile Marine (children struck off the lists at the age of 14). See Gen. Mag. Vol. 21 No. 6 (June 1984) pp. 196-199 and Vol. 21 No. 7 (Sep 1984) p.252. Army Lists have been printed since 1740 (gap 1741-53) and list all officers with their dates of commission, promotion and regiments. In addition there is Peterkin, Johnston and Drew's *Commissioned Officers in the Medical Services of the British Army: 1660-1960* published by the Wellcome Historical Medical Library in 1968. Many reference libraries have copies of both these publications.

Military wills of small estates did not have to be proved in court, so there is no record of these unless they have survived among pension applications and casualty returns in the War Office records. If a soldier died abroad before 1858 and left assets over a certain amount, grants of probate or administration were issued in the Prerogative Court of Canterbury.

The SOG Leaflet No. 19 *Army Research — A Selected Bibliography* gives useful addresses and for a selection of further reading we recommend:

Feature Article *The British Regular Army and its records* by Capt.(Retd.) Erik A. Gray, FHN&D, Vol.8 No.2 (Sep 1991).

In Search of Army Ancestry by Gerald Hamilton-Edwards (published by Phillimore).

My Ancestor was in the British Army: How can I find out more about him? by Michael J. Watts and Christopher T. Watts, SOG, 1992 price £5.95 inc. p&p.

By the same authors see also *In Search of a Soldier Ancestor* published in Gen. Mag. Vol.19 No.4 (Dec.1977). (SOG Leaflet No.24 of the same title.)

Military periodicals are dealt with under Naval Records.

Researching soldiers who served in the Great War of 1914-1918 often presents difficulties, owing to scarcity of records. The subject is dealt with in a series of publications: *World War I Army Ancestry*; *More Sources of World War I Army Ancestry* and *Location of British Army Records: A National Directory of World War I Sources* all by Norman Holding and obtainable from the FFHS.

See also a two-part article by the same author in FTM, Vol.2 No.6 (Sep-Oct 1986) and Vol.3 No.1 (Nov 1986), *Finding The Men Who Fought in The Trenches*.

Officers Died In The Great War 1914-1919 published by J.B. Hayward & Son, The Old Rectory, Polstead, Colchester CO6 5AE, price £18 plus £2 p&p. New edition of the original 1919 classic official work. In addition 2 appendices list over 1600 new entries and a new section 'Indian Army 1914-20, commemorates over 1400 officers. The original work lists some 34,000 officers.

Next-of-Kin Memorial Plaque

Soldiers Died in The Great War 1914-1919 published by J.B. Hayward & Son. Republishing of this 80 volume work, originally published by the War Office in 1921, began in 1988. This roll of honour lists the names together with other related information of soldiers from all parts of Great Britain and from all regiments and corps of the British Army. Costs vary between £10 and £15 per volume (apart from London £28). Details of volumes from publishers (see previous publication).

(Copies of the original volumes for London are in the IWM; the majority of local libraries will have at least the volume relating to their county.)

The lists of Officers and Soldiers Died in The Great War can be consulted on microfilm at the PRO. Printed copies of F & A Cook's *The Casualty Roll for the Crimea and the South Africa Field Force Casualty List, 1899-1902* are also available.

In The Cross of Sacrifice Series there are *Officers who Died in the Service of British, Indian and East African Regiments and Corps 1914-1919* by S.D. & D.B. Jarvis and *Officers of the Commonwealth and Colonial Regiments and Corps.* Alphabetical listings. Published by Roberts Medals Ltd, price in the region of £25.

After the 1914-1918 War a Next-of-Kin Memorial Plaque with scroll was commissioned as a memento, the cost to be borne by the State. The bronze plaque is just over 4″ in diameter; as well as the design (figures of Britannia and a Lion) it bears the inscription 'He died for Freedom and Honour' and the name of the deceased. The scroll is 11″ x 7″ and carries the wording adopted plus Rank, Name and Number. (These were decided upon as the result of a competition: see *The Times* 13 August 1917, 30 January and 20 and 23 March 1918; also The *Illustrated London News* 6 April 1918.)

Some 1,150,000 plaques and scrolls were issued from 1919 onwards to the next-of-kin of those of HM Forces (Army, Navy and RFC) who fell between 4 August 1914 and 10 January 1920 for Home Establishments, Western Europe and the Dominions (but not to Indian troops) whilst the final date for other theatres of war or for those who died subsequently as a direct result of the war was 30 April 1920.

See *The Dead Man's Penny: a history of the Next of Kin memorial plaque* by Philip Dutton, IWM Review No.3, 1988.

Canada, Australia and New Zealand had a similar commemoration in the form of a silver Memorial Cross but these were issued to wives and mothers only.

These plaques are now considered something of a collector's item and can sometimes be found in antique shops though it is rare to find the set of both plaque and scroll. It is worth keeping a lookout if it is known that one was once in the possession of your family.

The Roll of Honour (Class WO 304) for the War of 1939-45 has been transferred to the PRO by the Ministry of Defence. It comprises a list of army servicemen and women who died during the War of 1939-1945 and gives details of rank, regiment, place of birth and domicile (by town, county and country) and the theatre or country where the fatal wound was sustained. The Roll of Honour, which is dated 1947, is in two parts: one part arranged by regimental code, the other by surname in alphabetical order.

A little-known source of army casualties for the Great War is an eight- volume series called *Ireland's Memorial Books 1914-18* available at the SOG. They contain names, not only Irish, of soldiers, sailors, officers and other ranks. Regimental numbers, rank and regiment are given; also where born and died.

In Scotland Rolls of Honour are maintained on public display in the Memorial of the names of Scottish casualties of the 1914-1918 and 1939-1945 wars, and in campaigns since 1945; separate rolls are kept for each branch of the services, Scottish regiments, and Scots in other than Scottish regiments. 'Scottish casualties' include all those killed while serving in Scottish regiments, and all those of Scottish birth in other regiments, corps or units.

Specific enquiries should be addressed to the Secretary, The Scottish National War Memorial, The Castle, Edinburgh EH1 2YT. The staff are unable to undertake genealogical research.

There are a number of 'exceptions to the rule' when locating Medal rolls and we recommend that you read the relevant PRO Records Information leaflets. Basically, medal rolls for Campaign and War medals (except those for the First World War which are in WO 329) are in WO 100 (on microfilm) and Gallantry and Meritorious Service medals rolls are in classes WO 32; WO 108; CO 534 and CO 445 respectively.

The standard works of reference (obtainable through reference libraries) are *Headdress Badges of the British Army* by Kipling and King, *Uniforms of the British Army* by W.Y.Carman, published by Webb and Bower, and the books, published by Blandford, written by Michael Barthorp on British Infantry and Cavalry Uniforms since 1660.

Shire Publications (q.v.) have issued in their 'Discovering' series: *Military Traditions*, *English County Regiments*, *British Military Uniforms* all by Arthur Taylor and *Military Badges and Buttons*, and *The Artillery* by R.J. Wilkinson-Latham.

Badges of the British Army 1820 to 1960 is an illustrated Reference Guide for collectors by F. Wilkinson, Arms & Armour Press, 1971.

Study of photographs and postcards of a soldier in uniform will often reveal clues about him, his regiment and whereabouts he served. *Postcards and family history* and *Messages from men at war* by Andy Brooks, FTM Vol. 3 Nos. 5 and 9 (March/July 1987) explain more about this particular aspect.

The Military Museum and Visitors' Centre, Queen's Avenue, Aldershot, Hampshire, tells of the origins and history of the home of the British Army from 1854.

It is always worth visiting the relevant Regimental Museum which will have collections of medals, photographs, diaries, letters etc. and where you may well find a reference to your ancestor. *A Guide to Military Museums* by Terence Wise, Athena Books (20 St.Mary's Road, Doncaster, S.Yorks DN1 2NP), 1986, lists all these.

In the IWM (q.v.) *Tracing Individual Service Records and Medal Citations*; they are general guides to official documents held by themselves and elsewhere. Price £3 each of particular interest might be:

15A *Army*
15E *Household Cavalry and Guards Division*
15F *Prisoners of War*

The National Army Museum is at Royal Hospital Road, Chelsea, London SW3 4HT. It now has in its collections a large number of registers for the period 1901-1960 concerning money owed in the form of back pay to soldiers who died in service. The indexed registers give details both of the soldier and in some cases next-of-kin. Details of the records can be obtained from Head of Department of Archives, Photographs, Film and Sound, address as above. Please send sae or 2 IRCs. For administrative reasons it will be some years before all the records are available; it is therefore advisable to make enquiries prior to your visit.

If you have queries about some precise points any of the following may be able to assist you:

The Arms and Armour Society, c/o The Department of Metalwork, Victoria & Albert Museum, Cromwell Rd, London SW7 2RL

The Military History Society, c/o National Army Museum.

The Society for Army Historical, Ministry of Defence Army Historical Branch & Library Service, Old War Office Building, Whitehall, London SW1A 2EU.

Director General of Personal Services (Army), (for PS4 (Cas)(A)), Ministry of Defence (Army), Room 1012, Empress State Building, Lillie Road, London SW6 1TR.

The Army Central Library is situated at the Old War Office Building, Whitehall, SW1A 2EU and is available to the public by arrangement, as is the Scottish United Services Museum Library, Edinburgh Castle, and the Corps of Royal Engineers Library, Brompton Barracks, Chatham,Kent ME4 4UG.

The Police Gazette, known as 'The Hue and Cry', lists Army deserters. Information is very detailed as to origins and personal descriptions. Copies can be found at the PRO (Ref.HO75/11).

Australia: Army Deserters from H.M. Service Vol.1 1853-1858 by Yvonne Fitzmaurice has over 800 entries compiled from material held at the PRO, Melbourne and police records. All the men at this period came from the British Isles. Comprehensive details recorded. This is the first volume in a series intended to continue to 1900. Price $A10 plus $A3 p&p from the author, 23 Fuller Street, Mitcham, Victoria 3132, Australia.

Discharged in New Zealand: Soldiers of the Imperial Foot Regiments who took their discharge in New Zealand 1840-1870. Collated by Hugh and Lyn Hughes. Published by the New Zealand Society of Genealogists, Box 8795 Symonds Street, Auckland 1035, New Zealand and obtainable from them for $NZ8.50 plus postage. If you have a soldier ancestor who did not return to the UK you may find him in this book as having taken his discharge from one of the fourteen regiments and miscellaneous units covered. Index in alphabetical order for each regiment.

Also available from the same address is a *microfiche* publication: *Imperial Regiments in New Zealand 1856, 1862 & 1864. Officers Service Records — Harts Army Lists.* — names of the officers and dates of promotions, copies from the volumes at Auckland City Library. Not indexed. 1 fiche, $NZ3.00.

The titles of the Regiments of the British Army have changed many times since the first regular units were raised in the late 1600s. It was not until 1881, when Childers completed the Cardwell reforms by amalgamating units into Regiments of two Battalions and giving them territorial and other titles, that the familiar proud names of the Victorian Wars became standard. By and large, these remained in use until after the 1914-1918 war, and as this is the period in which most family historians will be researching their military ancestry, it is those names that are given, with the original numbers and date they were raised, in Appendix III.

Regiments of The Empire: A Bibliography of their Published Histories. Compiled and published (1989) by Roger Perkins, PO Box 29, Newton Abbot, Devon TQ12 1XU. Price £24.50 inc. p&p. Illus. In addition to the 1000 regiments and 900 book titles listed the Appendices cover Rolls of Honour, battle honours etc.

The British Army has always permitted fathers and sons, brothers and other relatives to serve together in the same regiment. Although regimental muster returns do not disclose relationships between men, the existence of namesakes should alert the astute family historian to the possibility of a relationship. A young lad who enlisted for Boy Service under age 18 may often be found to have had a father serving in the same regiment.

In general if nominated as his next-of-kin, the names of a soldier's parents may be found in his discharge document, where discharge took place after 1882. Earlier references to parents as next-of-kin normally only appear in regimental casualty returns.

Although army wives have followed their husbands on service from the earliest times, mention of them in regimental records before the mid-1860s is wholly exceptional, save when named as next-of-kin in casualty returns reflecting deaths. These normally show the names of next-of-kin and his or her last known place of abode.

From 1865 muster returns may include a married roll listing those wives who had permission to accompany the regiment. Such rolls normally provide the wife's Christian names; the date on which she was placed on the married establishment; and the ages and sexes (but not names) of any children accompanying her. The places at which the regiment was stationed, as shown by the returns, are often good indications of children's birth places.

An Army Pensioners Index is being compiled. It includes all surviving records of soldiers who were in service between 1793-1854 and discharged to pension. Eventually this will be published; meanwhile details are available from Mr Jim Beckett, 34 Eastwood Avenue, Droylsden, Manchester M35 6BJ. Please enclose sae or 2 IRCs. There is no search charge but donations are appreciated.

As a final resort, if you have unsolved queries try any or all of the following:

Capt. Erik Gray, 7 Mead Court, Walton-on-the-Hill, Surrey KT20 7RN, specialises in the regimental records of officers and soldiers who have served in the British Army. Write to him for further details and charges, enclosing sae or 3 IRCs.

The chairman of the Waterloo Committee is Mr D.P. Saunders, Delancey Cottage, 18A Albion Road, St Peter's, Broadstairs, Kent CT10 2UP, who is prepared to answer reasonable requests for information about soldiers who served at Waterloo. Please enclose sae or 3 IRCs.

Military Index for Wales: stray references from all sources to military men either in Wales or with obvious Welsh connections. Details from J.B. Rowlands, 18 Marine Terrace, Aberystwyth, Dyfed SY23 2AZ.

There is now a plethora of 'Army Indexes' in existence covering a wide range of rank, regiment, time-period etc. details of which can be found in *Marriage, Census and Other Indexes for the Family Historian* by Jeremy Gibson and Elizabeth Hampson, FFHS.

In collaboration with the Army Museum's Ogilby Trust, the Friends of the Public Record Office are engaged in a massive project to index the first section of Class WO 97, up to 1854 (discharge documents of British Army soldiers). Interim print-outs will be placed on the shelves at the PRO, with additional copies at the SOG and the National Army Museum. On completion there may be fiche available, volunteers are needed to speed things up. Write to Lesley Wynne-Davies, 47 Wyndcliff Road, Charlton, London SE7 7LP for more details. See also Feature Article by her *Indexing Soldiers' Documents*, FHN&D Vol.9 No.2 (Sep 1993).

ARTISTS Books of reference which may help are:
Samuel Redgrave's *Dictionary of Artists of the English School*.
M.H.Grant's *Dictionary of British Etchers* and *Dictionary of British Sculptors*.
A Dictionary of Artists who have exhibited works in the principal London exhibitions from 1760 to 1863 compiled by Algernon Graves. There is a copy in the Library of the SOG.

ASSESSION ROLLS Under the manorial system the assessment of rents was supposed to be carried out every seven years. They were recorded in Assession Rolls which also recorded land transactions.

ASSIZE Judges from the central courts went on circuit throughout the country twice a year to hear cases at the Assizes. Records were kept by the Clerks of the Assize, and have been deposited in the PRO; their Records Information leaflet 26 *Assize Records* deals with such records, though a number of them have not survived.

Serious cases of crime were dealt with at these courts. Remember, however, that what are now viewed as comparatively trivial offences were not so regarded formerly, so many apparently minor offences will be found here. You could be hanged (or at least transported) for theft.

There is little of genealogical value about the accused in the records, except the parish of residence. More, in fact, is given about those who made depositions — names, ages and places of residence. Few details of the circumstances of the crime are given.

Copies of Assize Calendars are often found in CROs. These are lists of prisoners to be tried with a statement of the charge against them. It is possible that some more colourful details appear in newspaper reports on the Assizes.

ASSOCIATION OATH ROLLS In 1695-96 all persons in England and Wales holding public office had to sign a pledge of loyalty to the Crown. These rolls are in the PRO. See *Hearth Tax, Other Later Stuart Tax Lists and Association Oath Rolls* by Jeremy Gibson, published by the FFHS.

ASYLUM see also Hospital. An Act of 1808 gave Justices in Quarter Sessions the authority to build a county asylum for lunatics. In 1815 parish overseers had to send lists of pauper lunatics to the Clerk of the Peace to be forwarded to the Quarter Sessions.

Asylum records are often found in CROs, but only those over 100 years old relating to individual inmates may be consulted by the public. PRO hold the records of Office of Commissioners in Lunacy which should not be overlooked.

See *19th century lunatic asylum records* by Michael Weller, FTM, Vol.9 No.10 (Aug 1993), and *Lunacy and the asylum, 1750-1860: A West Midlands Perspective* by L. D. Smith. Local History Mag. 35, (Sep/Oct 1992).

ATLAS AND INDEX (THE PHILLIMORE) see Parish Maps.

ATTAINDER Forfeiture of estate following sentence of death or outlawry.

ATTORNEYS see Legal Profession.

AUGMENTATIONS Court of: Created by statute in 1535 after the dissolution of the monasteries to administer the property of religious houses and foundations dissolved. Later on it dealt with chantries and the like, paying any revenues to the Crown. It was abolished in 1554 and its functions transferred to the Exchequer. At that time an Augmentations Office was established to keep the records of the Court, the keeper being appointed by the Clerk of the Pipe. When the Clerkship was discontinued in 1833 no further keepers were appointed so the very rich collection of records was taken over by the King's Remembrancer. The collection now forms part of the Exchequer Records in the PRO (see Guide to Contents of PRO, Vol.I).

AUSTRALIA see also Convicts, Emigration, Lacemakers and Transportation.

The Society of Australian Genealogists is situated at Richmond Villa, 120 Kent Street, Observatory Hill, Sydney, NSW 2000, Australia.

Researchers commencing Australian research should begin by reading *Compiling Your Family History* by Nancy Gray ($A7.95 plus $A3 postage from the Society of Australian Genealogists) as this gives an excellent introduction to the resources available in Australia and lists many useful addresses. In particular researchers should bear in mind that, unlike England, Australia is divided into states and each is responsible for its own record-keeping. There is no national system of recording birth, death or marriage information, nor are arrivals and departures centralised. It is therefore essential to determine an accurate location before commencing research.

Tracing Your Family History in Australia: A Guide to Sources by Nick Vine Hall, 2nd ed. 1994.

Directory of Archives and Manuscript Repositories in Australia has been published by the Australian Society of Archivists, PO Box 83, O'Connor, ACT 2601, Australia. It costs $A15 plus postage.

Two articles on Anglo-Australian Genealogy by Dr Anthony Joseph appeared in Vol.20 Nos.5 & 6 of Gen. Mag. (March and June 1981). See also FTM Vol.1 Nos.1&2 (Nov-Dec/Jan-Feb 1985), Vol.2 No.4 (May-June 1986), Vol.3 No.1 (Nov 1986).

The Australian Biographical and Genealogical Record (ABGR) has published a series of surviving Musters which were taken on a regular basis to provide the government with information on both free settlers and convicts. *Musters & Lists for NSW and Norfolk Island 1800-1802* ($A36 plus postage); *Muster of NSW and Norfolk Island 1805-1806* ($A40 plus postage); *The General Muster of 1811* ($A40 plus postage); the *General Muster and Land and Stock Muster of NSW 1822* ($A52 plus postage) and the *General Return of Convicts in NSW 1837* ($A48 plus postage) are all obtainable from the Society of Australian Genealogists. The 1814 Muster is out of print and the 1825 Muster is in preparation (as at 1994).

The Bicentenary Pioneer Register 2nd ed. Vol.3 from Bicentenary Pioneer Register, PO Box 307, Spit Junction, NSW 2088, Australia. Price $A33 plus p&p. Contains genealogical details of 500 pioneers and their families who arrived in New South Wales and Van Diemen's Land 1788-1820.

Perhaps not so well known is that many emigrants had assistance with their passage from the parish under the provisions of the 1834 Poor Law (PRO Class MH 12). Effective for rather a short time 1834-c.1860 it can account for that 'missing link'. Based on this, Pat Button has compiled *Passenger Lists of Emigrants who applied for Free Passage to South Australia 1836-1840*, published by South Australian Society, 1993.

Barefoot and Pregnant? Irish Famine Orphans in Australia by Trevor McClaughlin. About 4000 Irish girls, teenagers and orphans, who emigrated to Australia 1848-50 under a scheme instigated by Earl Grey, British Secretary of State for the Colonies. An interesting story, but the second part particularly, as it is a register of the orphans, listed alphabetically, according to the ship in which they travelled, with age, home town, names of parents (where known) and religion. Further information discovered since (e.g.marriage) is also given. Published 1991 by The Genealogical Society of Victoria Inc., 5th Floor, 252 Swanston St, Melbourne, Vic 3000, Australia. Price $A25 plus p&p.

Into History, the Guide to Historical, Genealogical, Family History and Heritage Societies, Groups and Organisations in Australia by R.S. & A.F. Reid, 3rd ed. 1992, is obtainable from the authors at 1 Ian Street, North Ryde, NSW 2113 at a cost of $A32 plus postage. The Australian Society of Archivists Inc. published the *Directory of Archives in Australia*, 1992. Obtainable from them at PO Box 83, O'Connor, ACT 2601.

Specialist Indexes in Australasia, A Genealogist's Guide, compiled by Judy Webster, 1990. Over 100 specialist indexes listed, divided into four categories — Localities and Pioneer Registers; Surnames; Newspapers and other topics. Details of the contents of the index, its location or publication, whether contributions are sought or search services available obtainable from the compiler, 77 Chalfont Street, Salisbury, Qld 4107, Australia. Price in Australia inc.postage $A8, overseas $A11 or £5 sterling.

Unrelated Certificates Index: Australia, Vol.4, also by Judy Webster. Prices of the four volumes available on application. Send return postage.

As with the BMSGHs National Collection of Unrelated Certificates (Civil Registration q.v.) this Australian index lists all legible names shown on the certificates contributed to the collection. Since many give parents' names, it is estimated that 20% of the people listed would have lived all or part of their lives in England, Scotland, Wales or Ireland. Full details of the certificates are available for a small fee.

A book recommended to readers on both sides of the world — not least for the chapter on Civil Registration in England and Wales — is *Searching Overseas: A Guide to Family History Sources for Australians and New Zealanders* by Susan Pedersen. Published by Kangaroo Press, PO Box 75, Kenthurst, NSW 2156, Australia, 2nd ed. 1990. Indexed. Price $A14. 95.

This publication explains clearly both what records can be obtained by researchers in Australia and New Zealand and how to ask for information from ROs, Libraries and FHSs in the UK. The second edition includes more details of how to obtain information from countries other than the UK and an expanded section of the facilities and holdings of the Church of Jesus Christ of Latter Day Saints.

The Australian War Memorial, GPO Box 345, Canberra, ACT 2601, Australia, is the repository for official Australian Commonwealth Government archival records relating to periods when Australia was involved in wars and warlike activities. Holdings are strongest relating to the period following the establishment of the Commonwealth, ie. since 1901. Colonial records are of a miscellaneous nature, as the various state archives hold the majority of records for this pre-Federation period. The records cover all branches of the armed services, though the Army has traditionally been the most prolific in generating records.

The printed books and maps, official records, and photograph collections include material from the Sudan War to date, with many items in these collections readily available for public access through computerised database searching.

Many personnel records are included in the official records, and there are good indexes to most of these. A strength is the official unit diaries, for both World Wars. They often mention individual soldiers. The embarkation Rolls and the Nominal Rolls for members of the 1st AIF (Australian Imperial Force) who served in World War I are published in microform. The embarkation Rolls list next of kin (who are sometimes living at overseas addresses), age and occupation. The Nominal Rolls include date of enlistment, date returned to Australia, or date killed. As published material, these are widely available in other libraries. The official histories of Australia in the two World Wars mention many individuals by name and frequently give date and place of birth and occupation, together with date of death (often many years after the war).

Collections preserved by private individuals or organisations such as the Red Cross are held by the Memorial. They include letters, diaries, and photographs. Recent acquisitions cover activities involving Australians in peacekeeping, for instance in Somalia and Cambodia.

There are many items in the collections relating to places where Australians served e.g. villages in France, air bases in England, stately homes in Scotland which supplied hospitality to servicemen. Many Allied servicemen feature in collections beside their Australian colleagues; for instance photographs of Australian prisoners of war may include British or Canadian airmen in the group, in many instances with their names.

The Memorial also has collections of medals, weapons, and a fine art collection.

The Memorial will supply a list of researchers on request, as it is unable to reply to mail enquiries unless they are specific.

Opening hours of the Information Services Section (which deals with enquiries): Tuesday to Friday 9am to 4.45pm, Saturday 2pm to 4.45pm.

Background reading: *A general guide to the library collections and archives in the Australian War Memorial* by Michael Piggott, 1953 and *Roll Call: a guide to genealogical sources in the Australian War Memorial.* Both Canberra: Australian War Memorial, 1986. *The Official History of Australia in the War of 1914-1918.* Twelve volumes. Sydney: Angus and Robertson, 1928-42. *Australia in the War of 1939-1945.* Twenty-two volumes. Canberra: Australia War Memorial.

BACSA see Cemeteries in South Asia.

BADGER see also Higgler and Pedlar. An itinerant trader, usually of food. Also refers to a corn dealer or miller. The term derives from an Act of 1697 which obliged paupers to wear a capital 'P' on their clothing (a badge). Also known in various dialects as Cadger, Hawker or Huckster.

Badgers had to be licensed by the Quarter Sessions. Their names, with those of sureties, were registered, sometimes with other details, and these records are known as 'Badgers' Recognizances'.

BAILIFF He was employed by the lord of the manor to administer some of the farms and lands of the manor. The overall administration, however, was in the hands of a Steward. See the booklet *The Mediaeval Bailiff* by T.F.T. Plucknett (University of London, Athlone Press) 1954.

BAIRMAN or **BAREMAN** A pauper.

BAKERS They had a London Livery Company — see *A Short History of the Worshipful Company of Bakers of London* by Sylvia Thrupp, 1933.

BANK OF ENGLAND The Bank has an extensive archive covering every aspect of its administration from the Bank's foundation in 1649 to the present day. In addition to offering an internal information service to its various departments it also provides research facilities for people worldwide. It holds a wide range of material of interest not only to genealogists but to social, economic and business historians and biographers.

The archive is catalogued on a database which researchers are permitted to use in the search room. A set of bound lists is also available.

The archive is open 10.00am-4.30pm Monday to Friday by appointment with the Archivist, Archive Section HO-M, The Bank of England, Threadneedle Street, London EC2R 8AH. An information leaflet is available on request.

A useful reference book is *A Guide to the Historical Records of British Banking* by L.S. Pressnell and John Orbell, 1985, Gower Publishing.

See also *An Index to the Bank of England Will extracts 1807-45* , price £18.00 plus p&p, from SOG (also on microfiche).

BANKRUPTCY In bankruptcy, proceedings are taken whereby the state gains possession of the property of a debtor through an officer appointed for the purpose. Such property is realised and, subject to certain priorities, distributed amongst the persons to whom the debtor owes money or has incurred pecuniary liabilities. An Act of 1914, subsequently amended, now regulates the proceedings in bankruptcy. Most debtors were subject to legal proceedings and to imprisonment if convicted of being unwilling or unable to pay their debts. From 1543-1841 those who were traders or who owed large sums were usually exempt from the laws relating to debtors, did not suffer imprisonment but were subject to proceedings for bankruptcy. After 1861 bankruptcy proceedings were extended to all those unable or unwilling to pay their debts although imprisonment for debt continued until 1970, in certain cases.

From 1684 notices appeared in the *London Gazette* (q.v.) of official proceedings of bankruptcy. These are indexed and in print from 1690. Indexes are variable; some names appear which are not found in the official records and some names are omitted which are. There are several competitive indexes all transcribed from the *London Gazette* and some from the *Scottish Gazette*. The series produced by Messrs William Smith & Co. Printers and Publishers, covers bankrupts with their dividends and certificates for the whole country at twenty year intervals from the 1780's. Previous lists by W. Bailey commence in 1772. Collections of these volumes are held at the IHGS and can no doubt be found elsewhere e.g. Guildhall Library (q.v.).

A typical entry shows a bankruptcy of 25th July 1795, James Horton, Flax Dresser of Kidderminster. His solicitors were Bigg of Hatton Garden and Hallen of Kidderminster.

Among the court and gaol records in the PRO are some which relate particularly to debtors. See Section 46 *Tracing Your Ancestors in the PRO* 4th ed. (see PRO).

BANNS After Hardwicke's Marriage Act, 1753, all marriages from March 1754 had to be by banns or licence and a banns register had to be kept. Unfortunately they have not always been preserved by the parish.

If you are unable to locate a marriage in the Marriage Register in the parish where you believe it should have taken place, see if a Banns Register has survived. It might contain the entry you want giving the name of the parish where the marriage was to take place — remember it was more usual for this to be the bride's parish, and this would be given in the banns' entry.

BAPTISM Religious rite signifying (for Christians) admission to the Church; generally accompanied by name-giving (i.e. christening). The two words are very often used interchangeably. Children christened privately (not in church) are sometimes referred to as 'half-baptised'.

BAPTISTS The Baptists were founded by an English refugee, John Smyth, in Amsterdam in 1609. They believed in adult baptism. They split into various factions with differing beliefs — the General Baptists and Particular Baptists. The General Baptists split into the 'New Connection' and the 'Old Connection', and the latter became Unitarians. A Baptist Union in 1813 attempted to bring about co-operation between the divisions. The Particular Baptists and the New Connection united in 1891.

As with other nonconformist registers, those of the Baptists up to 1837 were deposited with the Registrar-General and are now in the PRO.

The central repository for other records of the Baptist organisation is at the Baptist Church House, 4 Southampton Row, London WC1B 4AB. The Baptist Historical Society has its offices there. The Baptist Magazine from 1809 is a useful source of information for the family historian.

See *My Ancestors were Baptists: how can I find out more about them?* by G.R. Breed, SOG, 1988; revised edition 1995.

BAR THE RECOVERY see Entail.

BARBERS see also Royal Navy. Until 1745 barbers were also surgeons. From that year surgeons had their own identity. Records of the Barbers' (or Barber-Surgeons') Company of London are deposited at the Guildhall Library (q.v.). The following are background reading: *Annals of the Barber Surgeons' Company* by Sidney Young, 1890, *The Vicary*

Lecture by R. Theodore Beck, 1969 and *The Cutting Edge: Early History of the Surgeons of London* by R. Theodore Beck, 1974.

BARGES see also Boatmen and Canals. From 1795-1871 all boats and barges exceeding 13 tons burden used on inland navigations had to be registered with the Clerk of the Peace. Such records are with the Quarter Sessions Records in CROs.

Information on the history of the sailing barge can be obtained from the Thames Barge Sailing Club, c/o National Maritime Museum, Greenwich, London SE10 9NF and the Society for Spritsail Barge Research, Hon. Sec., 21 Grasslands, Langley, Maidstone, Kent. Data is available for some specific vessels.

BARKER A tanner of leather.

BARRISTERS see Legal Profession.

BASKETMAKERS This was a thriving trade in earlier times since baskets were used for transporting most goods. There are a number of books describing this craft, one of which is Shire Publication No.92 *Baskets and Basket Making*. An account of the London livery company is given in *The Basketmakers' Company* by Bobart & Perrin.

BASTARDY see Illegitimacy; Royal Descendants.

BEADHOUSE or **BEDEHOUSE** An almshouse or workhouse.

BEADLE He was a parish or ward officer who had various duties – he summoned parishioners to attend vestry meetings, kept children in order with a cane, whipped vagrants and is generally associated with administration of the poor law.

BELGIUM Write initially to the Belgian Embassy, 103 Eaton Square, London SW1W 9AB, who will supply advice. A list of useful contact addresses can be obtained from the Administrator of the FFHS in exchange for sae plus two extra 2nd class stamps, or 3 IRCs.

BERMUDA Three books on Bermuda records were published in 1992. Two by Juniperhill Press, 41 Juniper Drive, Pembroke, HM 13, Bermuda:

The Bermuda Index 1784-1914 has details of births, marriages and deaths recorded in Bermuda newspapers; 2 vols. compiled by C.F.E. Hollis Hallet, price US$95. *Early Bermuda Records 1619-1826*, 1 vol. compiled by A.C. Hollis Hallet, price US$75. There may be copies in the library at the SOG (q.v.) or locally.

Bermuda Settlers of the 17th Century by Julia E. Mercer, is from The Genealogical Publishing Co. Inc. Genealogical notes culled from abstracts of wills, deeds, letters, colonial and parish records etc. with an index of some 5,500 names referred to therein.

See also *Genealogical Research in Bermuda*, June A.Willing, Glasgow & West of Scotland FHS, Journal No.17 (Nov 1984).

BERNAU INDEX see also Chancery Proceedings. This Index was compiled by the late Charles Bernau, one of the founders of the SOG. It forms part of the Bernau Collection along with Bernau's Notebooks and Bernau's Correspondence Volumes in the possession of Pinhorns.

Although it does not give comprehensive coverage this is a most important index, the contents of which relate mainly to 18th century Chancery Proceedings although there are many references to Apprenticeship Books. Bernau employed a team of workers to examine every document in 2,793 huge bundles and to extract all names of those involved in each case. Evidence of witnesses — often people of humble origin — was taken by Commissioners sent to the Provinces. There is often genealogical information about these witnesses. The statements are known as depositions. Depositions in the Court of the Exchequer also figure in the Index.

A detailed description of the index appears in Gen. Mag. Vol.18 No.3 (Sept.1975). See also *Using Bernau's Index* by Guy Lawton, FTM. Vol.8 Nos.2, 3, & 4 (Dec 1991-Feb 1992). For a better understanding of this valuable index it is advisable to read at least one of these articles before consulting it.

The index was microfilmed by the LDS; it can be viewed at the Library of the SOG or at any FHC of the LDS though some of it is now worn and difficult to read.

Bernau's Notebooks are on microfilm in the SOG and are separate from the Bernau Index itself. See *Using Bernau's Notebooks* by Guy Lawton, FTM, Vol.10 Nos. 2, 3 and 4 (Dec/Jan/Feb 1993/4).

Bernau's Sources is a handwritten list of miscellaneous sources in part based on his extensive searches in the records of the Court of Chancery. The list has never been published.

The original Bernau Collection is held by Pinhorns, send 5 first class stamps or 5 IRCs for a guide to the collection and details of search fees.

The late Mrs R.M. Carne, C.A. Bernau's daughter, who actually helped to compile the index, writes about her father and this enormous task in The Journal of the BMSGH, No.26 (August 1972).

BIBLIOGRAPHY References to many books and pamphlets are made under appropriate sections of *Enquire Within*. Here we deal with a short selection of books about tracing ancestry in general, followed by suggested background reading for Social History. Bibliography for Local History and tracing ancestors in Scotland and Ireland will be found under the relevant headings.

How To Tackle Your Family History FFHS pamphlet

Starting Genealogy SOG Leaflet No.9

Beginning Your Family History George Pelling, published by the FFHS. Still the FFHSs best selling publication.

Planning Research: Short Cuts in Family History Michael Gandy, 1993. A 'must' in the FFHS's *An introduction to . . .* series.

Basic Sources for Family History 1: Back to the early 1800s Andrew Todd, 3rd ed. 1994, Allen & Todd. Obtainable from the FFHS.

Tracing Your British Ancestors C.R. Chapman, Lochin Publishing, 1993. Includes information on more than just England.

Tracing Your Ancestors Anthony J. Camp, published by John Gifford 1970. A concise informative book.

In Search of Ancestry Gerald Hamilton-Edwards, reissued 1983 by Phillimore. One of the 'classics', particularly good on military sources and East India Company archives.

Discovering Your Family History Don Steel, published by the BBC in conjunction with the television series *Family History*, 1980, revised ed. 1986.

Genealogical Research in England and Wales Frank Smith & David E. Gardner. 3 volumes first published 1956 and subsequently reprinted several times. Widely available through the library lending service.

The Family Tree Detective Dr Colin Rogers, Manchester University Press, 3rd ed. 1989. Originally reviewed in FHN&D, Vol.4 No.2 (Sep 1983). Valuable for hints on solving problems encountered in research.

The Parish Chest W.E. Tate. See under Parish Chest.

Tracing Your Family Tree Stella Colwell, published by Faber and Faber Ltd, London 1984. An introductory work illustrated by examples from the author's own family and two families from her home village of Grasmere, Cumbria.

Making a Pedigree J. Unett, David & Charles, 2nd ed. 1971. This book has more emphasis on early records than most general guides.

Discovering Your Family Tree David Iredale, Shire Publications Ltd. First published 1970 and still a popular book at a reasonable price.

The Oxford Guide To Family History David Hey, Oxford University Press, 1993.

Dictionary of Genealogy by Terrick V.H. FitzHugh. Published 1985, 3rd ed. 1991. Revised edition 1994, published by A & C Black. Subtitled A guide to British ancestry research this is a quick reference work to genealogical and related terms.

Raymond Bibliographical Series by Stuart Raymond
English Genealogy: An Introductory Bibliography
British Genealogical Periodicals A Bibliography of their Contents
    Vol. 1 *Collectanea Topographica et Genealogica* with *Topographica & Genealogist*
    and *The Ancestor* (3 separate publications).
    Vol. 2 *The Genealogist:* Part 1 *Sources;* Part 2 *Family Histories*
    Vol. 3 *Miscellanea Genealogica et Heraldica:* Part 1 *Sources;* Part 2. *Families.*
    Supplement 1. *British Genealogy in Miscellaneous Journals.*
Occupational Sources for Genealogists: A Bibliography
Londoners' Occupations: a Genealogical Guide
Genealogical Bibliographies: Counties – various published, on-going.
    Published by the FFHS. This is a series listing a wide range of books and articles, arranged by various categories, with brief notes on their content. Names of authors and titles of their works are given. Its aim is to assist researchers in identifying material relevant to their research.

Practice Makes Perfect – A Genealogical Workbook, compiled by members of the FFHS Education Sub-Committee, 1993. An excellent refresher for those who have progressed beyond a basic course in family history and a useful aid for those who teach.

Trace Your Family Tree Margaret Crush, Granada Publishing Ltd, 1983. An excellent paperback for young people. Simple text, interspersed with pages rather like questionnaires, on which children can enter details of their own families. An ideal book for use in schools for project work. Also by the same author, *The Family Tree Detective Book,* Young Library Ltd, 1988, price £6.50. Delightfully illustrated, step by step story-form book to help children trace their ancestry; each chapter in the relevant time-context from the 1970's to the 1840's

The World We Have Lost Peter Laslett, Methuen, 3rd ed. 1983. This book presents the social life of pre-industrial England.

Family History and Local History in England Dr David Hey, Longman, 1987. Reviewed in FHN&D Vol.6 No.2 (Sep 1987). This book shows how the two subjects complement each other and how the one must inevitably lead to the other to produce as full a picture as possible of one's ancestors, their lives and their environment.

Local Family History in England Colin D. Rogers and John H. Smith, Manchester University Press, 1991.

The History of Myddle Richard Gough, Penguin Books, 1981. A rare biographical profile of a complete village during the 17th century.

A History of Everyday Things in England 1066 to 1968 5 volumes, Marjorie and C.H.B. Quennell, 5th volume by S.E. Ellacott. A classic text book continually in print since 1918, published by B.T. Batsford.

Larger reference libraries probably have some, if not all, of the 270 volumes of *Notes and Queries*, founded in 1849 by the antiquary W.J. Thomas and originally for 'literary men, artists, antiquaries and genealogists'. Over 10,000 families in the British Isles were mentioned and their genealogy identified. Most importantly — there is an index!

Many archaeological and local history societies publish Transactions, Occasional Papers and Lists on related topics which are of interest to the family historian. These may be available at your local library or record office but if not they should be able to supply the address of the relevant society to whom you can write for help.

You would do well to read some of the late 18th century and early 19th century novelists, from H. Fielding's *Tom Jones* on to Jane Austen, and Mrs Gaskell's *Mary Barton*. Even Dickens gives you the 'feel' of mid-19th century England though it is very sentimentalised. Many similar books are listed in *Historical Novels* by Helen Cam, Historical Association Booklet No.48, first published 1961, Routledge & Kegan Paul.

BIGAMY Defined as 'crime of going through form of marriage while previous marriage is still in existence'. Until 1858 when it became easier to obtain a divorce (q.v.) bigamy appears to have been much more common than most people imagine and, unless the offence was discovered and brought to court, it is very difficult to detect or prove. Note that after 1837, even following a conviction, no correction was made to the Registrar General's records.

See *Bigamy in 19th Century England* by Stella Colwell, Gen. Mag. Vol.19 No.7 (Sep 1978).

In ecclesiastical law, bigamy (literally meaning 'twice married') can be used of a second marriage or of a marriage to a widow or widower.

BIOGRAPHIES see also Family Histories, Peerage. *The Dictionary of National Biography* is worth consulting if you have ancestors who achieved distinction in some field. It was published quarterly in 63 volumes, beginning in 1885 and ending in 1901 – a colossal work. Only those who had died were included. The 63 volumes contain 29,000 pages dealing with approximately the same number of people. Updates published at about ten year intervals.

Modern English Biography is another major work, written by Frederick Boase and published between 1892 and 1921. It was reprinted in 1965. The six volumes contain 30,000 biographies.

Between 1898 and 1912 W.T. Pike produced *A Dictionary of Edwardian Biography*, 33 volumes each combining a guide book with an illustrated dictionary of biography covering county areas and the cities of Belfast, Birmingham, Bristol, Cork, Dublin, Durham, Edinburgh, Leicester, Liverpool, London, Manchester and Sheffield. Each contains some 500 detailed and illustrated sketches of major local figures. The number printed was very limited, and except for Bristol and Manchester the titles are in the format *Hertfordshire in the Twentieth Century: Contemporary Biographies*. (Some are catalogued under the author of the topographical section, rather than under W.T.Pike.) These volumes are quite rare and their value to the family historian is often overlooked.

A reprint of some volumes of the biographical material, with a separate cumulative index, was published by Peter Bell, Booksellers, 4 Brandon Street, Edinburgh EH3 5DX.

See *Late 19th and 20th Century Biographical Directories* by C.J. Spittal, TMA, Vol.7 No.9 (September 1985).

Most useful, too, is *Who was Who* which covers all those in *Who's Who*, first issued in 1897, who had subsequently died.

There are numerous books in Reference Libraries on the lines of *Who's Who* but specialising in a particular field such as Art, Sport, the Theatre etc.

BISHOPS' TRANSCRIPTS In theory these were copies of the parish registers sent at intervals to the Bishop. No doubt most were, but there are cases where there are such considerable differences both of spelling and dates, omissions and inclusions, that the registers and transcripts would appear to have been maintained by different persons. Because of this it is worth checking entries you have extracted from original registers with those of the transcripts and vice versa.

Bishops' Transcripts started in 1598 but few have survived from such an early date, and they rarely go beyond the mid-19th century. There are usually gaps in the sequence either because of failure to make the returns or because they have been destroyed. There are none for the 'Commonwealth Period' 1649 to 1660.

You will find them in DROs or in CROs for sometimes the latter incorporates the former. For example, Warwick Record Office is also the DRO for Diocese of Coventry.

Bishops' Transcripts and Marriage Licences, Bonds and Allegations: A guide to their Location and Indexes by Jeremy Gibson is a survey on a county by county basis of where these may be examined. It is obtainable from the FFHS.

BLAZON A verbal description of arms in armorial terminology so that they can be accurately rendered from the verbal description.

Here is the blazon of Armorial Bearings granted in 1982 to Derek Aubrey Palgrave.

Chemistry is in evidence in the arms and badge of Derek Aubrey PALGRAVE, granted in 1982.

Azure a Cross embattled and conjoined with a Bordure also embattled Argent in the Azure four Lions rampant Argent.

Wreath: Argent and Azure Mantling: Azure doubled Argent.

Crest: A bittern booming Azure beaked legged and having looped about its neck a Polyanion Chain of Phosphate Tetrahedra reflexed over the back Gold.

Motto: Contendere Semper.

For a comment on Armorial terminology see under 'Heraldry'.

BLUECOAT SCHOOLS Charity schools, often boarding, whose uniform was a blue coat of varying design. Christ's Hospital was the first, and perhaps the best known, being one of the few survivors, and the only one where the boys wear the bluecoat as part of their normal dress, as do the girls in the winter. Formerly in London, and now at Horsham, the archives are at the Guildhall Library (q.v.)

There were at least 80 other bluecoat (and various other colour coat) schools known to have existed in such cities as Bristol, Coventry, Manchester and York. Local libraries should know if there was one in their area. Birmingham and Reading have Bluecoat Schools which are now run independently.

BOARDS OF GUARDIANS The New Poor Law of 1834 established these locally elected Boards in 'Unions' of parishes to arrange and oversee the relief of the poor through the provision of 'indoor' relief in workhouses and 'outdoor' relief for those remaining in their own homes. The idea was to encourage people to work hard rather than to rely on official charity, with the result that most of the inmates were the sick, infirm and chronic unemployed who could not do so.

31

These Unions rapidly became an important unit in local government, and the Boards of Guardians were asked during the next 70 years to take on other functions. Their records therefore contain not only matters relating to the relief of the poor (until 1930, when they were abolished) including the settlement laws, but also civil registration, rating, local health (including vaccination), sanitation, school attendance, and infant life protection.

The records, in CROs and the PRO, are extremely voluminous and can provide an immense amount of detail on individuals. You might find, for example, a workhouse inmate's date and place of birth, entry to the institution, religion, addresses of relatives or friends, medical examination, diet, punishment, state of clothing and many other features. They are described and located in the Gibson Guide series *Poor Law Unions* (3 volumes split geographically and the fourth, a gazetteer), published by the FFHS.

BOATMEN see also Barges, Canals, Salters and Watermen. The term Boatmen usually refers to those who worked solely on the boats of the inland waterways. Canalmen could be working in any capacity on the canal or its bank.

Flatmen worked on 'flats' (flat-bottomed boats) usually canal boats or those used for river or coastal traffic. These were very common in the Cheshire salt trade.

There is an Inland Waterways Index of Canal and River Boatmen and Allied Trades working on inland waterways. There are presently over 15,000 references from a wide variety of sources, covering many occupations. Enquiries may be made to Mr John Roberts, 52 St Andrews Rd, Sutton Coldfield, West Midlands B75 6UH. Please send sae. Mr Roberts would also like to receive references to boatmen from census returns, registers etc.

For more general details contact:

The Archivist, British Waterways, Llanthony Warehouse, Gloucester Docks, Gloucester GL1 2EJ. (Records relating mainly to canal life and history of the boatpeople and the companies who performed the carrying trade.)

The Manager-Curator, The Canal Museum, Stoke Bruerne, Towcester, Northants NN12 7SE (formerly known as The Waterways Museum).

The Boat Museum, Dock Yard Road, Ellesmere Port, South Wirral, Cheshire L65 4EF or The Salt Museum, 162 London Road, Northwich, Cheshire CW9 8AB.

There have been many books published on canals and the lives of those who lived on them; *Canal Boatmen 1760-1914* by Harry Hanson, reprinted 1984 by Alan Sutton Publishing is just one. A further selection should be in your local library.

See also *A Floating Population: Vessel Enumeration Returns in Censuses 1851-1921* by V.C.Burton, 'Local Population Studies' No.38 (Spring 1987) and *Boatpeople – from the 17th to 19th Century* by Barrie Trinder, Gen. Mag. Vol.23 No.10 (June 1991).

BODLEIAN LIBRARY Named after Sir Thomas Bodley who refounded it in 1602 on the site of an earlier structure. It is first of all the Library of the University of Oxford and one of the six copyright libraries holding a great deal of useful material for researchers. See *The Bodleian Library and The Genealogist* by Steven Tomlinson, Gen. Mag. Vol.22 No.8 Dec 1987.

BOND OF INDEMNIFICATION This term has two meanings. It relates to the sum of money obtained from a putative father to pay for the up-keep of his child. It was also the indemnity given by people respecting potential paupers who might be allowed to settle in a parish, or servants who gained settlement because of 12 months' employment.

BOOKPLATES Many Bookplates are either armorial, dated or give the name of an Estate, which may give clues as to the whereabouts of particular individuals, their alliances (impaled Coats of Arms) or their station in life. Bookplates can also be dated from their style in the same way as silver or furniture.

The best known collection is the Franks Collection of British and American Bookplates which is in the Prints and Drawings Dept of the British Library. A catalogue of 3 volumes was published in 1903. Other collections are the Percy Collection at the National Book League, London; Marshall Collection at the Heraldry Society, London. There are further collections at the SOG, and Society of Antiquaries, London, and Dublin Castle, Eire.

The Bookplate Society, 20a Delorme Street, London W6 8DT, publishes *The Bookplate Journal* and also a quarterly Newsletter.

BOOTMAKER see Shoemaker.

BOWYER A maker and dealer in archery bows or an archer. They had their London Livery Company which was in being in 1371.

BOYD'S MARRIAGE INDEX see also Marriages. This remarkable work — the index contains about seven million names — was the work of Percival Boyd, a Fellow of the SOG, and his many typescript volumes are one of the treasures of the SOG Library. It covers the period 1538-1837, and the information comes from Parish Registers, Bishops' Transcripts and Marriage Licences. Many CROs or libraries have microfilms of the volumes covering their own counties.

The index is divided by counties — but does not cover all counties by any means. The following is a list of the counties covered by individual volumes with the number of parishes included in each:

Cambridgeshire	170	Lancashire	101
Cornwall	202	London & Middlesex	160
Cumberland	34	Norfolk	146
Derbyshire	80	Northumberland	84
Devonshire	169	Shropshire	125
Durham	72	Somerset	120
Essex	376	Suffolk	489
Gloucestershire	121	Yorkshire	206

Each county is divided into ten periods, beginning 1500-1600 and then in approximately 25 year spans to 1801-1837. In most cases the Counties are indexed under the names of the men and women separately. There is also a parallel series of miscellaneous volumes covering some parishes in other counties.

It must be stressed that this is an index only, and the parish register must be consulted for full particulars of the entry, but it does enable one to find the entry without much searching since one is given the parish and the year of marriage. It does include a number of 'strays'. When the slips for the index were made, if it was found that one of the partners of a marriage came from a county *that was not adjacent to the county in which the marriage took place*, a second slip was made for that county's index. It was felt that any competent searcher would naturally search adjacent counties, so only the references to more distant counties were thus dealt with. So if at any time you are looking at Boyd's volumes for a particular county and see another county given alongside the entry, one of the partners to the marriage was from that given county.

See *Boyd's Marriage Index* by Anthony J.Camp, FTM Vol.1 No.5 (Jul-Aug 1985). Also *A list of parishes in Boyd's Marriage Index*, 54pp, SOG.

BREWERS (or BREWSTERS) They had their London Livery Company. See *A short History of the Worshipful Company of Brewers*. See *The Local Historian's Encyclopedia* (q.v.) for Legislation relating to Brewing and Public Houses.

The history of brewing is on display at the Bass Museum, Horninglow Street, Burton-on-Trent, Staffordshire DE14 1JZ.

The records of Courage Ltd include those of nearly 80 constituent companies and can be accessed by appointment with the Company Archivist, Courage Ltd, PO Box 85, Bristol BS99 7BT. Material includes records of licensees, deeds of public houses, tenants' registers, directors' minutes, photographs and magazines.

BREWSTER SESSIONS Instituted in 1729 when local Justices granted licences to sell alcoholic liquor. Why the word 'Brewster' was used is uncertain. Its origin is feminine — Brew(v) + ster — a woman that brews. Certain women were fined for charging too much for their ale, but usually referred to as the wives of their husbands, with no mention of their own surname and often without their christian name. Fransson (Middle English Surnames of Occupation) concludes that the difference between 'Brewer' and 'Brewster' is topographical, the former being common in the South and the latter more common in the Midlands and North.

BRIDEWELL A common term for a county gaol. Later the term referred specifically to a London prison at Blackfriars.

BRITISH ASSOCIATION FOR LOCAL HISTORY (BALH) see Local History Societies.

BRITISH FAMILIES ABROAD see also Civil Registration, Deaths Overseas, Emigration and Parish Registers. Records of British families in some foreign countries have been dealt with under separate headings where relevant.

There is an excellent article by Anthony J. Camp, Director of the SOG, entitled *Records of the English Abroad* in 'Family History', the journal of the IHGS, Vol.12 Nos.91/92, New Series Nos.67/68 (August 1982). Your FHS may have a copy.

The Guildhall Library (q.v.) holds many records called 'International Memoranda' from the Bishop of London's Registry, for the 19th and early 20th centuries.

BRITISH ISLES GENEALOGICAL REGISTER A major project under the auspices of the FFHS published in 1994 and registering nearly one-third of a million surnames being researched in the British Isles by over 17,000 family historians worldwide. Initially available on microfiche only (with the odd exception). The Register for England is published in county sections, each listing surnames being researched in that county only plus names and addresses of researchers. Separate sections for Isle of Man, Isle of Wight and Channel Islands. The rest of the British Isles is published in national sections for Ireland, Scotland and Wales. Copies of the complete register are on sale or may be consulted in various record repositories and libraries both in the UK and overseas — details from the Administrator of the FFHS in exchange for sae or 2 IRCs.

BRITISH LEGION see Royal British Legion.

BRITISH LIBRARY see also Oriental and India Office Collections. The British Library was formed in 1973 from four major national institutions: the British Museum Library Departments, the National Central Library, the National Lending Library for Science and Technology and the British National Bibliography.

The British Library is not administered by the British Museum. It is directed by a Board of Management and it is organised into 3 main Divisions: Reference, Lending and Bibliographic Services. Further information and lists of British Library publications can be obtained from Press and Public Relations, The British Library, 2 Sheraton Street, London W1V 4BH. Of special interest to family historians would be Reader Guides No.6 *English Places: Sources of information*, No.8 *Family and Personal Names, a brief guide to sources of information* and No.10 *British Family History, Printed Sources in the Department of Printed Books*. These are obtainable free from The British Library Reference Division, Department of Printed Books, Gt.Russell Street, London WC1B 3DG.

BRITISH OVERSEAS see Deaths Overseas.

BRITISH RECORDS ASSOCIATION This was founded in 1932 to co-ordinate and encourage the work of individuals, authorities, societies and institutions interested in the preservation and use of records. It should not be confused with the British Record Society (a different body).

See *The British Records Association* by Oliver Harris, Archivist, FTM Vol.5 No.2 (Dec 1988) and item by the same title in FHN&D Vol.9 No.2 (Sep 1993).

The BRA published its first *Newsletter* in September 1993, announcing at the same time a new form of subscription — Associate Membership £5 pa — which will be of interest to many, especially those supporting local record offices and other special interest groups. For an information leaflet and membership application form contact the Archivist, British Records Association, 18 Padbury Court, London E2 7EH.

BRITISH RECORD SOCIETY This was founded in 1889 and in the following year took over the 'Index Library' which had commenced in 1888. Many indexes have been published, especially of Wills. These can be seen in most major Reference Libraries, at the PRO and in CROs. Further details can be obtained from The British Record Society, Stone Barn Farm, Sutherland Road, Longsdon, Stoke-on-Trent, Staffs ST9 9QD.

See also *The British Record Society — A Centenary History* by Peter Spufford, (General Editor, the Index Library) Gen. Mag. Vol.22 Nos.9 & 10 (March/June 1988).

BRITISH TELECOM (BT) see Telephone Directories.

BRODERERS They were embroiderers. For an account of the Livery Society see *A Chat about the Broderers' Company* by Christopher Holford, 1910.

BURGAGE Tenure of land in town on yearly rent.

BURGESS ROLLS see Electoral Registers

BURIAL GROUNDS see Cemeteries, Monumental Inscriptions.

BURIAL INDEXES An increasing number of these indexes are being compiled either by individuals or as a family history society project. They comprise details taken from any or all of the following sources: Parish Registers and Bishops Transcripts, Church and Cemetery records, Monumental Inscriptions and War Memorials etc. covering all periods of time. In some instances details might be checked against the entry in the relevant burial register. Format varies from the good old-fashioned card index to the computer database version or the published form either as a book or on microfiche.

See *Marriage, Census and Other Indexes for the Family Historian* by Jeremy Gibson and Elizabeth Hampson, FFHS, or contact your local family history society for details, remembering to enclose sae or 2 IRCs. There is the possibility of a National Burial Index (computer database format) but this is still at the discussion stage.

BURIALS IN WOOLLEN see Parish Registers.

BUSINESS RECORDS see Companies.

BUTCHERS see also Slaughter Houses. For an account of the London Livery Company see *The Worshipful Company of Butchers*, 1962.

CADET An heraldic term referring to the younger son or junior branch of a family.

CADGER A carrier or pedlar of small wares by means of horse and cart. The word also refers to a street seller or a beggar (from which we get the verb 'to cadge').

CALAIS see Lacemakers

CALENDAR see also Dates and Regnal Years. England continued to use the Julian calendar up to 1751 whereas the Gregorian ('New Style') calendar had been adopted on the Continent in 1582 and in Scotland in 1600.

By 1751 the Julian calendar was 11 days out of step. In that year Chesterfield's Act stated that January 1st should be the first day of the year (previously the year commenced on March 25th). Thus 1750 had commenced on March 25th 1750 and ended March 24th 1750/51. 1751 commenced March 25th 1751 and ended on December 31st 1751. 1752 commenced January 1st 1752 and ended December 31st 1752. However, 11 days of September were omitted to bring it into line with the Gregorian calendar.

Dr R.Hetherington wrote an expansive article entitled *The Calendar* which appeared in TMA Vol.6 No.3 (December 1981).

Dates and Calendars for the Genealogist by Cliff Webb, published 1994 by and obtainable from the SOG, price £2.60 inc. p&p. Concise and easy to follow, this booklet is more than adequate for the needs of the majority of family historians.

When we shorten a date e.g. 3.4.79, we mean 3rd of April 1979. However, an American would write it as 4.3.79 i.e. putting the number of the month first. This explains why we might get a letter from an American friend which appears to have been received before it was written! It is advisable to use *letters* instead of numbers to denote months.

There is another sense in which the word 'Calendar' is used by archivists to describe a summary of the contents of a group of documents such as wills or estate papers.

CALLIGRAPHY A word describing handwriting, especially beautiful handwriting. An excellent introduction to the subject is *Creative Calligraphy* by Marie Lynskey, Thorsons, 1988.

CAMBRIDGE UNIVERSITY Lists of names of graduates and some information about them appear in a publication in several volumes entitled *Alumni Cantabrigiensis*, by J. & J.A. Venn, available in most Reference Libraries.

CANADA see also Children's Societies and Emigration. *Tracing Your Ancestors in Canada* is a free booklet published by the National Archives of Canada. Their address is 395 Wellington Street, Ottawa, Ontario, Canada K1A ON3; they will answer general enquiries.

Genealogical Research in Canada by Althea Douglas, Gen. Mag. Vol.23 No.6 (June 1990) warns that 'to trace your ancestors in Canada is not to trace them in a single country. Rather, you will be dealing with ten provinces and two territories, each of whom has a different history, holds different records...' She wrote in similar vein in an article of the same title in FTM Vol.8 No.7 and 11 (May and Sept 1992); Vol.9 Nos.1 and 2 (Nov and Dec 1992).

In Search of Your Canadian Roots by Angus Baxter, Macmillan of Canada, 1990, price $16.95 promises to guide you through this province-by-province minefield of sources!

The Canadian Emigrant Index contains about 10,000 references to emigrants to Canada and Newfoundland from all parts of the British Isles (including Ireland); covering the period 1749 to 1874 it was compiled by F.L.Leeson. It now forms part of the Emigrant Check held by Debrett Ancestry Research Ltd. Details of services/charges on request.

The National Personnel Records Centre, National Archives of Canada (see above) has made accessible the records of men who emigrated from Britain to Canada between 1900 and 1914, enlisted in the Canadian Expeditionary Force in the First World War, then demobbed in Britain and stayed there. Please supply name of unit and place of enlistment, or service identification number and full name and date of death; if the enquirer is not an immediate relative then the soldier needs to have been dead 20 years.

The same information is available for those in the Royal Canadian Navy and Canadian section of the Royal Flying Corps. No charge is made for this service but please expect delay of several months.

CANALS see also Boatmen, Barges, and Watermen.

A canal is an artificial watercourse for inland navigation or irrigation. Before the railways, the extension of water transport by cutting canals was the only means of significantly improving the transportation of many goods. Initiative by local companies who responded to the needs of the industrial revolution led to the creation of a national network of canals during the period 1750 to 1815. They were nationalised in 1947. *The Local Historian's Encyclopedia* (q.v.) gives dates for completion of the more important canals.

There is a series of books on the Canals of the British Isles, the greater number of which have been written by Charles Hadfield, published by David & Charles, Newton Abbot, Devon. There is also a Shire Publication (q.v.) entitled *Discovering Canals*. The Railway and Canal Historical Society has its headquarters at 64 Grove Avenue, London W7 3ES. It should be noted that their records do not include information about individuals.

CARPENTER Records of the Carpenters' Company were published in a number of volumes by Phillimore and there is a name index. See also *Historical Account of the Worshipful Company of Carpenters* by E.B. Jupp and W.W. Pocock 1887 and *A History of the Carpenters' Company* by B.W.E. Alford and T.C. Barker, 1968.

CARTER A waggoner or a stable headman.

CASHMARIE A fish pedlar — one who took fish from the coast to the markets inland.

CATAGMAN see also Cottar. One who lived in a cottage.

CATHOLICS see Roman Catholics.

CAVALRY see Household Cavalry. Shire Publication (q.v.) No.157 in the 'Discovering' series is entitled *British Cavalry Regiments*.

CAVEAT A warning notice — lodged at the appropriate court — that a will is to be disputed.

CEMETERIES see also Commonwealth War Graves Commission, Royal British Legion and War Memorials.

Burial Grounds (as distinct from parish churchyards) were started by nonconformists in the 17th century; many more were established in the 18th century. The first public cemetery was started in 1827 in Kensal Green, London, and other towns and cities followed suit. By 1850 some churchyards were full, so the General Board of Health was required to establish cemeteries to deal with the problem.

Cemetery records are maintained by Cemetery Registrars. Often they are indexed, and some contain details of memorial inscriptions. Registers of the old nonconformist burial grounds have been deposited with the Registrar General and are at the PRO. One important example is that of Bunhill Fields, London, 1713 to 1854.

London Cemeteries: Illustrated Guide & Gazetteer by H. Meller, Avebury Publishing Company, 1981; reviewed FHN&D, Vol.4 No.1 (Spring 1983). Also *Greater London*

Cemeteries and crematoria, and their registers revised ed. 1994, SOG and *A Handlist of Nonconformist, Roman Catholic and Jewish Burial Ground Registers at the Guildhall Library.* 2nd. revised ed., 1993. £3.25 inc. p&p.

CEMETERIES IN SOUTH ASIA The British Association for Cemeteries in South Asia (BACSA) was formed in October 1976 to bring together people with a concern for the many hundreds of European cemeteries, isolated graves and monuments in South Asia.

The Association would like to receive references to memorial inscriptions found in the British Isles which relate to soldiers or civilians who served in Asia but returned to their homeland. They also have memorial inscriptions for those civilians and soldiers who died in Asia.

Further information, and a list of BACSA publications, can be obtained from the secretary, Mr T. Wilkinson, 76½ Chartfield Avenue, Putney, London SW15 6HQ. (The ½ is not a printing error!) Mr Wilkinson is also author of the book *Two Monsoons* published by Gerald Duckworth & Co., 1976, revised 2nd ed. 1987, which tells of 350 years of European influence in India in terms of epitaphs and monuments left behind in Indian cemeteries.

See also *The British Association for Cemeteries in South Asia* by John Wall, Gen. Mag. Vol.24 No.1 (Mar 1992) and *In Other Lands To Die* by Brian George, FTM Vol.4 Nos.8 & 9 (June & July 1988): an article on British graveyards in India with references to specific names on tombstones.

CENSUS see also Ireland, Scotland and Ecclesiastical Census. The first official census was taken in 1801 and thereafter every 10 years, but up to 1841 they were purely numerical — individual names were not required. However, some enumerators took it upon themselves to make up their own lists of households, and these sometimes turn up in the parish records held by CROs. See PRO Census Information leaflet 5 *Censuses of Population, 1801-1891*.

The Public Record Office holds the census returns for England, Wales, the Isle of Man and the Channel Islands for 1841, 1851, 1861, 1871, 1881 and 1891: they are open to public inspection but *on microfilm or microfiche only.*

Scottish census returns are held by the Registrar General for Scotland, New Register House, Edinburgh EH1 3YT. Those for 1841 to 1891 are open to public inspection.

Census returns for all Ireland are held by the National Archives, Four Courts, Dublin 7, Republic of Ireland. Unfortunately, few 19th century Irish census returns have survived but the Irish returns for 1901 and 1911 are fairly complete, and are open to public inspection there.

Two very useful publications are *Census Returns 1841 to 1891 on Microfilm: A Directory to Local Holdings in Great Britain, Channel Islands and the Isle of Man* by Jeremy Gibson, obtainable from the FFHS and *Census indexes in the library of the Society of Genealogists*, 1994, SOG.

It is most helpful to have these guides since you may be able to avoid having to go to the PRO Census Room, Chancery Lane, London, where conditions can be very crowded, and you may find that all the microfilm readers are in use. If you do go there, you will find very clear instructions to enable you to find the required reference numbers needed to select the reels you want. A room has been set aside for the consumption of snacks (your own), and a drinks' dispenser has been installed. See PRO Census Information

The people were counted . . .

leaflets: 1 *First visit to the Census Rooms?* and: 2 *How To Find A Census Return*. Chancery Lane will be closing during 1996 and the records will be transferred to Kew. The Census Room, however, **will remain in London** as part of the central London microfilm Reading Room. At the time of publication the location for this has not been decided.

Further reading before a visit should be PRO Readers' Guide No. 1 *Making Use of The Census* by Susan Lumas, PRO Publications, obtainable from the FFHS. Also by Susan Lumas, from the FFHS in its *An introduction to . . .* series, is *The Census Returns of England and Wales*. See also *The Censuses 1841-1881: Use and Interpretation* by Eve McLaughlin; obtainable from FTM price £1.55 inc. p & p.

The 1841 census was the first to give the names of all people in a household, but except in the case of children under 15, the age is only approximate, to the nearest 5 years below. Thus those aged 15 to 19 are recorded as 15 years of age, 20 to 24 as 20 and so on. We are given the sex, occupation, and whether born in the same county as now residing in or not (indicated by a 'Y' for 'yes' or a 'N' for 'no'). Relationships are not given. For those born in Scotland we get an 'S' and in Ireland an 'I', and 'F' is used if born in foreign parts.

The subsequent census returns are much more useful since they give the relationship to the head of the household, exact ages (as reported by the informant, so there are possibilities of inaccuracy here), occupation and — most important of all — where they were born. If born outside England or Wales, however, only the country is generally given.

It helps to locate a family in the census of a town or city if you know an address, since often there is a street index, so it is worth consulting a directory of around the census date in case your ancestor appears in it. See PRO Census Information leaflet 3 *Additional Finding Aids: Guides to Places 1841-1891, and Surname Indexes 1841-1891*.

Marriage, Census and Other Indexes for Family Historians by Jeremy Gibson and Elizabeth Hampson will give you details of indexes being compiled by family history societies, whether a complete transcript is being undertaken or simply a surname index, cost of consultation and where to apply.

The FFHS is always willing to give advice to those contemplating a project of indexing census returns. Contact the Administrator — if only to check that a transcription has not already been done for the area you have in mind! You would also benefit from reading *Census Indexing* by Susan Lumas, FTM Vol.4 No.6 (April 1988).

The British Genealogical Record Users Committee (an informal group with representatives from FFHS, SOG, IHGS, PRO and the Genealogical Society of Utah among others) have made the 1881 Census the object of a national indexing project. The census returns for England and Wales — over 26 million names — are being fully transcribed and checked — after which they will be transferred to a computer data base which will facilitate separate indexes for each county: Surname Index, Birthplace (Strays) Index, Census Place Index, Arranged as Enumerated Index. There will be listings of vessels/ships and Institutions.

The resulting data will then be made available on microfiche, both as a full transcript of the returns and as an index to them. Initially the index will be arranged by county and then by surname and given name: a format easily recognisable to those who have used the IGI. Other arrangements will also be possible and no other census will be so easily accessible. It is an ambitious project but projected completion date is around 1995 since already over 30 counties have been published and can be consulted through any family history society, LDS FHC, library or Record Office that has acquired them. See *1881 Census Indexes of England and Wales (incl. the Channel Islands and Isle of Man)*, FHN&D, Vol.8 No.1 April 1991.

When using the census it is important to remember that members of the family who were not sleeping at home on the night of the census are not recorded with their family. A missing person in a family group in any of the census returns could be explained by the fact that the person was in hospital,in prison or in service. Soldiers and sailors serving abroad would not be included in their home census; those serving in Ireland however may be shown in the Irish census. Examples of these are given in three articles entitled *Missing From Home* by Colin J. Parry, FTM Vol.3 Nos.6,7 & 12 (April/May/Oct 1987).

If you find a 'mature' family in the census (i.e. where there are a number of children) it is worth exploring other entries in the area, for other relatives or older children who may have been 'living-in' with families where they were servants, or with tradesmen or craftsmen to whom they were apprenticed.

There is a much more realistic chance of tracing back several generations when searching censuses for a rural community than there is in an urban community. However, the next best thing is to find a common ancestral link in the urban community giving a rural birthplace. Search the immediate neighbourhood for an entry of a person(s) bearing the same surname — particularly if it is an unusual one. You may be fortunate enough to locate an older relative of your ancestor (an aged parent, grandparent, uncle or brother), whose birthplace was a rural area whereas your immediate ancestor found on that census will probably yield no such clue to further research! Unusual occupations can occasionally indicate the same link between families.

The dates on which the 6 censuses were taken are as follows:

1841 (June 6th),	1851 (March 30th),
1861 (April 7th),	1871 (April 2nd),
1881 (April 3rd),	1891 (April 5th).

Though you are not yet allowed to see the census returns for 1901, the staff at St Catherine's House (q.v.) will look at these census returns, but the service is limited to giving age and place of birth only for the specific family you request; you must give an exact address for that name and prove that you have the authority of the next of kin, or are a direct descendant. There is a considerable charge (of around £20) for this service so you may need to ponder whether such expenditure is justified! No searches are made on the 1911 census because it was never entered into enumerator's books but only exists on the original householders' schedules which are not in an order that can be easily searched.

See *Censuses and Census-taking in England and Wales in the 19th Century* by Edward Higgs, Gen. Mag. Vol.22 Nos 7 & 8 (Sept and Dec 1987) and his subsequent book *Making Sense of the Census: The Manuscript Returns for England and Wales, 1801-1901*, HMSO, 1989, price £9.95 which is an important guide to the historical and administrative background of these documents and the interpretation of the information therein.

Many family historians tend to think of the census only in terms of the 1841-1891 returns. *Local Census Listings 1522-1930: Holdings in the British Isles* by Jeremy Gibson and Mervyn Medlycott, FFHS, details other inhabitants' lists and their value to demographers, family and local historians alike. See also original article *Local Census Listings* by Mervyn Medlycott, Gen. Mag. Vol.23 No.8 (Dec 1990), and *Pre-1841 Censuses & Population Listings in the British Isles* by Colin R. Chapman, Lochin Publishing 2nd ed. 1991, obtainable from FTM price £5.45 inc. p&p.

People and Places in The Victorian Census: A review and bibliography of publications based substantially on the manuscript Census Enumerators' Books, 1841-1911 by Dennis Mills and Carol Pearce. An Historical Geography Research Series Publication No.23 (Nov 1989).

CENTURY period of 100 years. Bear in mind that in the context of family history any given century covers the preceding one hundred years — the nineteenth century covers the 1800s, the eighteenth century the 1700s and so on.

CHANCERY LANE see Public Record Office (PRO).

CHANCERY PROCEEDINGS see also Bernau Index. The Court of Chancery dealt with disputes over inheritance, lands, debts etc. and the records run from the 14th to the 19th centuries. They are held by the PRO and details appear in Records Information leaflets 30 *Chancery Proceedings (Equity Suits)* and 121 *Dormant Funds in Court; also known as Estates in Chancery or Money in Chancery* .

Articles by R.E.F. Garret entitled *Chancery and other Legal Proceedings* appeared in Gen. Mag. Vol.15 Nos.3 & 4 (Sep & Dec 1965). In Vol.18 No.3 (Sep 1975) of the same magazine there is an article by M.H. Hughes entitled *Notes on some finding aids to Chancery Proceedings in the library of the Society of Genealogists*.

Calendars of Chancery Proceedings up to the end of the reign of Elizabeth I have been published by HMSO and contain very many names. You can consult them in most large Reference Libraries.

The four volumes to the Index Society's *Calendar of Chancery Proceedings of the time of Charles I (1625-1649)* have been indexed by Mr Peter Coldham, 16 Foxley Hill Road, Purley, Surrey, CR2 2HB. He is prepared to make a limited search of the index for a nominal fee. Alternatively for those with access to the PRO, a bound copy should be on open shelves.

CHANGE OF NAME see Deed Poll.

CHANNEL ISLANDS Civil Registration began in Jersey in 1842 and in Guernsey in 1840. Official censuses were taken on a 10-year basis from 1841 onwards. Both Jersey and Guernsey have good library facilities in the form of their public libraries and those of Societe Jersiaise, 9 Pier Road, St Helier, Jersey and Societe Guerniaise, Candie, St Peter Port, Guernsey. Guernsey also has records for the other smaller Channel Islands.

A Biographical Dictionary of Jersey by G.R. Balleine contains details of 300 inhabitants who have achieved some distinction. An article by L.R.Burness entitled *Genealogical Research in the Channel Islands* appeared in Gen. Mag. Vol.19 No.5 (March 1978).

Family History in Jersey by Marie-Louise Backhurst, published by the Channel Islands FHS, 1992. Obtainable from Alex Glendinning, Little Eden, Maison St Louis, St Saviour, Jersey JE2 7LX, price £4.75 inc.p&p.

CHAPMAN A pedlar and dealer in small wares.

CHAPMAN COUNTY CODES When the English Place Name Society was established in 1923 a series of abbreviations was produced for the English counties in existence at that time. Many of these consisted of only one letter, some of two and a few of three letters. In 1973 the SOG extended this system to cover the other counties in the British Isles and published a list of abbreviations in Gen. Mag. Vol.17 No.6 (June 1973).

The Post Office and other authorities over the years have been using other standards for abbreviating county names. With the creation of new counties and the amalgamation of others in 1974 the accepted, if not acceptable, contractions multiplied. The FFHS, founded in 1974, not only brought together many individuals and groups all frequently having cause to mention county names within the British Isles but also created interest among many thousands of other people all requiring to abbreviate a county name, and each appearing to choose a different system.

The advent of computers and the desirability of standardisation, to enable coding of computer programs to be effected with the least confusion, led those working on such projects to devise a Three Letter Coded System for each of the counties within the British Isles. Wherever possible the systems proposed and used by the English Place Name Society and the SOG were retained within the present system; where necessary, these systems have had the abbreviations extended to three letters. This has not always produced the most logical abbreviation if the three letters chosen were already allocated by a previous system to another county, and in two cases the Utopian idea was impossible. For example, Co, the 1923 abbreviation for Cornwall, would logically be extended to Cor, but as this had been allocated in 1973 to Cork, the code of Con was chosen; Sx, now being Ssx for Sussex and IOW in place of Wt for the Isle of Wight (to bring it into line with the Isle of Man) are exceptions to the general rule used to derive the present coded system for the counties within the British Isles. As the post-1974 counties have also been included for completeness, and to obviate divergent applications in decades to come, other anticipated abbreviations could not be introduced; for example Cumberland, originally Cu, had to become Cul to prevent confusion with Cumbria which (post-1974) is abbreviated to Cma.

Colin Chapman, a Vice-President of the FFHS, was responsible for introducing the present County Codes when computerising some work on records. Over a period of time they have become generally known as the Chapman County Codes. With minor modifications (i.e. codes in current use ending in I or O have been altered to meet post office requests) this system has now been incorporated into the British Standard Specification *Codes for the representation of names of counties and similar areas* (BS 6879:1987). Obtainable from BSI, 2 Park Street, London W1A 2BS.

See Appendix IV for a full listing, also *Marriage, Census and Other Indexes for Family Historians* by Jeremy Gibson and Beth Hampson. They were also published in Vol.2 No.4 (Autumn 1980) of FHN&D and the *Genealogical Research Directory: National & International* lists not only the codes for the UK but those for a number of overseas countries too.

CHAPTER An ecclesiastical term meaning the full members of a monastic order or a meeting of the canons of a cathedral, the latter the most common in family history terms. The official who presided was the Dean.

CHARITIES Details of accounts etc had to be sent to Parliament by the Clerk of the Peace from 1786. Account books and other records of local charities often record in detail the charities dispensed with the names of the recipients; these are usually to be found in CROs. Charity Commissioners were appointed to examine and supervise the way charities were run, and they issued reports. These can be examined in the larger Reference Libraries. Documents in the keeping of the Charity Commissioners are open to inspection at their headquarters in St Alban's House, 57/60 Haymarket, London SW1Y 4QX. They may charge for supplying copies of records. Educational charities were removed from the Commission's control after 1899. See article by Brian Christmas on the Charity Commission, in Vol.2 No.3 (Summer 1985), *Journal of the Guild of One-Name Studies.*

CHATHAM CHEST A fund established about 1590 to relieve sailors hurt or wounded in service. It was maintained by regular deductions from the wages of all seamen in the Navy, and administered by a corporation of Officers stationed at Chatham, but within the jurisdiction of the Navy Board. In 1803 it came within the ambit of Greenwich Hospital, being known as 'the Chest at Greenwich'. The records include indexes of pensioners, records of payments made to them and other personal details relating in the main to the 17th and 18th centuries (see Guide to Contents of PRO, Vol.II). They are at the PRO.

CHECK BEFORE YOU GO! It is advisable to write or telephone any record repository you intend to visit to confirm that they *currently* hold the records you wish to view and can accommodate you on the date you wish to visit. With projected Local Government reorganisation, future changes at the PRO and the increasing use of microfilm, many records may have been transferred or be temporarily unavailable. A few minutes beforehand could save you a wasted visit.

CHELSEA, ROYAL HOSPITAL This is a home for army pensioners. There are records of baptisms (1691 to 1812), marriages (1691 to 1765) and burials (1692 to 1856) with the Registrar General. Records over 30 years old have been transferred to the PRO. Old soldiers who could not be accommodated were known as 'Out - Pensioners'.

By 1792 there were over 20,000 pensioners. As the Commissioners of the Royal Hospital were responsible for the payment of army pensions up to 1955, the term 'Chelsea Pensioner' tended to be used for all who received pensions from the Commissioners. An Army Pensioners Index is being compiled. It includes all surviving records of soldiers who were in service between 1793-1854 and discharged to pension. Eventually this will be published; meanwhile details are available from Mr Jim Beckett, 34 Eastwood Avenue, Droylsden, Manchester M35 6BJ. Please enclose sae or 2 IRCs. There is no search charge but donations are appreciated.

For those who would like to know more about the 'pensioners' and their home there is a book entitled *The Royal Hospital, Chelsea* by Captain C.G.T. Dean, MBE, published by Hutchinson & Co.Ltd., 1950. Probably out of print now but perhaps available at your local library.

CHEMISTS AND DRUGGISTS In 1893 Kelly's Directories published a Directory of Chemists and Druggists of England, Scotland and Wales and most principal towns in Ireland.

CHILDREN'S SOCIETIES

(Dr) Barnardo's – personal records dating from 1867 onwards. Requests for information in writing to the Head of After Care, Barnardo's, Tanners Lane, Barkingside, Ilford, Essex IG6 1QG. The records contain information about family circumstances and relatives, and subsequent information about the child whilst in Barnardo's care. A photograph of the child can often be supplied as part of the family background information. Enquiries from descendants ahould include consent of person concerned or nearest surviving relative. Those requiring background information on this organisation and its founder are recommended to *Barnardo* by Gillian Wagner, Eyre & Spottiswoode (Publishers) Ltd, 1980.

Barnardo's Photographic and Film Archive – dating back to 1871 – has been catalogued on computer. The collection covers social history and the history of child care in a unique and often evocative manner. Access to this research source is limited; for further information contact Head of Publicity Services, Barnardo's (address as above). See also *Barnardo's photographic and film archive* by John Kirkham, Local History Mag.41 (Nov/Dec 1993).

Records of some agencies who have ceased operating are also held by Barnardo's; in the event of them being unable to trace the subject of an enquiry in Barnardo's records they will also search the following: Children's Aid Society; MacPhersons Homes; Marchmont Home; Liverpool Sheltering Home; Sharmans Home.

Barnardo's Records deposited in the Archives Department of the University of Liverpool are **not** accessible to the public. All enquiries should be directed to the above address.

The Family Welfare Association was originally the Charity Organisation Society and its London records are at 40 Northampton Road, Clerkenwell. London EC1R OAB.

There were many other children's societies, and those listed here appeared in an article by Mrs S. Czech in TMA Vol.6 No.5 (June 1982).

Children's Aid Society (1856-The Reformatory and Refuge Union) amalgamated with Dr Barnardo's in 1966.

Children's Home and Mission (1899), 8-26 Crescent Road, London, E18 1HZ.

The Children's Society (formerly Church of England Children's Society — founded 1881 as Waifs and Strays Society), Edward Rudolf House, Margery Street, London WC1X OJL. Records not open to inspection but *specific* enquiries accompanied by sae can be directed to Mr Philip West, 91 Queens Road, London SE15 2EZ. Please supply as much information as possible to facilitate search.

Thomas Coram Foundation for Children, (1739 — started as the Foundling Hospital), 40 Brunswick Square, London WC1N 1AZ.

Incorporated Society of the Crusade of Rescue and Homes for Destitute Catholic Children (1905), 73 St Charles Square, London W10 6EJ.

Mr Fegan's Homes Inc.(1870), 1 Beulah Road, Tunbridge Wells, Kent, TN1 2NP.

John Grooms (1866), 10 Gloucester Drive, Finsbury Park, London N4 2LP.

Invalid Children's Aid Society (1888), 126 Buckingham Palace Road, London SW1W 9SB.

The Muller Homes for Children (1836), Muller House, 7 Cotham Park, Bristol BS6 6DA.

National Children's Home (1869), Highbury Park, London N5 1UD.

Shaftesbury Homes and 'Arethusa' (1843), 3 Rectory Square, London SW4 OEG.

Spurgeons Child Care, 74 Wellingborough Rd., Rushden, Northants NN10 9TY holds records for what was formerly Spurgeons Homes, Kent; founded as Stockwell Orphanage, 1867.

This list is by no means exhaustive. Other organisations are listed in *Family Welfare Association Charities Digest,* published annually by Butterworth; *Social Services Year Book,* published annually by Councils and Education Press. These should be available in the reference section of your local public library. It must be remembered that these books only give information about organisations which currently exist.

Between 1939 and 1965, over nine hundred children in the care of Catholic Diocesan child care agencies were sent to Australia. The emigration of children to Australia during this time was undertaken by a number of British child care agencies in England, Scotland, Wales and Northern Ireland, following government policy. Catholic child care agencies arranged the migration of children through the Catholic Child Welfare Council, a federation of Roman Catholic Diocesan Children's Societies, Religious Congregations and other Catholic organisations providing social care services for children and families in need, not necessarily Roman Catholics.

The principal Catholic agencies involved with the migration were:

> The Crusade of Rescue (Westminster Diocese)
> Father Hudson's Homes (Birmingham Diocese)
> Liverpool Catholic Children's Protection Society (Liverpool Diocese)
> The Catholic Children's Rescue Society (Salford Diocese)
> Southwark Catholic Children's Rescue Society (Southwark Diocese)

Children were also sent from independent Catholic children's homes such as those run by the Sisters of Nazareth.

The Catholic Child Welfare Council employs a researcher to help former child migrants and their families seeking information about their relatives and family background. Further enquiries should be directed to The General Secretary, Catholic Child Welfare Council, 120 West Heath Road, London NW3 7TY. All enquiries are treated in confidence and no charge is made.

Where the Catholic Diocesan child care agency is not known or an independent Catholic children's home was responsible, enquiries should be made to the Catholic Child Welfare Council, address as above.

If you are inquiring about a child in care in a charity which either closed its work or amalgamated with another organisation, or in one of the Public Assistance Authorities' Children's Homes which operated under the old Poor Law, it is suggested you make enquiries at the record office/reference library in the area of the place where you think care may have taken place. For instance, records of the Middlemore Charity (Birmingham) including files, minutes etc. of the emigration of children to Canada and Australia are now deposited in the Local Studies Department, Birmingham Reference Library.

An informative article entitled *Finding the History of a Deserted Child* by Mrs J. Penn was published in *The Cockney Ancestor,* Journal of East of London FHS, Winter 1983-84.

The British Child Emigration Movement began in 1869 and continued for about 70 years. *Off to A New Life* by Phyllis Harrison, FTM Vol.2 No.6 (Sep-Oct 1986) gives some background to this. *The Home Children* is by the same author, 3rd ed. in paperback published by Watson Dwyer in 1979.

On the same theme there is *The Little Immigrants* by Kenneth Bagnell, Macmillan of Canada, 1980 and *Barnardo Children in Canada* by Gail H.Corbett, Woodland Publishing, Ontario, 1981.

Records for the Kingsley Fairbridge Child Emigration Scheme are at the University of Liverpool Archives, Archives Unit, PO Box 147, Liverpool L69 3BX.

The National Archives of Canada, 395 Wellington Street, Ottawa, Ontario K1A ON3, Canada, have records of juvenile immigration — ships' passenger lists showing names of children. These are not indexed.

Children of the Empire by Gillian Wagner, published by Weidenfield and Nicolson, 1982 tells of the children shipped not only to Canada but to Australia, New Zealand and South Africa.

Do not confuse that book with the more recently published *Lost Children of The Empire* by Phillip Bean and Joy Melville, Hymans, 1989. 'Home Children',who were not necessarily orphans, were sent abroad (mainly to Canada, Australia and South Africa) as late as 1967. Often no records were kept of their origins and many suffered incredible hardships. This book tells of their plight. The Child Migrant Trust, 8 Kingston Road, West Bridgford, Nottingham NG2 7AQ, is an organisation formed to help these children find their records and in some cases relatives.

CHOLERA There were epidemics in Britain from 1831 and a very serious outbreak in 1849 which caused 53,000 deaths.

CHRISOM CLOTH see pp.59-60, Tate's *The Parish Chest*.

CHRISTADELPHIANS This is a religious denomination founded in the USA about 1848 by John Thomas, an Englishman from London. They claim to represent the simple apostolic faith of the 1st century. Branches of the sect were set up in this country. Their magazine *The Ambassador* was published between 1864 and 1871, when its name was changed to *The Christadelphian*. The magazines contain much useful genealogical information under 'Intelligence' which contained notices sent in by meetings all over the country concerning the movements of individuals, adult baptisms, marriages, removals, deaths etc. There are no central archives.

CHRISTENING see Baptism.

CHRISTIAN NAMES There is a considerable amount of information about Christian names in Vol.I of *The National Index of Parish Registers* by D.Steel. It also contains speculations on the influences on the choice of names and the practice of using a surname as a Christian name. There is a list of the Latin forms of Christian names found in early parish registers (a similar list is given in *The Local Historian's Encyclopedia* by J.Richardson (q.v.)). We have extracted a selection from Donald Steel's list, set out on pp.110-112 of the volume:

Aegidius – Giles	Hieronymus – Jerome
Agneta or Ana – Agnes	Hugo – Hugh or Hugo
Alberedus or Aluredus – Alfred	Homfridus – Humphrey
Alecia or Alicia – Alice	Imania – Emma
Alionora – Eleanor	Jacobus – James or Jacob
Aloysius – Lewis	Jocosa or Jodoca – Joyce
Andreas – Andrew	Johanna – Joan, Jane, Jean, Janet
Anna – Anne, Ann or Hannah	Johannes – John or Jonathan
Antonius – Anthony	Lionhardus – Leonard
Carolus – Charles	Lucas – Luke
Coleta – Nicholas (feminine)	Ludovicus – Lewis

Emelia – Emily	Marcus – Mark
Etheldreda – Audrey	Mauritius – Maurice
Eugenius – Owen	Misericordie – Mercy
Galfridus or Gaufridus – Geoffrey	Natalis – Noel
Godefridus – Godfrey or Geoffrey	Pero – Piers
Goisfridus – Geoffrey	Petrus – Peter
Gulielmus – William	Radulphus – Ralph
Hadrianus – Adrian	Seisillus – Cecil
Helena – Eleanor or Helen	Sidneus – Sidney
Helias or Helyas – Ellis	Silvanus – Silas
Henricus – Henry	Umfridus – Humphrey
	Villefridus – Wilfred

Many names have been omitted from the above list as they are easy to identify. Many Christian names were Latinised by adding 'us' (masculine) or 'a' (feminine) to the English form.

When Latin forms were abandoned, the English names were often abbreviated. Most of them are obvious, but below are some which might present difficulties:

Xpr – Christopher	Dy – Dorothy
Jas – James	Em – Emma or Emily
Jno – John	Hon – Honour
Jonth – Jonathan	Wm – William
Jos – Joseph	Mart – Martha (beware misreading as Mary
Josh – Joshua or Joseph	as Mary)
Alc – Alice	Tam – Tamsin or Thomasin
	Xian – Christian

In census records, for example, we often find that diminutives are used – sometimes called 'pet' names, and these even occur at times in the baptismal registers. Vol.I of the *National Index of Parish Registers* has a very long list of these. Most are very obvious, since they suggest the formal name; exceptions are 'Polly' which stands for Mary, often Mary Ann, 'Peggy' for Margaret 'Molly' for Mary, 'Jack' for John and 'Harry' for Henry, 'Sally' for Sarah and 'Kitty' for Catherine.

If you are interested in the subject of Christian names you could consult the following: *The Oxford Dictionary of English Christian Names* by E.G. Withycombe, reissued by Omega Books in 1988 as *The Concise Dictionary of English Christian Names*. Miss Withycombe gave a lecture on the subject which is reported in Gen. Mag. Vol.10 No.2 (June 1947).

Or more recently in Gen. Mag. Vol.21 No.8 (Dec 1984) *The Choice of A Christian Name* by Michael L. Nash and its subsequent 'Commentary' by Michael J. Wood in Vol.21 No.9 (March 1985). Tom Wood wrote further on the subject in FTM Vol.7 No.11 (Sep 1991), *Christian Names*.

A study of our Christian names appears in a book by Ernest Weekly entitled *Jack and Jill* published by John Murray, 1939. In the Shire Publications 'Discovering' series No.156 is entitled *Christian Names*. More detailed is *A Dictionary of First Names* by Patrick Hanks and Flavia Hodges, 1990, Guild Publishing by arrangement with OUP.

CHURCH ALE Mediaeval equivalent of church bazaar or vicarage garden party. (see pp.87-88 Tate's *The Parish Chest*).

CHURCH COMMISSIONERS FOR ENGLAND see also Queen Anne's Bounty. A body formed in 1948 by the amalgamation of Queen Anne's Bounty (q.v.) and the Ecclesiastical Commissioners (constituted in 1836). In 1856 the latter became responsible also for the duties of the Church Building Commissioners. Records of these three bodies, together with the records created since 1948, are held by the Church Commissioners at their offices at 1 Millbank, London SW1P 3JZ. They are primarily an archive of administrative records and are unlikely to be of interest to the family historian without a specialised interest in an individual parish. See *The Records of the Church Commissioners* by E.J. Robinson, Local Historian, Vol. IX, No.5, (Feb 1971).

CHURCH COURTS Their records, especially from Elizabethan times, are of immense value to the local, and family, historian, but suffer from two disadvantages. Where they have survived, they can be very extensive, when diligent and time-consuming searches may be necessary and, for the amateur, there is the problem of ancient handwriting. However, when an item of interest is found, the detail is usually far-reaching.

Church Courts were held by Archdeacons, Bishops ('Consistory' Courts) and Archbishops, as well as by priests who held title to a 'peculiar' (q.v.). They dealt not only with ecclesiastical matters but also with many aspects of 15th-19th century life. Thus attendance at, and especially behaviour in, church or churchyard, the conduct of parish officers, matters connected with the church fabric, furniture and its maintenance, parish dues and tithes were considered as well as all aspects of betrothal, marriage and wills. Offences against ethical codes such as libel, slander, defamation of character, bastardy, bigamy, incest, quarrels and much else were dealt with.

Penalties were awarded, usually private penance after lesser or public penance after more serious offences, though these could be accompanied by fines or castigation. The records survive in the form of the Court 'Act Books' in which an account of the proceedings was written by the Clerk, often as a verbatim record. The 'accused' was 'prosecuted' to the Court for his fault, usually by church-wardens or constables, 'witnesses' made 'depositions' on oath, and a judgement was pronounced by the ecclesiastic presiding. An accused could 'purge' his fault by producing witnesses who would make depositions on oath as to his innocence, but failure to appear before the court generally involved excommunication. Cases could last for many sessions, the account being correspondingly scattered throughout the text.

The availability of this class of record varies but the whereabouts of surviving Act Books is generally known by the Diocesan Archivist.

Records of the Church Courts, E.R.C.Brinkworth, appeared in 'The Amateur Historian', Vol II (2) (Oct-Nov 1984). Brinkworth also wrote *The Study and Use of Archdeacon's Court Records*, Transactions, Royal Historical Society, 4th Series, Vol.25 (1943). W.E. Tate deals with the subject on pp. 144-150 of *The Parish Chest* and *Introduction to Ecclesiastical Records* by J.S. Purvis is one of the St Anthony's Hall Publications, issued by the Borthwick Institute of Historical Research, York.

CHURCH OF ENGLAND see Anglican Church

CHURCH OF JESUS CHRIST OF LATTER-DAY SAINTS (THE) This is the correct title for what most people refer to as 'the Mormons' or the LDS. It was founded in 1830 by Joseph Smith in Fayette, New York, USA. Joseph Smith had a vision from God which instructed him to find some golden plates which were the basis of 'The Book of

Mormon'. Latter-Day Saints use the Book of Mormon alongside the Holy Bible and other scriptures in their services of worship.

This Church has a special interest in encouraging Family History studies. All members are encouraged to trace their family, since great emphasis is placed on the importance of family life.

They have a thriving genealogical society based on Salt Lake City where there is the largest genealogical library in the world. They operate a pedigree referral service. If you send in your family name with details of places and dates they may be able to give you information about others who may have been researching the same family group; a charge may be made for this service so it is advisable to ascertain beforehand what this will be.

Write to The Genealogical Society of Utah, The Church of Jesus Christ of Latter-Day Saints, Family History Library, 35 North West Temple, Salt Lake City, Utah 84150, USA. Send 3 IRCs or $1 bill. See also under USA.

In the UK *specific* enquiries are dealt with by The Area Manager, The Genealogical Society of Utah, 751 Warwick Road, Solihull, West Midlands B91 3DQ. The Area Manager *does not deal with genealogical research queries* but will help with matters relating to:

(a) Location and Use of Family History Centres
(b) International Genealogical Index
(c) Family History Library Catalogue
(d) Personal Ancestral File – (PAF) a genealogical database programme.
(e) Family Search (a powerful computer system, designed to assist researchers).

Two of the Church's greatest achievements are the creation of the International Genealogical Index (q.v.) and the Family Search computer system. In addition they have microfilmed a great many records, and have set up Family History Centres all over the world. The use of these is not restricted to members of the Church, and genealogists are grateful for the facilities they offer. See *Family History Centres of Church of Jesus Christ of Latter Day Saints*, FHN&D, Vol.6 No.4 (Sep 1988).

It is possible to order microfilms of records you would like to consult in one of these Centres and the fee for this service is a modest one.

The Family History Centres in the UK are located as follows:

North Anderson Drive, *Aberdeen,* Scotland AB2 6DD. (Tel: 01224 692206)
401 Holywood Road, *Belfast,* Co.Down, Northern Ireland, BT4 2GU. (Tel: 01232 768250)
The Linkway, *Billingham,* Cleveland TS23 3HG. (Tel: 01642 563162)
Warren Drive, Cleveleys, *Blackpool* Lancs FY5 3TG. (Tel: 01253 858218)
721 Wells Road, Whitchurch, *Bristol,* Avon BS14 9HU. (Tel: 0117 983 8326)
670 Cherry Hinton Road, *Cambridge,* Cambs CB1 4DR. (Tel: 01223 247010)
Heol y Deri, Rhiwbina, *Cardiff,* S.Glamorgan CF4 6UH. (Tel: 01222 620205)
Langrigg Road, Morton Park, *Carlisle,* Cumbria CA2 5HT. (Tel: 01228 26767)
Thirlestaine Road, *Cheltenham,* Gloucs. (Tel: 01242 523433)
30 Clifton Drive, Blacon, *Chester,* Cheshire CH1 5LT. (Tel: 01244 390796)
33-41 Water Street, *Chorley,* Lancs. (Tel: 01257 269332)
Scarsfield Road, Wilton, *Cork,* Republic of Ireland.
Riverside Close, Whitley, *Coventry* West Mids. (Tel: 01203 301420)

Old Horsham Road, *Crawley,* Sussex RH11 8PD. (Tel: 01293 516151)
Woodside, Woodbourne Road, *Douglas, Isle of Man* . (Tel: 01624 675834)
The Willows, Finglas, *Dublin 11,* Ireland. (Tel: 010 353 462 5609)
36 Edinburgh Road, Albanybank, *Dumfries,* Scotland.
Bingham Terrace, *Dundee,* Tayside, Scotland DD4 7HH. (Tel: 01382 451 247)
30A Colinton Road, *Edinburgh 10,* Scotland EH4 3SN. (Tel: 0131 337 3049)
Wonford Road, *Exeter,* Devon. (Tel: 01392 50723)
Wynols Hill, Queensway, Coleford, *Forest of Dean,* Gloucestershire.
   (Tel: 01594 542480)
35 Julian Ave, *Glasgow,* Strathclyde, Scotland, G12 ORB (Tel: 0141 357 1024)
Linwood Avenue, Waltham Road, *Grimsby,* DN33 2PA. (Tel: 01472 828 876)
38 Lordswood Road, *Harborne, Birmingham* B17 9QS (Tel: 0121 427 9291)
Clodgey Lane, *Helston,* Cornwall. (Tel: 01326 564503)
Huddersfield, Dewsbury Chapel, 86 Halifax Street, Dewsbury, W.Yorks.
   (Tel: 01924 460929)
725 Holderness Road, *Hull,* North Humberside HU4 7RT. (Tel: 01482 701439)
Hyde Park, 64/68 Exhibition Road, South Kensington, *London,* SW7 2PA.
   (Tel: 0171 589 8561)
13 Ness Walk, *Inverness,* N3 5SQ, Scotland. (Tel: 01463 231220).
42 Sidegate Lane West, *Ipswich,* Suffolk IP4 3DB. (Tel: 01473 723182)
Rue de la Vallee, *St Mary, Jersey,* Channel Islands. (Tel: 01534 82171)
Whatriggs Road, *Kilmarnock,* Ayrshire, Scotland KA1 3QY. (Tel: 01563 26560)
Reffley Lane, *Kings Lynn,* Norfolk PE30 3EQ. (Tel: 01553 670000)
Winifred Crescent/Forth Park, *Kirkcaldy,* Fife, Scotland. (Tel: 01592 640041)
Onangle Road, *Morecambe, Lancaster.* (01254 33571)
Vesper Road, *Leeds,* West Yorkshire, LS5 3QT. (Tel: 0113 258 5297)
Wakerley Road, *Leicester* LE5 4WD. (Tel: 0116 221 4991)
South Road, *Lerwick,* Shetland. (Tel: 01595 5732)*
Purcell Ave, *Lichfield,* Staffs. (Tel: 01543 414 843)
Skellingthorpe Road, *Lincoln,* LN6 0PB. (Tel: 01522 680117)
4 Mill Bank, *Liverpool,* Merseyside L13 OBW. (Tel: 0151 228 0433)
Racecourse Road, Belmont Estate, *Londonderry,* Northern Ireland.*
Corner London Rd/Cutenhoe Rd, *Luton,* Bedfordshire LU1 3NQ,
   (Tel: 01582 482 234)
165 Yarmouth Road, *Lowestoft,* Suffolk. (Tel: 01502 573851).
76B London Road, *Maidstone,* Kent ME16 ODR. (Tel: 01622 757811)
Altrincham Road, *Wythenshawe, Manchester* M22 4BJ. (Tel: 0161 902 9279)
Southridge Drive, *Mansfield,* Nottinghamshire NG18 4RT. (Tel: 01623 26729)
Nanty Gwenith Street, George Town, *Merthyr-Tydfil,*
   Mid-Glamorgan, CF48 1NR. (Tel: 01685 722 455)
PO Box 285, The Brampton, *Newcastle-under-Lyme,* Staffs ST5 OTV.
   (Tel: 01782 620 653)
Chestnut Close, Shide Road, *Newport, Isle of Wight* . (Tel: 01983 529643)
137 Harlestone Road, *Northampton* (Tel: 01604 587630)
19 Greenways, Eaton, *Norwich,* Norfolk NR4 7AX. (Tel: 01603 52440)
Hempshill Lane, Bulwell, *Nottingham* NG6 8PA. (Tel: 0115 927 4194)
Cottesmore Close off Atherstone Avenue, Netherton Estate, *Peterborough*
   (Tel: 01733 263374)

Paisley, Campbell Street, Johnstone, Strathclyde, Scotland PA5 8LD. (Tel: 01505 20886)
Hartley Chapel, Mannamead Road, *Plymouth,* Devon. (Tel: 01752 668666)
8 Mount Road, Parkstone, *Poole,* Dorset BH14 OQW. (Tel: 01202 730 646)
Kingston Crescent, *Portsmouth,* Hampshire. (Tel: 01705 696243)
Haslingden Road, *Rawtenstall, Rossendale,* Lancs BB4 OQX. (Tel: 01706 213460)
280 The Meadway, Tilehurst, *Reading,* Berkshire RG3 4PF. (Tel: 01734 410211)
321 Evesham Road, Crabbs Cross, *Redditch,* Worcs B97 5JA. (Tel: 01527 550657)
Rhuddlan Road, *Rhyl,* Clwyd, N.Wales.*
Tweedale Street, *Rochdale,* Lancashire OL11 3TZ. (Tel: 01706 526292)
Romford, 64 Butts Green Road, *Hornchurch,* Essex RM11 2JJ. (Tel: 01708 620 727)
Stepney Drive/Whitby Road, *Scarborough,* N.Yorks.
Wheel Lane, Grenoside, *Sheffield,* S. Yorks S30 3RL (Tel: 0114 245 3231)
41 Kingston Road, *Staines,* Middlesex TW14 OND. (Tel: 01784 462627)
Linden Rd off Queen Alexandra Road, *Sunderland,* Tyne & Wear SR2 9BT.
    (Tel: 01915 285787)
185-187 Penns Lane, *Sutton Coldfield,* Birmingham, West Midlands B76 1JU.
    (Tel: 0121 386 1690)
Cockett Road, *Swansea,* W.Glamorgan.*
Telford Chapel, 72 Glebe Street, *Wellington,* Shropshire.
149 Nightingale Lane, *Balham,* London SW12 (*Wandsworth*). (Tel: 0181 6736741)
Linthouse Lane, *Wednesfield,* Wolverhampton, West Midlands. (Tel: 01902 724097)
Goring Street, *Worthing,* West Sussex. *
Wellington Road, *Yate,* Avon. (Tel: 01454 323004)
Forest Hill, *Yeovil,* Somerset. (Tel: 01935 26817)
West Bank, Acomb, *York.* (Tel: 01904 785128)

* Contact Area Manager at Solihull for details of opening times.

An appointment should be made to use the library. There is no charge but a donation
towards administrative costs would be gratefully received. A short article entitled *The
LDS libraries and how they work* by John E.Wiles will give you a peep 'behind-the-
scenes'. See FTM Vol.3 No.6 (Apl 1987).

Overseas readers are advised to contact their relevant family history society or Church
of Jesus Christ of Latter-Day Saints for details of FHCs elsewhere in the world.

CHURCH MONUMENTS see Monumental Inscriptions.

CHURCH RATES Land or real property whether owned or leased was liable to a
church rate. These were abolished in 1868. They were sometimes called Easter Dues, as it
was then that payment was required to be made.

CHURCH REGISTERS see also Deaths Overseas and Guildhall Library. In general
this means parish registers but it should not be overlooked that there are other churches
that have registers e.g. Nonconformists (q.v.). The subject is dealt with in *Church
Registers* by Lilian Gibbens, FFHS in its *An introduction to...* series.

CHURCHWARDENS/CHURCHWARDENS' ACCOUNTS Churchwardens – two or
four according to the size of the parish – were elected by the Vestry (q.v.) usually on
Easter Tuesday.

They had a great many duties which included managing the parish property and income, maintaining the church fabric, allocating pews, helping to keep the parish registers and the arranging of burials of strangers and baptisms of foundlings. Their accounts may survive among parish papers.

CHURCHWARDENS' PRESENTMENTS These were reports to the Bishop relating to misdemeanours of parishioners. Here is an example:

'A presentment made by the Churchwardens of Badsey and Aldington in the Diocese of Worcester delivered at the Visitation of the Right Rev'd Father in God John, Lord Bishop of Worcester, holden in the parish church of All Saints in Evesham, May 27th 1718.

We present Mary Miland for being guilty of ye heinous sin of Adultery by having a child in the absence of her husband Anthony Miland'.

Between 1660 and 1760 there are many presentments for non-attendance at Church; those so named were usually Roman Catholics or Quakers.

CIRCUS FAMILIES Travelling circuses and fairgrounds employed numerous people, not only as entertainers but as support staff. In addition to their nomadic lifestyle many of the entertainers often adopted performing names. It therefore follows that these families could pose a worse-than-usual research problem!

The secretary of the Circus Friends Association is John Exton, 43 Waterloo Lane, Skellingthorpe, Lincoln LN6 5SJ. The Association Librarian, Dr Turner, 15 Lingdales, Formby, Liverpool L37 7HA wrote *Circus family histories*, FTM Vol.4 No.7 (May 1988) and *Circus Roots,* Vol.6 No.12 (Oct 1990). The articles have extensive bibliographies.

Dr Turner has a detailed index of over 2000 performers for 1845-1924, with greatest emphasis on pre-1900; he will search this in exchange for sae or 3 IRCS. A short article on how to research circus history is available for £1 inc.p&p.

See also *George Sanger, Showman* and *'Lord' George Sanger and other circus families* by Julie Goddard, FTM, Vol.5 No.7 (May 1989); Vol.10 No.10 (Aug 1994) respectively.

CITATION A summons to appear before a court.

CITATION INDEXES When writing an article or more substantial work for publication, the author frequently 'Cites' or refers to previously published material. The citations or references appear as footnotes or in a section at the end. Most entries specify the previous author, his subject matter and the book or journal in which it was published.

For a given field of research it is possible to compile Citation Indexes by taking the references from all the articles and books published in that field over a given time interval, and arranging them in alphabetical order of author and subject matter.

Each entry in the index links to the article or book in which it was cited. This is particularly useful from the historical point of view because a modern author may well cite a source which is several centuries old. This enables the historian to gain access to earlier instances of a sought-after surname.

Citation Indexes have been compiled for Science, Social Sciences, Arts and Humanities. Copies are available in the larger libraries.

The Public Record Office General Information leaflets 24 and 25 *Citation of Documents in the PRO* and *How to Cite Documents in the PRO* recommend the way in which the records in its custody should be cited in books, articles or theses.

CIVIC TRUST see Local History Societies.

CIVIL REGISTRATION see also Register Office. The requirement to register a birth, marriage or death came into effect on 1 July 1837 in England and Wales. The indexes of all registrations since that date are open to inspection by the public at St Catherine's House (General Register Office) in London. It is situated on the corner of Kingsway and The Aldwych (10 Kingsway, London WC8 6JP). Please note, however, that all *postal applications* for certificates should be made to the OPCS, General Register Office, Postal Applications Section, Smedley Hydro, Trafalgar Road, Birkdale, Southport, Merseyside PR8 2HH.

People Count: A History of the General Register Office, by Muriel Nissel, HMSO, 1987, was published to mark its 150 years in existence. It tells of the origins and developments of civil registration and of the statistical work, including the census, of the Office plus results of social and economic changes on the service. Illustrated and indexed it is well worth the price of around £6.00.

Up to 1983 Births, Marriages and Deaths are in separate alphabetical indexes, each covering the preceding three month period and dated March, June, Sept and Dec; from 1984 the indexes are arranged in alphabetical order for the full year. They are handwritten to December 1865 and typewritten thereafter. The earlier volumes are gradually being replaced by typewritten indexes. The GRO indexes are compiled from the entries sent in from local Register Offices and, inevitably, omissions occur. If you are fairly certain that an entry should be in a particular area but there is no suitable reference at the GRO it is worth contacting the local Register Office and asking them to check their records.

The quarter in which the event took place is not necessarily the quarter in which it is registered. Always check at least the following quarter.

The indexes give only the Surname, Christian names, name of Registration District, Volume and page reference. It is these details which you have to enter on an application form for a copy of the certificate you require. The current cost of a certificate is £6 if ordered *in person* from St Catherine's House, or by post from a local Register Office; £12 if ordered by post quoting the *reference number* (including quarter and Registration District), £15 otherwise. For the latter a search over a period of five years will be made but half of the fee is forfeited if the search proves negative. The cost includes airmail postage overseas and second class post in U.K.

The GRO will only issue a certificate if the details match exactly with those on your application form. It is possible to put a 'check' on an application giving some known fact which will identify the correct entry or stating that you will accept certain variant spellings or occupations. This check is free if the certificate is issued, £3.00 is charged if the entry appears incorrect and no certificate is issued.

There are professional searchers who specialise in searching the indexes at the GRO and whose rates are reasonable. A number of FHSs have followed the example of the North Middlesex FHS which was the first to organise a scheme whereby their members carry out a search for members or non-members for a modest fee — provided a lengthy search is not involved. Enquire of your local family history society. Remember to enclose sae or 3 IRCs.

Prior to 1900, 4 marriages were entered on one page of the Register (since 1900 this has been reduced to 2). Births and Deaths Registers can have up to 8 entries on the same page. This can cause confusion when, for example, cousins bearing an unusual surname are born, in the same area, some days apart but are registered on the same day, thereby receiving an identical registration reference and making it seem like a registration of twins. It can also be misleading when searching for a marriage between a couple who both bear common (for the area in question) surnames as, with 8 names on the page, it is possible to find an apparent 'match' which, on checking, turns out to be the groom from one marriage on the page and the bride from another.

Identical entries in the indexes in successive Quarters can also occur. This is basically due to a flaw in the administrative system; if application is made for two identical certificates due to such duplication, the GRO will refund the cost of one certificate and correct the index.

The McLaughlin Guide *St Catherine's House – the General Register Office*, is a very useful booklet dealing with the procedures for obtaining certificates; it has maps and diagrams of the layout of St Catherine's House. Obtainable from FTM price £1.55 inc. p&p.

There are also leaflets issued free at St Catherine's House, or obtainable by post in return for sae. They are:

General Register Office: Tracing Records of Births, Marriages and Deaths (ARC 1)
Reference Checking System (CAS 62)
General Register Office: Information for visitors (CAS 63)
Tracing the whereabouts of persons (CAS 6
Fees and Searches for Certificates

At St Catherine's House you will also find indexes to the following:
Births and Deaths at Sea since 1st July 1837: events occurring at sea on any ship registered in Great Britain and Northern Ireland (Marine Register Book).

Births and Deaths in Aircraft from 1949: events occurring in any part of the world in any aircraft registered in Great Britain and Northern Ireland. (Air Register Book)

Service Records: events among members of H.M.Forces and certain other persons working for or attached to H.M.Forces. Army Registers date mainly from 1881, Royal Air Force from 1920 and Royal Navy 1959.

Consular and High Commission: events of British subjects in most foreign countries registered by British Consuls; births and deaths of British subjects in most Commonwealth countries registered by British High Commissioners.

Miscellaneous Records (including certain Regimental Registers).

There are separate registers containing the registration of deaths of Servicemen in World Wars I and II: certificates of marriage forwarded by the British High

Commissioners in India, Bangladesh, Sri Lanka and Ghana from 1950 and foreign certificates of marriage forwarded by British Consuls: births and deaths aboard British registered hovercraft and deaths occurring on off-shore installations.

Copies of Records of Still-Births registered in England and Wales since 1st July 1927 can be obtained only with special permission of the Registrar General.

See also PRO Records Information leaflet 39 *Records of Births, Marriages & Deaths*.

Readers of this book will almost certainly have seen a birth, marriage or death certificate, so the contents need not be described. For examples see *Beginning Your Family History* by George Pelling, obtainable from the FFHS. However, a few words of advice (and warning!) at this stage might ensure that you obtain the correct certificate first time round. Here the editor acknowledges in greater part, entries from FHN&D Vol.5 Nos.1 & 2, *Did you Know...?* *"They"* did, you may not.

Errors and omissions do occur both in the Indexes and on certificates issued for a variety of reasons. Handwriting and dates can be mis-read — both by staff and by researchers! Bear in mind that the Registrar or Incumbent wrote down what he *thought* he heard and, as many people could not read or write in the early years of Civil Registration, there was no way of checking his entry. Regional accents, speech impediments, even the common cold can affect what is written on a certificate. (One very useful tip when trying to find a 'missing' entry is to hold your nose, say the name out loud, and listen to what comes out — it may sound silly but it can be very revealing!)

Remember that the spelling of surnames varied — and that the difference of one letter, even using one 't' instead of 'tt' (as in Whit(t)aker) can put entries pages apart in the indexes. Beware of any surnames beginning with a vowel or with an H (the former may well collect an H; the latter lose it). Always check, for example, MacDougall and McDougall (which come pages apart) and look out for such names as (K)Nowles, W(Roe), and (Y)Eardley

Births. During the early years of civil registration many births, particularly those of illegitimate children, were not registered. Until 1875 when it became compulsory, there was no penalty for failure to do so. Parents were given 6 weeks (42 days) to register; after 6 weeks and up to 6 months the birth could be registered on payment of a fine. After 6 months, with very few exceptions, a birth could *not* be registered. It was fairly common for parents, arriving to register a child a few days late, to 'adjust' the birth date to come within 42 days. Since 1875 the father of an illegitimate child can only be named on the birth certificate if he is present at the registration and consents.

A child which had not been named at the time of registration may be found at the end of entries for the surname in question, listed under 'Male' or 'Female'. Reversing of christian names was common — a man married as 'Henry John' may well have been registered as 'John Henry'.

If the time of birth is given on a certificate, it frequently implies a multiple birth.

From the September Quarter 1911 the birth indexes give the maiden surname of the mother.

Marriages After the December Quarter 1911 the Marriage Indexes give the maiden name of the bride alongside that of the groom and vice-versa. There is a separate entry alphabetically for bride and groom so assuming you know the bride's maiden name you can cross check (in the index for the same Quarter) to ensure that the volume and page references coincide. You then know that you almost certainly have the correct entry.

Ages on marriage certificates are often unreliable! '21' and 'of full age' both mean that the person was 21 and upwards — if they were telling the truth. In theory, a marriage certificate should state if father of bride or groom is deceased; in practice, this requirement was often ignored. It is not safe to presume he is still alive because the certificate does not state that he is deceased.

Do not assume that a marriage took place nine months or more before the birth of the first child. A high percentage of brides were pregnant when they married and a surprising number of couples did not marry until after the birth of their first child. One instance can be cited where the couple married *14 years after* the birth of the first child!

A widow will be listed in the index under her previous married name and not under her maiden name but her maiden surname will appear on the certificate. Marriages which took place in non-conformist chapels prior to 1898 had to be carried out in the presence of a (civil) Registrar. Such marriages will often be located in the Registrar's own register (also used to record marriages which took place in the Register Office) and *not* in the Register of the chapel concerned. They will appear in the indexes at St Catherine's House but may not be easily traced in a local Register Office.

Remember also that a marriage register need only be deposited with the local Registrar when it is full — a church where few marriages take place may still be using a register commenced in 1837 and the local Register Office will have no copy of this book.

Deaths In 1837 a death had to be registered within 8 days; in 1875 this was reduced to 5 days. From 1866 onwards Death indexes give the age of the deceased at death. Do not place too much reliance on the age given on a death certificate. The only person who should know the true facts was not there to give them! The accuracy of the age given depends on the person giving the information (relative/employer/neighbour/workhouse master) and, particularly in the early days when there were no birth certificates to verify the statement, it may be years 'out'. Many people deliberately 'lost' several years from their age at some stage in their lives and actually came to believe their 'new' age. Also, you will sometimes find a discrepancy between the age given on a death certificate and that given in the burial register.

'Present at the death' means what it says; 'In attendance' means that the person registering the death was *not* actually present at it but is attending at the Register Office to register it.

With very few exceptions, a death cannot be registered until a positive identification of the body has been made. This can cause considerable confusion to the family historian!

If there is no body, a death cannot be registered. If the body is recovered (e.g. from a mining accident or a shipwreck) several years later and is identified, the death will be registered as at the date of recovery *but* the age given will be that which applied when the person actually died.

Unless a body is legally identified, it cannot be registered under a specific name — hence entries in the indexes at St Catherine's House for, for example, 'Old Joe aged about 65', for an itinerant worker with no known surname, and the pages of entries to be found at the end of each volume listing 'unknown' or 'unidentified' bodies with estimated ages. If you have 'lost' a death, particularly in the early days of civil registration, it would be worth checking these lists to see if you can spot a likely entry in the correct Registration

District. If an inquest was held, the death will be registered in the quarter when the inquest was completed. Particularly if there was an adjournment, this may be some time after the actual death and the entry may be in a later quarter than you anticipate.

If a ship goes down at sea with no survivors then, generally speaking, none of the deaths of those on board can be registered because the bodies cannot be legally identified.

It is still legal in the United Kingdom for a person to be buried on private land and *not* in a churchyard or cemetery.

It is worth drawing on the experience of others — see an article entitled *Certified Correctly* by Pat Stanbridge, first published in Vol.1 No.2 of the East Surrey FHS journal. It contains very detailed advice for those unfamiliar with St Catherine's House, to which some more has been added in another article in the same journal Vol.10 No.2.

Sometimes you are faced with a choice between two or more entries, and the place of registration could lead you to the entry most likely to be correct. However, the name of the registration district does not always give you a clear idea as to where it was located. Sometimes old 'Hundred' names for the area are used, names which no longer appear on modern maps. It is a help to be able to locate the county by a knowledge of the 'code' (the first part of the reference you have to quote on your application form). The reference numbers that follow are only a guide, however, for often the same reference is used for more than one county, though these are usually adjacent.

From 1837 to 1851 Roman numerals were used. From 1852 we have Arabic numerals followed by a letter.

Anglesey	XXVII 11b	Lincolnshire	XIV 7a
Bedfordshire	VI 3b	London (with suburbs)	I, II, III, IV,
Berkshire	VI 2c		1a, 1b, 1c, 1d
Brecknockshire	XXVI 11b	Merionethshire	XXVII 11b
Buckinghamshire	VI 3a	Middlesex	I, II, III
Caernarvonshire	XXVII 11b		1a, 1b,1c,3a
Cambridgeshire	XIV 3b	Monmouthshire	XXVI 11a
Cardiganshire	XXVII 11b	Montgomeryshire	XXVII 11b
Carmarthenshire	XXVI 11b	Norfolk	XIII 4b
Cheshire	XIX 8a	Northamptonshire	XV 3b
Cornwall	IX 5c	Northumberland	XXV 10b
Cumberland	XXV 10b	Nottinghamshire	XV 7b
Denbighshire	XXVII 11b	Oxfordshire	XIV 3a
Derbyshire	XIX 7b	Pembrokeshire	XXVI 11a
Devonshire	IX, X 5b	Radnorshire	XXVI 11b
Dorset	VIII 5a	Rutland	XV 7a
Durham	XXIV 10a	Shropshire	XXVI, XVIII 6a
Essex	XII 4a	Somerset	X, XI 5c
Flintshire	XIX, XXVII 11b	Staffordshire	XVI,XVII,XVIII 6b
Glamorganshire	XXVI 11a	Suffolk	XVI, XII, XIII, 3b, 4a
Gloucestershire	XI, XVIII 6a	Surrey	IV, 1d, 2a
Hampshire	VII, VIII, 2b, 2c	Sussex	VII 2b
Herefordshire	XXVI 6a	Warwickshire	XI, XVI, XVIII
Hertfordshire	VI 3a		6b, 6c, 6d
Huntingdonshire	XIV 3b	Westmorland	XXV 10b
Kent	V, 1d,2a	Wiltshire	VIII 5a
Lancashire	XX, XXI, XXV,	Worcestershire	XVIII, 6b, 6c
	8b,8c 8d,8e	Yorkshire	XXI, XXII, XXIII,XXIV,
Leicestershire	XV 7a		9a, 9b, 9c, 9d

Another useful aid can be obtained from the IHGS. They have published two maps showing the Registration and Census districts; one covers the period 1837 to 1851, and the other 1852 to 1946.

See also *St Catherine's House Districts* by Ray Wiggins. Obtainable from FTM price £2.25 inc. p&p. An alphabetical listing of civil registration districts in England and Wales for the 19th and early 20th centuries. The Genealogical Society of Victoria has published *Registration Districts of England and Wales 1837-1851, 1852-1946* by Talbot and Les Hill. Available from the GSV, 5th Floor, 252 Swanston Street, Melbourne 3000, Victoria, Australia, price $A12. Both books are particularly useful now that microfilm/fiche copies of the indexes can be seen at other locations.

Births, Marriages and Deaths Indexes have been microfilmed and microfiched. Some ROs and the larger Public Reference Libraries have purchased these, though perhaps not full coverage of dates available. Before visiting a repository check the current extent of holdings on microfilm and microfiche and whether you need to book a reader. It may take a little longer to locate an entry in these forms than it would by consulting the index at St Catherine's House but you may consider this a minor inconvenience if you can travel more easily to a library or record office that has the indexes on film or fiche.

If after all that, you still got it wrong, a national unwanted certificates index has been compiled! Many people have purchased certificates which turned out to be the wrong ones for their purpose and have subsequently donated them to the index. *All* names on the certificate have been indexed i.e. parents, witnesses, registrars etc.

Published by the BMSGH and obtainable from them c/o The Kingsley-Norris Room, BMI. Collections 1 & 2 combined £2.40 (UK), £2.65 (o/s surface); Collection 3 £2.90 (UK), £3.20 (o/s surface); Collection 4 £1.40 (UK) £1.60 (o/s surface). All three collections at a special price of £5.80 (UK), £6.30 (o/s surface).

Contributions to the index should be sent to Mr & Mrs R. Andrews, 16 Rock Road, Solihull, West Midlands, B92 7LB, who will also answer *specific* enquiries accompanied by sae or 3 IRCs.

CIVIL REGISTRATION IN IRELAND The general registration of births, marriages and deaths did not begin until 1864 and until 1921 it covered the whole of Ireland. Registration of Protestant marriages began in 1845.

These records are held by the Registrar General, Joyce House, 8/11 Lombard Street East, Dublin 2, together with those for Eire since 1921.

Registrations for Northern Ireland after 1921 are at Oxford House, 49/55 Chichester Street, Belfast BT1 4HL.

CIVIL REGISTRATION IN SCOTLAND Registration commenced on 1st Jan 1855. Certificates for that year gave an astonishing amount of information; however, the authorities found it too difficult to keep up such a standard and modifications were introduced. Birth certificates in 1855 and from 1861 give the date and place of the parents' marriage. Marriage certificates give the names of both parents of each party. Death certificates give parents' names.

In Scotland, the public is allowed to see not just the indexes but the full details on the certificates themselves, subject to certain limitations. Some local Registrars also allow limited access to the Registers, by arrangement. See Scottish Ancestry for details of procedure at New Register House, Princes Street, Edinburgh EH1 3YT, where the records are kept.

CIVIL SERVANTS Records will usually be amongst those of the Department in which they served – e.g. Customs and Excise – and will generally be found in the PRO. See *Tracing Your Ancestors in The Public Record Office* 4th ed., obtainable from FFHS.

CLANDESTINE see Marriage.

CLASSMAN A term used particularly in Suffolk in the 1840's to describe unemployed labourers.

CLERGY Crockford's *Clerical Directory* was first published in 1858, listing the names of all Church of England clergy, and it has been published at frequent intervals since. Almost all Reference Libraries stock Crockford.

Prior to Crockford, the *Index Ecclesiasticus* compiled by Joseph Foster lists clerical appointments from 1800 to 1840. The Institution Books held at the PRO list earlier appointments of clergy. John le Neve's *Fasti Ecclesiae Anglicanae* in various volumes gives details of all the higher clergy of the Church of England from early times to the mid-19th century.

Noblemen were allowed to have their own chaplains, the number depending on their rank. Certain Officers of State were also allowed to have them. These chaplains were permitted to enjoy two benefices.

There is a record of the appointment, death or dismissal of such people in the Faculty Office (q.v.) from 1660. The 18th century volumes have been indexed at the beginning of the book under the names of the Peers who appointed. These records can be consulted at Lambeth Palace Library, London SE1 7JU. A prior appointment is not necessary but a letter of introduction is required on the first visit. A Reader's Ticket from another manuscript library (e.g. British Library) or the PRO is acceptable.

In the case of Clergy of the Church of Scotland, *Fasti Ecclesiae Scoticanae* is regularly reissued, and details ministers in parish churches from 1560.

There are Year Books issued by other denominations listing the names and churches of ministers. You could also write to the Archive Repository of that denomination (see under denomination name).

There was a school for the orphans of clergy (boys only). The Register of the Clergy Orphan School for Boys, 1751 to 1896, edited by M.J.Simmonds was published in 1897. The school was in Yorkshire 1751 to 1804, Acton 1804 to 1812, St Johns Wood 1812 to 1855, and Canterbury 1855 to 1896. It then became St Edmund's School. The Register gives the year of birth, date of admission, name of father and the parish where he served. There are some footnotes stating to whom some children were apprenticed or a profession entered.

CLERK In addition to its present meaning, this term was often applied to a clergyman who was officially a 'Clerk in Holy Orders'.

CLIMBING BOYS see Sweeps.

CLOCKMAKERS AND WATCHMAKERS see also Oriental and India Office Collections. Clockmakers were originally a part of the Blacksmiths' Company, but were granted a charter in 1631. The Company owns an extensive library of books, documents and portraits. There is a book entitled *Some Account of the Worshipful Company of Clock-makers,* Aikens & Overall, 1881.

Old Clocks and Watches and their Makers by F.J. Britten has a list of nearly 12,000 makers. *Index of British Mathematicians: 1701-1800* by R.V. and P.J. Wallis contains many references to clock and watchmakers. Published by Project for Historical Bibliographies, Newcastle upon Tyne, 1993. Price £22.

Westmorland Clocks and Clockmakers (1974) and *Lancashire Clocks and Clockmakers* (1975) are two of a series by Brian Loomes. Each has an alphabetical list of clockmakers, with considerable genealogical information. In the Westmorland book there are two five-generation pedigrees of clockmaking families. There is also *Shropshire Clock and Watchmakers* by D.J.Elliot, Phillimore 1979.

There is a Clockmakers' Company Museum at the Guildhall Library (q.v.) and the Gershom-Parkington Collection of Time-keeping Instruments is at the Manor House Museum, Honey Hill, Bury St Edmunds, Suffolk (Tel: 01284 757072).

CLOSE ROLLS These documents are in the PRO. They are records of deeds, conveyances between individuals, sales of lease and release and many other similar transactions. They date from as early as 1204 and calendars have been printed by HMSO to 1500. As an example of the bulk of these records, the calendars for 1272 to 1435 fill 37 very large volumes. These are full of names!

CLOTHWORKER The Clothworkers' Company was an amalgamation of the Fullers and Shearmen. See *The Golden Ram. A Narrative History of the Clothworkers' Company 1528 to 1958* by Thomas Girtin.

COACHMAKER AND COACH HARNESSMAKER They also had a London Livery Company. See *A History of the Worshipful Company of Coach Makers and Coach Harnessmakers of London* by G. Eland, 1937.

COASTGUARD An index of coastguards is being compiled from such sources as census records, directories, parish records as well as some PRO sources. Contributions are welcome; a modest charge is made for searches in the index. Details from Mrs Eileen Stage, 150 Fulwell Park Avenue, Twickenham, Middlesex TW2 5HB. Please send sae or 3 IRCs.

See also PRO Records Information leaflet 8: *Records of HM Coastguards*. Further reading *Coastguard!* by W. Webb, HMSO, 1976.

COAT OF ARMS see Heraldry

CODICIL An addition to a will, either modifying or revoking it.

COINAGE In records likely to be used by genealogists the coins most likely to be found referred to by researchers are Guinea (21s.), shillings, groats (worth 4 old pennies) and pennies. Remember that there were 240 pennies in a £, 12 pennies in a shilling and 20 shillings in a £, before the introduction of decimal coinage in 1971! Prior to 1799 a penny was larger and thicker than those of our pre-decimal coinage.

COLLEGES Many of the admission registers of Colleges have not only survived but have been printed. See *Registers of the Universities, Colleges and Schools of Great Britain and Ireland* by P.M. Jacobs.

COLLEGE OF ARMS see also Heraldry. This is the name usually given to the Corporation of the Kings, Heralds and Pursuivants of Arms. The present College, built after the Great Fire of 1666, stands on the site of Derby House, and the address is Queen Victoria Street, London EC4V 4BT. A Grant of Arms can only be made by the Kings of Arms. The College houses a great variety of records and many thousands of pedigrees. You can call at the College between 10 am and 4 pm Mondays to Fridays for advice from one of the Officers on duty. However, you *cannot* consult the College's records personally. Professional research is undertaken by members of the college and fees are, of course, charged.

COLLIER Originally a charcoal seller, later the name came to mean a coal miner, *or* coal-ship (or sailor on it).

COMBMAKER A Combmakers Index is being compiled by Mr R.C. Bowers, Road End Cottage, Stockland, Honiton, Devon EX14 9LJ and contains over 2,300 entries. Principally compiled from City of London Alphabets of Freedom 1681 to 1893 but also from York, Bristol, other leading cities and overseas records. There is no charge for consulting the index but please remember to send sae or 3 IRCs.

As a result of his research into the subject Mr Bowers has published a booklet *Combs, Combmaking and the Combmakers Company*, price £2.30 by post.

A small supplement to this index is one of combmakers of Gloucester and other parts of the country whose names do not appear in the Bowers index (published 1987). Contact Mr Robert Watts, 34 Cherry Orchard, Wotton-under-Edge, Glos GL12 7HT. Please send sae or 2 IRCs.

COMMON PLEAS see Court of.

COMMON RECOVERY see Entail.

COMMONWEALTH (The) 1649 to 1653 but period 1649 to 1660 usually referred to as 'Commonwealth Period'. This was the English republic established after the execution of Charles I and ruled by the Rump Parliament and a Council of State. The Commonwealth proper ended with the establishment of Oliver Cromwell's Protectorate (1653). This is a difficult period for the family history researcher; there is a hiatus in many of the records (especially parish registers). Virtually all wills for this period should be in the PRO.

COMMONWEALTH WAR GRAVES COMMISSION The Commission was established in 1917 and its duties are to mark and maintain the graves of the members of the forces of the Commonwealth who were killed in the two World Wars, to build memorials to those who have no known graves and to keep records and registers, including after the Second World War, a record of the Civilian War Dead. (Records include sunken ships and the Runnymede Memorial to Royal Air Force personnel whose bodies have remained undiscovered.)

Records are held at head office which enable a grave to be traced and in most cases a photograph can be supplied. The more information enquirers can supply the more easily a record can be traced but conversely the Commission may be able to supplement even the scantiest of information from their records, once located. The CWGC hold a copy of the Roll of Honour Civilian War Deaths 1939-1945, the original of which is in Westminster Abbey.

This service is free to relatives or ex-comrades, otherwise there is a charge of £1 (under review). The address to write to is The Information Officer, Commonwealth War Graves Commission, 2 Marlow Road, Maidenhead, Berks, SL6 7DX.

Cemetery and memorial registers published by the Commission are usually housed in register boxes on site and are also available for consultation at the Commission's offices.

War Graves within British civil cemeteries of the Empire in India and now unmaintained are commemorated on memorials to the missing. The CWGC are still responsible for graves in the actual War Cemeteries in India.

A video film entitled *I Will Make You A Name* illustrates the work of the commission and can be hired for showing by societies, schools etc. or purchased for £3.50 from the above address. The film is in colour with narrative.

See also *The Records of the Commonwealth War Graves Commission* by Peter J. Bilbrough, FTM Vol.9 Nos.8-10, (June-Aug 1983); *The Unending Vigil: history of the Commonwealth War Graves Commission 1917-1964* by Philip Longworth, Constable, 1967 and *Before Endeavours Fade* by Rose E. Coombs, Battle of Britain Prints International, 6th ed.1990: a guide to the battlefields of the First World War.

Graves other than those of the two World Wars are recorded by the Ministry of Defence at PS4(CAS)(A) Room 1012, Empress State Building, Lillie Rd, London SW6 1TR.

COMPANIES. Since the 1850's a Register of Companies has been maintained on behalf of the Department of Trade and Industry. Records give details of people associated with companies — addresses, relationships etc. See PRO Records Information leaflet 54 *Registration of Companies and Businesses*.

The main office of the Registrar of Companies is at Crown Way, Maindy, Cardiff, CF4 3UZ where there is a Reading Room open Mon to Fri 9.00am — 5.00pm. Details of the key documents of individual companies are kept here. You can make a search yourself, pay the cost of a search by the Bureau or employ a record agent.

There is a London Search Room at Companies House, 55-71 City Road, London EC1Y 1BB, open Mon to Fri 9.00am-5.00pm where microfilm copies of the key details can be seen. A charge of £3.00 per company record inspected is made. The records come on microfiche and become the searcher's property. There may be a wait of up to two hours before the fiche becomes available but it may be posted to the searcher at a charge of £2.50 per fiche, so avoiding the wait. Copies of the pages can be made on microfiche printers at the Search Room (charge 10p per page) by the searcher. Postal applications for searches of the indexes are accepted and a leaflet describing the service is available. If a personal visit is not possible a professional record agent would have to be employed or your local reference library may be willing to apply for the loan of microfilm copies of specific companies for you.

Companies House now has Satellite Offices at:

75 Mosley Street, Manchester M2 2HR. (Tel: 0161 236 7500)

Birmingham Central Library, Chamberlain Square, Birmingham B3 3HQ.
(Tel: 0121 233 9047)

25 Queen Street, Leeds LS1 2TW. (Tel: 0113 233 8338)

Records of companies dissolved before microfilming began (c1973) are only available in hard-copy and have to be sent from Companies House, Cardiff to the London Search Room. The records of old companies much before this date may have been destroyed.

The Business Archives Council, 4 Maguire Street, Butlers Wharfe, London SE1, is a registered charity founded in the 1930s. It is the leading agency in the UK concerned with the preservation of historical records of British industry and assists in the rescue and preservation of records, advises companies on archives policy, publishes an annual journal and a quarterly newsletter.

Records of Scottish Companies can be found in Companies House, 100-102 George Street, Edinburgh EH2 3DJ (Satellite Office: 108 Bothwell Street, Glasgow G2 6NR) or The Business Archives Council of Scotland, Glasgow University Archives, The University, Glasgow G12 8QQ and for Irish Companies in Companies Registration Office (N.Ireland), IDB House, 64 Chichester Street, Belfast BT1 4JX or the Public Record Office of Ireland, Four Courts, Dublin 7. There are facilities for searching in Edinburgh and Belfast.

A very detailed article entitled *Company Records as a Source for the Family Historian* by C.T. & M. Watts, appeared in Gen. Mag. Vol.21. No.2 (June 1983).

Company Archives: The Survey of the Records of 1,000 of the First Registered Companies in England and Wales by Lesley Richmond and Bridget Stockford, is the result of a survey of 1,200 companies, the only survivors of the 30,334 registered between 1856 and 1889 and extant in 1980. Published by Gower Publishing 1986, price £45. There is a copy in the SOG.

At a more modest price of £15 Gower Publishing brought out in 1987 *A Guide to Tracing the History of a Business* by John Orbell. Family historians should not be put off by the title as the book recommends a number of sources for locating a business plus addresses of the main repositories where research material is available. There is a useful bibliography.

See also *Business and Company Records* by Eric Probert, FFHS.

An Index to the Archives of Industrial Companies, based primarily on the unpublished lists and reports held in the National Register of Archives, is available in the Search Room of the Royal Commission on Historical Manuscripts, Quality House, Quality Court, Chancery Lane, London WC2A 1HP.

The index covers the period 1760-1914 and contains information about the surviving records of some 12,000 companies, including details of the present whereabouts or ownership of these. The Commission would welcome brief details of any collections of historical importance that are at present unlisted.

Three of the oldest Trading Companies are the Levant Company (records, PRO), Hudson's Bay Company (records, Hudson's Bay Company Archives, Provincial Archives of Manitoba, 200 Vaughan Street, Winnipeg, Manitoba, Canada R3C 1T5; copies on microfilm at the PRO) and the East India Company (records at the Oriental and India Office Collections (q.v.)).

COMPTON CENSUS Instigated by Bishop Henry Compton. This census, taken in 1676, gives statistical returns of parishes in the Midlands, Wales and the South, including estimates of population and numbers of dissenters. Copies are at the William Salt Library, Stafford and the Bodleian Library, Oxford. Nineteen parishes have actually been found with names. See *Local Census Listings 1522-1930: holdings in the British Isles* by Jeremy Gibson and Mervyn Medlycott, FFHS.

COMPUTER FILE INDEX (CFI) now International Genealogical Index (IGI) (q.v.).

COMPUTERS IN GENEALOGY This is the title of a quarterly journal issued by the SOG and possibly for the more experienced user. It reports progress in the application of computers to genealogy, shares experience to minimise effort involved in designing programs and organising information, provides a forum for discussion and advertises future events and meetings. The subscription is modest and further details can be obtained from the SOG in exchange for sae or 3 IRCs.

Highly recommended and having proved its worth is *Computers for Family History: An Introduction*, David Hawgood, published by Hawgood Computing Ltd. Obtainable from the FFHS. It is intended for the family historian with no previous knowledge of computers and as each new technique is introduced the background to it is described in simple terms. An ideal starting point for anyone considering a computer for their family history.

Also by David Hawgood *Genealogy Computer Packages* gives a listing of programs available both sides of the Atlantic and for all types of machines. Obtainable from the FFHS, as is *Spreadsheet Family Trees* by Guy Lawton, published by David Hawgood, 1994. The author has used a particular computer package to produce and edit a set of drop-line trees for his family. He gives examples of trees and details of method used to produce them.

GEDCOM Data Transfer: Moving Your Family Tree by David Hawgood, Hawgood Computing Ltd, obtainable from FFHS. Different genealogy packages have different ways of holding information. GEDCOM is a method of transferring genealogy data between different computer systems, and different genealogy packages.

Computer Programs for the Family Historian (8 volumes). This series of booklets by John Bloore and published by the BMSGH, is designed to give an evaluation by comparison of some of the reasonably priced available programs for the MSDOS PC. (A similar book for the PCW user is in preparation.) Both commercial and shareware programs are included. These booklets are well written, 'easy readers', no mean achievement when considering the subject matter! Anyone seeking further knowledge on the relevance of the computer to family history should read these before going any further. Obtainable from the FFHS.

CONGREGATIONALIST see also Dr Williams's Library and United Reform Church. This denomination believed in the control of their church by the congregation. They were also known as Independents. In the 19th century many became Unitarians (q.v.). There are many records in the Congregational Library, 15 Gordon Square, London WC1H 0AG.

The Congregational Historical Society since 1901 has published a number of early records in its 'Transactions'. Registers were handed over to the Registrar General in compliance with the 1840 Act and are now in the PRO.

See also *My Ancestors were Congregationalists in England and Wales: with a list of registers* by D.J.H.Clifford, SOG, 1992, price £4.90 inc. p&p.

CONSISTORY COURT see also Ecclesiastical Courts and Wills. This was a bishop's court – the Episcopal Consistory Court – through which wills were proved.

CONSTABLE As the name suggests, in simple terms he was the parish policeman; he was appointed by the Vestry, his appointment being confirmed by the Justices.

He had to supervise 'Watch and Ward' (q.v.), maintain the local prison and the stocks, remove itinerant strangers, apprentice pauper children, was involved in the training of the local militia, and had many other duties.

Any parishioner might be nominated to act as Constable. It was not a popular job, and the parishioner chosen often opted to pay someone else to act in his place.

CONVEYANCES A conveyance was the process of transferring property, and also the name of the document relating to it.

There are many thousands of conveyances both of crown and private property in the PRO. There is no composite index, but there are a number of indexes and calendars, usually arranged according to the names of the parties concerned.

You are advised to consult the PRO Records Information leaflet 48 *Private Conveyances in the PRO* which deals in some detail with a complicated series of records.

CONVICTS see also Assize, Prisons and Transportation. Ask at your CRO if they have any records of convicts awaiting transportation. As an example, the Cheshire Record Office has records which supply names, 'make' (e.g. stout), visage (e.g. round), complexion (fair, sallow etc), eyes, hair, town, character, before whom and when convicted. PRO Records Information leaflet 94, *Australian Convicts; Sources in the PRO* should also be consulted.

Relevant to anyone who is trying to trace the subsequent life of a person sentenced to transportation is *A Convict's Life: A Guide To Tracing Your Convict's Life* by Janet Reakes, PO Box 937, Pialba, Queensland 4655, Australia. Price $A10.95 plus p&p.

Recommended reading is *Bound for Australia* by David Hawkings, Phillimore, 1987, illus. This is a guide for family historians wishing to follow the movements and destiny of an ancestor who was transported to Australia. It sets out a systematic sequence by which a convict can be traced from his conviction at court to his life in Australia. It also provides assistance with establishing the convict's place of origin. However, we would suggest that some previous experience of research technique is necessary to obtain a satisfactory result.

The Founders of Australia: a biographical dictionary of the First Fleet by Mollie Gillen with appendices by Yvonne Browning and others, Sydney, 1989, indexed, £32. This comprehensive work — researched from primary documents in England and Australia — will be an invaluable source of information to those seeking details of the men and women who landed at Sydney Cove on 26 Jan 1788.

Two of the twelve appendices are particularly important: details of those First Fleeters who have previously appeared in error in published works and 'The Waysiders', those who were originally on the First Fleet but who never reached Australia.

The Second Fleet, Britain's Grim Convict Armada of 1790 is a companion volume to *Founders* and provides similar information, including biographies of the second fleet convicts. Written by Michael Flynn it was published in Sydney by the Library of Australian History in 1993.

The Convict Ships 1787-1868 by Charles Bateson, published 1983 by the Library of Australian History, Sydney, N.S.W. tells the story of the convict transportation system —

that of the actual conveyance of prisoners to Australia from England and Ireland and of the convict ships, officials and merchants who despatched them.

A.G.L. Shaw's *The Convicts and the Colonies*, London 1966, is still regarded as a standard reference work on the subject.

Ms Marilyn Chowney, 76 Middle Gordon Road, Camberley, Surrey GU15 2HT is compiling The Convict Register. In addition to convicts' details, the compiler aims to help researchers in Britain contact descendants of their convict ancestor in Australia and vice versa. Send sae or 3 IRCs for details. Information for the register welcomed.

COOKS There was a London Livery Company. See *The Cooks' Company — Short History* by F.Taverner Philips, 1966.

COOPERS These were makers and repairers of barrels, and other wooden vessels such as tubs, buckets etc. much in demand in earlier times. See *A Short History of the Worshipful Company of Coopers of London* by Sir William Foster, 1961, and Shire Publication No.28 *The Village Cooper*.

COPEMAN Originally he was a dealer, but by the 18th century the word had come to mean a receiver of stolen goods.

COPYHOLD see also Freehold. This term is often found in old wills. It refers to lands held by title written into the Manorial Court rolls. On the death of the tenant, the land reverted to the Lord of the Manor who normally transferred it to the deceased's heir. This was only abolished in 1922; all copyhold land became freehold.

COPYRIGHT see also Stationers' Hall. This is covered by the 1988 Act entitled Copyright Designs and Patents Act. (The 1911 Copyright Act having been repealed.) It requires that, within 1 month of publication, British and Irish publishers must deposit one copy of each of their publications at the Legal Deposit Office, The British Library, Boston Spa, Wetherby, W.Yorks, LS23 7BY.

Certain other libraries are entitled to free copies of publications *provided that they make written demand within 12 months after publication* (i.e. they cannot demand back numbers published over 12 months ago). These libraries are Cambridge University Library; the Bodleian Library, Oxford; the National Library of Scotland; Trinity College, Dublin and the National Library of Wales. These have a joint agent, Mr A.T. Smail, at 100 Euston Street, London NW1 2HQ, to whom publications can be sent, thus economising on postage.

In general, copyright of published work remains in force for 50 years from the author's death. In the case of documents, it cannot be assumed that as 50 years have elapsed since the death of the originator of the document, one cannot infringe copyright. It is worth seeking some sort of waiver from the owner of the document.

For a more expansive note on copyright (infringement of etc) see FHN&D Vol.4 No.4 (Sep 1984) and Vol.5 No.1 (April 1985) and PRO General Information leaflets 15, 16 and 17 *Copyright*, *Copyright: A Brief Guide to Publication of material among records held in the PRO*, *Copyright: A Brief Guide to restrictions on the provision of Copies of Records and Published Works in the PRO*.

Understanding Copyright: A Practical Guide by Eric Thorn. Clearly written. Comprehensive, covering copyright relating to audio, video, computers etc. as well as print. Indexed. Published by Jay Books, 30 The Boundary, Langton Green, Tunbridge Wells, Kent, 1989. Price £4.95.

CORDWAINER Worker in leather — from leather bottles and shoes to horse harnesses. The term was most commonly used of shoemakers. See *A Descriptive and Historical Account of the Cordwainers of the City of London*, 1931.

CORONERS' INQUESTS Unfortunately many records of coroners' inquests have been destroyed, though there are exceptions. Those for the City of London have survived and are in the Guildhall Library (q.v.). From the late 19th century more are available. It is worth enquiring at your local CRO. Newspapers often give very detailed reports of Coroners' Inquests and it is worth checking the relevant newspaper in the absence of any other record.

If an inquest into a suspicious death was held and adjourned then the death cannot be registered until the inquest has been closed. In certain circumstances this may be several months later and will account for why the death registration does not appear in the GRO indexes when you would expect it to (i.e. at the time of actual death).

The FFHS has published *A Guide To Coroners' Records in England and Wales* compiled by Jeremy Gibson and Colin Rogers.

COSTERMONGER Originally he was a seller of apples. It later became a general term for a seller of fruit and vegetables from a barrow.

COST OF LIVING see Inflation.

COTTAR He was a cottager with a small landholding, obliged to provide labour on the estate of the lord of the manor.

COUNCIL FOR BRITISH ARCHAEOLOGY see Local History Societies.

COUNTESS OF HUNTINGDON'S CONNEXION This was connected with the Methodist denomination. The Countess Selina (1707-1791) warmly advocated the principles of Methodism and appointed George Whitfield, a notable preacher, as her chaplain. Her name was given to Whitfield's followers. The Countess founded a college in Wales and built many chapels. She had been widowed in 1746.

The earliest register of this sect comes from Norfolk and dates back to 1752. The movement spread throughout the country. Registers were deposited with the Registrar General in accordance with the 1840 Act and are in the PRO. Most CROs have information of chapels in their own counties.

COUNTY CODES see Chapman County Codes.

COUNTY HISTORY The *Victoria History of the Counties of England* (familiarly known as the VCH) was begun in 1899 and, with her approval, named after Queen Victoria. Its aim is to narrate the history of the English counties based on original research and ranging from earliest times to the present.

For each county there is planned a set of volumes, containing both 'general' and 'topographical' volumes therein. Broadly speaking the former consider the pre-history, ecclesiastical and economic history, Domesday Book entries etc., on a county-wide basis, whilst the latter describe in depth each individual city, town and village in that county. Each volume is illustrated and includes maps and plans.

Fourteen county sets are complete, work is in progress on at least twelve others. Further particulars may be obtained from VCH, c/o the Institute of Historical Research, University of London, Senate House, London WC1E 7HU.

Volumes less than three years old are distributed by Oxford University Press, Walton Street, Oxford, OX2 6DP. Older volumes and facsimile reprints are distributed by Dawson Book Service, Cannon House, Folkestone, Kent CT19 5EE. Price in the region of £50-£60 each volume. Copies of the volumes may be ordered from any good bookseller and, of course, most larger libraries should have at least the volumes for their counties.

An article entitled *The Victoria County History* by G.C. Baugh (editor of the Victoria County History of Shropshire) appeared in TMA Vol.6 No.5 (June 1982) and one of the same name written by Christopher Currie appeared in FHN&D, Vol.9 No.1 (April 1993). The latter is supported by a map showing the progress of the VCH to 1992.

COUNTY MAPS see Maps.

COUNTY RECORD OFFICES Quite early in your family history researches you will find yourself wanting to visit a CRO.

An excellent booklet from the FFHS is *Record Offices and How to Find Them*. Compiled by Jeremy Gibson and Pamela Peskett, it is mainly composed of sketch maps showing the position of the Record Office in relation to roads and public transport. It gives the addresses and telephone numbers. A brief practical introduction gives good advice, such as 'phoning to ensure that the office is open when you wish to visit it, and whether it is necessary to book a microfilm reader if the records you want (e.g. the census) are on microfilm, and a reminder that only pencils may be used if you are handling books or manuscripts.

In and Around Record Repositories in Great Britain and Ireland compiled by Rosemary Church and Jean Cole, edited by Avril Cross. More detailed in that it gives additional information on facilities for the disabled, procedure for document ordering, nearby places of interest, but omits the useful sketch maps. Published by FTM, 2nd ed. 1990, obtainable from the FFHS.

You will find a visit to a record office much more rewarding if you do your homework beforehand and arrive well prepared. A helpful leaflet is *You and Your Record Office: a code of practice for family historians using County Record Offices*. Issued by the Association of County Archivists in conjunction with the FFHS (2nd ed. 1990), obtainable from the Administrator of the FFHS in exchange for sae plus an extra 1st class stamp or 3 IRCs.

The County Archivist and staff are usually most helpful. If you have a specific enquiry and know that it would take only a little time for a reference to be verified or a photocopy produced, you can write and ask for this, remembering to enclose sae or 3 IRCs. A modest charge may be made, of course, if only to cover the cost of photocopying and some Record Offices have a minimum charge for supplying photocopies by post.

If any long search is required, you may be supplied with a list of local researchers who undertake such work for a fee (see Professional Searchers).

Cities and large towns usually have their own record offices, often associated with the local reference library.

COUPER One who buys and sells, especially in cattle and horses. Sometimes used in combination, e.g. a horse-couper or a herring-couper. Confusion can arise from its being mis-spelt 'cooper'.

COUPLE BEGGAR An itinerant 'hedge-priest' (priest of low status, often illiterate) who performed marriages (before 1754).

COURSES (in family history) see Family History Societies, Institute of Heraldic and Genealogical Studies, Society of Genealogists.

COURT OF ARCHES This was the Court of Appeal for the Province of Canterbury dealing with matters such as disputed wills, probate and other causes. The Court now meets at Church House, Westminster. Muniment Books are kept at Lambeth Palace Library, London SE1 7JU. There is a printed index to wills, admons. and inventories (in disputed cases) 1660-1857, (British Record Society, Vol.85).

COURT BARON This was part of the manorial system and the Court Baron concerned itself mainly with the changes of copyhold tenancies and the organisation of open fields, meadows and common land. Its records are found with other manorial documents (q.v.).

COURT OF COMMON PLEAS This Court was in operation from 1194 to 1875 and was concerned with disputes between subjects of the Crown. There is much family history hidden away in the proceedings of this court. The records are in the PRO and some in the British Museum.

COURT OF KING'S BENCH This Court ran parallel with the above Court: it was used if Crown property was involved.

COURT LEET This manorial court dealt with matters relating to law and order on the manor. In some cases the jurisdiction extended over a wider area than the Manor — often that of a Hundred. It was also known as the Court Customary since it dealt with customary tenants i.e. those who held land according to the custom of the manor as against those who were copyholders dealt with by the Court Baron. The functions of the two courts were apt to overlap.

COURT OF REQUESTS Between 1485 and c1642 this court dealt with land and monetary matters. The records are in the PRO. There is a printed surname index and place name index though the dates for these may not coincide exactly.

COURT ROLLS These were the written documents which set down the decisions of the manorial courts. They contain much genealogical information where they survive; a notable series is the Wakefield Court Rolls — the early ones are being printed in the Wakefield Court Rolls Series. The originals can be consulted at the Yorkshire Archaeological Society Archives, Claremont, Clarendon Road, Leeds LS2 9NZ.

COURTS MARTIAL see Army.

COUSIN GERMAN A first cousin.

CREST The crest is an heraldic device, modelled onto the top of the helm and part of an achievement of arms. The term is frequently used incorrectly for the whole achievement.

CRIME AND CRIMINALS A brief study of the quarter sessions records will bring home the realisation that until the late 19th century these words implied something very different than they do now, as people were transported or hanged for acts which today would be considered more a misdemeanour (e.g. stealing clothing). Between 1688 and the early 19th century the number of offences for which the nominal penalty was death had risen from about 50 to over 200.

Criminals, like paupers, were often well-documented, though the location of records is not so easy, since criminal justice was administered locally but prisons might be organised locally or nationally. *Criminal Ancestors: A Guide to Historical Criminal Records in England and Wales* by David Hawkings, Alan Sutton Publishing, 1992, is an expansive book dealing with criminals' records in considerable detail. The eight appendices list hundreds of classes of criminal records and their whereabouts, there is a glossary plus indexes of place names (though not subjects), prison hulks and ships. Based on the author's own research and outlined in an article *Criminal Ancestors in England and Wales*, FTM Vol.8 No.5 (March 1992).

The Hangman's Record is a 16pp booklet listing principal executions in this country for 400 years (1600-1906). Printed by Mrs Burgess in London early this century (the flyleaf describes it as "a marvellous book for settling a dispute"!).

CRIMEAN WAR After twenty five years extensive research into the records of the Crimean War, Mr Ken Horton, 15 Bartestree Close, Matchborough East, Redditch, Worcs B98 0AZ, can provide from his copious files, information on all the Regiments and personnel that participated, including some of the womenfolk who accompanied the expedition. His files also include details of the nurses who were part of Florence Nightingale's contingents. Mr Horton was consulted by the British Authorities when they provided a list of inscriptions to be placed on the memorial obelisk to the British dead in the Crimea built by the Russian Authorities. Any enquiry should be accompanied by sae or IRC.

Honour the Light Brigade by Canon Lummis gives a record compiled from the Muster Rolls in the PRO, of the services of Officers, Non-commissioned Officers and men of the five Cavalry regiments that made up the Light Brigade at Balaclava in the Crimea, though there are many omissions and errors.

CROCKFORD'S CLERICAL DIRECTORY see Clergy.

CROFTER This is the usual term for a Scottish smallholder — there are regional variations. It is also used for a bleacher or dyer in textile trades.

CURATE Usually the vicar's or rector's assistant. A Perpetual Curate was in fact a vicar.

CURATION see also Tuition. Guardianship over orphaned minors, under 21 but over 14 (boys) or 12 (girls).

CURIA REGIS ROLLS These relate to the records of the Court of King's Bench covering the period 1193 to 1272. The Rolls, later known as Common Pleas, record the proceedings of the Bench and the court 'Coram Rege'. They are held in class KB26 at the PRO and include all the surviving rolls of itinerant justices for the reign of Richard I and some for those for King John.

Many of the Rolls have been transcribed and published; they are useful not only to those studying Mediaeval Law but also as a source reflecting the social and economic life of the times.

CURRER-BRIGGS see Indexes

CURRIER Curriers were dressers of leather for further treatment, and were originally linked to the cordwainers. See *The Curriers and the City of London* by Edward Mayer, 1968.

CURSITOR A clerk in a Chancery Court who drew up wills.

CURTILAGE This is a term sometimes found in wills and means a plot of land near the house, usually a vegetable garden.

CUSTOMAL This was a written document setting out the 'customs' of the manor and the services owed by tenants, the duties of town burgesses and the rights and duties of the lord of the manor.

CUSTOMS AND EXCISE Customs duties are imposed on goods imported into or exported from the country, excise duties are imposed on goods within the country.

Customs duties date back to the reign of Edward I and until 1671 were administered by the Exchequer. In that year six commissioners were appointed and formed a Board of Customs which set up Customs Houses with salaried officers throughout the country. The administration of Excise duties on the manufacture, sale or consumption of goods began in 1642 and was transferred to Customs in 1909.

There are 300 volumes at the PRO, dating from the late 17th century relating to provincial ports (Headquarters' records were destroyed by fire in 1814). The correspondence in these volumes contains much information about government staff, such as recommendations, adverse reports, baptismal certificates and notes about sickness and death. Excise Board records in the form of indexed minute books from 1695 to 1867 fill 749 volumes and contain similar information. See 'Information' Series 106 *Customs and Excise Records as sources for Biography and Family History*.

The library of HM Customs and Excise is at New King's Beam House, 22 Upper Ground, London SE1 9PJ whilst their Museum is in the Georgian Custom House, Lower Thames Street, London EC3.

A report of a lecture by Rupert Jarvis on the subject appears in Gen. Mag. Vol.10 No.7 (Sep 1948) and more recently in FTM Vol.5 No.10 (Aug 1989) Joy Lodey asks *Was Your Ancestor a Customs Officer?*.

CUTLER Made swords, knives and instruments. There was a London Livery Company. See *History of the Cutlers' Company of London* by Charles Welch, 1923, and *A Brief History ...* by Dudley Hayton, 1956. The term 'cutler' later applied to those who made domestic cutlery also — Sheffield being the centre of the modern industry.

DANISH ANCESTRY The Danish Embassy, 55 Sloane Street, London SW1X 9SR, has issued a leaflet on Genealogical Research in Denmark. Enclose sae or 3 IRCs. For the same postage a list of family history societies in Denmark can be obtained from the Administrator of the FFHS.

DATA PROTECTION ACT In 1984 new legislation was passed about the way personal information is handled in computers. It affects everyone who owns a computer or who has any data processed on someone else's equipment. The Act is highly complex! For details of how this might affect you see SOG Leaflet No.18 *The Data Protection Act and Genealogists*.

DATES see also Calendars and Regnal Years.
Dates and Calendars for the Genealogist by Cliff Webb, SOG, 1994. Obtainable from them price £2.60 inc.p&p. This booklet is more than adequate for the needs of the majority of family historians. Concise and easy to follow it even has short sections dealing with the Roman, French Revolutionary, Jewish and Moslem Calendars in addition to the more familiar Julian and Gregorian Calendars.

Every family historian should read this at least once, preferably during the earlier stages of research; they may make fewer errors of calculation later.

Handbook of Dates for Students of English History, ed. C.R.Cheney, published by the Royal Historical Society as Historical Society Guides and Handouts No.4, 1984, price around £5. Obtainable from the IHGS. A copy may be available in your local library. More comprehensive than the previously recommended publication; includes six-page bibliography.

Also Haydn's *Dictionary of Dates,* various editions from 1841; copies may be available in libraries or can be purchased secondhand.

DEAN He presided over the Chapter (q.v.). A rural dean, like the Archdeacon, was a bishop's deputy, but inferior in status.

DEATH DUTIES Death duty was a tax payable on legacies and residues of personal estates of deceased persons and was initiated by a series of statutes starting in 1796. Initially it was a tax on particular legacies but it was gradually extended until by 1811 all estates going through probate courts were included except those that were very small.

The registers of abstracts for the whole country from 1786-1903 are now in the PRO (IR 26). They record the date of probate, names of beneficiaries, details and value of property and the duty paid.

There are three main uses of the Death Duty registers. Firstly as a finding aid to ascertain in which court a will was proved or an admon. granted. Secondly, because the registers give you a list of people who shared the estate and its value you can discover what actually happened as opposed to what was intended. Thirdly, in the case of an admon. which will simply tell you the name and address of the administrator or next of kin, the register will tell you the value of the estate. See PRO Records Information leaflet 66 *The Death Duty Registers* for details.

The Indexes to the Registers are available at the PRO and are on film from 1812-1857. From 1796-1812 and 1858-1903 they are obtainable upon application to the Search Room officer and do not have to be ordered by computer.

There are no copies of the Devon and Cornwall wills, which were destroyed during the Second World War, at the PRO, according to that Office.

Recommended reading is *Affection Defying the Power of Death: Wills, Probate & Death Duty Records* by Jane Cox, FFHS (*An introduction to...* series). Also articles *A Note on the Death Duty Registers* by Jane Cox, Gen. Mag. Vol.20 No.8 (Dec 1981) and *Death Duty Registers — A Users' Guide* appeared in the journal of the West Middlesex FHS Vol.3 No.1 (April 1982).

DEATHS see also Funeral. Parish Registers are the obvious source; from 1837 we have the use of Civil Registration and a number of FHSs are now compiling Burial Indexes. Publications such as *The Gentleman's Magazine* and *Miscellanea Genealogica et Heraldica* (published from about 1880-1920) contain a vast amount of assorted genealogical information and can be consulted at the SOG and larger reference libraries. Whilst not exclusively genealogical, *Notes and Queries etc.* also include Obituaries and MIs. Besides the national edition some counties seem to have had their own editions.

Boyd's London Burials can be consulted at the SOG. It is an index of about a quarter of a million entries from burial registers of London churches and cemeteries 1538-1852, including a large part of the registers of the Nonconformist burial ground of Bunhill Fields. The index contains names of males only and no children. Whilst far from complete it remains an extremely useful 'lucky dip'.

See *Boyd's London burials and citizens of London* by Anthony J. Camp, FTM Vol.1 No.6 (Sep-Oct 1985).

DEATHS OVERSEAS see also BACSA and Commonwealth War Graves Commission. There are various registers of deaths of British subjects overseas and of servicemen in the indexes at St Catherine's House (see Civil Registration).

The British Overseas: a guide to the records of their births, baptisms, marriages, deaths and burials, available in the UK, The Guildhall Library Research Guide (q.v.), 3rd ed. 1994. It deals primarily with sources pre-1945 and Part: I Introduction to the Sources, is particularly helpful. Part II: *Lists of known Registers for Individual Places Overseas* deals with everywhere from Aden (South Yemen) to West Indies. Price in the region of £6.

It is also worthwhile checking *Parish Register Copies in the Library of the Society of Genealogists,* 1992, price £5.65 inc. p. & p., since they hold a considerable amount of material relating to events overseas.

The Anglican Church Registers of Lisbon, Portugal contain details of baptisms, marriages and burials of naval men from 1721 to 1867. Extracts were printed in Vol.8 of

Gen. Mag. (1938 – 39). A large number of ships of the British Navy were stationed from time to time in the Tagus.

The registers of marriages solemnised in the British Chapel at Lisbon 1822 to 1859 are at St Catherine's House.

The Bishop of London's Registry, St Paul's Churchyard, London has a Lisbon register of Marriages 1812 to 1890 and baptisms 1830 to 1848.

There is a Protestant Church Cemetery at Macao (Portuguese overseas province, South East China). Memorial Inscriptions appeared in Gen. Mag. Vol.8 No.6 (June 1939).

Corfu: Baptisms 1865 to 1880, Marriages 1866 to 1902 and Burials 1865 to 1878 were transcribed by a Mr Hopwood who died in Corfu and is buried in the cemetery there. The transcriptions appeared in 'The Manchester Genealogist' (journal of the Manchester & Lancashire FHS) Vol.13 No.3 and Vol.14. Nos 1 and 2, respectively.

Mr D. Pearce, 'Wayside', Roman Road, Twyford, Hampshire, SO21 1QW is custodian of "An Index of Britons Dying Overseas". This index contains more than 300,000 names of persons born in the UK from the 16th century to the present day, but who died overseas. Entries are culled from innumerable sources. A considerable number of names of persons who have spent part of their lives overseas have also come to light so a parallel index has been started of Britons who have Lived/Served Overseas. Contributions of obituary notices from local newspapers, MIs and personal pedigrees are welcome. Enquiries should be accompanied by 5 x 2nd class stamps and sae, or 3 IRCs. See *Index of British born People Dying Abroad* by Doreen Pearce, FTM Vol.8 No.10 (Aug 1992).

DEBRETT ANCESTRY RESEARCH see Indexes

DECEASED WIFE'S SISTER – Marriage to: see Marriage.

DEED POLL There is no law to prevent you from changing your name – you do it merely by using the new name you have chosen. There would come a time, however, when you would need legal proof of your identity. It is advisable, therefore, to make a simple statutory declaration, drawn up by a solicitor, of your change of name.

If you want complete formality use a process called Deed Poll; you do this through the Central Office of the Supreme Court, Royal Courts of Justice, Strand, London WC2A 2LL. There is a charge for this service.

You are probably more interested in those who changed their names in the past. It was sometimes done in order to inherit an estate or title. You should read the PRO Records Information leaflet 38 *Change of Name* which deals with the records relating to this and the method of making a change of name. It is of interest to note that between 1939 and 1945 British subjects could change their names by publishing details in the London, Edinburgh or Belfast Gazette for 21 days beforehand.

W.P.W. Phillimore and E.A. Fry compiled *An Index to Changes of Name 1760 to 1901*, London 1905, which you can probably locate in a large Reference Library. *Pinhorns' Index to Changes of Name, 1901 to 1915* was originally compiled to follow the above volume; it is unpublished but can be consulted for a search fee on request to Pinhorns.

DEEDS REGISTRY see Title Deeds.

DELEGATES Court of. This was a Court of Appeal for the provincial courts of Canterbury and York.

DELINQUENT A word used mainly during the Commonwealth Period (q.v.) to describe those who took the Royalist side in the Civil War or those who were described as Papists or Recusants.

DEMESNE This term refers to the lord's land, as distinct from the tenant's land. An 'ancient demesne' refers to Crown land. In effect, tenants of land belonging to the Crown had special privileges, even though the land may later have been given to another lord. The word is pronounced 'Domaine'.

DEMISE Another word for a conveyance of land. It can also mean to lease land or to bequeath or transmit to a successor (all involving death).

DENIZATION see Naturalization.

DENTIST The library of the British Dental Association, 64 Wimpole Street, London W1M 8AL has an index to articles from periodicals which have contained names of dentists. This index commences in 1839. There is little other archive material available.

DEPOSITIONS These are statements of evidence, usually relating to a court case. Disputes between individuals were heard in the Court of Chancery. If your ancestors were people of humble origin they would be unlikely to resort to such a court. However, they may have been required to give evidence in support of plaintiff or defendant.

The names of the deponents have been indexed — see Bernau Index.

DESERTER During the 18th and early 19th centuries notices of deserters from the armed forces were printed in local newspapers and the *Police Gazette and Hue and Cry*. These give detailed physical characteristics and often place of birth and trade, so there was a good chance that a deserter who returned home might be caught.

Here is an example from 'Aris's Birmingham Gazette' for 15th March 1756:

'Deserted from Serjeant Bland, of Colonel Anstruther's Regiment of Foot, from Birmingham, THOMAS OWEN who enlisted the 26th February and deserted the 10th of March. He was born in the parish of St Chad in Shrewsbury, is 16 years of age, 5ft 6 inches and a quarter high, dark brown hair, very much marked with the Small-Pox, a dimple on his chin, by trade a leather dresser; had on a dark brown wig, a dark brown frize coat, greasy leather breeches and a black velvet stock with ribbons to it, round his neck'.

Army Deserters from HM Service Vol.1 1853-1858 Yvonne Fitzmaurice, 1988. Price $A10 plus $A3 p&p. Obtainable from the author, 23 Fuller Street, Mitcham, Victoria 3132, Australia.

Over 800 entries compiled from material held at PRO, Melbourne and from police records. Gives comprehensive details of the men, all of whom at this period came from the British Isles. First volume of a series intended to continue to 1900.

DEWEY CLASSIFICATION A decimal index system for the subject classification of books using 3 digit whole numbers, starting with 000, and decimal subdivisions. Perhaps the most important for Family Historians are 900, Geography and History, and 929

Genealogical Reference Books. It has to be remembered that the shelving of a particular book depends very much on the view of the contents taken by the librarian concerned.

For a detailed consideration see the series of articles by D.J.Steel in the Journal of the Bristol and Avon FHS (and a parallel series published by the West Surrey FHS) starting in Journal No.1 (Autumn 1975) and ending in Journal No.8 (Summer 1977).

DEXTER He was a dyer. It is also a heraldic term referring to everything placed on the right hand side of the shield, as opposed to Sinister, the left hand side. The terms right and left in heraldry are as seen from the back by the person holding the shield and are therefore the reverse of the normal positions.

DICTIONARY OF NATIONAL BIOGRAPHY (D.N.B.) see Biographies.

DICTIONARY OF NAVAL BIOGRAPHIES Can be consulted at Plymouth Central Library, Drake Circus, Plymouth, PL4 8AL.

DIOCESAN RECORD OFFICES Records were deposited in what was called the Diocesan Registry, and these have formed the basis of the Diocesan Record Offices which are open to the public — but check whether access is available by appointment only. In the case of some of the newer dioceses, their record offices are administered by the local Reference Library (e.g.Birmingham) or by the County Record Office. Many CROs are also DROs.

DIOCESE The district over which a bishop has authority.

DIRECTORIES see also Kelly's and Poll Books. Directories of large towns date from the middle of the 18th century and County Directories from early 19th century: they serve both as gazetteers and as a guide to people living in the area although the early ones contain only the names of persons of substance or people in business.

A useful reference book is *British Directories: A Bibliography and Guide to Directories Published in England and Wales (1850-1950) and Scotland (1773- 1950)* by Gareth Shaw and Alison Tipper, Leicester University Press, 1988. Indexed. Price around £50 but there should be a copy available in your local library! Divided into three parts: Introduction and Evolutionary trends in directory publication; Bibliography and its organisation; Library Holdings by location and Index by place and subject. Well-written and informative.

See also *Guide to National & Provincial Directories of England and Wales (excluding London) before 1856* by Jane Norton,1950: for London see *London Directories 1677 to 1856* by C.W.F.Goss, 1932. The SOG has published a *Catalogue of Directories and Poll Books in the Possession of the Society of Genealogists* (new ed 1994), and chapter 9 of *Town Records* by John West (Phillimore 1983), entitled *Commercial Directories 1763-1900,* contains a 6pp gazetteer of Commercial Directories for those dates.

When using directories make allowances for the lapse of time between the collection of information and the publication year. Thus, a Directory of 1845 may well be recording addresses of residents a year or more earlier. Also valuable as a source of information are trade and professional directories and telephone directories.

DIRECTORIES: GENEALOGICAL Publications on a National and International scale (see also Directories of Members' Interests) listing names and addresses of subscribers and the names which they are researching, usually with areas and dates.

A *Genealogical Research Directory: National and International* is published annually by Keith A. Johnson & Malcolm R. Sainty. This is regarded as a key work for worldwide family history research; especially useful for contact addresses is its section 'Directory of Societies', many of whom are not members of the FFHS. In addition to the Chapman County Codes for the British Isles it also lists codes for many overseas countries.

There are worldwide representatives from whom the directory can be obtained; British Isles enquirers can obtain further details from Mrs Elizabeth Simpson, 2 Stella Grove, Tollerton, Nottingham NG12 4EY, otherwise send 3 IRCs to the Administrator of the FFHS who will supply the relevant address.

DIRECTORIES OF MEMBERS' INTERESTS see also *British Isles Genealogical Register.* These are produced by almost all the regional Family History Societies or by a group of Societies in an area. They contain names and addresses of members together with the names (and areas and dates) which they are researching and they aim to put family historians in touch with each other to avoid duplication of effort. Although interests in the geographical area covered by the publishing society do tend to predominate, most people have widespread interests and it is advisable to consult Directories for areas in which you do not have a personal interest as well as those covering the territory where your ancestors lived. Write to the Secretary of the Society which covers the area in which you are interested to ask if they have a Directory of Members' Interests and the cost of obtaining a copy by post.

A series of 'County Families' Directories has been produced with entries relating specifically to research on people living in a particular county. Some 15 volumes were produced but these are largely out of print and dated. The series has been replaced by the relevant sections of the *British Isles Genealogical Register* (q.v.).

DISSENTER see Nonconformist.

DISTRESSED PROTESTANTS IN IRELAND 1642 (Collection for) On the eve of Civil War in England rebellion broke out in Ireland. Thousands of Protestant 'planters' were massacred, thousands more fled to the fortified garrison towns or to England. There was an urgent need to provide emergency relief to the refugees and to pay for a small force to suppress the rebellion. Parliament and King passed an emergency act to receive loans and free gifts for these purposes.

Those charged with collecting the gifts were also charged with submitting the names and contributions of the donors. Many of the returns survive, and are in the PRO, though they are little-used. The returns are split between two separate classes: Lay Subsidies (E179) and State Papers Domestic (SP 28). The returns for Buckinghamshire and East Sussex have been printed.

See *Protestation Returns 1641-42 and Other Contemporary Listings* by Jeremy Gibson and Alan Dell, FFHS. This gives names of all places covered by the returns, originally researched by Cliff Webb, Gen.Mag. Vol. 21 No. 9 (Mar 1985).

To find a person interested in the name **SWINNERTON**

First use the index section which comprises a list of surnames being researched. This list has often been placed in strict alphabetical order. Please make sure you check all possible variants of the surname you are researching.

SWINGWOOD	Anywhere	STS	E	All	2236
SWINLEY	Anywhere	ALL	A	All	13015
SWINNERTON	Anywhere	ALL	A	All	**3505**
SWINNERTON	Whitmore	STS	E	1500 +	7908
SWINNINGTON	Anywhere	ALL	A	All	3505

A person interested in SWINNERTON (in bold type) has the number **3505** in the right hand column. This person is interested in SWINNERTON anywhere. He may be interested in hearing from anyone interested in SWINNERTON, whereas the other person interested in SWINNERTON is probably only interested in hearing about the SWINNERTON family from Whitmore in Staffordshire 1500 +. As your SWINNERTON family came from Yorkshire then it is to **3505** you could write. If you were interested in Staffordshire you could write to 7908.

You now need to go to the address section which comprises a list of names and addresses of the contributors. Each person has a number which corresponds to a reference number usually to be found in the right hand column in the surname section or at the end of the relevant section.

3505   Mr A Swinnerton, 20 A Street, Anytown, Anyshire HG2 0PL.
7908   Ms R.A Smith, 12 Our Street, Ourtown, Ourshire SY8 2ET

So you can write to A. Swinnerton and he may be able to help you with your Yorkshire SWINNERTON family or you may be able to help him.

When writing to someone please give a brief outline of your interest. The exchange of information can begin after you have established a positive connection.

An example page of a Genealogical Directory.

DISTRICT PROBATE REGISTRY See also Wills. Where probate was taken out at a district registry, that registry retained the original will and made a copy before forwarding a further copy to the Principal Registry in London. District Probate Registries generally covered the counties in which they lay and there were none in the Home Counties. See *A Simplified Guide to Probate Jurisdictions* by Jeremy Gibson, FFHS, and *Wills, Probate and Death Duty Records* by Jane Cox in the *'An introduction to...'* series.

DIVORCE You are advised to read PRO Records Information leaflet 127 *Divorce Records in the PRO* which gives a history of the Divorce Law, its complexities and the whereabouts of relevant records.

Under early catholic church law there was no such thing as divorce; although Henry VIII had annulled two of his marriages there was no general 'divorce' in the sense that these marriages were dissolved by a formalised legal process. By the end of the sixteenth century and despite the introduction of a reformed Protestant religion, England was the only European Protestant country to have no divorce law as such. There was no legal change in the law of divorce before 1857.

In practice, however, various ways were found to separate partners in unsatisfactory marriages and the remedies were available through the church courts, common law courts and through parliament but only to those who could afford them. Within the poorer classes of society separations were straight forward desertions. Between 1670 and 1857 divorce was obtainable only by an Act of Parliament and private divorce acts are mainly to be found at the House of Lords Record Office (q.v.).

The 1857 Divorce Act finally became law as the Matrimonial Causes Act on 1 January 1858 and made divorce possible by use of the civil courts. The 1857 Act did not apply to Ireland (Scotland had a fairly liberal divorce law by the 17th century). Before searching for divorce records in the PRO it is necessary to have an idea of when the separation took place, or whether an appeal was made from a local court in questions of separation before 1858.

After 1858 all divorce cases in England and Wales were heard before the new court for divorce and after 1873 by the Probate, Divorce and Admiralty Division of the Supreme Court of Judicature. Files from these courts can be found in PRO Principal Probate Registry Divorce Files, 1858 to 1938. Some files are restricted under a 75 year closure, but the indexes are subject to the normal 30 year rule. Permission to see closed files may be sought from the Principal Registry of the Family Division, at the address given below.

Records from 1938 to the present (England and Wales only), and copies of records from 1858, are at the Principal Registry of the Family Division, Somerset House, The Strand, London WC2 1LP. The index is not open to the general public but a search service is available at a cost of £5 for a block of ten years searched with an additional charge of £5 for each subsequent block of five years (dates as supplied by the enquirer). If the search is successful then this charge includes the cost of a copy of the Decree Absolute.

Records of Marriage and Divorce in Lambeth Palace Library by Melanie Barber appeared in Gen. Mag. Vol.20 No.4 (Dec 1980) and *Divorce and Separation* by Jean A. Cole in the journal of the Rossendale SGH Vol.4 No.2 (May 1983), now Lancs. FH & HS.

See *Road to Divorce — England 1530-1987* by L.Stone, 1990, and *Broken Lives, separation and divorce in England 1660-1857* also by L.Stone, Oxford University Press, 1993. £12.95 and £16.95 respectively, plus p&p. Obtainable from SOG.

Divorces were extremely newsworthy items. An index to divorces reported in *The Times* 1788-1910 is in the care of Mrs Annie Weare, 5 Berwick Close, Beechwood, Birkenhead, L43 9XA. The search fee is £1.50 ($A3.75; NZ$5). Australian and New Zealand cheques are acceptable and should be payable to Mrs Weare. Return postage is not required as it is included in the fee. The index is available for purchase on microfiche (9) for £8 ($A22; NZ$30), inclusive of airmail postage.

The sale of wives was one means used by poor people to obtain a separation. The practice is described in Thomas Hardy's *The Mayor of Casterbridge*. In Borrow's *Romany Rye* the jockey bought Mary Fulcher for 1s.6d and married her three weeks later, the husband having died on the day of the sale.

Wives for Sale by Samuel Pyeatt Menefee, Blackwell, Oxford, 1981 makes fascinating reading.

DOCKYARD EMPLOYEES Until 1832 dockyards and naval establishments were the responsibility of the Navy Board, but victualling yards and depots were controlled by the Victualling Board, itself answerable to the Navy Board. Gunwharves, jetties used specifically for loading gunpowder and ordnance stores onto warships were the responsibility of the Ordnance Board.

After 1832 all yards and establishments in each port, excepting gunwharves, were amalgamated under a single authority.

There are records at the PRO, relating to employees prior to 1832, referring to tradesmen as well as to salaried staff. After that date there are pension records of salaried staff, but yard musters survive only to the mid 19th century.

A detailed summary of the records is given in PRO Records Information leaflet 15 *Dockyard Employees: Documents in the Public Record Office* They relate to establishments all over the world.

DOCTOR see Medical Profession.

DOCTORS' COMMONS see also Proctors. College of Doctors of Civil Law in London. Five courts were held in the buildings, Prerogative Court of Canterbury, Court of Arches, Court of Faculties, Consistory Court and High Court of Admiralty. Business included divorce suits, marriage licences, probate matters, ecclesiastical law, Prize claims, etc. It ceased to function after 1858.

Hatred Pursued Beyond The Grave by Jane Cox draws on material from the records of Doctors' Commons — not so much a text book but stories taken from the unique and invaluable records of these courts; the voices of our ancestors. Published by HMSO in association with PRO, available from FFHS.

Dr BARNARDO see Children's Societies.

Dr WILLIAMS'S LIBRARY Births of many London nonconformists were registered at this theological Library, 14, Gordon Square, London WC1H OAG. The register was intended for nonconformists living within 12 miles of central London but there are entries for those living further afield. The registers are now in the PRO, and cover the period 1742 to 1837.

Amongst the special collections at the library are many histories of individual congregations, both printed and duplicated, of the different nonconformist denominations and of nonconformity generally on a geographical basis.

There is an invaluable card index of brief biographies of all Congregationalist ministers, and complete runs of the 'Congregational Year Book' which contain obituary notices of ministers.

An annual subscription entitles a member to borrow up to 3 books at one time. Books may be sent to borrowers by post. There is also a short term subscription. Further information may be obtained from the Librarian.

DOCUMENTS The preservation of any document of value, either historical or sentimental, is of paramount importance. *Caring for Books and Documents* by A.D. Baynes-Cope is most informative on all aspects of this subject. Published by and obtainable from British Museum Publications Ltd, 6 Bedford Square, London WC1B 3RN. £3.00 inc. p&p.

See also *Care of books and those things that hold your heritage treasures* Althea Douglas, FTM Vol.4 No.6 (April 1988): gives chart of desirable levels of humidity, temperature and light. *The Creation and Care of Documents* T.J.Collings, FTM Vol.5 Nos.5,6 & 7 (March/April/May 1989), *The Conservation and Care of Documents* Richard Harris, Gen. Mag. Vol.23 No.8 (Dec 1990).

In *Modern Papers Used for Recording a Family History*, East Surrey FHS, Vol.16 No.1 (March 1993), John Bishop quotes names and addresses of suppliers of preservation materials (which may not be cheap but look upon it as an investment). The SOG (q.v.), too, stock a product for this purpose and will supply details on request.

If in doubt as to how to tackle this problem then contact your local archivist for advice — if they cannot help then who can!

DOMESDAY BOOK Survey of England drawn up by order of William the Conqueror in 1086. The Survey's function was to register all taxable holdings; since many lands and buildings were exempt from taxation, especially those owned by religious houses, not all are noted.

Before its rebinding in the 1980s (into a more-manageable five volumes) the Survey consisted of two volumes. One covering Essex, Norfolk and Suffolk, the other the remainder of England with the exception of Cumberland, Durham, Northumberland and northern Westmorland. London and Winchester are also omitted. (Northumberland and Durham were subsequently covered by what is known as the Boldon Book.)

The two volumes of the survey acquired the name 'Exchequer Domesday' (Great and Little) as there was no appeal against the judgements based on the evidence in their pages.

The original Survey is in the PRO. See PRO Records Information leaflet 75 *Domesday Book*. The appropriate volume of *Victoria County History* gives a transcription and summary or Phillimore (q.v.) publish the complete edition in 35 (County) volumes plus three index volumes.

See also FTM Vol.1 No.5 (July-Aug 1985), *Can you trace your family back to the Domesday Book* by Jane Cox, Vol.2 No.2 (Jan-Feb 1986), *Domesday and The Family*

Historian by Cecil R.Humphery-Smith and Vol.2 No.3 (Mar-Apr.1986) *The Domesday Exhibition or How The PRO Went Public* by Jane Cox.

DORMANT FUNDS see Funds in Chancery.

DOWER A widow's share for life of one third of her deceased husband's land (not just his 'estate' which would include cash, investments etc.) The word is also used for dowry (property brought by woman to husband at marriage) a practice quite common amongst the middle and upper classes until the 20th century.

DRAPER The London Drapers' Company was an important and influential one. There are two books about the Company – *The Triple Crowns* by Tom Girtin and *The History of the Worshipful Company of the Drapers of London* by the Rev. A.H. Johnson.

DUBLIN UNIVERSITY *Alumni Dublinienses 1593 to 1860* gives names of graduates.

DUGDALE SOCIETY Named after Sir William Dugdale, one time Garter King of Arms, author of *Antiquities of Warwickshire* and a series of Heralds' Visitation Pedigrees compiled during the years 1662-66 when he visited personally all 10 counties in his province (north of the River Trent). The Society has published several volumes of material starting in 1921. Details from Hon. Sec., The Shakespeare Centre, Stratford-upon-Avon, Warwickshire CV37 6QW.

DYERS There was a London Livery Company. See *A Short History of the Ancient Mystery of the Dyers of the City of London*, by J.N. Daynes, privately printed.

EAST INDIA COMPANY see Oriental and India Office Collections.

EASTER DUES see Church Rates.

ECCLESIASTICAL CENSUS In 1851 the Home Office took a census of all places of worship in the country. It contains the address of every church or meeting house of all denominations, gives the location, date of erection or foundation, and size of congregation.
It is in the PRO (Ref.HO129), and is arranged by county or by Poor Law Unions. Often, however, the information is incomplete because of the ignorance or reluctance of the informant. See PRO Records Information leaflet 51 *Ecclesiastical Census of 1851*.

ECCLESIASTICAL COURTS These dealt with the clergy and matters of heresy. The lowest court was that of the Archdeacon. Appeals could be made to the Bishop's Court – also known as the Consistory Court. The highest courts were the Court of Arches for the Province of Canterbury, and the Court of Chancery for the Province of York.
Recommended reading *Ecclesiastical Courts, Their Officials and Their Records* by Colin R. Chapman, Lochin Publishing (1992). Obtainable from FTM price £5.45 inc. p&p.

ECCLESIASTICAL LAWYER see Proctor.

EDUCATION Many famous schools are of very old foundation; many were set up originally to educate poor boys, but developed into Public Schools (which, for the benefit of overseas readers unfamiliar with the quirks of our educational system, are now private schools).

The old school registers of most of the Public Schools have been published, together with other records; they can contain valuable genealogical information such as names of parents, and even details of what subsequently happened to the pupils, e.g. marriage, careers and distinctions obtained. Details will be found in *Registers of the Universities, Colleges and Schools of Great Britain and Ireland*, by P.M. Jacob.

Other useful reference books are *Histories of Old Schools; a revised list for England and Wales* by P.J. Walesby, published by the Dept. of Education, University of Newcastle upon Tyne in 1966 and *Reformatory and Industrial Schools* (certified by the Home Office 1854-1933), compiled by D.H.Thomas, Newcastle upon Tyne Polytechnic Products Ltd, 1988, and obtainable from the Library, Newcastle upon Tyne Polytechnic, Ellison Building, Ellison Place, Newcastle upon Tyne NE1 8ST, price £1.95 plus p&p.

The SOG Library has a fine collection of these printed records, and copies are likely to be found in libraries in the locality of the individual school. See *School, University and College registers and histories in the library of the Society of Genealogists*, price £2.60 inc. p&p.

See also PRO Records Information leaflets 77 *Records relating to Elementary and Secondary Schools*; 78 *Education: Records of Teachers*; 79 *Education: Records of Special Services* and 80 *Records Relating to Technical and Further Education*.

Before the provision of education by the state, schools were set up by the church authorities; you may find records of them with other parish documents.

Industrial schools were set up from 1857 for children in need of care and protection, and magistrates sent children there to learn a trade. There were numerous private schools, which charged a small weekly fee, some run by women teachers being known as Dame Schools.

Ragged Schools were begun in 1818 by John Pounds who provided a school which was free for the poorest children. In 1844 Lord Shaftesbury helped to organise an official union of these schools and by 1869 there were about 200 establishments.

The Sunday School movement was popularised by Robert Raikes who founded a school in Gloucester in 1780, although it is thought the first Sunday School was in Yorkshire in 1763. He charged pupils a penny each week. The Sunday School Union was founded in 1803 to improve such schools in the London area.

Forster's Education Act of 1870 divided England into areas and arranged that schools should be set up where provision was insufficient. Legislation in 1876 laid down the principle that all children should receive elementary education, but it was not until 1880 that school attendance became compulsory up to the age of 10.

The National Society, The Church of England Record Centre, 15 Galleywall Road, London SE16 3PB (formerly The National Society for Promoting the Education of the Poor in the Principles of the Established Church) holds indexed registers of teachers trained at their Central School 1812-51, plus admission registers for training colleges at St Marks, Chelsea 1841-48 and Battersea 1844-48. Unindexed copies of *National Society Monthly Paper* 1849-74 and *School Guardian* 1875-1930s can be consulted by appointment. They contain many references to teachers.

Please send sae or 2 IRCs with enquiries or for free leaflet *Brief Notes for Family Historians using Church of England Records*.

The archives of the British and Foreign School Society are held at the West London Institute of Higher Education, Borough Road, Isleworth, Middlesex TW7 5DU. See *The Records of the British and Foreign School Society* by George F.Bartle, Gen. Mag. Vol.23 No.3 (Sep 1989).

These and numerous other aspects of schooling are dealt with in *The Growth of British Education and its Records* by Colin R. Chapman, Lochin Publishing, 1991. Obtainable from FTM price £5.39 inc. p&p.

Records of the old School Boards, and of the schools themselves, are often to be found in CROs. School Log Books sometimes contain references to an individual's parents. These are useful sources from which to enrich your family history.

Mr Tim Cockerell, The Old Mill House, Weston Colville, Cambridge, CB1 5NY has over a hundred School, College and University Registers in his possession which he is willing to search in exchange for a fee of £5 plus sae or 2 IRCs per surname. There is no central index so he would need a clue e.g. where and when someone was thought to have been at school, college or university.

The *National Union of Teachers' War Record 1914-1919*, Hamilton House, 1920, contains details which could be useful if your teacher-ancestor served during this period. A copy may be in your local library otherwise Mrs A. Jones, Rookery Farm, 16 New Lane, Walton on the Wolds, Loughborough, Leics LE12 8HY will consult her copy in exchange for sae or 2 IRCs. Please print all names clearly and if possible it would help to mention where your ancestor came from.

The Museum of the History of Education is located at The University of Leeds, Parkinson Court, Leeds LS2 9JT.

The Institute of Education Library, University of London, 11-13 Ridgmount Street, London WC1E 7AH, specialises in the history of education.

PRO General Information leaflet 20 *Teachers and the Public Record Office* indicates to present-day teachers the types of records held by the PRO, what facilities it can offer for educational use relative to current syllabuses and equally, what services it is not in a position to provide for students.

ELECTORAL REGISTERS see also Poll Books.

Electoral Registers since 1832; and Burgess Rolls: A Directory to holdings in Great Britain by Jeremy Gibson and Colin Rogers, FFHS.

The 1832 Reform Act greatly widened the franchise, and enacted that the names of all those qualified to vote be published annually. The resultant Electoral Registers continue to this day, but the printed lists for the 19th and earlier 20th centuries survive much more rarely than might be expected. This is the first ever attempt to list those in record offices and local studies libraries throughout England, Wales and Scotland and shows just where these amazingly informative lists can be consulted.

A burgess is defined in the Oxford Dictionary as 'Inhabitant of a borough with full Municipal rights, citizen'.

Burgess lists of those entitled to vote, mostly for Borough representatives, continued in parallel into the 20th century, but sometimes survive from much earlier (even mediaeval) times. These, and 18th century lists of county free-holders, are also included in this guide to much neglected sources for family, local and social historians.

See also *Electoral Rolls in Genealogy* by Alexander Sandison, Gen. Mag. Vol.22 No.10 (June 1988).

EMIGRATION see also Children's Societies, Passports and Population. The chief sources of information are in the numerous classes of Colonial Office records, and in a few classes of Home Office, Board of Trade and Treasury records. You are strongly advised to obtain a copy of PRO Records Information leaflet 71 *Emigrants: Documents in the Public Record Office* or Family Fact Sheet 10 *Tracing an Ancestor who was an Emigrant* ...

Some References to Emigration Records at the PRO featured in FTM Vol.1 Nos.1,2 & 3 (Nov-Dec 1984/Jan-Feb/Mar-Apl 1985).

The amount of material is vast, so much so that chances of tracing particular persons is related to the amount of information one has to start from. If one knows only a name, the chances of success are remote. Note that it is far easier to locate a person from within the country to which they emigrated as shipping lists usually survive at the port of arrival and not that of departure. The numerous family history societies in the respective countries may also be able to advise on what records are available.

The National Archives and Records Service, Constitution Ave, Washington DC 20408, USA has indexes and passenger lists for various years covering the USA in the period 1800 to 1952. However, they will search them only if you can supply the name of the passenger, port of entry, name of vessel and approximate year of arrival OR name of port of embarkation and exact date of arrival. They also have naturalization documents from about 1787 for some areas, but again they need the name of the petitioner and approximate date of naturalization.

The United States Government kept Passenger Lists starting in 1820 and they still do so. The earlier records were kept by the Customs Bureau (1820-1883) and are called Customs Passenger Lists. In 1883 what is now the Immigration and Naturalisation Service was given the responsibility of keeping the records which are called Immigration Passenger Lists. The Customs Passenger Lists provide only the immigrants' name, age, sex, occupation, nationality (place of origin) and their destination.

The Immigration Passenger Lists were much more informative giving the immigrants' name, age, sex, marital status, occupation, last residence, final destination in the US, date of previous arrival and place of previous residence in the US, name, address, and relationship to relatives or friends they are joining. In 1903 they added race to the form. In 1906 they added a personal description, and in 1907 they added the name and address of the immigrants' nearest relative in the country they had come from. Records less than 50 years old can only be consulted through the Immigration and Naturalization Service, New York NY 10007, USA.

Only records 1800-1820 are Baggage Lists for the port of Philadelphia. There was a tax on recovering luggage and these lists name the owner and describe his baggage.

In the PRO, under Treasury Papers there are details of 'bound servants' (indentured servants) between the ages of 15 and 21 who entered into an indenture for a term not exceeding 8 years in return for a passage to the Plantations in North America. The records follow an Act of 1717. They are important in that in addition to names, ages, and occupations they give the former place of residence.

Original lists of emigrants in bondage from London to the American colonies 1719 to 1744 edited by M. & J. Kaminkow is in the Library of the SOG. The book is based on a series of documents in the Guildhall Library (q.v.) entitled *Memoranda of Agreements to serve in America and the West Indies*. They date from 1718 to 1759 and are records of 3,000 Englishmen who emigrated to the colonies as indentured servants.

The Complete Book of Emigrants ... (4 vols: (1) 1607-1660, (2) 1661-1669, (3) 1700-1750, (4) 1751-1776), *Emigrants from England to the American Colonies, 1773-1776* and *American Wills and Administrations in the Prerogative Court of Canterbury 1610-1857* all compiled by Peter Wilson Coldham are just a few of the books on the impressive list of The Genealogical Publishing Co. Inc. Publications list sent on request

The Gale Research Co. also publishes similar books, an example is *Passenger and Immigration Lists Index* by P.W. Filby and M.K. Meyer in 13 volumes with supplements to 1993. This mammoth work - an index to *published* lists not manuscript materials — covers nearly half a million passengers who reached North America c.1583 to 1900. It may be in some larger Reference Libraries, as might *Ships' Passenger Lists* by Carl Boyer and others, published by him in a series of volumes. There is also the earlier *A Bibliography of Ships Passenger Lists 1538 to 1825* by Harold Lancour.

English Adventurers and Virginian Settlers by Noel Currer-Briggs, published by Phillimore in 3 volumes, is based on a very detailed study of relevant 17th century British and American records. The index contains more than 12,000 names and places mentioned in the abstracted documents.

For information about Canadian immigrants pre-Spring 1908 write to the National Archives of Canada, 395 Wellington Street, Ottawa, K1A ON3. The earliest record is 1865. Details of emigrants to Canada after 1908 can be obtained from Records of Entry Visit, Canada Employment and Immigration Commission, 10th Floor, 140 Place du Portage, Phase IV, Ottawa, Canada K1A OJ9.

The F.L. Leeson Emigrant Index 1600-1855+ (America, West Indies and Canada) is based on a wide variety of printed and manuscript sources. Details of service/charges from Debrett Ancestry Research Ltd.

Currer-Briggs "Colonial Records" Index 1560-1690 consists mainly of unpublished wills, Chancery and High Court of Admiralty Depositions and Libels, many PR extracts, lists of Indentured Servants from Bristol etc. Relates purely to English families (not Welsh, Irish or Scottish). Also Dutch Notorial records and Virginia Colonial records pre-1700. Send sae or 3 IRCs for details and charges to Noel Currer-Briggs, 3 High Street, Sutton-in-the-Isle, Cambs, CB6 2RB.

It must be remembered that not all the early settlers in Australia were convicts! For instance, many of the crew of the 'First Fleet' remained in Australia, as did those of the Second and Third Fleets. The census of New South Wales and Tasmania for 1828 is the most complete record for the early years and contains names of more than 35,000 persons with their ages, religions, families, land held etc. In addition there is an indication of whether they came to the colony free or in bond or were born in the colony, and the ship and year of arrival.

A copy of this census is on microfilm at the PRO (HO10 21-27). Transcripts of the returns have been published by the Library of Australian History, PO Box 795, North Sydney, NSW 2060, Australia.

National Register of Shipping Arrivals: Australia & New Zealand ed. Andrew Peake, published by the AFFHO and obtainable from them c/o 120 Kent Street, Sydney, NSW 2000, Australia. Price $A10.00 posted from AFFHO. This publication lists the extant records of arrivals into the various Australian and New Zealand ports. It includes a bibliography and list of record repositories.

Parish Assisted Emigrants, 1834-1860; an index of several thousand names from Poor Law records at PRO and for some counties cross-referenced to CRO records. Being added to continually. Destinations include USA (mid-1830's only), Canada, Australia, Tasmania, New Zealand and South Africa. Details of search and charges from Miss J.M. Chambers, 54 Chagny Close, Letchworth, Herts SG6 4BY.

See *Marriage, Census and other Indexes for the Family Historian* by Jeremy Gibson and Elizabeth Hampson for further references under this heading which may assist in your research. Obtainable from the FFHS.

The Long Farewell by Don Charlwood, Penguin, 1981 provides a good backcloth to the lives of the early settlers in Australia. It has an extensive bibliography.

There is also publication No.2 in the Great Expectations Series, *The British To The Antipodes* by Jill Kitson, Gentry Books Ltd, 1972.

Prior to 1834 British subjects could not go to India without the consent of the East India Company. Application records and permission to trade are with the Oriental and India Office Collections (q.v.). Lists of East India Company employees up to 1794 are also there.

For Scottish emigrants, consult *A Dictionary of Scottish Emigrants* edited by D.Whyte, Baltimore: Magna Carta Book Co., 1973; *The Scots Overseas: Selected Bibliography* by Donald Whyte, published by the FFHS, 1988 and *The Emigrant Scots* by James Lawson, Aberdeen & N.E.Scotland FHS, price £3.75 plus p&p.

The Original Scots Colonists of Early America 1612-1783 by David Dobson, published by Genealogical Publishing Co.Inc., 1988, lists 7000 people.

For Irish emigrants, *The Famine Immigrants: Lists of Irish Immigrants arriving at the Port of New York, 1846-1851*, Ira A. Glazier, The Genealogical Publishing Co. Inc., 1983-86 (7 vols). Not strictly within the category of either emigration or immigration there is a class of records covering a thirty year period which could be overlooked. They are the Records of Cross-Channel Passengers at Boulogne, 1822-58.
These include:

Passenger Embarkation Lists: Departures to England 12 Nov 1824 – 9 Nov 1858 with 2 short gaps; 26 Oct 1833 – 26 Aug 1834 & 29 July – 11 Oct 1836.

Passenger Disembarkation Lists: Arrivals from England 21 Sep 1825 – 14 Apl 1858 with a short gap 4 July 1836 – 12 Oct 1836.
Alphabetical Indexes to Passenger Lists 1826-1844.
Registers of Visas 26 Dec 1822 – 31 Dec 1855 with 2 gaps 6 Jan 1836 – 19 Oct 1843 and 28 Nov 1845 – 31 Jan 1846.
Ferry Movements: January 1853-September 1855.

Records are with the Archivist, Monsieur Jean-Pierre Eloy, Archives Communales, Hotel de Ville, Place Godefroy de Bouillon, 62321 Boulogne-sur-Mer, France. Access to records is by prior notice. Details from the Archivist.

The records give a cross-section of persons travelling to and from Britain; whilst British passengers are in the majority there is an astonishing range of nationalities from all over the world.

See *Travellers through France: Records of Cross-Channel Passengers at Boulogne, 1822-58, and Related Records Elsewhere* by Brian V. Meringo, Gen. Mag. Vol.22 No.5 (March 1987).

Whether or not you have emigrant ancestors, an article well worth reading is *Europe is the Lesse... the Human Background to Colonial Emigration* by Elizabeth Simpson, Gen. Mag. Vol.22 Nos. 5 & 6 (March and June 1987).

Other books which will give you background information are:

The great migration: the Atlantic crossing by sailing ships since 1777 by E.C. Guillet, University of Toronto Press, 1937, paperback 1963.

Emigration from the British Isles by W.A. Carrothers, published by P.S. King, 1929.

Passage to America by T.Coleman, first published by Hutchinson, 1972. Published by Penguin Books 1974 and reprinted by them 1976.

The Maritime Record Centre, Merseyside Maritime Museum, Albert Dock, Pierhead, Liverpool L3 1DN has a section devoted to emigration through Liverpool — very useful for social, local and family history.

ENCLOSURE AWARDS Between 1760 and 1860 a process of enclosing and re-allotting open fields, common meadows, commons, heaths, greens or forests took place as part of what has come to be called the Agrarian Revolution.

A Parliamentary Enclosure Act was necessary, and then Commissioners were appointed to work out the details. Their decisions, generally accompanied by maps showing the land involved with details of owners and tenants, can be invaluable to family historians since they pinpoint just where particular lands were. They are usually found in CROs. In some areas Enclosure Maps and Awards are found where Tithe Maps (q.v.) are not. The term 'Inclosure' is often found to describe these awards. See PRO Records Information leaflet 40 *Enclosure Awards*.

ENTAIL An estate of freehold land but unlike Fee Simple (q.v.), inheritance was limited to defined classes of descendant. A General Entail was created by the words "to X and the heirs of his body"; a Special Entail was created by the words "to X and the heirs of his body by his wife Z".

Entails could be limited to the male or female side of the family: Tail Male or Tail Female. In such cases the property could only descend to a male or female depending upon what type of entail had been created. The person entitled to the entail was a Tenant in Tail. He (or she) could Bar The Entail. This would convert the Fee Tail or entail into a Fee Simple.

A Common Recovery was the method used to bar the estate tail. A fictional Court Action was brought against the Tenant in Tail. The Fines and Recoveries Act 1833 abolished the Common Recovery and a Disentailing Assurance was substituted to effect the barring of the entail.

EPIPHANY The 6th of January (12th Night). The term was applied to that Court of Quarter Sessions held sometime between 25th December and 25th March.

ESTATE Very many of our ancestors worked as servants or labourers on the estates of the landed gentry or nobility. The Farm Bailiffs kept careful records of payments made to workers and details of the work assigned to them.

Usually these vast collections of records, which include a great many property deeds, have been deposited at a record office - but not necessarily in the record office of the county you would expect, for many landowners held estates in various parts of the country and preferred to have their muniments kept intact as a collection. Some of the larger estates have their own archives offices; the principal ones are listed in *The Local Historian's Encyclopedia* (q.v.).

The Historical Manuscripts Commission with its headquarters at Quality House, Quality Court, Chancery Lane, London WC2A 1HF has listed a great many collections of estate papers and their whereabouts.

It is a good idea to find out the names of the landowners in the parish in which your ancestor lived. An easy way to do this is to study the monuments in the church. You can then enquire, first at the CRO and then at Quality House if necessary, as to the estate records of those families. If you do manage to track them down you may learn a great deal about the way your ancestors earned their livings. Many estate records are voluminous; some collections are calendared, others unsorted. Estate maps may have the names of occupiers of farms marked on them. With the maps there may be schedules describing the nature of the farming done and the acreage.

Much land was held by the Crown, and the bulk of the Crown Estate papers is either at the PRO (particularly land in the Duchy of Lancaster), or at the Crown Estate Commissioners, 13-15 Carlton House Terrace, London SW1Y 5ES. Papers relating to the Duchy of Cornwall are at the Estate Office, 10 Buckingham Gate, London SW1E 6LA.

See *Estate Surveys as a Source for Names* by John Beckett, Gen. Mag. Vol.24 No.8 (Dec 1993).

ESTATE DUTY OFFICE REGISTERS see Death Duties.

EUROPEAN ANCESTRY see Worldwide Family History.

EXAMINATION An Act of 1662 empowered two justices to order intruders into a parish to leave and return to the one from which they had come. They might, however, apply for a 'settlement' (q.v.) to allow them to stay.

To determine whether a person should be granted a settlement certificate an 'Examination' was made of the person's background. These documents are of great value to the family historian. They are full of factual information – virtually autobiographies in miniature – giving details of parentage, family, occupation and movement from place to place.

Where these Examinations survive you should find them with the poor law records of the parish in the CRO.

EXCISE see Customs and Excise. A tax on goods for the home market; tax paid for a licence to carry out a trade or sport.

EXCOMMUNICATION(S) Exclusion from communion and from privileges and public prayers of the church. Lists of those excommunicated for serious misdemeanours are to be found amongst ecclesiastical records in DROs.

EXTRA-PAROCHIAL DISTRICT see also Liberty. This was an area outside the jurisdiction of the parish. Neither poor rates nor church rates were paid, though tithes, in theory, went to the Crown. A resident could choose to worship in the adjoining parish of his choice. In 1894 extra-parochial areas were abolished, and either added to an existing parish or given parish status.

FACTORY ACTS From 1801/2 onwards numerous Acts of Parliament were passed relating to conditions in factories and mines, many of them concerned with the exploitation of children. Briefly they were as follows:

1801/2 Workhouse apprentice children were not to work more than 12 hours a day, and were to receive elementary education.

1819   Applied to cotton mills. No children under 9 to be employed, others not to work more than 12 hours a day.

1831   Workers not to be paid in kind nor by tokens exchangeable only in employers' shops (known as the Truck Act).

1833   Applied to textile mills and laid down hours of work for young people.

1842   Mines Act. No women or boys under 10 to be employed in mines.

1844   Textile mills. Women not to work more than 12 hours a day and children to spend half their day at school.

1853   Textile mills. Children to be employed from 6 a.m. to 6 p.m. with one and a half hours for meals.

1867   Provisions of previous Acts to apply to all industries employing more than 50 people in one place.

1867   Inspection of workshops by local authorities. No employment of children under 8. Those aged 8 to 13 to work only half a day.

Further Acts gradually improved the situation with regard to children, but it must be realised that there was little enforcement of some of the earlier Acts. It gives us some idea of the terrible conditions endured by some of our ancestors as children.

FACULTY OFFICE see also Marriage Licences. In simple terms this is the Archbishop of Canterbury's Legal Department. Historical records issued by this office survive from 1660 and are now housed in Lambeth Palace Library, London SE1 7JU. The archivist will supply details of the types of records available on request. No prior appointment is necessary but a letter of introduction or reader's ticket from a recognised manuscript library (e.g.British Library) is required on the first visit.

FAMILY BIBLES It was a custom to record family events (births, marriages and deaths) in a family Bible which would then be handed down. Ask your relatives if they recall ever having heard of such a volume — it may be in the hands of a descendant of a collateral line to your own. If it can be located, the information in it will save you much tedious research.

If you locate one, check whether the date the Bible was printed was before or after the first event noted. If it was after, then the entries could have been from memory —

notoriously unreliable where years are concerned, though day and month of a birthday may be correct. It is also possible that the entries have been copied from an older Bible.

A Family Bible Surname Index is being compiled by Mrs E.R. King, 16 Upper Shott, Cheshunt, Herts EN7 6DR. Entries are taken from Bible inscriptions for birth, marriage and death dates and places 1600 onwards; there is occasional mention of emigration, army regiment, godparents, vicars etc. Many overseas related families. Owners of existing bibles are encouraged to register for possible contact from other family branches. Initial surname search free, otherwise £2 plus sae or 3 IRCs per surname. Request thereafter of photocopies of pages of information relevant to surname £2 per name.

FAMILY HISTORIES Make sure that your family history has not already been written — or at least the history of some branch of your family!

To ascertain this, you need to consult *all* of the following books but remember that they record only *printed* pedigrees.

(*a*) George Marshall's *Genealogist's Guide*; the edition published in 1903 records all known family histories to that date.

(*b*) Major J.B. Whitmore's *A Genealogical Guide* published in 1953, brought the listings up to that date.

(*c*) The task was continued by Geoffrey Barrow in *The Genealogist's Guide; an index to printed British pedigrees and family histories 1953 to 1975*. This was published by the Research Publishing Company, 1977.

(*d*) T.R. Thomson's *A Catalogue of British Family Histories* appeared in a 3rd ed. in 1980. In the back of this catalogue is an Appendix of family histories printed between 1975 and 1980, the only compilation of its kind for this period.

Those interested in Scottish families should consult *Scottish Family History* by Margaret Stuart, 1930, and *Scottish Family Histories Held in Scottish Libraries* by Joan P.S. Ferguson, 1960; revised and reprinted 1986. The latter details some 3200 entries held in libraries, including separately printed histories and articles in periodicals.

For Irish families consult *A Bibliography of Irish Family History and Genealogy* by Baron Brian de Breffny, 1973. Also Edward MacLysaght's *Irish Families*, 1957; *More Irish Families*, 1960; *A Guide To Irish Surnames* 1964 and *Bibliography of Irish Family History*, Irish Academic Press, 1981. This bibliography was previously published in MacLysaght's *The Surnames of Ireland* (revised and corrected 1978) but was omitted from the 4th ed. (1980) and subsequently published separately.

The LDS has organised a Family Registry. You submit details of your research and by this means may be able to contact others working on the same family. The service is free. For further details write to Genealogical Department, Family Registry, Fourth Floor, West Wing, 50 East North Temple St, Salt Lake City, Utah 84150, USA.

You should also endeavour to see the card indexes and large collection of manuscript and typescript family histories in the library of the SOG. When you have written yours, you should deposit a copy with them for the sake of posterity!

See *Has It Been Done Before* SOG Leaflet No.21 and *The Great Card Index* by Lydia Collins, FTM Vol.3 No.7 (May 1987).

The British Museum Library Catalogue might be consulted too, but it does not cover all privately printed family histories, since there was no obligation under the Copyright Acts to deposit a copy there — though a sensible author would have done so. Again — try to produce sufficient copies of your family history so that you, too, can send them a copy. *How To Record Your Family Tree* by Patrick Palgrave-Moore, obtainable from the FFHS, gives helpful advice on this matter.

There are some books to guide the would-be author. *How To Write A Family History* by Terrick V.H. Fitzhugh, published by Adam & Charles Black (Alphabooks), 1988. Price £12.95. The chapter entitled 'Writing the Narrative' has been described as "stimulating and provocative". Try to see *Preserving your past: a painless guide to writing your autobiography and family history* by J.T. Dixon and D.D. Flack, published by Doubleday, New York in 1977. Another book is *Your Family History* by A.J. Lightman, published by Random House, New York, 1978. John Titford passes on a few tips in *Writing up your family history – you know you've always meant to get around to it!* FTM Vol.3 No.12 (Oct 1987). You should try to make your book something of a social history by putting in plenty of background. *Family History in Schools* by D.J. Steel & L. Taylor, published in 1973 by Phillimore will give you lots of ideas.

Two more suggestions about books you might consult – *Sources for English Local History* by W.B.Stephens, 2nd ed. 1981, Cambridge University Press and *Writing Local History, A Practical Guide* by David Dymond, Bedford Square Press, 1981. The technique of writing a family history is similar to that of writing local history.

Family photographs, copies of family documents, and old postcards can all help to bring your narrative to life. Study the way other people have written up their family histories to get some ideas.

To link up with a fellow genealogist who has been researching some of your branches is a great bonus. Many FHSs have produced Directories of Members' Interests (q.v.).

FAMILY HISTORY CENTRE(S) see Church of Jesus Christ of Latter Day Saints.

FAMILY HISTORY NEWS AND DIGEST (FHN&D) see also Publications. This is the journal of the Federation of Family History Societies (q.v.). Published twice a year (April and September) it contains news of the activities of all Member Societies and the Digest section carries over 400 abstracts of articles appearing in family history, genealogical or heraldic journals or other publications of interest to its members. The Digest section is classified and is an effective cumulative index to current literature for family history. As each issue carries an up-to-date list of Member Societies with addresses of all secretaries, its value is considerable to individual subscribers and institutions all over the world.

FAMILY HISTORY RECORD SHEETS 15 A4 charts, maps and forms of use to the family historian, including Pedigree Charts, the St Catherine's House Codes, maps of British Isles Counties before and after 1974, forms for recording details of Census Returns and Parish Register entries etc., available from FFHS.

Record Offices and Libraries are, however, very crowded these days, restricting space for use of large files and forms. To meet the requirements for 'on-the-spot' notetaking, "Genfile" has been produced. This consists of preprinted forms for taking down details from GRO indexes, Census Returns, Wills, MIs, Directories, Parish Registers etc. all punched with 6 holes to fit the standard 4 or 6-ring Filofax or similar personal organisers. Alternatively Genfile has its own purpose-made ringbinder.

A sample set of forms can be obtained by sending sae plus 2 separate first class stamps to Genfile, PO Box 35, Ludlow, Shropshire SY8 2ZZ.

FAMILY HISTORY SOCIETIES see also Directories: Genealogical. There has been a phenomenal growth of these societies in the period from 1970, not only in the size of their membership but in their number. Virtually every county has its society – for some areas there are several e.g. for Yorkshire and the London area. The BMSGH, however, covers the counties of Worcestershire, Warwickshire and Staffordshire with Birmingham as a central point.

For a map of the areas covered by London FHSs consult *London FHSs and Registration Districts* published by the SOG and obtainable from them price £1.95 plus £1 p&p (it comes in a tube). On the reverse of the map is a list of places in London and where you can find them.

Yorkshire is similarly dealt with in the useful booklet *Yorkshire Family History Societies* compiled by David P. Jepson, 1994 and obtainable from him at 39 St James's Road, Marsh, Huddersfield, W.Yorks HD1 4QA, price £1 inc. p&p.

Such organisations hold regular meetings (often in more than one centre), produce a journal which is issued free to members, organise courses at all levels on 'Tracing Your Ancestors' and allied topics, give advice on local matters relating to ancestry tracing and, most important of all, are engaged on numerous projects which are designed to help to preserve records and cut down the time it takes to consult them. Typical of such projects are the production of Marriage Indexes, the recording of memorial (or monumental) inscriptions, indexing local census returns and indexing other valuable source materials particularly those relating to the Poor Law and to the Ecclesiastical Probate Courts.

Researchers would be well advised to write to the Secretary of the Society in the area of their interest and ask for details; subscriptions are very modest, in the region of £6 per year. A comprehensive list of family history societies who are members of the FFHS can be obtained from the Administrator of the FFHS in exchange for sae plus two extra 2nd class stamps or 3 IRCs.

See *The advantages of belonging to a family history society* by Pauline Saul, FTM Vol.7 No.11 (Sep 1991).

FAMILY TREE MAGAZINE (FTM) This publication has proved a popular addition to the many family history periodicals now available. A 56-paged commercially produced monthly 'glossy' magazine, it costs £1.70 per issue. It provides an excellent Postal Book Service. Subscriptions to Family Tree Magazine, 61 Great Whyte, Ramsey, Huntingdon, Cambs PE17 1HL (Tel: 01487 814050). Many family history societies are now selling this magazine so if you are a member of one you may be able to subscribe that way if you prefer.

Readers are welcome to visit Family Tree Magazine's Family History Shop, at the above address, to view books before purchasing. There is also a small reference section available for visitors to peruse. Open Mon - Fri 8.30am - 4.30pm.

FANMAKER There was a London Company of Fanmakers – see *A Short Account of the Worshipful Company of Fan Makers* by Bernard Ross, 1950.

FARMING see Rural Life.

FARRIER He was a shoeing smith (of horses). See *The Farrier and his craft* by L.B. Prince, published 1980, and *History of the Farriers of London to 1948* by R.C. Robson.

FEDERATION OF FAMILY HISTORY SOCIETIES (FFHS) This was formed in 1974, as a result of the growing interest in the study of family history. Since its inception, its membership has grown to over 150 societies throughout the world, including national, regional and one-name groups. Its principal aims are to co-ordinate and assist the work of societies or other bodies interested in British Family History, Genealogy and Heraldry and to foster mutual co-operation and regional projects in these subjects. It was granted charitable status in 1982.

Membership of the Federation is open to any Society or body specialising in family history or an associated discipline.

Federation Council, comprising representatives of the Member Societies, meets in Britain twice a year; representatives can thus exchange views and debate matters of importance to family historians. Council defines policy, which is implemented by an elected executive committee, with a Chairman, Vice-Chairman, Secretary to the Council, and Treasurer as Chief Officers, and a (paid) part-time Administrator, Publications Manager and Finance Officer.

National projects are co-ordinated by the Federation so that the work of several societies can be integrated to the benefit of all concerned. At the present time a plan is under way to transcribe all British Monumental Inscriptions; moreover, a considerable contribution is being made to the National Inventory of War Memorials (q.v.) established by the IWM in 1988. Other projects include developing more indexes, particularly marriage indexes for the period 1813 to 1837 and the co-operative 1881 British Census Project (see Census Returns).

Education in family history is a vital element within the Federation. This is achieved informally through regular meetings and discussions conducted by its Member Societies and by visits made to other organisations; also formally through the many courses on family history organised around the world. The Federation's *List of Lecturers* (3rd ed. 1993) was initiated by its Education Liaison Officer. The Subject Index of that publication gives some indication of the wide range of interests and knowledge acquired by family historians over the past decade. *Practice Makes Perfect – A Genealogical Workbook* compiled by members of the Education sub-committee is an excellent aid for those who teach family history and a refresher for all who have progressed beyond a basic course in the subject.

Conferences are organised on a national basis both by the Federation and by Member Societies in conjunction with the Federation. These draw the attention of the general public to the study of Family History, thereby encouraging new members to join family history societies. Those attending conferences meet others with similar interests and, quite apart from the formal proceedings, many ideas are exchanged during informal discussions and social events. As a result of the experience gained and as an encouragement to societies contemplating a conference *Organising a Family History Conference* (Guidelines) was published in 1987.

Representations are made to official bodies on matters affecting the study of family history and related topics. The Federation has a seat on the Record Users Group, is represented on the British Association for Local History, and has established regular liaison with the Society of Antiquaries, the Society of Archivists, the Historical

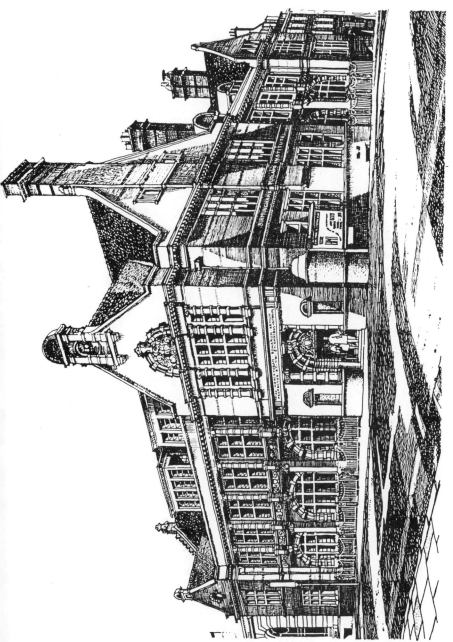

The Birmingham and Midland Institute, postal address of the Federation of Family History Societies.

Association, the British Records Association, and the British Records Society. The Federation provides an authentic, audible and respected voice for the many thousands of individual family historians belonging to local and national societies.

The Federation's journal *Family History News and Digest* (q.v.) is published twice-yearly; each issue provides a list of FFHS publications and Member Societies.

A more detailed account of each member society and its officers can be found in the Federation's *Handbook* published annually. Size of membership, annual subscription, meeting place, title and frequency of journal is just some of the useful information given along with contact addresses for the relevant officers of each society; around 300pp, either coil bound or punched for an A5 ring binder.

Family History Society Bookstalls (Guidelines for Organising) 1992, and *Publishing Family History Society Journals* 1993 were both produced in an effort to assist member societies.

Tracing Your Ancestors in Britain is a pamphlet published by the British Tourist Authority in co-operation with the FFHS and SOG. It is written **specifically for overseas enquirers** to guide them (hopefully) in the right direction early on in their research. Gives concise information, relevant addresses and maps. Obtainable from the Administrator of the FFHS, price or British Tourist Authority offices. *Research Services: A code of practice for Family Historians* (Susan Lumas); originally written to assist those overseas but now generally accepted as sound advice on what to expect when (i) providing a research service (ii) requesting a service.

Publications, covering aspects of family history research and the whereabouts of relevant records, are commissioned by the Federation, with a view to assisting Member Societies and individuals with their research. These are available at discount to Societies for sale to their members and to the general public. Many of these publications are referred to throughout this book and a full list, with prices, can be obtained from the Administrator, The Benson Room, Birmingham and Midland Institute, Margaret Street, Birmingham B3 3BS.

See *The Federation of Family History Societies* FTM, Vol.7 Nos.9 & 10 (July/Aug 1991).

FEE ENTAIL see Entail.

FEE SIMPLE An estate of Freehold Land not the subject of feudal service of a servile nature to the lord. After 1540 freehold land could be given away by will. Fee simple was described therefore as an estate by inheritance, free of conditions unlike copyhold land where the land could not pass to an heir unless it was 'surrendered' back to the Lord of the Manor first, a 'Fine' paid before the heir was 'admitted' as the new tenant and his name added to the Manor Court Roll. Fee Simple land was inheritable by heirs generally, regardless of whether they were male or female, descendants or collaterals.

FEET OF FINES The term Fine refers to an agreement relating to land transactions kept by the King's Justices. The fine was written three times on a skin, then divided by wavy cuts or 'indentures', there being an upper, a lower and a transverse section, the latter being termed the foot. The Foot was filed among the rolls of the Court of Common Pleas; the collection of these in the PRO is familiarly known as 'Feet of Fines'.

The word 'Cyrographum', with variant spellings, was written where the cuts were to be made. Thus identification could be assured by matching not only the jagged cuts but the cut letters of the word, making forgery almost impossible. The procedure was only abolished in 1834.

With the exception of the Commonwealth period the earlier records were written in Latin, but those for several counties have been translated and printed. They cover several centuries from the early 12th century. Only an approximate date of the actual agreement can be surmised as the date shown on the writ summoning the parties to appear is that on which it was due to be returned to court. In many cases there is also an additional record known as a Note of Fine and a Concord which is a duplicate.

These are useful early references to those of our ancestors who owned land. The Fine was regarded as putting an end to any controversy as to ownership.

FELL MONGER A dealer in hides, especially sheepskins. Sometimes written as one word.

FELTMAKERS see also Hatting Industry. They had their London Livery Company. See *History of the Worshipful Company of Feltmakers of London* by J.H. Hawkins, published in 1917.

FEOFFEE A person to whom freehold estate in land is conveyed by a feoffment (a particular mode of conveying freehold estate) or a trustee invested with such estate.

FERONER see Ironmonger.

FIRE BRIGADES Fire fighting became the responsibility of the parish as long ago as 1575 when orders were given that buckets, hooks and ladders were to be kept in churches. The equipment was, however, not always kept up to standard!

Fire insurance companies came into being in the late 1600's and many formed their own fire brigades to protect the properties of their clients, mainly in towns and cities. During the 18th century and first half of the 19th century fire fighting was principally organised and run by the various fire insurance companies. It was common practice for them to place a metal plate called a fire-mark on the wall of the insured property. This not only proved to the fire brigade that the premium was paid, it also acted as an advertising plaque. These plaques quite often had the insurance policy number beneath the company emblem. Folklore has it that if the first fire fighters to reach the scene were rivals of the company who insured the property at risk they were most likely to leave the fire burning!

The second half of the 19th century saw the formation of the municipal brigades who took over responsibility from the parish and insurance companies.

The Auxiliary Fire Service manned by volunteers was formed in 1937 in readiness for war and they worked with the full-time brigades. In 1941 the National Fire Service (incorporating the Auxiliary Fire Service) replaced the independent fire authorities. This service continued until 1948 when the brigades were restored to local authorities and no further changes took place until the local government reorganisation in 1974 when many of the smaller brigades were merged with the larger ones.

There are very few references to early fires and extant records vary greatly, as do those of the insurance brigades and companies. You are advised to check with your local CRO. Occasionally parish records contain details of fire equipment purchased and may even name the person in charge.

Industrial fire brigades were run by many large firms and railway companies; any surviving records should be with their archive material at the CRO or local Reference Library. By law there must be a fire brigade present anywhere that planes or helicopters are flown. A minimum standard of operation is laid down. Large airports have their own fire stations and fire services which are independent of the local authority fire brigade.

See *History of Fire Fighting* edited by John L.Kirk, revised ed. 1960, published by Castle Museum, York, *A History of the British Fire Service* by G.V. Blackstone, 1957 and *Images of Fire: 100 Years of Fire-Fighting* by Neil Wallington, David & Charles, 1989. Fire marks are dealt with in *Footprints of Assurance* by A.E. Bulau, 1953.

FIRE INSURANCE see also Fire Brigades and Insurance. A comprehensive list of some of the earlier Fire Insurance Companies, with their dates of foundation, is given in *The Local Historian's Encyclopedia* (q.v.).

The records of some companies have been deposited in CROs, the SOG has a collection of claims documents of the Sun Fire Office for 1770-88 but by far the largest collection is probably that at the Guildhall Library (q.v.) which holds records of over 80 London based insurance companies, approximately half of which were involved in insuring property against fire. These include the Hand-in-Hand Fire and Life Insurance Society (est. 1696), Sun Insurance Office (est.1710 as Sun Fire), and the Royal Exchange Assurance (est. 1720).

Fire insurance offices were established in London from the late 17th century, in the provinces from early 18th century (almost exclusively local-based). Some London-based companies initially restricted their business to that area, gradually developing throughout Britain working through provincial agents. Insurance of property in Ireland and overseas was not undertaken by them in a significant way until the 19th century.

Where fire policy registers exist they generally include policy number, name of agent/location of agency; name, status, occupation and address of policy holder; names, occupations and addresses of tenants (where relevant); location, type, nature of construction and value of property insured; premium; renewal date; and some indication of endorsements. Entries are generally arranged in chronological order i.e. policy number order.

Indexes to the policy registers deposited at the Guildhall Library (q.v.) vary with each collection so searching can be a lengthy business. An article by M.W. Beresford *Building History from Fire Insurance Records*, Urban History Yearbook, 1976, suggests ways of reducing search time; a copy of the book is available at the library.

Other records available are committee minutes, agents' records, share records, endorsement books, claims records, investment records, surveyors plans and reports, accounts and correspondence. Some records are on restricted access.

See free leaflet *Fire Insurance Records at Guildhall Library*.

FIRST FLEET see Convicts, Emigration and Transportation.

FIRST FRUITS An expression used to describe the profits of an ecclesiastical benefice for the first year after a vacancy. Records from mid 16th century to early 19th century are held at the PRO and include details of payments made or defaulted, arrears, usually the names of the incumbents, vacant livings and valuation data.

FLATMAN see Boatman.

FLEET see Marriage.

FLETCHER see also Bowyer. A maker of, or dealer in, (bows and) arrows. See *The Fletchers and Longbow String Makers of London* by Prof. James E.Oxley, 1968.

FOGGER He was a pedlar — but the term is also used to mean a headman at a farm, a groom or a manservant. The term has also been used for a middleman in the nail and chain trade, for a low-class lawyer (usually Pettifogger), or for a farm labourer.

FOLIO A folio is two pages so folio numbers occur on every other page. The two sides are distinguished by recto (right side) and verso (reverse side) or obverse and reverse. Folio numbers are often referred to in connection with census returns/transcriptions and manuscripts.

FOREIGN ANCESTRY see Worldwide Family History.

FOUNDER see also Gunfounding. A worker in brass and brass alloy or tin plate. They had their London Livery Company. See *Annals of the Founders' Company* by W.M.Williams, 1867, and *History of the Worshipful Company of Founders of the City of London* by W.N.Hibbert, 1925.

FOUNDLING An abandoned baby. Baptisms and burials of foundlings are commonly found in Parish Registers, especially in London and particularly in the sixteenth and seventeenth centuries. Foundlings were often named after the church where they were baptised, the vicar who baptised them, the person on whose property they were found or the geographical location where they were found e.g. Church, Field, Meadow.

The Greater London Record Office holds records of the Foundling Hospital (Thomas Coram Foundation).

With luck, it may just be possible to trace a foundling's parentage if he/she was in the Foundling Hospital. See *The History of the Foundling Hospital* by R.H. Nichols & F.A. Wray and *The Foundling Hospital and its children* by Pauline Litton, FTM Vol.2 No.4 (May-June 1986). Also *Thomas Coram Foundation for Children* by Colin Masters, 'Cockney Ancestor', No.46 (Spring 1990).

Lying-in hospitals (q.v.) were often patronised by women living away from home and sometimes it can be beneficial to consult the registers of these. Those for Chelsea, Greenwich and British Lying-in Hospitals are in the PRO. A transcription of the Middlesex Hospital register is in the Greater London Record Office.

FOUR AND TWENTY MAN Member of a Select (Close) Vestry (q.v.)

FRANCE see also Prisoners of War. The Anglo-French Family History Society was formed in 1993. The aims of the society include the sharing of information between members and to provide advice and information to aid their research; collating and publishing information on sources; liaison with French organisations and establishing networks; maintenance of a directory of members' interests and a quarterly journal *French Ancestor*. Further details from Anglo-French FHS, 31 Collingwood Walk, Admiral's Way, Andover, Hants SP10 1PU.

There are over 130 local family history societies in France most grouped in regional associations covering several departements. The addresses of the majority of these are published in the *Genealogical Research Directory* (see Directories: Genealogical). Many of these societies also belong to the French federation of genealogical societies, from whom the address of specific local societies may be obtained. Write to Federation Française de Genealogie, BP 63, 75261 Paris-Cedex 06 enclosing 2 IRCs. Note, when writing to France, writing in French will usually encourage a helpful response! (see entry on Translators).

The founder of the Anglo-French FHS, Patrick Pontet, has produced two guides: *Researches in France* and *Researches in Paris*, both of which describe sources and where and how to use them; also a *Directory of French Genealogical Associations and Genealogists*. Further details as per Anglo-French FHS. *Huguenot Ancestry* by Noel Currer-Briggs and Royston Gambier, published by Phillimore (q.v.), whilst dealing mainly with the French Protestants, also contains a wealth of advice and information on French ancestral research in general. The library at the IHGS (q.v.) has several French publications on the subject, including French heraldry. A copy of the late Margaret Audin's thesis, *British Hostages in Napoleonic France — The Evidence: With Particular Reference to Manufacturers and Artisans*, is held by the library of the SOG. Details of other publications are contained in Patrick Pontet's *Researches in France* mentioned above.

Worldwide Family History (q.v.) by Noel Currer-Briggs devotes a chapter to French ancestry and records; there is also an article in Gen. Mag. Vol.10 No.15 (Sep 1950). A later issue, Vol.20 No.8 (Dec 1981) has *Tracing Ancestry in France* by the late Mme Margaret Audin.

Mme Audin subsequently wrote a series of articles dealing with French genealogy and its attendant research procedures for FTM. See Vol.1 Nos.3-7 (1985) and Vol.2 Nos.2-5 (1986).

FRANCIS FRITH see Photographs.

FREE AND VOLUNTARY PRESENT TO KING CHARLES II This was a voluntary levy collected in 1661. The lengthy lists of subscribers, by county or borough, are in the PRO and make useful comparison with the Hearth Tax (q.v.) first levied the following year. Full details are given in Jeremy Gibson's *The Hearth Tax, Other Later Stuart Tax Lists and the Association Oath Rolls,* published by the FFHS.

FREEHOLD Freehold tenure was not subject to the custom of the manor and after death could pass to anyone named to inherit in the will of the deceased.

FREEMASONS The Seditious Societies Act of 1799 required that each Freemasons' Lodge should submit a list of members to each Quarter Sessions with addresses and occupations. As a rule these lists will be found with the other Quarter Sessions records deposited in CROs though quite often they are incomplete.

If you have an ancestor whom you think may have been a Freemason details of his date of entry and name of his lodge can be obtained from the Secretary, The United Grand Lodge of England, Freemasons Hall, 60 Great Queen Street, London WC2B 5AZ. A charge is made for search of the Membership Registers. Details on request.

A Freemasons Index is being compiled from an extensive collection of notes made by the late Frederick Humphery-Smith to references to Freemasons and others in similar societies from the 18th and 19th centuries. Details from the IHGS (q.v.).

FREEMEN In Corporations, a freeman is a person who has inherited or acquired by adoption, purchase or apprenticeship the rights of a citizen. By the Municipal Corporations Reform Act (1835) persons who had hitherto enjoyed the right of voting were placed on the Freemen's Roll, whilst those who obtained privileges by virtue of the act were placed on a separate list called the Burgess Roll. The title is now an honorary one.

Records of Freemen of the City of London are in the Guildhall Library (q.v.); those of other towns will be found in the local County or City ROs.

See *The Archives of the Freedom of The City of London 1681-1915* by Vivienne E. Aldous, Gen. Mag. Vol.23 No.4 (Dec 1989) and *Freemen of England and Wales* by David Clark, FTM, Vol.9 No.3 (Jan 1993).

FRIENDLY SOCIETIES Registers of Friendly Societies were kept after 1793. Those for 1846 onwards should be with the Registrar of Friendly Societies, 15-17 Gt.Marlborough Street, London W1V 2AX or the Registry of Friendly Societies (Scotland), 19 Heriot Row, Edinburgh EH3 6HT.

See *The Friendly Societies in England 1815-1875* by P.H. and J.H. Gosden, Manchester University Press, 1961 and PRO Records Information leaflet 54 *Registration of Companies and Businesses*.

FROBISHER An armour polisher. Sometimes spelt Furbisher.

FRUITERER There was a London Livery Company. See *History of the Worshipful Company of Fruiterers of London* by A.W.Gould, 1912.

FUNDS IN CHANCERY Also known as 'Dormant Funds' these are monies from the estates of deceased persons which have remained unclaimed for a minimum of 15 years. A list is published periodically in *The London Gazette* of amounts of £50 or more; amounts are generally not large and information is only disclosed, on payment of a fee, to those believed to have a beneficial interest. Applications giving details of such an interest should be sent to the Court Funds Office, Royal Courts of Justice, Strand, London WC2A 2LL.

FUNERAL A ceremony at which a dead person is buried or cremated. An authority on English funeral customs is Julian W.S. Litten, who lectures and writes on various aspects of ecclesiology in an informative and entertaining manner. See *Journeys to Paradise:*

Funerary Transport 1600-1850, Gen. Mag. Vol.23 No.5 (March 1990) and *The English Way of Death: the common funeral since 1450* published by Robert Hale, 1990.

He was commissioned by Portsmouth Cathedral to organise the obsequies of the Unknown Mariner from the *Mary Rose* in 1984 and in 1987 the re-organisation of the Undercroft Museum, Westminster Abbey with its unique collection of royal funerary effigies.

Funeral Directors' Records can be a very useful source of information if you know when and where an ancestor died but cannot locate the burial place. Though not bound by law to preserve them, funeral directors may keep records for some considerable time (upwards of thirty years). Usually filed by date — not alphabetically — they include a number of personal details in addition to the funeral arrangements and will note if a burial is to be in a family grave. Trade and telephone directories would list local funeral directors.

FURBISHER see Frobisher.

FURNITURE HISTORY SOCIETY This Society was founded in 1964 to study furniture of all periods, places and kinds, to increase knowledge and appreciation of it, and to assist in the preservation of furniture and its records. They publish an annual journal and a quarterly newsletter in addition to holding meetings and lectures.

A Dictionary of English Furniture Makers 1660-1840 eds. Geoffrey Baird and Christopher Gilbert was published by the Furniture History Society and W.S.Maney & Son Ltd in 1986. It costs around £100. The Dictionary covers the same period as Sir Ambrose Heal's *London Furniture Makers* and includes both London and Provincial makers and their apprentices along with other details.

Further information about the society can be obtained from the Secretary, The Furniture History Society, c/o Department of Furniture and Woodwork, Victoria and Albert Museum, Cromwell Road, London SW7 2RL.

Shire Publications have published *Discovering Furniture 1500 to 1720* and *Discovering Furniture 1720 to 1830*.

There are Furniture Museums located at the Victoria and Albert Museum and the Geffrye Museum, Kingsland Road, Shoreditch, London E2 8EA.

F.W.K. see also Stockinger. A common abbreviation for a Framework Knitter in the textile industry.

GAFFMAN A bailiff. It is considered by some that this is the origin of the slang word 'Gaffer' much used in the building trade. However, there is a possibility that Gaffer was derived from 'grandfather' or 'godfather'.

GAME DUTY Between 1784 and 1807 manorial gamekeepers and all who killed or sold game had to register with the Clerk of the Peace and pay a fee. These registers are useful since they also record the name of the lord of the manor and at what date he 'deputed' the power of killing game to his keeper. The registers are likely to be found with the Quarter Sessions records in a CRO (q.v).

GAOL DELIVERY These are registers of prisoners delivered from gaol to stand trial at Quarter Sessions. Gaol Delivery Rolls can be seen at the PRO (see Guide to PRO Vol.1, p.126); see also *English local administration in the Middle Ages* by Helen M. Jewell, published by David & Charles, 1972, pp.144-145. More recent records, because of their close association with Quarter Sessions etc., are more likely to be found in CROs.

GARTH(MAN) An enclosed court, yard or dwelling. A yardman or herdsman. Also used for one who owned or worked in a fish-garth. This was a dam or a river for catching fish.

GAVELKIND This was a custom, followed in Kent and as normal practice in Wales, by which land was divided equally between the male heirs on the death of the father.

GENEALOGICAL SOCIETY OF UTAH see Church of Jesus Christ of Latter-Day Saints.

GENERAL REGISTRATION see Civil Registration.

GENERATION Generally reckoned to last about 30 years.

GENFILE see Family History Record Sheets.

GENTLEMAN'S MAGAZINE This monthly publication was begun in 1731 and continued until 1908. It is of particular value to genealogists because until 1861 it published notices of births, marriages and deaths. These were not, as one would have supposed, only of the upper classes — middle class people and those in trade or commerce were often included. There are also obituary notices. Bound volumes are to be found in many libraries — there is a complete run in the Library of the SOG and of the BMSGH.
    There is a cumulative index for 1731 to 1786, and from 1786 to 1819. Specialist indexes of particular interest to family historians have been produced. In 1891 the Index Society produced an Index to the Obituary and Biographical Notes in the Gentleman's Magazine 1731 to 1780.
    There are also:-
Index to Births and Marriages 1731 to 1862, by R.H. Farrar, 2 vols.1886.
An Index to Marriages 1731 to 1768, by E.A. Fry, 1922.
    If you do find an entry of interest it is worth checking on newspapers of the time, since the Magazine used them as its source and often considerably pruned the original entry.
    The Gentleman's Magazine also contains endless reports of unusual events involving people.

GENTRY Records of landed families other than those with titles — what one might call the lesser nobility — can be found in Walford's *County Families* and also in *Burke's Commoners* which later became *Burke's Landed Gentry*. Available in most Reference Libraries.

GERMANY The Anglo-German Family History Society was formed in 1987. Further details can be obtained from the Secretary, Mrs J. Rushton, 11 Church Lane, Teddington,

Middlesex TW11 8PA. Members receive a Journal and a large 'Strays' index (q.v.) for German names that are found in more unusual places is being compiled. Help can be given with formulating letters to Germany when enquiring about church records.

The society has also published *The German Hospital in London and the Community it Served 1845-1948*, price £2.50. Obtainable from the secretary.

How To Find My German Ancestors and Relatives by Dr Heinz F. Friedericks, Degener & Co., 1969 is a booklet written in English, primarily for those living in the USA with German ancestry. It contains much useful information and lists of addresses for source material in Germany. Obtainable from Nurnbergerstr.27, Postfach 1340, D-8530 Neustadt, West Germany.

See also *Basic German Sources* by Susan Pearl, FTM Vol.5 Nos.5 and 6 ((March/April 1989) and the more expansive *In Search of Your German Roots: A Complete Guide to Tracing Your Ancestors in the Germanic Areas of Europe* by Angus Baxter, Genealogical Publishing Co. Inc., 1987.

In FTM Vol.3 No.4 (Feb 1987) there is an article entitled *The gentle Palatines* by John Leonard Alton. The term Palatine describes one of a group of about 14,000 emigrants who fled their homeland in the area of the Upper Rhine during the period May to October 1709. Many eventually settled in London. A document series at the PRO (T1/119) gives invaluable information on these people, though they are difficult to read. A list printed in the USA, taken from these records, can be consulted at the Library of the SOG. See also *The Early Eighteenth Century Palatine Emigration* by Walter Allan Knittle, published in Philadelphia, 1936.

German-English Genealogical Dictionary by Ernest Thode, Genealogical Publishing Co.Inc, Baltimore, 1992, $29.95. For the researcher who has little or no knowledge of German; it covers thousands of German genealogical terms. With a standard German-English dictionary the user should be able to make a translation of any document.

Address Book for Germanic Genealogy by Ernest Thode, GPC, 1994, $24.90. Among the contents are new German postal regions, maps of the 1871-1918 German Empire, and archives with German-related collections in the English-speaking world.

GIBRALTAR Civil registration similar to that of the British Isles, commenced thus: Births 1848 (compulsory 1887); Marriages 1862 (compulsory 1902); Deaths 1859 (compulsory 1869), although some civil authorities registered Anglican Marriages from 1845. Jews and Roman Catholics tended to register their events with their own religious authorities though there are many instances of Catholics marrying in Protestant churches or the register office.

The LDS has microfilmed the Civil Registers of BMDs and the card indexes to them and these films are available through FHCs.

Searches of the card indexes to the registers and to the registers themselves are permitted in person on a daily fee-paying basis. If names and approximate dates of events are known copies of certificates can be obtained by post on payment of the fee (plus an overseas handling charge). Write to the Registrar, 277 Main Street, Gibraltar.

Full censuses of the population were carried out by British Authorities in 1834, 1868/71, 1878/81, 1891, 1901, 1911, 1921 and 1931 though some, notably 1901, are incomplete. The records are in the care of the government archivist, 6 Convent Place, where they can be viewed by appointment. Again, microfilm is available through FHCs.

For details of further sources for research in Gibraltar see *Genealogical Research in Gibraltar* by Lawrence R. Burness, Gen. Mag. Vol.21 No.1 (March 1983) updated by an article of the same title by John A. Bryden in Gen. Mag. Vol.24 No.7 (Sep 1993).

GIPSIES see gypsies.

GIRDLER A belt maker. See *The Girdlers' Company — a second History* by Dr.T.C. Baker, 1957. Unfortunately the records of the Company were destroyed in the air raids of World War II.

GLASGOW UNIVERSITY The Matriculation Albums of the University of Glasgow from 1728 to 1858 have been published (1913). There is a copy in the Library of the SOG.

GLASS see also Glaziers. The Broadfield House Glass Museum, Barnett Lane, Kingswinford, West Midlands, DY6 9QA is situated in what was the heart of the glass making industry; it is well worth a visit to provide a background to the glass trade. It is open Tues to Fri 2.00pm — 5.00pm; Sat 10.00am — 1.00pm and 2.00pm — 5.00pm; Sun 2.00pm — 5.00pm; Bank Holiday Mondays 2.00pm-5.00pm. There is a small admission charge. They will answer written enquiries on receipt of sae or 3 IRCs.

There is a Shire Publication entitled *Glass and Glass Making* but for more specialised reading try *From Broad-Glass to Cut Crystal — A History of the Stourbridge Glass Industry*, D.R. Guttery, London, 1956; *Notes on the Stourbridge Glass Trade,* H.J. Haden, Stourbridge, 1949, reprinted by Dudley Library 1969 and *Collections for a Genealogy of the Noble Families of Henzey, Tyttery and Tyzack*, H.S.Grazebrook, Stourbridge, 1877.

An Index of Glassmakers in the UK is being compiled by Mr B. Hardyman, 26 St Anne's Drive, Coalpit Heath, Bristol BS17 2TH. The index covers the period 1600-1900 and contains occupations of glassblower, glass bottlemaker, glasscutter, glass beveller together with any other occupations connected with the making and enhancing of glass. Contributions to the index are welcome; enquiries should be accompanied by sae or 3 IRCs.

GLASS-SELLERS There was a London Livery Company. See, *The Worshipful Company of Glass-Sellers of London* by G.A. Bone, 1966.

GLAZIERS: PAINTERS OF GLASS: STAINED GLASS see also Mediaeval Records. See *The Worshipful Company of Glaziers* ...otherwise... *Glaziers and Painters of Glass* by C.H.Ashdown, 1919, and *English Glass Painting*, by F.M. Drake, London, 1912.

Stained Glass in England by June Osborne, Frederick Muller, London, 1981, contains many individual names of artists and firms throughout this country; useful contact addresses are given.

The British Society of Master Glass Painters, 11 Lansdowne Road, London N10 2AX, may be able to supply further information.

GLEBE TERRIERS These are to be found in Diocesan archives. They are records of Church lands and property. Often the location of these is given in relation to non church-owned property, with the tenants or owners named, which enables us to locate the sites of the latter. Sometimes the names of the occupiers of the church lands or property are given. To be able to pinpoint just where your ancestors lived will add much interest to your family history.

GLOSSARY OF TERMS FROM PROBATE INVENTORIES see Inventories.

GOLDSMITH see also Oriental and India Office Collections. The term 'hallmark' means the mark originally applied at Goldsmiths' Hall, the headquarters of the London Livery Company. See Vol.2 *History of the Twelve Great Livery Companies* by W. Herbert, 1968.

The London Goldsmiths, 1200 to 1800 compiled by Sir Ambrose Heal and published by the Cambridge University Press, 1936, would be of considerable interest to anyone whose ancestor was a member of this craft or trade. There is a list of nearly 8,000 goldsmiths, jewellers, bankers and pawnbrokers in London up to the year 1800. Similarly, published in 2 vols. 1987, *The Directory of Gold and Silversmiths, Jewellers and Allied Traders, 1838-1914* by John Culme, Antique Collectors Club, 5 Church Street, Woodbridge, Suffolk IP12 1DS, price £145.

GOSSIP A Gossip was a sponsor in baptism; a god-father or god-mother. Can also mean a close friend, especially a female friend present at childbirth.

GRAVEYARDS see Cemeteries and Monumental Inscriptions.

GREAVE A bailiff or foreman. A Gr(e)ave or Greeve also meant a grove.

GREENWICH HOSPITAL This was a home for navy pensioners. Registers, baptisms (1720 to 1856), marriages (1724 to 1754) and burials (1705 to 1857) are at St Catherine's House. Details of apprenticeships of pensioners' children and registers of the admission and discharge of pensioners 1704 to 1869 are at the PRO.

GREENWICH HOSPITAL SCHOOLS These were established to provide education for children of disabled or deceased officers of the Royal Navy.

The PRO has a collection of registers which include school admission papers 1728 to 1870. The latter are arranged under first letters of surnames and give details of the birth or baptism of the children, marriage of parents and father's naval service.

The registers themselves include registers of claims and candidates, admissions, apprenticing etc.of boys and girls. Most are indexed. The Reference is ADM 73. A second group which is similar in nature covers the period 1883 to 1922, reference ADM 163.

See *Royal Hospital School Greenwich* by H.D.T. Turner, Phillimore, 1980, price £11.95.

GRETNA GREEN MARRIAGES (term widely used for Irregular Border Marriages which were performed at a number of places close to the English/Scottish border). Marriages recorded at Gretna since 1st January 1855 are in duplicate, one held by the local Registrar, the other by the Registrar General for Scotland at New Register House, Edinburgh EH1 3YT. The Old Parochial Registers of Gretna relating to the years 1730 to 1855, are also in the care of the Registrar General. These were kept by the ministers and/or session clerks of the parish church.

Old Registers of irregular marriages prior to 1855 are known to be in the care of the following (numbers of entries given in brackets):

The Ewart Library, Catherine Street, Dumfries, DG1 1JB. 1829 to 1855, 1 vol. (1130 entries); 1832 to 1845, 3 vols. (342 entries).

Wright, Brown & Strong, Solicitors, 7 & 9 Bank Street, Carlisle, CA3 8HQ. 1843 to 1865 (over 6,000).

Robert Muckle Son & Hall, Solicitors, Norham House, 12 New Bridge Street, Newcastle-upon-Tyne, NE1 8AS. 1783 to 1895 (4 volumes).

Registrar – Gretna, 50A Annan Road, Gretna CA6 5DG. 1843 to 1862 (910).

Mr C.R. Hudleston, Flat 1, 3 Palmeira Square, Hove, Sussex, BN3 2JA. 1807 to 1840 (Approx.25 small notebooks, rough notes and fragments).

Registrar, 25 Hide Hill, Berwick-on-Tweed, TD15 1EQ. 1804 to 1816 and 1849 to 1855 (Index only).

Rev M.D. Ryan, The Vicarage, Cornhill-on-Tweed, Northumberland, TD12 4EQ. 1793 to 1797.

A charge is made for searching. For further information consult *Irregular Border Marriages* by Meliora G. Smith (using the pseudonym 'Claverhouse') published by the Moray Press, Edinburgh & London 1934.

There were other marriages than those in the collections above, but whereabouts of the records is not known, or access is denied. Details about these records are contained in the article *Irregular Border Marriages* by G.S. Crighton in Gen. Mag. Vol.20 No.8 (Dec 1981). See SOG Leaflet No.10 of the same name.

GRIEVE An alternative spelling of Greave – a bailiff or foreman.

GROAT A small silver coin of the value of 4 pence, the groat was mediaeval in origin and about an inch in diameter. There were 60 groats to the £.

GROCER see *Some Account of the Grocers' Company* by Baron Heath, 1869.

GUERNSEY see Channel Islands.

GUIDE BOOKS A great many were published for various areas, towns etc. from the mid-19th century. You will find them in libraries and they provide interesting background material for your family history and may provide clues to changes of occupation etc.

GUILD see One-Name Studies, Guild of.

GUILDHALL LIBRARY Located at Aldermanbury, London EC2P 2EJ. This public library houses a fine collection of genealogical material, printed books, manuscripts and maps. It holds especially records relating to the City of London and the London area with the printed sources relating to England as a whole and also registers and transcripts of the Anglican and diplomatic communities abroad. *A Guide to Genealogical Sources in the Guildhall Library* compiled by Richard Harvey, (revision in progress; new edition due 1995) will point you in the right direction.

GUILD(S) see also Apprenticeship Records. Guilds of craftsmen flourished in the towns from the later Middle Ages, and the Guild records for such towns as Shrewsbury, Norwich, Bristol, Coventry etc. give us glimpses of our ancestors in pre-parish register times as well as in later centuries. There are records of both masters and apprentices. You should enquire at the relevant record offices.

In London the Guilds were known as Livery Companies. There is an excellent book by John Kennedy Melling, first published in 1973 with subsequent editions in 1978 & 1981 by Shire Publications Ltd, entitled *Discovering London's Guilds and Liveries*. The chapter entitled 'Historical Introduction' is well worth reading. Unfortunately the book does not give much information about the whereabouts of records. Most are in the Guildhall Library (q.v.) and details can be found in *City Livery Companies and Related Organisations*, Guildhall Library Publications, 3rd ed. 1989. Price £5.80 inc. p&p. Some Livery Companies still surviving have their own Archives.

The present City Livery Companies, with their addresses, are listed in *The Local Historian's Encyclopedia* (q.v.)

GUNFOUNDING AND GUNFOUNDERS *A Directory of Cannon Founders from Earliest Times to 1850* by A.N. Kennard, the Arms & Armour Press, 1986. It outlines the gunfounding process and includes an international list of Gunfounders, with biographical information.

GUNMAKERS The making of hand guns, as distinct from the casting of cannon, started in the 14th century; from that time records exist of the various makers, and of the specialist makers of gun components. Several books have been published which although primarily intended for those interested in the history and collecting of guns, do outline the business and biographical details of many of the people in the trades.

Useful for London is *A Dictionary of London Gunmakers 1350-1850* by Howard L Blackmore, Phaidon & Christies, 1986. For England and Wales, there is *The English Gunmakers*, sub-titled *Birmingham and Provincial Gun Trade in the 18th & 19th Century*, by DeWitt Bailey & Douglas A. Nie, Arms & Armour Press, 1978; this same firm published *Scottish Arms Makers, 15th century to 1870* by Charles E. Whitelaw, 1977.

Much of the early trade was concentrated in the Tower Hamlets area of London, often contracting to the Board of Ordnance whose records are at the PRO, or to trading companies such as the Hudson's Bay Company. The Worshipful Company of Gunmakers was established by Royal Charter in 1637/8, and they set up their Proof House in Whitechapel. The Highland Scots were noted for producing pistols. 'Black Country' towns such as Darlaston and Wednesbury (Staffordshire) became major suppliers of gunlocks and barrels. The first evidence of the Birmingham (Warwickshire) trade was in the supply of guns to the Parliamentarians in 1643. The 1851 census recorded 7731 gunsmiths and workers in England & Wales, of which 5167 were in Birmingham and 1223 in London. The trade was noted for work being done in family groups subcontracting to others. However after 1860, more industrialisation occurred with the setting up of large companies.

An Index of London Gunmakers is being developed to include all British gunmakers and gun trade workers, working in the years up to 1880. Information from Mr Stan Cook, 20 Cautley Close, Quainton, Aylesbury, Bucks HP22 4BN. Enclose sae or 2 IRCs.

GYPSIES Though tracing Gypsy ancestry is difficult many Gypsy families lived semi-sedentary lives or had family connections who lived in houses.

In some cases the broad term 'Traveller' can serve to conceal the identity of a Gypsy family. There were a number of associated occupational groups which were often of Gypsy origin or covered by Gypsies. These include: Braziers, Tinkers, Chair-bottomers, Sieve-makers, Pot-hawkers, Peg-makers and inevitably Horse-dealers.

References to any of the above occasionally occur in parish registers, especially in the Burial Registers.

A list of publications of interest to those researching Gypsy ancestry can be obtained from The Gypsy Studies Section, Sydney Jones Library, University of Liverpool, PO Box 123, Liverpool L69 3DA. The library's Special Collections Section holds the archives of the Gypsy Lore Society, which includes some pedigree notes on Gypsy families.

A useful starting point for family enquiries is the Romany and Traveller Family History Society. Details from the secretary Mrs Janet Keet-Black, 6 St James Walk, South Chailey, East Sussex BN8 4BU. Please send sae or 2 IRCs. A notable member of this society is the well known lecturer on the subject, David Smith, 81 Narborough Road, Cosby, Leicester LE9 5TB.

For a modest charge (six 2nd class stamps or 3 IRCs) Alan McGowan, 22 Orchard Way, Aldershot, Hants GU12 4HW, will provide a copy of *On The Gypsy Trail* – a practical guide to family history research for travelling families. This article first appeared in 'Hampshire Family Historian' Vol. 20 Nos. 3 & 4 (Nov 93 & Feb 94). See also two articles by David Lazell *Romany in the family* FTM, Vol.8 No.4 (Feb 1992), *A return to the Romany Camp* FTM, Vol.8 No.11 (Sep 1992).

HABERDASHERS They were originally part of the Mercers' Company, and divided into the Haberdashers of hats, who came to be known as milliners, and those of small wares e.g. ribbons. See *A Short Description of the Worshipful Company of Haberdashers* by Commander Prevett, 1971.

HALF-BAPTISED Privately baptised.

HAMLET A grouping of houses but with no church. A hamlet was thus part of a larger parish unit.

HANDWRITING see Palaeography.

HANWAY ACTS Jonas Hanway was an English philanthropist (1712-1786). There are a number of references to him in *English Society in the 18th Century* by Roy Porter, Pelican Social History of Britain, 1982, and *Illustrated English Social History* by G.M.Trevelyan, Pelican ed. 1964, Vol.3.

Following the persistent lobbying of Jonas Hanway, Parliament passed 2 Acts:
1761 – required parish authorities to keep accurate records of infants in their care.

1767 – directed parish authorities to send infants out of the city when placing them for care and nursing. He also founded a hospital for fallen women.

HARLEIAN SOCIETY Founded in 1869 for 'the publication of heraldic visitations of counties and any manuscripts relating to genealogy, family history and heraldry'. It publishes 2 series; Visitations and Registers, the latter predominantly of London. Details from The Secretary, The Harleian Society, College of Arms, Queen Victoria Street, London EC4V 4BT.

HATCHMENT Diamond-shaped funeral hatchment, on which the coat of arms of the deceased was painted. These are to be found in many of the older churches. A series of books entitled *Hatchments in Britain* by Peter Summers is being published by Phillimore (q.v.). The hatchments are recorded on a county basis. An informative article on the subject entitled *Funeral Hatchments* by C.J. Smith, was published in 'The Blazon', journal of the Suffolk Heraldry Society, Autumn 1984, No.29.

HATTING INDUSTRY This was an important industry especially in London, Cheshire, Lancashire, Gloucestershire and South Wales. It was a very mobile industry with hatters frequently moving between these areas. For further information see *The Felt-Hatting Industry c.1500 to 1850 with special reference to Lancashire and Cheshire* by P.M. Giles. Transactions of the Lancashire and Cheshire Antiquarian Society, Vol.LXIX 1959.

The expression 'Mad as a Hatter' derived from the fact that many hatters suffered from mercury poisoning; mercury being extensively used in felt hat making processes.

Straw hats have been made in the villages of South Bedfordshire since before 1680; the reasons for the trade being in this area are not known. It became a cottage industry and the plait was often made by children in 'Plait schools'. The product was then sold in the weekly plait markets in Luton and Dunstable. In 1869 a 'Plait Hall' was built at Luton for these markets.

Hat manufacturers worked from home or had small factories. The trade produced many allied occupations e.g Blockers, plait-dealers, dyers, Leghorn merchants (hat manufacturer, from the high quality Italian plait from Leghorn), ribbon merchants and card board box makers (to pack the finished product). Hats were trimmed by out workers who finished the rough 'hoods' at home.

The History of the Straw Hat Industry by Dr J.G.Dony, Gibbs Bamforth, 1942 is the standard book but see also Shire Album no.78 *Straw Plait* by Jean Davis, 1981.

HAWKER A travelling salesman who carries his wares. The Pedlars Act, 1871, required travelling traders, on foot, to be licensed by the police and the Hawkers Act, 1888, required travelling traders with horse or other beast of burden, to be licensed by the County or County Borough Council.

HEARTH TAX This tax was levied from 1662 to 1689, though the lists of taxpayers only survive, and then spasmodically, from 1662 to 1674. The records are useful to the family historian in that they indicate the size of the house, and thus the degree of affluence or otherwise of our ancestors.

Persons with houses worth less than 20/- per annum were exempt as were those in receipt of poor relief. Otherwise, 2/- per hearth was payable. The parish constable made lists of householders with the number of hearths, and the lists were submitted to the Justices at the Quarter Sessions. The tax was collected twice a year, at Michaelmas and Lady Day. Lists are headed 'in bonis' for the humble, and 'in terris' for the wealthy.

A person with only one hearth was probably relatively poor; a yeoman or 'Gent' might have three or four, an esquire six or more.

Occasionally CROs have contemporary copies retained in Quarter Sessions records, and some have photocopies or microfilms of the relevant PRO holdings for their county. A good many have been published, usually with indexes, or there may be locally held indexes to unpublished modern transcripts. Exact details of the records surviving in the PRO and elsewhere, plus published and other copies, are given in *Hearth Tax Returns, other Later Stuart Tax Lists and the Association Oath Rolls* by Jeremy Gibson, FFHS.

Pinhorns hold an indexed transcript to the London and Middlesex Hearth Tax 1666. Details of search charges in exchange for sae or 3 IRCs.

HELLIER A slater or tiler sometimes found as Hillier.

HERALDRY The social status of your ancestors will determine whether a knowledge of heraldry will assist your researches although that is no reason why you should not enjoy the subject for its own sake.

There are many books which have been published on the subject. *Boutell's Heraldry* 1950, revised ed. 1978 by J.P. Brooke-Little, published by Frederick Warne, *A New Dictionary of Heraldry*, Alphabooks, 1987 and *Heraldry for the Local Historian and Genealogist* both by Stephen Friar, are excellent hardback publications. More modestly priced and perhaps for the novice is the FFHSs *Heraldry Can Be Fun*, *The Observer's Book of Heraldry*, published by Frederick Warne or *How To Read A Coat of Arms* by Peter Summers, A & C. Black, 1986.

Heraldic matters are controlled by The College of Arms, Queen Victoria Street, London EC4V 4BT, which has a fine collection of pedigrees of Armorial families. New Register House, Princes Street, Edinburgh, EH1 3YT is the Headquarters of the Court of Lord Lyon King of Arms and can advise on matters of Scottish heraldry. Their Information Leaflet No.5 *Ancestry Research* explains that the onus of proof of ancestry is upon the Petitioner applying for Arms – the Court does not do research. The Chief Herald of Ireland, Kildare Street, Dublin 2, deals with heraldic matters in that country.

The Heraldry Society, 44-5 Museum Street, London WC1A 1LH, specialises in Heraldic studies as does the IHGS (q.v.).

If you come across a copy of a coat of arms in your family documents, do not assume it belonged to one of your ancestors. It could have been those of a family to whom he or she was a servant! See *The Right To Arms* Leaflet No.15 published by the SOG. *Papworth's Ordinary of British Armorials* will help you to identify a coat of arms and most Reference Libraries have a copy. This unique work lists most known coats of arms according to 'Ordinaries' or 'charges' on the shields. Thus, if axes appear on the arms, you look up 'axes' in the book and there you will find them listed and described.

A good introduction to Civic Heraldry is the Shire Publication of the same name in the 'Discovering' series, and of equal interest is the booklet *Church Heraldry* by J.G. Storry, published by The Nettlebed Press, 1983.

HERALDS' VISITATIONS In the 15th century the Senior Heralds, known as Kings of Arms, were given the right to grant arms. The Heralds began to compile registers both of the arms already in use and of those that they granted. Early in the 16th century conditions became more stringent when certain property requirements had to be proven before a grant of arms would be approved.

From 1530 onwards, at intervals of about thirty years, the Heralds made tours of the country to examine gentlemen's claims; they took account of records of previous visitations, family muniments and traditions before allowing a claim.

The Herald was empowered 'to put down or otherwise deface at his discretion' all unlawful arms, crests, cognizances, and devices, 'in plate, jewels, paper, parchment, windows, gravestones, and monuments or elsewhere wheresoever they be set or placed'. They could also summon before them any person who had unlawfully 'usurped and taken upon him any name or title of honour or dignity as esquire, gentleman or other'.

Visitations continued until 1686. The Harleian Society has printed copies of visitation pedigrees although some of them are suspect! Nevertheless, many are genealogical records of value.

Visitation Pedigrees and the Genealogist by G.D.Squibb, Norfolk Herald Extraordinary, appeared in Gen. Mag. Vol.13 No.8 (Dec 1960). It was subsequently published with a short inserted passage and a few extra notes, by Phillimore (q.v.) in 1965 and Pinhorns in 1978 (limited ed).

HIGGLER (or Higler) see Badger. An itinerant dealer, usually with horse and cart. One who haggles or bargains.

HIGHWAYS Public roads, usually main routes. Originally the upkeep of the highways was the responsibility of the Manor, but from 1555 the Parish became responsible for their maintenance. Each parishioner owning a ploughland in tillage, or keeping a plough, had to supply a cart for 4 days a year. If able-bodied, he also had to give 4 days labour a year. In 1691 this was increased to 6 days. The custom arose to commute this obligation by payment. The Accounts of the Surveyors of Highways which record expenses and payments received are a valuable source of information for the family historian, and where extant can be found in CROs, see *County Records* by Emmison & Gray, Historical Association Booklet H62, 1973, and Chapter IX of W.E. Tate's *The Parish Chest* (q.v.).

The appointment of Surveyor was made by the justices. The person chosen (from a list supplied by the parish) sometimes commuted the office.

A very useful early book containing details of the main routes of the time is *A new and accurate description of all the direct and principal cross roads in England and Wales and part of the roads of Scotland*. It includes references to some of the principal houses and their occupants. The book was compiled by Lt.Col.Daniel Paterson and by 1808 had reached a 14th ed.

HILLIER see Hellier.

HIND A farm labourer; a household servant.

HIRING FAIR see Market Towns.

HISTORICAL ASSOCIATION (The) see Local History Societies.

H.M.S.O. Her Majesty's Stationery Office (Publishers). See Useful Addresses at the front of this book.

HOSPITAL see also Census and Lying-In Hospitals. The majority of the early ones were charitable foundations: their records can often be found in the PRO, the Greater London Record Office or CROs. The number of hospitals increased after c.1750 (a list of hospitals and asylums with foundation dates can be seen in *The Local Historian's Encyclopedia*) (q.v.).

In the 19th century many hospitals/infirmaries were associated with workhouses; these often had their own burial grounds and burial registers (many now deposited in CROs or local libraries).

The Hospital Records Project computer database contains full details of all hospital records held in public repositories; information on more than 1,000 hospitals. The appearance of a hospital on this list does not mean that all its records will be found as the quantity of records held for any particular hospital varies. The records are also subject to the '30 year' rule for administrative records and the '100 year' rule for patient records. Enquiries about the Project should be addressed to the PRO where the database is maintained. See *Hospital Records in the Greater London Record Office* by Janet Foster, Gen. Mag. Vol.24 No.3 (Sep 1992).

See *The Story of England's Hospitals* , Courtney Dainton, 1961; *The Hospitals,* Brian Abel-Smith, 1964; *The Mediaeval Hospitals of England* by Rotha Mary Clay, 1909 (in which mediaeval hospitals are arranged under counties); *Hospital Records* by Adrian Phillips, TMA Vol.7 No.4 (June 1984).

HOSTELLERS see Innkeepers.

HOSTLER see Ostler.

HOUSE OF CORRECTION A county gaol used to house vagrants, beggars and unmarried mothers where, by hard labour and other deprivations, an attempt was made to reform the prisoners, not merely punish them.

HOUSE OF LORDS RECORD OFFICE see also Parliamentary Records. The bulk of its records consists, of course, of Acts of Parliament and there are at least 60,000 in the Record Office. Many are private bills and these include such matters as divorce and naturalisation.

There are investigations of peerage claims from 1628 and these contain much genealogical information. There are, too, many documents dealing with problems of succession to family estates. They also hold the 1641 Protestation Returns.

The House of Lords Record Office, House of Lords, London SW1A OPW, is open Mon to Fri 9.30am — 5.00pm. It is preferable, but not essential, to make an appointment about a week in advance.

HOUSEHOLD CAVALRY The Household Cavalry Museum collection relates to The Life Guards, Horse Grenadier Guards, Royal Horse Guards (The Blues) and The Blues and Royals, covering over three hundred years of the history of the Sovereign's mounted bodyguard.

The collection contains uniforms, weapons, standards, medals, and Horse Furniture plus paintings, prints and many other curios of the Regiment.

The Library contains Officers and Soldiers records from the latter part of the 17th century, Order Books, Courts Martial records, Historical records of the Regiments, marriage and birth records, private letters, journals and war diaries. There are also records of State occasions and photographic records from mid-19th century.

For details of access contact the Curator, Household Cavalry Museum, Combermere Barracks, Windsor, Berkshire.

HOUSES - HISTORY OF Sources of information will be located in County or City Record Offices.

If the house is a very old one, consult the Victoria County History for the appropriate county. The relevant county in Pevsner's *Buildings of England* should also be consulted. Below are listed some records which may help (see also under relevant heading in this book):

(1) Ordnance Survey maps - both 6" and 25". (2) Early maps of towns if applicable. (3) Enclosure maps and awards (late 18th or early 19th century), usually have houses marked on them. The Schedule, if available, lists names of owners or occupiers, and sometimes these are recorded on the maps. (4) Tithe Maps and Awards. (5) Estate Surveys. (6) Family Histories. (7) Wills (8) Manorial Records (9) Parish records (especially 'Terriers') (10) Sale catalogues (11) Land Tax Records (12) Rate Books (13) Census Returns (14) Registers of Electors.

The Shire Publication *Discovering This Old House* by David Iredale, has been reissued as *Discovering Your Old House*.

HUCKSTER A street seller of ale (often a woman) or a retailer of small wares in a shop or booth.

HUDSON'S BAY COMPANY see Companies

HUGUENOT AND WALLOON RESEARCH ASSOCIATION The Association publishes a twice yearly journal aimed to assist its members with presumed or known Huguenot, Walloon or Flemish ancestors. Details may be obtained from: Mrs J. Tsushima, 'Malmaison', Church Street, Great Bedwyn, Wilts SN8 3PE, by sending large sae or 3 IRCs.

HUGUENOTS French Protestants. The first Huguenot refugees arrived in England in the mid 1500's. In 1685 there was an influx of at least 40,000 after the Revocation of the Edict of Nantes. They tended to concentrate in London, the Cinque Ports, Norwich, Bristol and the West Country.

They had their own churches, and most of the registers have been published by the Huguenot Society, which has its headquarters at The Huguenot Library, University College, Gower Street, London WC1E 6BT. The Huguenot Library which can be visited by appointment only, is open free to members, and to fee-paying readers on a daily basis; on Tues Wed Thurs 10.00am-4.00pm. Application to join should be made to the

Administrative Secretary at the Library. The Society has also published volumes listing naturalisations and aliens 1509 to 1800. Naturalisations are also in *Index to Local and Personal Acts, 1801 to 1947* published by HMSO. The 'Proceedings' of the Huguenot Society are worth study by anyone with a Huguenot ancestor in the family.

A valuable *General Index* to its publications 1855-1991 compiled by C.F.A. Marmoy has now been published. The State Papers, Domestic, Edward VI, Mary and Elizabeth (the Calendars have been printed) contain references to strangers in London from 1560 onwards, many of whom were Huguenots. A useful book entitled *Huguenots, Their Settlements, Churches and Industries in England and Ireland* by Samuel Smiles was published in 1867.

Huguenot Heritage by Dr Robin Gwynn, Routledge & Kegan Paul, 1985, (hardback £15.95) is the first full-length study of the Huguenots in England to appear this century and marked the tercentenary of the Revocation of the Edict of Nantes.

Published in the same year was *In Search of Huguenot Ancestry* by Noel Currer-Briggs and Royston Gambier, Phillimore, price £8.95.

See also a series of articles in FTM Vol.1 Nos.1,2, and 5 (Nov-Dec 1984/Jan-Feb/Jul-Aug 1985).

HUNDRED A subdivision of a county or shire, having its own court. Hundred names and areas are detailed in the Victoria County History series and their derivations in English Place Names Society series (Place Names).A number of taxes, including Land Tax, are arranged under Hundreds (or equivalent names in certain areas) and many Registration Districts are named after the old Hundreds.

HUSBANDMAN A tenant farmer.

I.G.I. see International Genealogical Index.

ILLEGITIMACY To be born of parents who were/are not married to each other at the time of birth (father often unknown). Parish Poor Law Overseers usually tried to establish the name of the father of an illegitimate child, so that he could be made to pay weekly amounts to the mother and thus spare the Poor Rate funds. The matter was dealt with by the issue of a Bastardy Bond. Many cases are mentioned in Quarter Sessions records.

Under the Poor Law Amendment Act of 1834 mothers of illegitimate children could apply to the Petty Sessions for a Bastardy Order against the father. When an illegitimate child was registered, the father's name was normally omitted.

The term 'illegitimate' was not employed in parish registers until the 18th century, though the Latin form 'Illegitima' may be found, as also 'Filius naturalis et legitimus' (which in English might appear as 'Natural and lawful son').

However many other phrases − some quite extraordinary − have been found in registers. An article appeared in the Journal of the BMSGH February 1975 by Dr R.J. Hetherington, containing a collection of no fewer than 87 which he has noted including:

Bantling, Base, Base-born, Bastardus, Begotten in adultery, Begotten in fornication, Born extra, By-blow, By-chip, By-scape, By-slip, Chance begot, Child of shame, Come by chance, In sin begotten, Love begot, Lovechild, Merrybegot, Misbegotten, Scape-begotten-child, Son of no certain man, Spuriosus, Supputed son, Whoreson. Illegitimacy is very common; there are few families without an example. *Illegitimacy* by Eve McLaughlin, is not only a helpful booklet but tends to put the matter into perspective! Obtainable from FTM price £1.55 inc. p&p.

IMMIGRATION see also Aliens, Emigration, Naturalisation and Population.

See PRO Records Information leaflet 70 *Immigrants: Documents in the PRO* and Family Fact Sheet 9 *Tracing an Ancestor who was an Immigrant*. There are a great many records to help you, though a lot of searching may be necessary. A summary of the PRO information is printed in Gen. Mag. Vol.16 No.5 (March 1970).

IMPERIAL WAR MUSEUM see also Army, Royal Air Force and Royal Navy.

Situated in Lambeth Road, London SE1 6HZ, the IWM illustrates and records all aspects of the two World Wars and other military operations involving Britain and the Commonwealth since 1914. The Museum was founded in 1917, and has been in its present home (formerly the Bethlem Royal Hospital or Bedlam) since 1936.

The Department of Documents is a repository for documentary records of all types relating to warfare in the twentieth century. The Collections fall into two main groups, one consisting of British private papers and the other largely of captured German material.

There is a photographic library which has over five million First, Second and Post War photographs. It is necessary to make an appointment to visit both of these departments which are open 10.00am - 5.00pm Mon - Sat. Visitors are admitted free to the Reference Departments but there is a charge for touring the Museum galleries — well worth the money though.

The IWM has a selection of publications the series title of which is *Tracing Individual Service Records and Medal Citations:* they are general guides to official documents held by themselves and elsewhere. Price £3.00 each; titles listed under relevant headings in this book.

INCLOSURE AWARDS see Enclosure Awards.

INCOME TAX This was first levied in 1799 to pay for the war against France. The rate was 2/- in the £. It was abolished in 1802 but revived the following year.

INCUMBENT A general term which covered rector, vicar, parson, minister or perpetual curate (all q.v.). The incumbent was in charge of the parish.

INDENTURE This was originally a document cut into two pieces, the authenticity of one piece being proved when matched with the other. The contents of the document were written twice, and it was usual to add the word 'Cyrographum' where a jagged cut between the two copies was to be made. In very early times indentures were used for wills and later for contracts, title deeds etc. The word has now come to be associated with apprentices, articles and leases.

INDENTURED SERVANT see Emigration.

INDEXES Most researchers consult indexes as often as, if not more than, actual source material. They are an invaluable working tool. Where appropriate we have directed you to a relevant index and details of many others can be found in *Marriage, Census and Other Indexes for the Family Historian* and *Unpublished Personal Name Indexes in Record Offices and Libraries*, FFHS and a series of articles *Indexers and their indexes*, FTM Vol.8 No.6 (Apr 1992) ongoing.

Pinhorns hold a number of indexes and genealogical collections. The more specific ones are detailed under the relevant headings in this book (e.g. Change of Name Index) but there are others not so easy to classify which may prove a 'lucky dip' for you (the East of England Index or the Cotton Collection). Send sae or 3 IRCs for details. Enclose 2 additional first class stamps for a list of publications.

The Currer-Briggs Genealogical Index covers the period from about 1550-1700, and is made up of several hundred thousand names of persons derived from unpublished sources. These include wills, proceedings in the Courts of Chancery and Requests, notarial records of Amsterdam and Rotterdam having to do with the 17th century tobacco and fur trades, parish registers and other miscellaneous manuscript sources. It is supplemented by an extensive library of Virginian and other colonial records and land grants, an index of five hundred ships and their crews and much more. Send sae or 2 IRCs for details and charges to Noel Currer-Briggs.

Debrett Ancestry Research Ltd, offers a number of **Surname Services**. Write for a copy of their pamphlet which gives details of their indexes: Francis Leeson's Surname Archive; an Emigrant Check, Annuity Check and a Surname Report. There is a scale of fees for these services (some of which may be regarded as costly).

However, at some time you may need to compile an index (a task not always as easy as it sounds!); before embarking upon this it would be worth reading one or more of the following books:

Indexes and Indexing by Robert L. Collinson, published by Benn, 1972.

Recommendations: The Preparation of Indexes, British Standards Institution, 1976.

How to let your fingers do the walking and not lose the way, K. Bakewell, The Times Higher Educational Supplement, 26 Sept. 1980.

Indexing for Editors by R.F. Hunnisett, British Records Association, 1972.

There is a Society of Indexers and details of courses, training and publications on indexing can be obtained from the Secretary, Society of Indexers, 16 Green Road, Birchington, Kent CT7 9JZ. Or perhaps of particular interest would be the Genealogical Group of that organisation formed in 1993 and still comparatively small (but keen!). Details from Mr H.A. Rydings, 29 Eastwood Road, Shrewsbury, Shropshire SY3 8YJ.

INDIA see Oriental and India Office Collections, also Cemeteries in South Asia and Emigration.

INDUSTRIAL ARCHAEOLOGY You can find useful references to such things as mines, railways etc. by consulting *The BP Book of Industrial Archaeology* by Neil Cossons, Newton Abbot, 1975. It lists sites, museums and organisations connected with these topics.

A comprehensive list of the various Industrial History Museums is also given in *The Local Historian's Encyclopedia* (q.v.)

INFLATION   see also Wages. Although we think of this as largely a modern phenomenon, there was a period of considerable inflation in the 16th century, one cause of which was the flow of gold and silver from the Americas. Do remember that the value of money has altered dramatically over the past 400 years. For further reading see *History of the Cost of Living* by John Burnett, Pelican, 1969.

INHIBITION The period during the visitation of a bishop to an archdeaconry, when the archdeacon's court would be closed and probate business conducted in the consistory court. In theory the visitation of an archbishop to a diocese would have the same effect on a consistory court but in post-mediaeval times this was likely to be 'pro forma' only. Some peculiars were entirely exempt from visitation and inhibition, others subject to visitation by a dean or a dean and chapter. Visitations would normally last several months at intervals of several years.

INLAND REVENUE see Valuation Office.

IN-LAW This phrase had a different meaning in the mid 19th century, and indeed much earlier, from that which it has today. In the 1851 census, for example, the term daughter (or son) -in-law could mean 'step-daughter' or 'step- son', i.e. children of the wife of the head of the household by a previous marriage. In Dicken's *Pickwick Papers*, Sam Weller addresses his step-mother as 'mother-in-law'. It is important to remember this when studying early wills from which much important information about relationships can be gleaned.

INNKEEPERS They were also known as ostellers or Innholders. See *A History of The Innholders' Company* by O.Warner, 1962.

INNS OF COURT see Legal Profession.

INQUESTS see Coroners' Inquests.

INQUISITIONS POST MORTEM If a person held land belonging to the Crown, on his death an inquiry was made into his possessions, services due, and his rightful heirs. These enquiries, known as Inquisitions Post Mortem, often contain useful genealogical information.   They cover a period of some 400 years up to the end of feudal tenures in 1660. Though they tended to relate to important people, often quite humble folk were called upon to give evidence, relating to the age of the heir. The person giving such evidence was named, his age given, and such information as: 'He has lived in . . . for 45 years, and remembers . . . was baptised the same week as his son John'.
　　These records are in the PRO. There are Calendars of the early Inquisitions, and it is worth enquiring at the appropriate CRO to see if they exist for the area to which you have traced your ancestors if you have been fortunate in getting back to the early registers. Those for a number of counties have been printed by local record societies.

INSTITUTE OF HERALDIC AND GENEALOGICAL STUDIES (IHGS) (Northgate, Canterbury, Kent CT1 1BA) see also Pallot Index. The Institute is constituted as a registered charity and is an educational trust. It made its home in a mediaeval building in Canterbury in 1961 and provides for training, study and research in genealogy and the history of the family. It acts as a qualifying body for genealogists, setting and maintaining professional standards. The Institute is supported by Achievements Ltd which also provides practical experience for students of the Institute in genealogical and related research.

It is constituted to train those who wish to acquire skills in family history research. It organises day, evening and residential courses at several levels. A full-time course for a small number of students is provided at the Institute giving practical experience under tutorial guidance. The Institute conducts a series of evening classes in conjunction with universities and there is also a popular correspondence course. The Institute's training courses can lead to examinations in the method and practice of genealogy and heraldry.

The Institute's syllabus of Study and Qualifications provides for several stages of progress from beginners to more advanced classes. They follow a guided course structure which leads teachers and students through the topics which should be covered in a thorough introduction to the study of family history. The syllabus can be adapted to suit the time available in various courses. It is hoped that teachers who follow the beginners' syllabus will encourage their students to test their acquired knowledge by sitting the graded assessment tests. Details of these tests and higher levels of qualifications are contained in the syllabus which is available from the Registrar on receipt of £1.00 plus an A5 self-addressed envelope, to the address above. See *Examinations in Genealogy* by Richard Baker, FTM, Vol.9 No.7 (May 1993).

Membership of the Institute: Fellows are elected by Council. The Licentiateship is awarded to those fulfilling qualification requirements. Graduate membership is also available to those qualified through examination. Associate membership is open to all wishing to support the Institute. Members may be granted free access to the library during normal opening hours. The journal *Family History* and newsletters are issued to members and subscribers. All members are required to pay an initial fee of £30 (reduced after 31st March in any year to £22.50) and thereafter £15. Non-members can obtain the journal for a subscription of £12.00 for one year or four issues, £30.00 for three years or twelve issues.

A large number of publications on heraldry, genealogy and related subjects are available from the Institute's Family History Bookshop (on which members receive a discount). Also within the Institute there are accredited specialists who will advise on heraldry and associated artwork.

Along with other aids to research and the *Family History Diary* the Institute publishes *parish maps of the counties of England, Wales and Scotland* and produced the *Phillimore Atlas and Index of Parish Registers* (see Parish Maps).

Teachers Packs of overhead projection slides, covering a variety of subjects (e.g. General Registration, Censuses, Trades & Occupations, Heraldry), have been produced to meet the difficulties teachers of family history have experienced in finding good examples. Packs are accompanied by brief notes highlighting the main points which can be demonstrated with each slide. They are not teaching notes.

The library contains an extensive collection of works on heraldry, genealogy and local history, providing invaluable finding aids and useful background material. There are sources for the whole of the UK along with special collections for the counties of London, Kent, Sussex and Hampshire along with many specialist indexes such as the IGI, Scottish OPR Indexes, Catholic Marriage Index, indexes of census returns, monumental inscriptions, marriage licences and armorials, and an indexed archive collection of genealogical research into some 20,000 genealogical cases. Non-members may use the library which is open between 10.00am and 4.30pm (except Thursdays) for a fee of £12.00 per day (£8.75 half day). All visitors should make an appointment with the librarian as space is at a premium. A research and advisory service is available for those who cannot visit the library.

INSURANCE see also Fire Insurance. The Guildhall Library (q.v.) holds the records of over 80 London based insurance companies or subsidiaries. Brief details of the records held there and elsewhere are given in *The British Insurance Business 1547 to 1970* by H.A.L. Cockerell & Edwin Green, Heinemann Educ.Books, 1976.

The original registers of the Sun Fire Office are in the Guildhall Library, together with an index of policy holders between the years 1714 to 1730, arranged by counties, but excluding London, Scotland and Wales. See *Life Insurance Companies* — Pinhorn Handbook No.3 obtainable from Pinhorns.

The surviving registers of both the Royal Exchange Assurance and the Sun Fire Office 1775-1787 are now on microfiche, covering some 150,000 policies. The microfiche is available for viewing at many libraries and record offices throughout the country.

INTERNATIONAL GENEALOGICAL INDEX (IGI) This remarkable index has been produced by the LDS. The index contains many millions of baptisms and marriages but virtually NO BURIALS. The most recent date for entries (1992 edition) is about 1885 but the majority are much earlier. By no means all parish or non-conformist registers are included and even where the index contains some entries from a particular register this does not necessarily indicate coverage of the whole period of the register.

For ENGLAND, SCOTLAND and IRELAND, the entries are arranged as follows:

1. under COUNTIES
2. within counties, under SURNAMES in alphabetical order
3. within surnames, under CHRISTIAN NAMES of individuals christened or married, in alphabetical order — note that, for example, all Wm. entries follow ones for William and Wm and are not combined in a single sequence
4. within christian names, in DATE ORDER

For Wales, the IGI is similarly arranged as for England, Scotland and Ireland described earlier. However it has the addition of a GIVEN NAME arrangement in alphabetical order within counties.

The ISLE OF MAN and CHANNEL ISLANDS follow the same arrangement for names but each of these is treated as a single unit, corresponding to an English, Welsh or Scottish county.

Most editions of the IGI have variant surname spellings combined under one standard spelling. The 1981 edition, due a computing error, did not follow this format. Researchers using this edition should beware!

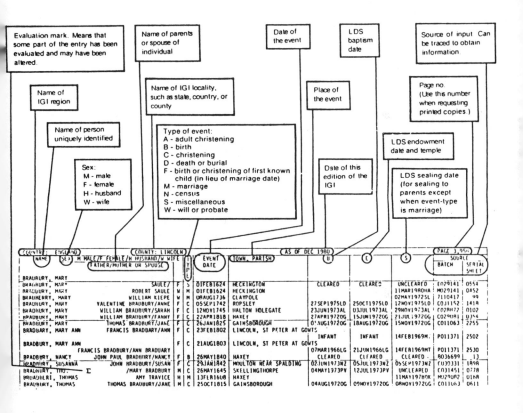

Evaluation mark. Means that some part of the entry has been evaluated and may have been altered.

Name of parents or spouse of individual

Date of the event

LDS baptism date

Source of input. Can be traced to obtain information.

Name of IGI region

Name of IGI locality, such as state, country, or county

Place of the event

Page no. (Use this number when requesting printed copies.)

Name of person uniquely identified

Type of event:
A - adult christening
B - birth
C - christening
D - death or burial
F - birth or christening of first known child (in lieu of marriage date)
M - marriage
N - census
S - miscellaneous
W - will or probate

LDS endowment date and temple

Sex:
M - male
F - female
H - husband
W - wife

Date of this edition of the IGI

LDS sealing date (for sealing to parents except when event-type is marriage)

COUNTRY: ENGLAND   COUNTY: LINCOLN   (AS OF DEC 1980)   PAGE 3,954

NAME	SEX	FATHER/MOTHER OR SPOUSE	TYPE	EVENT DATE	TOWN, PARISH	B	E	S	SOURCE BATCH	SERIAL SHEET
BRADBURY, MARY										
BRADBURY, MARY	F	SAULE/	S	01FEB1624	HECKINGTON	CLEARED	CLEARED	UNCLEARED	E029141	0554
BRADBURY, MARY	W	M ROBERT SAULE		01FEB1624	HECKINGTON				M029141	0452
BRADBERRY, MARY	W	M WILLIAM RIEPE		08AUG1736	CLAYPOLE			02MAY1972SL	7110417	99
BRADBURY, MARY	F	C VALENTINE BRADBURY/ANNE		05SEP1742	ROPSLEY	27SEP1975LD	25OCT1975LD	12NOV1975LD	C031152	1418
BRADBURY, MARY	F	C WILLIAM BRADBURY/SARAH		12NOV1745	HALTON HOLEGATE	23JUN1973AL	03JUL1973AL	29NOV1973AL	C028H77	0102
BRADBURY, MARY	F	C WILLIAM BRADBURY/FANNY		22APR1818	HAXEY	27APR1972GG	15JUN1972GG	21JUL1972GG	C029081	0354
BRADBURY, MARY	F	C THOMAS BRADBURY/JANE		26JAN1825	GAINSBOROUGH	01AUG1972GG	18AUG1972GG	15NOV1972GG	C011063	2255
BRADBARY, MARY ANN	F	C FRANCIS BRADBARY/ANN		23FEB1802	LINCOLN, ST PETER AT GOWTS	INFANT	INFANT	14FEB1969N.	P011371	2502
BRADBURY, MARY ANN	F	C FRANCIS BRADBURY/ANN BRADUARY		21AUG1803	LINCOLN, ST PETER AT GOWTS	07MAR1966LG	21JUN1966LG	14FEB1969MT	P011371	2530
BRADBURY, NANCY	F	B JOHN PAUL BRADBURY/NANCY		26MAY1840	HAXEY	CLEARED	CLEARED	CLEARED	B036699	13
BRADBURY, SUSANNA	F	C JOHN BRADBURY/SUSAN		29JAN1842	MOULTON NEAR SPALDING	02JUN1973NZ	05JUL1973NZ	05SEP1973NZ	C030331	189A
BRADBURY, THO.	M	C /MARY BRADBURY		26MAY1645	SKELLINGTHORPE	04MAY1973PV	12JUL1973PV	UNCLEARED	C031451	0778
BRADBERI, THOMAS	H	M AMY TRAVICE		13FEB1608	HAXEY			11MAY1978OK	M029082	016A
BRADBURY, THOMAS	M	C THOMAS BRADBURY/JANE		25OCT1815	GAINSBOROUGH	04AUG1972GG	09NOV1972GG	08NOV1972GG	C011063	0611

Interpreting a print out from the International Genealogical Index (IGI).

123

It can be a useful 'finding aid', as long as you do not expect it to be the answer to all your problems. If you find a likely ancestor listed in the index you should *always refer back to the original register* to authenticate the entry.

The IGI can be used for at least three purposes. (1) To find genealogical information. (2) To avoid duplication in research (3) To determine if someone else is researching a given line. This is done by noting the batch number in the last two columns. (Not all the names in the IGI were compiled through genealogical research. The name may simply have been extracted as part of an indexing project.) Contact with other researchers can only be made via the LDS.

Many family history societies, libraries and record offices now have copies of the index on microfiche; some have only the section which relates to their county, others have a complete set for the British Isles and the Channel Islands and the SOG, among others, has world-wide coverage. The PRO Census Reference Room S has the microfilm indexes covering England, Wales, the Channel Islands and the Isle of Man. Other copies are available at the PRO. See Census Information leaflet 4: *The International Genealogical Index* and *Making the Most of The IGI* by Eve McLaughlin obtainable from FTM price £1.55 & £1.83 respectively inc. p&p.

A number of societies and repositories offer a print-out service at a modest cost (about 40p a page, which contains approximately 50 entries).

You can obtain a print-out of all instances of a given surname within a county; you can obtain a print-out of a particular christian name and surname for a given county, you can even limit that to within a certain time span e.g. John Brown for years 1780 to 1810 in Warwickshire. However, the arrangement of the index makes it *impossible* to abstract entries for a *surname only* within a given time span.

It is not possible to obtain a print-out of a given name just for a particular parish either, as the arrangement is geographical only by County, after that it is alphabetical by names not parishes. It can be useful to know which parishes have been included for a particular County and a list with dates of the entries can be found in the separate index entitled *Parish and Vital Records List.*

See Pitfalls for the Unwary by Colin Atkinson, 'Hampshire Family Historian' Vol.10 No.1 (May 1983); *Beware the IGI* and *IGI: Always read the Instructions* by Pauline Litton, FTM, Vol.7 No.10 (Aug 1991), and Vol. 8 No.4 (Feb 1992); *Using the I.G.I.for Wales and Monmouthshire* by Chris Pitt Lewis, Gwent FHS Journal, No.3 (April 1982) and *The International Genealogical Index* by Lance J. Jacob in Gen. Mag. Vol.21 Nos.2 and 3 (June/Sep 1983). (This does relate especially to the 1981 edition of the IGI.)

The International Genealogical Index 1992 is a very informed article by Elizabeth L.Nichols a User Specialist at the Family History Library, Salt Lake City. In two parts, the second of which is largely devoted to More About Temple Records and Supplementary Sources. See Gen. Mag. Vol.24 Nos.7 & 8 (Sep/Dec 1993).

During the early 1990s, The Church of Jesus Christ of Latter-Day Saints published the IGI on compact disk (CD ROM) as part of its Family Search computer system. These compact disks are similar to audio compact disks sold in record shops. They are capable of storing vast amounts of information. The disks are read by a computer with a special compact disk player. This edition of the IGI includes many features not possible on microfiche, such as listing all names alphabetically within a country or region.

Information can be stored in a 'holding file' and printed onto paper or transferred to a floppy diskette as required. It is a *very* sophisticated database which brings a new perspective to searching the IGI. Unlike the microfiche edition of the IGI, the CD-ROM version is not available for sale to private individuals. It is however freely available for use in the main Family History Library in Salt Lake City as well as at the majority of the Church's FHCs.

INTERNATIONAL REPLY COUPONS If you wish to write to someone overseas, you will naturally wish to send them the cost of replying to your letter. You can do this by going to your post office and purchasing some International Reply Coupons (IRCs). Coupons can be exchanged in any post office in the world for a stamp sufficient to reply to your letter by air mail postage. Remember that the basic air mail rate only allows for 10g or one sheet of A4 paper.

A 'poundage' has to be paid for the coupons and this makes them very expensive. Indeed, this has been described as "a rip off"! If you are writing to a society they would prefer to receive a $1 (Canada or USA) or $2 (Australia and New Zealand). They will get more and you pay less.

Occasionally the issuing office will omit to stamp the IRC or will have stamped the 'exchange' box instead of the 'issuing box' on the coupon, in which case the receiving post office will almost certainly refuse to accept it. In the UK these can be redeemed by sending them with a covering letter to International Reply Coupons, Royal Mail International, Chetwynd House, Chesterfield, Derbyshire, S49 1PF. A small commission is levied so it may be worthwhile waiting until you have accumulated a number of void coupons.

If you live overseas and assuming you are likely to write to people in the British Isles, it would be worthwhile obtaining a supply of British stamps by writing to the British Philatelic Bureau, 20 Brandon Street, Edinburgh EH3 5TT, Scotland, enclosing a remittance, and asking them to send you a supply of stamps of the denomination needed to send air mail letters to your country from Britain.

Many overseas FHSs purchase British stamps in bulk and will supply these to their members.

INTERNATIONAL STANDARD BOOK NUMBER (ISBN) Occasional publications (such as Directories of Members' Interests) can be allocated an ISBN by the Standard Book Numbering Agency, 12 Dyott Street, London WC1A 1DF. Publishers can apply to the Agency for a block of numbers which they can allocate as and when new titles are published.

INTERNATIONAL STANDARD SERIAL NUMBER (ISSN) Serial publications which appear at regular intervals are allocated an ISSN by The Director, ISSN UK Centre, The British Library, Boston Spa, Wetherby, W.Yorkshire LS23 7BQ, who will be pleased to supply useful leaflet describing the ISSN system and its value.

The ISSN number should appear on the cover of each issue. It is possible to apply for an ISSN number in advance of publishing the first issue of a periodical by sending proofs of the title page; otherwise a number should be allocated by the British Library on receipt of first issue. The number consists of two sets of four digits separated by a hyphen; this should be printed at the top right hand corner of the cover preceded by the letters ISSN.

INTERREGNUM (1649-1660) Term used to describe the period between the execution of Charles I (1649) and the Restoration (1660), embracing various governments of the Commonwealth and Protectorate. During this period many ecclesiastical records are fragmentary and probate records will be found in the PCC records in the PRO.

See PRO Records Information leaflet 88 *Confiscations, Sales and Restoration of Crown and Royalist Land 1642-1660: sources in the PRO* and *The Civil War and Interregnum, sources for Local Historians* by G.E. Aylmer and J.S.Morrill, Bedford Square Press, 1979. The latter is obtainable from the SOG price £3.50 inc. p&p.

INTESTACY A person who dies without leaving a will is said to have died 'intestate'. Many people die without leaving a will. Their goods are then divided between the children or taken over by a surviving partner by mutual agreement. If no property is owned, no legal process is involved.

If, however, property is involved or there is money in a bank or savings scheme, an application for probate has to be made, and 'letters of administration' (admon.) are granted to enable the heirs to sell the property or obtain the money. See article by Malcolm Pinhorn in Gen. Mag. Vol.17 No.1 (March 1972).

INVENTORIES These were lists of the belongings of a deceased person, and were part of the process of obtaining probate. Common until mid - C18 but uncommon later except in Peculiars.

They are fascinating documents and give a vivid picture of the contents of the houses in which our ancestors lived; from the inventory we can often judge whether they lived in affluence or in poverty. Many of the items listed, however, may puzzle you.

You are recommended to obtain a copy of *A Glossary of Household, Farming and Trade Terms from Probate Inventories* by Rosemary Milward, 3rd ed. 1986, published by Derbyshire Record Society. Obtainable from the FFHS.

Another book you might consult is *The Goods and Chattels of our forefathers* edited by J.S. Moore, published by Phillimore in 1976. It has a useful glossary.

Probate Inventories and Local History by Jill Groves, 'Local History' No.23 ((Sep 1989). An interesting article which brings a slightly different approach to the subject; a good introduction for anyone who hasn't used an inventory.

IRELAND see also Civil Registration in Ireland, Parish Registers of Ireland, Emigration and Family Histories.

Most of the valuable archival records deposited at the Public Record Office in the Four Courts, Dublin, were destroyed in 1922 as a result of the Civil War in Ireland. Therefore, it is no use pretending that tracing Irish ancestry is going to be easy. However, contrary to popular belief, it is not impossible. Records which were not housed at the Four Courts in 1922 were not affected by the Civil War.

For complete beginners in researching Irish ancestry the best "text" book available at present is *An Introduction to Irish Research* by Bill Davis, FFHS. A more in-depth guide is *Tracing Your Irish Ancestors – The Complete Guide* by John Grenham, Gill & Macmillan, Dublin, 1992. Also useful are *Irish Genealogy: A Record Finder* edited by Donal Begley, Heraldic Artists, Dublin, and *The Irish Roots Guide* by Tony McCarthy, Lillliput, Dublin, 1991. For more obscure sources *Irish and Scotch-Irish Ancestral Research* by Margaret Falley, 2 vols. 1962, reissued 1989 Genealogical Publishing Co.Inc, is very good, but difficult and somewhat out of date. *Sources for Irish Genealogy in the Society of Genealogists* compiled by Anthony J. Camp, 1990, is an essential guide to research in that repository. (Price £1.10 inc. p&p.)

Since 1921 Ireland has been divided into two parts, the Republic of Ireland (sometimes referred to as Eire, though rarely within Ireland) with Dublin as the seat of Government, and Northern Ireland (still part of the UK), governed for a time from Belfast and now from London. Northern Ireland consists of the counties of Antrim, Armagh, Down, Fermanagh, Londonderry (referred to by Nationalists as Derry) and Tyrone. It is sometimes called the Six Counties. The other twenty-six counties form the Republic.

Most genealogical records are centralised in either Dublin or Belfast. The relevant repositories are:

Dublin

The National Library of Ireland, Kildare Street, Dublin 2.

National Archives, Bishop Street, Dublin 8.

General Register Office, Joyce House, 8-11 Lombard Street East, Dublin 2.

Representative Church Body Library, Braemor Park, Churchtown, Dublin 14.

Registry of Deeds, King's Inns, Henrietta Street, Dublin 1 (land registration dates from 1708).

Genealogical Office, 2 Kildare Street, Dublin 2.

(See *National Archive of Dublin* by Dennis C.N. Allen, FTM, Vol.8 No.5 (Mar 1992).)

Belfast

Public Record Office of Northern Ireland, 66 Balmoral Avenue, Belfast BT9 6NY.

General Register Office (post-1922 Northern Ireland only), Oxford House, 49-55 Chichester Street, Belfast BT1 4HL.

The Association of Professional Genealogists in Ireland (APGI), c/o The Genealogical Office, will provide a membership list (enclose 1 IRC). It represents most professionals in the Republic and Northern Ireland and has a complaints investigation procedure. Research may also be commissioned with indexing or "heritage" centres throughout the country which are in the process of indexing church registers in their locality. *Directory of Parish Registers Indexed in Ireland* (Irish Family History Society) is the most up-to-date history of these centres and their holdings. Most centres are affiliated to the Irish Family History Foundation. While they will conduct searches in their indexes, they do not usually allow direct access to them.

For those visiting Ireland to research their ancestry it is advisable to begin with the Consultancy Service at the Genealogical Office. It is run by the G.O. in conjunction with APGI. It consists of a personal consultation of up to an hour with an APGI member. The current fee is IR£20.

There are a number of amateur organisations which have membership facilities. The oldest is the Irish Genealogical Research Society, founded in 1936 and based in London (c/o Irish Club, 82 Eaton Square, London SW1W 9AJ) where its library is located. The IGRS publishes *The Irish Genealogist* annually. It has a worldwide membership and there is an 'Ireland Branch' for members within Ireland (Republic and N.I.); details available from Dermot Blunden, 6 Eaton Brae, Orwell Road, Rathoar, Dublin 14. The Irish Family History Society (PO Box 36, Naas, Co.Kildare) also has a worldwide membership and publishes an annual journal. The North of Ireland Family History Society (c/o Dept.of Education, Queen's University, 69 University Street, Belfast BT1 1HL) has eight branches in Northern Ireland and issues a journal.

Details of other family history societies in Ireland may be obtained from the Administrator of the FFHS in exchange for sae or 2 IRCs or see current issue of FHN&D.

There is an Anglo-Irish Branch of the Liverpool and South West Lancashire FHS which meets most months in St Helens, Lancashire. Details from Mrs J.McCann, 46 Stanley Avenue, Rainford, St Helens, WA11 8HU.

The Irish Genealogical Congress was first held in September 1991 at Trinity College, Dublin and attracted 400 participants, amateur and professional. The second took place in September 1994 and the event is planned to be held on a regular three year cycle. Information is available from the IGC Committee, c/o The Genealogical Office, 2 Kildare Street, Dublin 2.

The following books may help you in your research:

Handbook on Irish Genealogy published by Heraldic Artists, Dublin and obtainable from the FFHS.

A Simple Guide to Irish Genealogy ed. by R. ffolliott, 1967 published by the Irish Genealogical Research Society.

Irish Church Records: Their History, Availability and use in Family History Research from Flyleaf Press, 4 Spencer Villas, Glengeary, Co. Dublin, Ireland, price approx. £24.

Irish History from 1700, a guide to sources in the Public Record Office by Alice Prochaska, British Records Association, Archives & User No.6, 1986, price £6.75 inc. p&p. This publication refers to records in the PRO, London, which have Irish connections.

There is a PRO Records Information leaflet 11 entitled *The Records of the Royal Irish Constabulary*. Microfilm copies of these records are now held at the PRO of Northern Ireland and the National Archives.

Wills for the period 1858-1899 probated at the Principal Registry (i.e.Dublin) were destroyed in 1922. Those probated in local offices (i.e. outside Dublin) for that period survive in Will Copy Books for places like Belfast, Armagh, Derry, Limerick etc. Wills 1900-1922 survive, those relating to people in what became Northern Ireland were transferred to the PRO in Belfast. The National Archives in Dublin have abstracts of many pre-1858 wills.

Index to the Prerogative Wills of Ireland, 1536-1810 by Sir Arthur Vicars (1897) reissued 1989 by Genealogical Publishing Co. Inc.

Genealogical abstracts were made by Sir William Betham of the wills dating from 1536 to 1800. Sir Arthur Vicars indexed Betham's abstracts in 1897 and his index is the only printed guide to the wills and the only means of access to the mass of abstracts.

The index contains 40,000 entries arranged alphabetically by the name of the testator, showing his rank, occupation or condition, his town and county of residence, and the year of probate.

A time saver when searching for Irish wills and admons. for the years 1859-1876 inclusive at Somerset House, is to look under the letter 'Z' rather than the testator's name. Following the 'Z' Admons. appear: Irish Probates, sealed, Irish Admons. sealed and Scottish Confirmations, sealed.

In each of these three sections testators' names are arranged in strict alphabetical order. These could be of great value since though calendared in the PRO, Dublin, these wills and admons. are missing from some courts including the Principal Registry. A number of these admons. refer to persons deceased before the Letters of Administration were taken out.

Memorials of the Dead in Ireland, a series of volumes published by the Irish Memorials Association, contains many thousands of inscriptions from gravestones and other memorials. Many of these are indexed in the Great Slip Index at the SOG.

Heraldic Artists, The Genealogy Bookshop, 3 Nassau Street, Dublin 2, Ireland, can supply the the following:

Genealogical and Historical Map of Ireland (folder map with over 3000 Irish Family names in their historical location)

Family Tree Charts and Story Map of Ireland

The Surnames of Ireland (lists over 4000 Family names with information on practically every surname found in Ireland).

Recommended is *History in the Ordnance Map: An Introduction for Irish Readers* by J.H. Andrews, republished 1993 by David Archer, The Pentre, Kerry, Newtown, Montgomeryshire, Wales SY16 4PD and available from him price £7.90 inc. p&p. The introduction to the book is an evaluation of the historical and demographical use of ordnance survey maps; following on is a detailed analysis of each type of map: boundary sketches, fair plans etc. Sources and references are quoted and there is a bibliography.

For family historians researching for Irish connections *Barefoot and Pregnant? Irish Famine Orphans in Australia* by Trevor McClaughlin, could prove extremely valuable. The book is about 4000 Irish girls, teenagers and orphans, who emigrated to Australia in 1848-50 under a scheme instigated by Earl Grey, British Secretary of State for the Colonies. An interesting story, the second part particularly so, as this is a register of all the orphans, listed alphabetically, according to the ship in which they travelled, with age, home town, names of parents (where known) and religion. Any further information discovered since (e.g.marriage) is also given. Published 1991, by The Genealogical Society of Victoria Inc., 5th Floor, 252 Swanston St, Melbourne 3000, Australia. Price $A25 plus p&p.

Various indexes for Ireland are being compiled either by individuals or family history societies. Details in *Marriage, Census and Other Indexes for Family Historians* by Jeremy Gibson and Elizabeth Hampson, FFHS.

IRONMONGER Also known as a 'Feroner' or dealer in iron. There was a London Livery Company, and there are several books on the subject: *Worshipful Company of Ironmongers* by E.Hawkes, 1896, *A Brief History* by T.C. Noble, 1889, *Some Account of the Worshipful Company of Ironmongers*, by J.Nicholl, 1866, and the Shire Publication *Victorian Ironmonger*.

IRREGULAR BORDER MARRIAGES see Gretna Green Marriages

ISLE OF MAN Civil registration of marriages on the Isle of Man commenced in 1849, but not until 1878 for births and deaths. The records are held by the Island's General Registry, Finch Road, Douglas, Isle of Man. Information about wills can also be obtained from the Registry. Other records are to be found in the Manx Museum Library, Kingswood Road, Douglas, Isle of Man.

The censuses for England and Wales also cover the Isle of Man and the IGI (q.v.) for Manx baptisms and marriages is virtually complete.

See *The Manx Family Tree: A Beginners' Guide to Records in the Isle of Man* by Jane Narasinham, Isle of Man, 1986, reprinted 1994.

Details of the Isle of Man Family History Society can be obtained from the Administrator of the FFHS in exchange for sae or 3 IRCs.

Please note that mainland stamps are invalid on sae's sent to the Isle of Man as they have a separate postal authority from the UK; IRCs are acceptable.

In 1979 there were celebrations to mark the 1000 years of Tynwald, the world's oldest continuous parliament which was founded when the Vikings ruled the island.

The *Express and Star* newspaper reported that the Island had launched 'Operation Roots' to help trace a million people of Manx descent. The report stated 'Anyone who thinks he is of Manx descent should drop us a line. Our surnames are very distinctive — they usually begin with the letters C, K or Q'. These types of enquiries are now directed to the secretary of the Isle of Man FHS.

Further information, microfiche records and publications are available at the society's library, Athol Street, Peel, Isle of Man, which is open Tues, Wed, Fri and Sat 2.00pm-5.30pm.

ITALY see relevant chapter in *Worldwide Family History* by Noel Currer-Briggs, Routledge & Kegan Paul, 1982. However, Cecil R.Humphery-Smith in FTM Vol.5 No.2 (Dec 1988) warns that it is not an easy country in which to arrange research from overseas; you would do well to read his article *Research your Italian Ancestry*.

Dr Michela D'Angelo the author of works on English merchants in Sicily and Malta is researching British merchants in Italy, with emphasis on the period 1750-1850. Correspondence with anyone who has such connections would be welcomed by her at Via Milano 11, 98124 Messina, Italy.

JAGGER An itinerant pedlar or hawker, carrier or carter — often used for a seller of fish. It also has a more specialised meaning in mining — the man who carried ore on a pack-horse from a mine to be smelted, or a boy in charge of the 'jags' or train of trucks in a coal mine.

JAPANNING This was a thriving industry especially in Birmingham in the 18th and 19th centuries, and was often allied to Papier-Mache manufacturers, both trades usually being carried out in small factories.

If an ancestor was engaged in this work any of the following books would be of interest. *English Papier Mache of the Georgian and Victorian Periods*, Shirley Spaulding Devoe, London, 1971.

English Papier Mache: its origin, development and decline, George Dickinson, London, 1925.

Lacquer of the West: the history of a craft and industry, 1550-1950, Hans Huth, Chicago and London, 1971.

Georgian and Victorian Japanned Ware of the West Midlands, Yvonne Jones, Wolverhampton Art Gallery & Museums, 1982.

Papier Mache in Great Britain and America, Jane Toller, London, 1962.

JERSEY see Channel Islands.

JEWELLERS see Goldsmiths and Oriental and India Office Collections.

JEWISH ANCESTORS Part of the National Index of Parish Registers, Vol. III (q.v.) is devoted to Jewish genealogy and family history, and lists the principal sources likely to be useful in searching for Jewish ancestors.

The Bevis Marks Hall, 2 Heneage Lane, London EC3A 5DQ has a collection of Jewish registers 1687 to 1837. Its publications include birth registers 1780-1887 and Circumcisions performed between 1715-1785, with many details of parentage, grandparentage and godparentage. A book entitled *Anglo-Jewish Notabilities* has been published by the Jewish Historical Society, whose headquarters are at 33 Seymour Place, London W1H 5AP and at University College, Gower Street, London WC1E 6BT. The Anglo-Jewish Association, Woburn House, Upper Woburn Place, London WC1H OEZ can be very helpful. There is a Jewish Museum at the same address.

The genealogical collection of Anglo-Jewish Archives is deposited at the SOG; this includes the important Collyer-Fergusson and D'Arcy Hart papers; Miss Isobel Mordy's collection of Jewish pedigrees and indexes can also be consulted at the SOG.

Sources of Anglo-Jewish Genealogy by Wilfred S. Samuel is a pamphlet; a copy is in the Library of the SOG who have also published *My Ancestor was Jewish*, ed. Michael Gandy, 1983, revised edition 1995. *Jewish Records* by Dr A.P. Joseph was published in 'Family History', Vol.12 87/88 (Jan 1982). See *Anglo-Jewish Genealogical Records* FTM, Vol.8 No.9 (July 1992).

The Jewish Genealogical Society of Great Britain was formed in March 1992. Advantages of membership include receipt of the Society's magazine, the opportunity to attend cultural and specialist activities and access to the Society's library. Help and advice is available from the many experts within the field of worldwide Jewish genealogy. Details from Ms Caroline Dresden, 32 Tavistock Street, Covent Garden, London WC2E 7PD.

There are active Dutch, French, and Swiss Jewish Genealogical Societies which all publish regular journals or newsletters. Enquiries will be forwarded to them via the British agency: Dr A.P. Joseph, 25 Westbourne Road, Edgbaston, Birmingham B15 3TX, England. Dr Joseph is Chairman of the Birmingham Branch of the Jewish Historical Society of England.

Details of the Australian Jewish Genealogical Society can be obtained from Mrs Sophie Caplan, PO Box 154, Northbridge, Sydney, NSW 2063, Australia. Alternatively Australian Jewish historical or genealogical enquiries can be sent either to Dr Joseph or direct to Mrs B. Davis, PO Box 255, Camberwell, Victoria 3124, Australia.

Avotaynu is an International Review Magazine on Jewish genealogy published since 1985, obtainable from 1485 Teaneck Road, Teaneck, New Jersey 07666, USA.

The First International Jewish Genealogical Seminar was held in Jerusalem in 1984; the Third in Salt Lake City 1991 and the Fourth in Jerusalem 1994. All the lectures were taped and are available via *Avotaynu*.

Proceedings from the Second IJGS held London 1987 are available from Dr Joseph (see above).

JOINER The records of the Joiners and Upholders (i.e. upholsterers) are in the Guildhall Library (q.v.). There was a London Livery Company — see *The Worshipful*

Company of Joiners and Ceilers or Carvers, a chronological history by Sidney E. Lane, 1969.

JOINT TENANT see also Tenant in Common. A person who owns property in common with one or more other persons, where there is a right of survivorship i.e. on the death of a joint tenant the property wholly rests in the surviving joint tenants. Eventually the last survivor is entitled outright. The property held by joint tenants *cannot* be left by will but passes on the death of one to the survivors automatically as described above.

JURORS There were various property qualifications necessary before a person could serve on a jury. In 1825 service was limited to men between 21 and 60 who owned property worth at least £10 a year, or leased property worth at least £20 a year, or rented property worth at least £30. Lists of jurors are found with Quarter Sessions records.

JUSTICES OF THE PEACE The office of Justice of the Peace (JP) was instituted in 1361 but the duties of the office had been performed by 'Keepers of the Peace' since 1195, when Richard I commissioned certain knights to preserve the peace in unruly areas, and an act of 1327 had provided that in every county 'good and lawful men' should be appointed to guard the peace.

For centuries those appointed to the Commission of the Peace were either landowners or men of substance, whose social position was so strong that their authority went undisputed.

An act of 1361 provided that JPs should meet four times a year - the origin of Quarter Sessions, which continued until replaced by Crown Courts in January 1972. Between sessions, JPs could meet to settle very small matters in Petty Sessions. and they oversaw the administration of the Poor Laws. They are named in the Quarter Sessions rolls, but they were not all obliged to be present at every court.

JUVENILE OFFENDERS From 1847 monthly returns of juvenile offenders were compiled with details of punishments. They are with Quarter Sessions records, usually in CROs.

KELLY'S DIRECTORY see also Directories. Generally regarded as the most important series of local directories. They began in 1799 with a volume for London and subsequently covered all counties and large cities of England. Whilst they largely ceased in 1939 some volumes appeared as late as the mid 1970's. Publication was about every eight years for county volumes, city volumes appeared more frequently.

Earlier volumes contained names and addresses of commercial organisations, expanded to include those of wealthier private householders and eventually of all householders. Entry was free but the directory had to be purchased.

Archives of Kelly's Directory (e.g. Minute Books and Ledgers), can be consulted at Westminster City Archives, Victoria Library, 160 Buckingham Palace Road, London SW1W 9UD. If you wish to consult the records it is advisable to telephone beforehand. The most comprehensive set of directories is held at the Guildhall Library (q.v.); the SOG has a good collection as do many local libraries.

KEW see Public Record Office.

KIN in the phrase Kith and Kin, strictly the former are friends and the latter are blood relatives although the phrase is often loosely interpreted. Next-of-kin is generally defined as a person's closest relative and nowadays is usually taken to mean a person's spouse. However, technically a person's next of kin is their child, parent, sibling etc. as a spouse is not a blood relative and this should be borne in mind particularly when interpreting wills.

KING'S BENCH see Court of.

KITH AND KIN see Kin.

LACEMAKERS Mrs Jennifer Hanney of 155 Ridgeway Drive,Bromley, Kent, BR1 5DB who teaches lacemaking is compiling an Index of Lacemakers.

There are details of lacemakers in the UK, but mainly East Midlands and Devon. Others connected with the cottage industry are included e.g. Bobbin makers. Although no specific years, the industry thrived from the early 17th to late 19th century when lacemaking almost died out due to the advent of machines.

Any enquiries for the index or general information on lacemaking will be answered on receipt of sae or 3 IRCS and any additions to the index will be welcome.

See also: *A History of Lace*, by S.M. Levey and W.S. Maney, Victoria and Albert Museum, 1983; *A Dictionary of Lace* by Pat Earnshaw, Shire Publications, 1982.

The Australian Society of the Lacemakers of Calais represents descendants of machine lacemakers who worked in Calais 1815-1848. Recent holdings include French records of English births and deaths, copies of Methodist Register for Calais to 1877, NSW births, deaths and marriages, and Society's own files collected from members and representing immigrants from Nottingham, Derby, Leics., and Kent and their families in Australia. Files include genealogy lines, personal records, historical fact, especially relating to history of machine lace. Archivist willingly follows enquiries in Australia. Enquiries to Gillian Kelly, 10 Sorrell Place, Queanbeyan 2620, NSW, Australia.

LADY DAY (25th March) Until 1752, the year began on Lady Day. Traditionally the day on which hiring-fairs for servants etc. took place.

LAND OWNERSHIP see also Ireland, Scotland and Title Deeds. Most useful volumes are *Returns of Owners of Land*, published 1873 to 1876, and arranged on a county basis. Most large reference libraries and record offices have a copy.

LAND TAX This tax was first introduced about 1692, and was not finally abolished until the 1950s. The rate was usually 4/- in the pound. The annual lists contain names of owners and tenants of houses and land, sometimes with names of houses and fields. These records survive mostly in CROs, in Quarter Sessions collections, in particular for 1780 to 1832, when the Clerks of the Peace used the tax lists as indicating those entitled to vote in parliamentary elections. County taxpayers' lists for earlier years survive only rarely but some boroughs (London, Bristol etc) have long runs. For just one year, 1798, there is a duplicate set of taxpayers' lists for the whole of England and Wales (except Flintshire) in the PRO. Post-1832 lists are of less use, as they omit the growing number of landowners who had commuted payment. *Land and Window Tax Assessments* by Jeremy Gibson, Mervyn Medlycott and Dennis Mills, FFHS, explains the purpose and collection of the tax, with a county-by-county list of surviving records and their location.

LATHE A term used in Kent for a grouping of several Hundreds.

LATIN see also Relationships. Many ecclesiastical, manorial and legal records up to the early 18th century were written in some form of Latin.

There are a number of published guides to reading Latin as it was used in material likely to be of interest to the family historian. (Many 15th century wills were in Latin.) There is *A Latin Glossary for Family Historians* by Janet Morris, FFHS, and the Eve McLaughlin *Simple Latin for Family Historians* obtainable from FTM price £1.55 inc. p&p.

A list of Latin Christian Names is given in *The Local Historian's Encyclopedia* by John Richardson (q.v.), and a selection in this publication under Christian Names.

Possibly one of the most useful books is *Latin for Local History* by Eileen A. Gooder, published by Longmans, 1979, (6th impression 1988). However, you will want also the *Shorter Latin Primer* by Kennedy, published by Longmans. Both are available in paperback editions.

The Record Interpreter compiled by Charles Trice Martin, facsimile of 2nd ed. published by Phillimore 1982, with introduction by David Iredale, is a collection of abbreviations, Latin words and names used in historical manuscripts and records. It is accepted as one of the standard local history reference sources.

LATTENER Latten was a yellow metal compound very similar or identical to brass. It was used for the 'brasses' found in churches. A lattener was a worker in this metal.

LAVENDER A washerwoman (French 'Laver' to wash).

LAW TERMS A precise definition of law terms is impossible since not only are they dependable on moveable ecclesiastical feast days but there are variations over the centuries. A rough guideline is sufficient, therefore, when searching legal records, bearing in mind that in Chancery records the legal year begins with the Michaelmas term.

Michaelmas – from late September to the end of November.

Hilary – from mid January to mid February.

Easter – from just after Easter to mid April or May, (depending on the date of Easter).

Trinity – anywhere from mid May until June 24th.

However sittings customarily took place outside the terms as well.

LAWYER see Legal Profession.

LAY SUBSIDIES see Subsidies.

LDS see Church of Jesus Christ of Latter-Day Saints

LEATHERCRAFT A Museum of Leathercraft (through the ages) is at 60 Bridge Street, Northampton NN1 1PA. It is open Mon – Sat 10.00am-5.00pm; closed Good Friday, Christmas Day and Boxing Day.

There are indexes for (leather) Objects and (leather) Craftsmen; the curator will answer specific enquiries in exchange for sae or 3 IRCs. Contributions to either index also welcomed.

Walsall Leather Museum houses a small but very wide ranging library covering most aspects of leatherworking past and present. Within the museum itself there are regular demonstrations by highly experienced leatherworkers, who are happy to discuss their craft with visitors. The museum is at Wisemore, Walsall, WS2 8EQ, and is open Tue — Sat 10.00am-5.00pm and Sunday 12 noon-5.00pm. Researchers wishing to use the library should ring first (Tel. 01922 721153).

The social history of the industry is poorly recorded. An initial contribution is: *Stitching and Skiving: Women in the Walsall Leather Industry* by M. Glasson, Walsall M.B.C 1991.

LEATHERSELLERS There was a London Livery Company — see *History and Antiquities of the Worshipful Company of Leathersellers* by W.H. Black, 1887.

LEET see also Court Leet. Equivalent of a Hundred in East Anglia.

LEGAL PROFESSION Barristers were admitted through the Inns of Court — Lincoln's Inn, Middle Temple, Inner Temple and Gray's Inn. Printed lists of entrants to the legal profession via the Inns of Court exist from 1775 for all but the Inner Temple. The Librarian might be willing to supply information regarding admissions to Inner Temple, though earlier admissions have been published.

Barristers were usually University graduates, so records of them may be in the *Alumni* — see Universities. Judges had first to be barristers. The term Serjeant applied to a type of English barrister who practised in the Common Law courts. He took precedence over 'ordinary' barristers. This ceased in 1875. There was a Serjeants Inn of Court in London.

Solicitors were less frequently graduates, so are harder to trace. Their place of practice may be determined from the 'Law List' first published in 1774 and thence annually. Once a name disappears from these lists one might conclude that one has the year of death or retirement. Solicitors usually left wills.

The Law Society (110-113 Chancery Lane, London WC2A 1PL) has records of the Register of Attorneys and Solicitors which include lists of admissions from 1845 (earlier to some courts) and Registers of Articles of Clerkship from 1860. Earlier Articles of Clerkship (plus indexes), Certificates of Admission and Chancery Oath Rolls are in the PRO. See PRO Records Information leaflet 112 *Records of Attorneys and Solicitors in the PRO*.

Enquiries regarding Scottish solicitors should be directed to The Law Society of Scotland, 26/28 Drumsheugh Gardens, Edinburgh, EH3 7YR.

An article by Christopher T.Watts entitled *Solicitors' Records and the Family Historian* appeared in Vol.20 No.5 of Gen. Mag. (March 1981), and a card Index of Solicitors, Attorneys, Notaries, Proctors and Conveyancers is being compiled by Brian Brooks, Cambria House, 37 Pembroke Ave, Hove, Sussex, BN3 5DB. It has about 6000 entries to date; additions are welcome. Send £5.00 plus sae or 3 IRCs for search of index. Mr Brooks also has an almost complete collection of old Law Lists from 1780, plus a large manuscript collection.

Timothy Cockerell also has a card index of lawyers, which consists of a little less than 4000 entries. He charges £5 plus sae or 3 IRCs for a search of his index. (See under Educational Records for address.)

LEGENDS Family legends, stories of our ancestors handed down by word of mouth, e.g. from an elderly relative, should be carefully recorded in every detail, but should, of course, be treated with great circumspection, and checked against the memories of other elderly members of the family if possible. There is usually a grain of truth in them. Exaggeration − especially of property ownership etc. − is the most common snag. There was a tendency for people to assume, with no foundation of fact whatsoever, that there was a relationship with some person of importance or renown who had the same surname. Another common fault is for the legend to refer to events which took place several generations earlier than the teller says.

LEIGHTONWARD In spite of his important sounding name, he was a gardener.

LETTERS PATENT These are documents granting rights or privileges, in the form of open letters. A Grant of Arms is a typical example. The records run from 1201 to 1920 and are included in Chancery Records PRO.

LEVANT COMPANY see Companies

LIBERTY Area with freedom, generally by Royal Grant, from Royal Officials and jurisdictions. Marriages could be performed in some Liberties and, being exempt from normal ecclesiastical jurisdiction, they became, until 1754, local Gretna Greens (e.g. Peak Forest, Derbyshire).

LIBRARIES see also British Library and Guildhall Library. We have made frequent references to standard works of reference which should be found in libraries. Remember there is an Inter-Library Loan Scheme, by which your library can obtain on loan a book you need which they do not stock; possibly the only charge to you is for postage. Sometimes, instead of having to obtain the book itself, the owning library will make a photocopy of the reference you are seeking, which, of course, reduces the postal charges and saves you copying it out. Make enquiries at your own public library about the scheme.

A detailed list of Specialist Libraries, with addresses, is given in *The Local Historian's Encyclopedia* (q.v.). For a comprehensive listing of addresses and telephone numbers see *Libraries in the United Kingdom and the Republic of Ireland...* published bi-annually by Library Association Publishing Ltd.

Directory of Information Sources in the UK, E.M. Codlin, 6th ed. ASLIB Library, 1990: has details on over 5000 institutions with separate volume of subjects index.

The members of the Association of Independent Libraries are all subscription libraries, founded between 1768 and 1841, before the creation of the public library service. They are not controlled or financed by outside bodies, and many of them are still owned by their members. They combine care of their historic buildings with the supply of the latest books and periodicals. Some of the libraries house rare and important books.

For further details write to the secretary: Mrs Janet Allan, Portico Library, 57 Mosley Street, Manchester M2 3HY.

The Friends of the National Libraries was founded in 1931 to give the Nation's libraries and record offices the same kind of help that art galleries and museums receive from the National Art-Collections Fund. The purpose was to ensure that books and documents of national importance were retained in this country in suitable institutions, well cared for and accessible. The Friends have achieved this in many instances by making grants towards purchases of books and documents and by organising appeals and publicity. If you would like further information write to Friends of the National Libraries, c/o The British Library, Great Russell Street, London WC1B 3DG.

Genealogy for Librarians by Richard Harvey, Library Association Publishing, 2nd ed. 1992. Since librarians are not very often genealogists this is aimed at helping them overcome the ever-increasing number of questions posed to them on the sources available. On that score alone the genealogist would benefit from reading it too, particularly as it has a 28 page bibliography. At £27.50 the price is a little high but perhaps you could browse through the copy that will hopefully be in your library!

LIFE ASSURANCE see Insurance.

LIGHT BRIGADE see Crimean War.

LISTS OF NAMES see also Deeds. Genealogists — especially those who concentrate on 'One-Name Studies' (q.v.) — delight in such lists. Telephone Directories, Directories of towns and counties, Poll Books, Census Returns, and thousands of different kinds of records are mainly lists of names.

One unusual one might be mentioned here. *Palaeography, Genealogy and Topography, 1930 to 1937* was intended primarily as a sale catalogue. The descriptions of the various documents which this extensive list contains are so full and completely compiled, that almost as much information can be derived from the abstracts as from the originals. The catalogue was published by Herbert R. Moulton. As a separate volume he published an index of names — some 30,000 of them — occupying 120 pages. The price of the book in 1937 was 6/- post free!

LIVERY COMPANIES see Guilds.

LLOYDS MARINE COLLECTION see Seamen.

LOCAL HISTORIAN'S ENCYCLOPEDIA *The Local Historian's Encyclopedia* by John Richardson; published by Historical Publications Ltd., 2nd ed. 1986. £12.95.

This is an invaluable reference work both for local history and family history researchers. The first ed. (1974, reprinted 1975 & 1977, 1981) in softback was an ideal companion for the briefcase; the second ed. (1986) in hardback is less suited to that but is nonetheless as indispensable. It has been updated, enlarged and illustrated with line drawings. The Bibliography Section as such has been abandoned in favour of reference to relevant titles at the end of each section.

The arrangement is in sections, by subject, with an overall alphabetical index, leading to sub-headings. Contents of the first edition covered Land and Agriculture, Local Community and its Administration, Taxes, Rents, and Rates, Archives, Archaeology, Education, Social Welfare, Law and Order, Public Utilities and Services, Transport, Religion, Local Militia, Architecture, Place Names, Coins and Tokens, Heraldry, Trade, Commerce and Industry. The second ed. appears to have absorbed Place Names elsewhere and has new sections on Palaeography, Museums and Libraries, Organisations and Societies and Genealogy — albeit a general introduction to the subject!

Used in conjunction with this book you should rarely be stuck for an answer!

LOCAL HISTORY see also Bibliography. This is the title of an interesting and informative magazine first published in 1984. It is geographically wide-ranging and frequently includes articles and items of interest to family historians. The section on new books is most useful.

Published by Susan and Robert Howard, 3 Devonshire Promenade, Lenton, Nottingham NG7 2DS. Subscription £10.80 for six issues inc. p&p. £2 per single copy including postage.

LOCAL HISTORY SOCIETIES see also Newspapers. If your aim is to write your family history you need as much interesting background material as you can get for the area in which your ancestors lived.

In many counties, towns and even villages there are local history societies, and in some cases they have published pamphlets about the way of life of people who lived there in the past. There is a British Association for Local History (BALH), whose headquarters are at Shopwyke Hall, Chichester, Sussex PO20 6BQ. They will be pleased to supply details of their activities, subscription rates, a list of publications, and the contact address for any local history society.

Alternatively, it may be simpler to write to your area's Record Office. The PRO Records Information leaflet 24 *English Local History: a note for Beginners* is also available and the following organisations will supply helpful literature.

Council for British Archaeology, 112 Kennington Road, London SE11 6RE.

Civic Trust, 17 Carlton House Terrace, London SW1 5AW.

Historical Association, 59A Kennington Park Road, London SE11 4JH.

There is a wide range of books on the subject from modestly-priced paperbacks to the more expensive hardback. In no particular order of preference:

The Batsford Companion To Local History by Stephen Friar, B.T. Batsford Ltd, 1991.

Local History in England by W.G.Hoskins with David Hey, 3rd ed, published by Longman, 1984.

Family History and Local History in England by David Hey, Longman, 1987.

Discovering Local History by David Iredale, Shire Publications 1973.

Local History, a Handbook for Beginners, 1983 and *Record Sources for Local History*, 1987 both by Philip Riden, published by Batsford Ltd.

English Local History, an introduction by K. Tiller, Alan Sutton, 1992.

Village Records (1962 reprinted 1982) and *Town Records*, 1983 both by John West, published by Phillimore. These were reviewed in FHN&D Vol.4 No.4 (Sep 1984).

LONDON see also Maps and Occupations. The Greater London Record Office and History Library is at 40 Northampton Road, Clerkenwell, London EC1R OAB. There is now much enlarged accommodation for the enormous collection of archive material about the Greater London area.

For clarification on the whereabouts of records for 'London' read *Local Archives in Greater London* by Elizabeth Silverthorne, FTM Vol.3 No.2 (Dec 1986) and Vol.3 No.3 (Jan 1987). Or preferably *London Local Archives, A Directory of Local Authority Record Offices and Libraries* by Elizabeth Silverthorne, Guildhall Library and Greater

London Archives Network, 1990, 2nd edition expected 1995. Price in the region of £4.00 plus p&p from the Guildhall Library (q.v.).

See also *An Introductory Guide to the Corporation of London Records Office* edited by Hugo Deadman and Elizabeth Scudder, Corporation of London, 1994, price £5.60 inc. p&p. This office is situated in Guildhall reached from Basinghall Street. NB **not** *The Guildhall*.

The London Archive Users Forum is open to all who have an interest in London, or who use London Archives. Information can be obtained from Dr P. Croot, Victoria County History, 34 Tavistock Square, London WC1.

Tracing ancestors who lived in London in the years between the late 18th century and civil registration in 1837 can be very difficult as people mostly lived in rented accommodation and changed their addresses frequently. The Pallot Marriage Index (q.v.) can be very helpful.

Boyd's Citizens of London is a collection of 238 volumes covering the 15th to 19th centuries, and is in the Library of the SOG. A microfilm copy of the index to this collection is in the Guildhall Library (q.v.). See *Boyd's London burials and citizens of London*, Anthony J. Camp, FTM Vol.1 No.6 (Sep-Oct 1985).

There are numerous books available on London and its environs; which of them you read will depend very much upon what period of time you are researching and whether your research is centred on a particular sphere of interest. Two fairly general but useful publications are *An Encyclopaedia of London* by William Kent (revised by Godfrey Thompson), published by J.M. Dent & Sons Ltd., 1970 and *The Shell Guide to The History of London*, W.R. Dalzell, published by Michael Joseph Ltd, 1981.

The books written by Henry Mayhew supply detailed background to the living and working conditions of mid-19th century Londoners; in particular a series of four volumes called *London Labour and the London Poor; a Cyclopedia of the Condition and Earnings of Those That Will Work, Those That Cannot Work, and Those That Will Not Work*, published in 1861, reprinted 1968 by Dover Publications Inc.

London and Middlesex: A Genealogical Bibliography by Stuart A. Raymond, FFHS, attempts to identify some of the many useful books and journal articles which give an appreciation of the sort of life Londoners have lived through the centuries. *Lists of Londoners* by Jeremy Gibson and Heather Creaton, FFHS, is a guide to unpublished indexes or biographical listings of people who lived or worked in London at various periods of history.

Greater London Local History Directory 2nd ed, compiled and published by Peter Marcan and available from him at PO Box 3158, London SE1 4RA, price £16 inc. p&p. This edition complements rather than supersedes the first edition of 1988. The two volumes taken with *London's Local History* 1983 form a bibliography of local and family history publications over a 25 year period. Much useful reference material and listing of organisations and an extensive index.

The Centre for Metropolitan History has been set up at the Institute of Historical Research in collaboration with the Museum of London and other organisations. Further details about the Centre's activities can be obtained from Miss H. Creaton, Institute of Historical Research, Senate House, Malet Street, London WC1E 7HU.

The London Topographical Society has published a number of books, plans, maps and views which could interest family historians with London connections. For a list, write to the Hon. Secretary, 36 Old Deer Park Gardens, Richmond, Surrey TW9 2TL.

For those with much stranger 'connections', the London Dungeon Ancestors Club consists of people who can either trace their ancestry to rogues and heretics who were put to death in any gruesome way in this country during the Middle Ages — or those whose ancestors were responsible for carrying out the death sentence. Details from the Hon. Secretary, 28/34 Tooley Street, London SE1 2SZ.

LONDON GAZETTE This is the official publication of the British government. It was first issued in February 1665/6 and originally appeared on a Tuesday and Friday though for many years it has been issued daily. There are quarterly indexes from the early 1800s.

It publishes official civil, naval, military, church and legal appointments and promotions; notices on the formation and dissolution of business companies and partnerships, settlements of claims and other financial and legal matters related to individuals and corporate bodies, including bankruptcies and insolvent debtors.

There is a complete set of the *Gazette* in both the Guildhall Library (q.v.) and the British Library (q.v.). Some larger libraries may also have them. See *A History of the London Gazette, 1665-1965*, by P.M. Handover, HMSO, 1965.

LORD-LIEUTENANT He was appointed by the Crown, eventually replacing the Sheriff, his main concern being the control of the county militia. His importance dates from 1662. He was, and is, the Sovereign's representative in the county and still holds the office of Custos Rotulorum or keeper of the records of the county although this is now actually exercised by the Clerk of the Peace.

LORIMER A lorimer was a maker of bits, spurs and other small ironware for horses. Sometimes known as Loriner.

LUNATICS see Asylums.

LYING-IN HOSPITALS From mid-18th century these maternity hospitals were established in London and later in other cities. They can be a useful source for missing baptisms of migrant ancestors.

Records of the British Lying-In Hospital, Holborn are included in the IGI (q.v.) (the originals are in the PRO and a transcription of the Middlesex Hospital register is in the Greater London Record Office).

The British Lying-In Hospital at Holborn catered for the distressed poor, with special attention to the wives of soldiers and sailors, though many women appear to have been the wives of servants. Admission was supposedly by recommendation. The baptismal registers are supplemented by the hospital's own records of admissions which give vital and interesting details for the genealogist. The hospital records, 1749-1868, cover over 42,000 admissions and 30,000 baptisms, by no means all of Londoners.

Two articles concerning the Lying-In Hospitals appeared in the journal of the North Cheshire FHS: *Moving Around*, Vol.8 No.4 (Nov 1981) and *Why was he in a Charity Hospital*, Vol.9 No.1 (Feb 1982).

MACHINE BREAKERS see Swing Riots.

MAGISTRATE see Justices of the Peace.

MAKER-UP A term used in the textile industry for a garment assembler; but it can also refer to a chemist or druggist.

MANORIAL RECORDS These could be extremely useful when tracing back to pre-parish register times, and also give background information about one's ancestors. Most are in the keeping of Record Offices, but some are still in private hands. A great many have, unfortunately, been destroyed.

Manorial boundaries did not coincide with those of a parish; any one parish might include portions of several manors. The Royal Commission on Historical Manuscripts, Quality Court, Chancery Lane, London WC2A 1HP, will advise on which manors were in a given parish and where records of those manors may be found if they have survived. The Manorial Documents Register is available for public use in its search room.

The Court Rolls (q.v.) up to 1732 were often in Latin. They list cases for the consideration of the Lord of the Manor and are full of details relating to the tenants — their tenancies, activities and misdemeanours.

See *My Ancestors Were Manorial Tenants: How can I find out more about them?* by Peter Park, published by and obtainable from the SOG; 1994. *How to Locate and Use Manorial Records* by Patrick Palgrave-Moore, is obtainable from the FFHS price £1.80. *Using Manorial Records* by Mary Ellis, is one of the PRO Readers' Guide series. Published 1994, price £6.95.

Manorial Records by P.D.A. Harvey, published by the British Records Association. *Archives and the User* No.5, 1985, is a more comprehensive book available from BRA, Master's Court, The Charterhouse, Charterhouse Square, London EC1M 6AU.

Further reading: *The Manor and Manorial Records* by N.J. Hone, Methuen, 1906 and *Life on the English Manor* by H.S. Bennett, Cambridge University Press, 1956. The Manorial Society of Great Britain, 104 Kennington Road, London SE11 was founded in 1906. It publishes a journal for its members; information about recent sales of Manorial Rights may be available from the society though there is no obligation on their part to disclose this.

MANX see Isle of Man.

MAPS see also Parish Maps and Tithes. It is well worth enquiring at Record Offices about the availability of maps for the areas in which you are interested. Some early maps even give the names of property owners and tenants.

Enclosure Award maps and Estate maps are particularly useful. There were two copies of the former — one deposited in the 'parish chest', and this copy has usually found its way to the CRO, and a second deposited with the Clerk of the Peace for the county, and this may have been similarly deposited. There is, therefore, a good chance that at least one has survived.

Tithe maps were produced mainly between 1838 and 1854 in connection with the Tithe Commutation Act of 1836 which converted tithe payments into an annual rental. The scale of the maps was generally between 13 and 26 inches to the mile, so all buildings are usually shown. Three copies were made, one for the parish authorities (this copy is now usually in the CRO (q.v.)), the second went to the Bishop (and may be in the Diocesan Archives) and the third to the Tithe Redemption Commission.

The Ordnance Survey, founded in 1791, and originally called the 'Trigonometrical Survey' had as its aim to map Great Britain to a scale of 1 inch to the mile.

The 'Old Series' was produced between 1805 and 1873, but the actual date of publication may have been anything up to 20 years after the survey was made. Before this was completed a 'New Series', commenced in 1840, was undertaken, taking 20 years to complete. It covered 300 sheets. From the 1890s there were numerous other series. For some areas a scale as large as 60 inches to the mile was used and thus individual buildings and even outhouses are shown. There are even a few drawn at 10.56 ft to the mile! A study of these — if you know town addresses — and a copy of the part which shows the street in which your ancestors lived would greatly enhance your family history.

The 110 maps of the original edition have been reduced to 97 by transferring small sections of coastline into spare space on adjoining maps, and reproduced by David & Charles, of Newton Abbot, Devon TQ12 4YG. Send for their leaflet.

The maps are also being published in 8 volumes by Harry Margary, Lympne Castle, Kent CT21 4LQ. Send for leaflet for further details.

> Vol.1 Kent, Essex, East Sussex & South Suffolk.
> Vol.2 Devon, Cornwall & West Somerset.
> Vol.3 Surrey, West Sussex, Hants., Dorset, East Somerset & South Wilts.
> Vol.4 Central England
> Vol.5 East Anglia, Lincs., and Cambs.
> Vol.7 North-central England.
> Vol.8 Northern England.
> Vol.6 Wales.

Ordnance Survey Maps: A Concise Guide for Historians, by Richard Oliver and published by the Charles Close Society for the Study of Ordnance Survey Maps, to whom cheques should be made payable. Price £12.95 post free; obtainable from Dave Watt, Flat 9, 33 Cotswold Way, Langley Avenue, Worcester Park KT4 8LN

Ordnance Survey Indexes to the 1:2500 and 6 inch scale maps of England and Wales with foreword by Richard Oliver.

Ordnance Survey of Great Britain: Scotland. Indexes to the 1:2500 and 6 inch scale maps. First published by the Ordnance Survey, now reprinted in a new enlarged edition by David Archer, The Pentre, Kerry, Newtown, Montgomeryshire, Wales SW16 4PD, from whom they are obtainable, price £15.93 inc. p&p.

History in the Ordnance Map: An Introduction for Irish Readers by J. H. Andrews publisher David Archer as above, price £7.90 inc. p&p.

Information about current maps can be obtained from Ordnance Survey, Romsey Road, Maybush, Southampton SO9 4DH. However, if there is a branch of Her Majesty's Stationery Office within easy reach, you will find they can produce any map you require, printed direct from the negatives they stock.

The PRO Map Room houses several hundred thousand items — including the Tithe Apportionments and Maps (IR 29 and IR 30). See PRO General Information leaflets 4 and 28 *The Map Room, Kew* and *Maps and Plans at Chancery Lane* and Records Information leaflet 91 *Maps in the PRO*.

Copies of early 6" maps and others can be obtained from the Curator of Maps at the British Museum, Great Russell Street, London WC1B 3DG. Also a series of reproductions of 6" maps are published by Alan Godfrey, 57-58 Spoor Street, Dunston, Gateshead, Tyne & Wear NE11 9BD.

Local Studies, which are a department of the Public Library Service in many towns, also hold stocks of, and publish, copies of the maps of their area. The London Topographical Society includes amongst its publications maps of 18th and 19th century London. (See under London for address.)

For an explanation of the boroughs, registration districts, family history societies and boundaries of London as we know it today consult the map London Family History Societies and Registration Districts, published by the SOG and available from them price £1.95 plus £1 p&p (it comes in a tube). On the reverse of the map is a list of places in London and where you can find them.

Yorkshire is similarly dealt with in the useful booklet *Yorkshire Family History Societies* compiled by David P. Jepson, 1994 and obtainable from him at 39 St James's Road, Marsh, Huddersfield, W.Yorks HD1 4QA, price £1 inc. p&p.

You may also like to read *Maps for the Local Historian: a Guide to the British Sources* by J.B.Harley, published by Blackfriars Press Ltd., 1972, and by the same author, *The Historian's Guide to Ordnance Survey Maps*, Standing Conference for Local History, 1964.

Maps for Local History by Paul Hindle, and *Maps and Plans for the Local Historian and Collector* by David Smith. Both published by Batsford, 1988. The latter is particularly intended as a guide to the maps of the British Isles produced before 1914.

Maps for Genealogy and Local History by Geraldine Beech, Gen.Mag. Vol.22 No.6 (June 1987) is the text of a lecture given at the SOGs 75th Anniversary Congress, September 1986.

See Appendix V for County Maps showing the historic counties of England, Wales, Ireland and Scotland *before* 1974 and the administrative counties and regions *after* 1974.

MARINE SOCIETY see National Maritime Museum.

MARINES see Royal Marines.

MARKET TOWNS Towns which had been granted Charters permitting them to hold markets and/or fairs on particular days. By the 18th century, these towns were usually well-placed on the road network and market day served as the main social gathering point for the surrounding areas. Couples often met there from villages many miles apart — and married there: for elusive marriages always check the nearest market town which will often be in a neighbouring county. A comprehensive list of Market Towns is given in *The Local Historian's Encyclopedia* (q.v.). See also PRO Records Information leaflet 45 *Markets and Fairs*.

Owen's Book of Fairs published in 1813 gave a county by county, place-by-place listing of all fairs for the sale of cattle, pigs, sheep, cheese, pedlary etc. followed by a monthly list of fairs and an index of places. A second-hand copy might be expensive but provide unusual reading matter!

MARRIAGE see also Gretna Green Marriages, Parish Maps and Strays. In the case of Marriages for Scotland see Old Parochial Registers series in the General Register Office for Scotland (Scottish Ancestry q.v.)

Until the Middle Ages the church had only a limited role in marrying couples, who performed a simple ceremony themselves, usually exchanging vows in a public place before witnesses. This gradually changed and by the seventeenth century most weddings were carried out by the clergy, although many marriages did not comply with the laws of the church (canon law) in some way or other. Church weddings are recorded in parish registers from their commencement in 1538.

During the Commonwealth period (q.v.) when, in 1653, 'Parish Registers' were appointed, a marriage could only take place after a certificate had been obtained from the Register to state that banns had been called on three Sundays after the morning service, or on three successive market days in the market place. The marriages were solemnised by a Justice of the Peace. An Act of Parliament at the Restoration in 1660 legalised such marriages.

After the Restoration in 1660 the marriage scene became particularly chaotic. Clandestine weddings (without banns or licence, usually in a parish in which neither bride nor groom were resident) became common practice, with two London centres – St James Duke's Place and Holy Trinity Minories – leading the way. At Duke's Place some 40,000 weddings are recorded from the start of the registers in 1665 to 1694: these entries are included in Boyd's Marriage Index (q.v.) but parishes of origin of the parties are not regularly noted in the registers until 1696. At the Minories although clandestine marriages appear to start in 1644, there is no continuous register sequence until 1676, and although weddings before 1663 are in Boyd, those after that date are not. However, an index to weddings there, so far covering 1676-1693 (around 12,000 entries) has been produced on microfiche by the East of London FHS. Almost all register entries at the Minories contain details of the origins of those marrying. Between them, these two marriage centres accounted for around half of all marriages in London in the late 17th century; those marrying came not only from surrounding east London and City parishes, but also all over the South East and even further afield, including all social classes from the very rich to very poor, although mariners made up the largest group. After 1695 all weddings there were by licence, as various Acts of Parliament restricted the scope for carrying out clandestine weddings.

From the late 1690s marriages in the chapel of the Fleet Prison became more common, despite the effects of this legislation, and by around 1710 the area around the prison, known as "The Rules", became the centre of the clandestine trade, with the weddings carried out in "marriage houses". Marriages in the Fleet reached a peak in the late 1720s and by the late 1740s some 6500 weddings annually (over half the London total) were performed there, again attracting custom from far and wide. The Fleet became notorious for abuses of the marriage trade and some doubt has been cast over the accuracy of the registers. Nevertheless, despite these concerns, dubious entries form a small minority and the registers are mostly well-kept, containing details of occupations, status and origins. There are 230,000 or so weddings, making these registers one of the greatest unindexed genealogical sources. The registers and notebooks covering the period 1675-1754 are held in class RG7 (with two volumes covering 1726-35 in PROB 18/50) at the PRO. Registers for other clandestine centres at the King's Bench Prison, the Mint and the Mayfair Chapel (also a major centre in the 1740s) are also found in RG 7.

For further information see *Irregular marriage in London before 1754* by Tony Benton, SOG, 1993 price £4.50 inc. p&p; *Marry'd in their Closets* by the same author

The Marriage Ceremony.

Gen. Mag. Vol.23 No.9 (Mar 1991); the chapter on clandestine marriages in Vol. I of National Index of Parish Registers (q.v.), *General Sources of Births, Marriages and Deaths before 1837*; *The Rise and Fall of the Fleet Weddings* by R.L. Brown in R.B. Outhwaite *Marriage and Society*, 1981.

Clandestine marriages were not confined to London and all over the country before 1754 local marriage "hot spots" are to be found.

The introduction of Hardwicke's Marriage Act on 25 March 1754 curtailed the activities of the clandestine centres.

With the coming of Civil Registration in 1837 (q.v.), Superintendent Registrars were allowed to issue licences for marriages either in the Registrar's Office or in a non-conformist church.

Huguenot registers continue to show marriages beyond 1754 though they were not exempted from the provisions of Hardwicke's Act whereby marriages had to take place in the Parish Church or a Public Chapel.

The Age of Marriage Act of 1929 forbade marriage under the age of 16. Until then, girls of 12 and boys of 14 could legally marry in England. It might, therefore, be worth checking back those few extra years for a 'missing' marriage.

Marriage to a deceased wife's sister was not permissible under Canon law until 1907 as the relationship was within the 'prohibited degrees'. However, such marriages did take place — usually well away from the couple's home area. Up to 1835 such marriages were not void but were voidable by legal action. Few such actions were instituted but the risk was always there.

A marriage is most likely to be found in the bride's parish which was often different from that of the bridegroom, and hence marriages can be elusive. Remember that banns were valid for 3 calendar months after the third calling. There are a number of aids to the genealogist in the form of various indexes. Boyd's Marriage Index has already been dealt with, as has the International Genealogical Index (see under their respective headings). Many County family history societies and individuals have embarked on ambitious schemes to compile marriage indexes for their areas. You should consult a most useful publication by the FFHS entitled *Marriage, Census and Other Indexes for the Family Historian*, and also *Phillimore's Atlas and Index of Parish Registers* (see Parish Maps).

For Better, For Worse: British Marriages 1600 to the Present by John R. Gillis deals with the whole subject of marriages and has an extensive bibliography. Published by Oxford University Press, Inc., New York, 1985 but obtainable from SOG £8.50 inc. p&p.

The UK Marriage Witness Index is being compiled and as a 'strays' index is of value to any family historian seeking a missing ancestor. The computerised index has over 17,000 entries and a search can be made for a specific surname at a charge of 30p (50 cents) per name plus sae or 2 IRCs. State geographical limit for more common surnames. Details from Mr Ted Wildy, 167 Carlisle Road, Browns Bay, Auckland 1310, New Zealand.

MARRIAGE LICENCES, BONDS AND ALLEGATIONS Licences were issued so that marriages could take place without the necessity for banns to be called. This was useful if both parties were away from their normal place of residence, or if the parties did not wish to wait for the three week period during which the banns were called. It was also something of a status symbol to be married by licence — it avoided what was regarded as a private family affair being proclaimed to all and sundry.

The licence, which was valid for 3 calendar months from the date of issue, was generally granted by the Bishop or his surrogate of the diocese in which both parties lived. If they lived in different dioceses other rules applied but surviving documents can usually be found in the records of the diocese where the marriage took place.

A licence gives names, places of residence, occupations, whether single, widow or widower, ages, parishes and, in the case of minors, fathers/guardians and their consent, and the place where the marriage was to take place.

In 1822 an Act required applicants for licences to produce documentary evidence of their birth or baptism, and these certificates were attached. However, owing to administrative difficulties the Act was repealed within a year.

The licence itself would be given to the parties who were being married but an 'Allegation', i.e. a statement made by the parties affirming their intention to marry, was kept by the Diocesan registry. With it would be 'Bonds' — assurances by bondsmen — often friends or relatives (one was usually the groom himself), in which the sureties undertook to ensure that the couple would be married in a specified church or chapel.

Bonds and Allegations can be seen in DROs or CROS. Those for York Province are at the Borthwick Institute of Historical Research (York University), St Anthony's Hall, Peasholme Green, York YO1 2PW, Published indexes currently cover 1750-1839. Province of Canterbury records are at Lambeth Palace Library, London SE1 7JU. For a useful guide as to the location of these records see Jeremy Gibson's *Bishops' Transcripts and Marriage Licences, Bonds and Allegations.*

Many collections of these related documents have been indexed, the indexes having been published, or produced in typescript. A booklet entitled *Marriage Licences: Abstracts and Indexes in the Library of the Society of Genealogists*, ed. by L.Collins,

4th ed. 1991 can be obtained from the Society (by post £2.80) and should be used in conjunction with the book by Jeremy Gibson previously referred to.

Sometimes extensive searches for marriages fail — yet the evidence for a marriage survives in these documents. *Using Marriage Licences*, by Patrick Palgrave-Moore, FTM Vol.3 No.10 (August 1987) offers possible explanations. Before 1754 marriages will often be found in the church of the clergyman issuing the licence and not in the church(es) specified in the licence. It is interesting to note that Shakespeare's marriage entry has not been found in a register. Yet at the Worcester Diocesan Registry two allegations have been found — one for the marriage of a William Shakespeare dated 27th November 1582 to Anne Whateley and another dated 28th November 1582 to Anne Hathaway. This strange duplication has been attributed to a clerical error!

MARRIAGE TAX see Registration Tax.

MARSHALSEA Former prison in Southwark, London: principally a Debtors' Prison.

MASONS The Masons had their Livery Company in London. Freemasons were originally what their name implied i.e. Freemen Masons — members enjoying all the privileges of the guild of masons. These craftsmen travelled about to take part in building, and were recognised and accorded hospitality after exchanging certain signs known only to members of the guild. A master was at the head of the central organisation, and wardens presided over branches of it. Modern Freemasonry has, of course, no connection with a specific trade. The movement became worldwide, and at times was regarded as a subversive movement, but not in England, for when, in 1799, an Act for the suppression of secret and unlawful societies was passed, freemasons' lodges were specifically exempted.

However, annual returns of members of freemasons' lodges had to be made after 1799 to the Quarter Sessions. Names and descriptions of the members are given. You will find these lists in the Records at your CRO.

See *The Hole Crafts and Fellowship of Masons* by E.Conder, 1894, and *The Worshipful Company of Masons* by Raymond Smith.

MECHANICAL ENGINEERS (INSTITUTION OF) The Information and Library Service of the Institution of Mechanical Engineers holds two sets of records which yield biographical information. The first set of records which are unique to IMechE are the proposal forms, giving details of date and place of birth, schooling and early career of individual members, in many cases information otherwise unobtainable. The second group are IMechE proceedings which list dates of election to membership, any publications written and memoirs of the members.

IMechE records are supplemented by published biographical dictionaries, autobiographies, technical histories, indexes etc. The initial cost for the genealogical search service is £5. Further details from the Librarian, Information and Library Service, Institution of Mechanical Engineers, 1 Birdcage Walk, Westminster, London SW1H 9JJ.

MEDALS Records of medal rolls are at the PRO. They do not give detailed information about individuals. There are records for medals awarded to those who served in the

Army, Royal Navy, Royal Marines, Royal Air Force, Fleet Air Arm, Merchant Navy, Military Nurses, Police and for Home Guards and Civilians.

Because of the complexity of classification of records you are advised to read the relevant sections in *Tracing Your Ancestors in the Public Record Office* 4th ed. (see PRO). See also PRO Records Information leaflets:

108 *Records of Medals*
101 *Service Medal and Award Rolls: War of 1914-1918*
105 *First World War: Indexes to Medal Entitlement*

Leaflet 108 deals with three types of medals — those awarded for gallantry and meritorious service; those awarded for war service (known as Campaign or War Medals); and commemorative medals. Earliest records are 1793.

With a few exceptions Gallantry and Meritorious Service Awards are published ("gazetted"). The PRO holds a complete set of the *London Gazette*.

The Army Medal Office, Government Office Buildings, Worcester Road, Droitwich, Worcs WR9 8AU, has documents relating to awards since 1920 which includes the Second World War 1939-1945 and subsequent Campaigns. They do not have administrative records, neither do they handle enquiries relating to personal awards.

Soldiers of the First World War 1914-1918 were sent their medals automatically; officers had to apply for them. Circumstances made it impossible to adopt this procedure during the Second World War.

The Army Medal Office advises that "unissued medals awarded in respect of deceased personnel can be claimed and issued to the Legal Beneficiary or Next-of-Kin after the completion of certain necessary formalities. Entitlements to medals for campaigns and service prior to 1920 are given in the Medal Rolls held by the PRO. The Army Medal Office would only accept that an issue or re-issue of medals could be authorised if those Rolls clearly indicated that the awards were never issued or had been returned for some other reason. All awards since 1920 would have to be verified and approved by the Army Medal Office after examination of the individual service records." Some delay may occur; be patient!

Further information on medal awards to the other services may be obtained from:
Ministry of Defence, RAF Personnel Management Centre, P.Ma.3 (d) (4), RAF Innsworth, Gloucestershire GL3 1EZ.

Ministry of Defence, NPP Acs 3 (b) 4, HMS Centurion, Grange Road, Gosport, Hampshire PO13 9XA.

Ministry of Defence, Drafting and Record Office Royal Marines, HMS Centurion, Grange Road, Gosport, Hampshire PO13 9XA.

Registrar General, General Register and Record Office of Shipping and Seamen, Block 2, Government Buildings, St Agnes Road, Gabalfa, Cardiff CF4 4YA.

The Orders and Medals Research Society holds monthly meetings and issues a quarterly journal. Further details can be obtained from the General Secretary:
Mr N. Brooks, 21 Colonels Lane, Chertsey, Surrey, KT16 8RH.

There are a number of books and articles to help you identify medals and, in the case of 'war' medals, to tell you more about the campaigns for which they were awarded:

British Gallantry Awards by P.E. Abbott and J.M.A. Tamplin, 1981.

British Battles and Medals by L.L. Gordon, 1962.

Guide to Medal Rolls by A. Farrington, India Office Library, 1980.

The Register of the Victoria Cross and *The Register of the George Cross* both published by This England, PO Box 52, Cheltenham, GL50 1YQ.

Observer's Book of Awards and Medals by Edward C. Joslin, published by Frederick Warne, 1972.

British Orders, Decorations and Medals by Don Hall, Balfour Publications, 1973.

Ribbons and Medals by H. Taprell Dorling, published Geo. Fhillip & Son, first ed. 1916, new ed. 1974.

War Medals of the British Army by Carter & Long, originally published 1893, republished by Arms and Armour Press, 1972.

Family History from Medals, by M. Walcot, Liverpool FHS Journal, Vol.3 No.3 (Autumn 1981) and, in the same journal Vol.4 No.2 (Spring 1982), *Family Medals* by D.L. Bray, and *Agricultural Medals* by D. Higham.

War Medals as Tools for the Genealogist, by J.E.G. Hodgson, Cumbria FHS Newsletter No.6 (Feb 1978).

MEDIAEVAL Denotes records kept before about 1485. If your research has progressed thus far, read *Mediaeval Records* by Peter Franklin, FFHS, to discover the various types of records available (Inquisitions Post Mortem, Close Rolls, Pipe Rolls, Manor Court Rolls, Feet of Fines etc.) and, more particularly, which of these, mostly written in Latin, are available in English translation. A further volume, detailing more mediaeval records, is in hand. See *A glimpse of medieval family life* by Peter Franklin, FTM, Vol.10 No.12 (Oct 1994).

To encourage the resurgence of interest in the country's mediaeval period The Ranulf Higden Society has been formed. Named after the monkish author of the *Polychronicon* it is principally a society for self-help to develop skills for those who read mediaeval manuscripts. Further information available from the Secretary, J.C. Sutton, 5 Beechwood Drive, Alsager, Stoke on Trent, Staffs ST7 2HG or the Departments of History at the Universities of Keele and Liverpool or the John Rylands University Library, Deansgate, Manchester.

MEDIAEVAL STAINED GLASS Under the auspices of the Royal Commission on the Historical Monuments of England the *Corpus Vitrearum* is a project for recording mediaeval stained glass. The principal aim is to publish details of all surviving European mediaeval window glass, including material of European origin now in USA and Canada. Five British catalogues have been published together with a bibliography of conservation – ongoing.

Material in the photographic archive may be consulted; windows are identified by number with details of location, subject matter, date, donor and craftsman. The CVMA archive may be consulted in: The National Buildings Record, Royal Commission on the Historical Monuments of England, Fortress House, 23 Savile Row, London W1X 2JQ (Tel 0171 973 3088). Open 10.00am-5.30pm Monday to Friday. No appointment necessary.

The archivist is willing to answer queries and welcomes information and records relating to mediaeval glass. A full guide to the archive is available. See also *Stained Glass in England 1180-1540* by Sarah Crewe, HMSO, 1987, price £9.95 plus p&p; published using photographs from the files.

MEDICAL PROFESSION see also Apothecaries and Barbers. The medical profession included physicians, doctors, surgeons and apothecaries, and their comparative status was in that order. The vast majority of records relating to these are deposited at the Guildhall Library (q.v.). See also *Records of the Medical Profession* by Susan Bourne and Andrew Chicken, 1994 £3.

Physicians were usually university men or members of the College of Physicians. The internal records of the Royal College of Physicians of London are in the library of the College, 11 St Andrews Place, London, NW1 4LE. Information concerning the medical profession in Scotland is available from the Royal College of Physicians of Edinburgh, 9 Queen Street, Edinburgh, EH2 1JQ (lists of members since its foundation in 1681) and important collections are also held at the Royal College of Physicians and Surgeons of Glasgow, 234-242 St Vincent Street, Glasgow, G2 5RJ which was established in 1599.

Eighteenth Century Medics by P.J. & R.V. Wallis with the assistance of J.G. Burnby and the late T.D. Whittet, 2nd ed., published by the Project for Historical Bio-Bibliography, Newcastle upon Tyne, 1988. It is advisable to read the Introduction before embarking upon the contents of this book — brief summaries of the 80,000 entries for medical practitioners, physicians, surgeons, apothecaries, pharmacists, distillers, chemists, druggists, dentists, opticians, midwives and patent-medicine sellers. There is a bibliography and the Index of Places is printed as a separate booklet.

Monk's Roll of Physicians gives details of well-known members of the profession. From the early 19th century medical Directories can be helpful, with an obituary notice in the volume covering the year of the physician's death.

Many medical men qualified at Trinity College, Dublin, or at the universities at Glasgow or Aberdeen (q.v. Alumni) so records of these establishments could be helpful. Leyden, in Holland, was also a popular place at which to qualify, and a list of English students has been published.

Medical Registers first appeared in 1858 and contain biographies of practitioners. The London and Provincial Medical Directory began in 1861.

Surgeons up to 1745 were associated with the Surgeons and Barbers Company of London. The Company of Surgeons was established in 1745. Detailed lists of Apprentices, Surgeons and Company Officials, those fined or disenfranchised and relevant bibliographies appear in the following:

The History of the Surgeons' Company 1745 to 1800 by Cecil Wall, 1935.

The History of the Royal College of Surgeons of England by Sir Zachary Cope, 1959.

The Royal College of Surgeons was founded in 1800 and led to an improvement in status. Details of deceased Fellows from 1843 to 1973 have been published in *Lives of the Fellows of the Royal College of Surgeons (England)*. A further volume covering those who died between 1974 and 1982 is in preparation.

Records held by the College include the following:
Examination Books of the College from 1800 and the Examination Book of the Surgeons' Company 1745-1799. 1541-1745 are in the Guildhall Library (q.v.). These give

names of candidates, examinations sat, whether passed or failed and, occasionally, place of residence.

An Apprentice Book 1784-1846.

The Medical Directory 1845 to date.

Miscellaneous publications listing graduates of various universities and members of the Army and Indian Medical Services etc.

Specific enquiries should be addressed to Mr E.H. Cornelius, The Librarian, Royal College of Surgeons, 35-43 Lincoln's Inn Fields, London WC2A 3PN. There is no fee but a donation is appreciated. Please send sae or 3 IRCs.

Information about surgeons in the Army or Navy should be sought in military records (q.v.), but see also *Commissioned Officers in the Medical Services of the British Army 1660-1960, Volume I: 1660-1898*, by Peterkin and Johnston, *Volume II: 1898-1960*, by Drew, each volume 600pp. published by The Wellcome Historical Medical Library, 1968. Between 1580 and 1775 licences to practise Medicine and Surgery were issued by the Archbishops of Canterbury. A pamphlet on this by Dr R.R. James is in the Library of the SOG.

Royal Society of Medicine, 1 Wimpole Street, London W1M 8AE, keeps the papers of the important societies which were amalgamated to form the society in 1907.

The Wellcome Institute for the History of Medicine houses the medical history library at 183 Euston Road, London NW1 2BP. Records are available to the public by arrangement.

Glasgow University Library has a fine medical section with a particular emphasis on the William Hunter collection of maunuscripts and books.

Death notices and obituaries often appeared in *The Lancet* (first published 1823), *The British Medical Journal* (first published 1857) and *The Medical Directory* (1845-1914 only). There are indexes to the first two publications. Enquire at your local library.

MEMBERS' INTERESTS see Directories of.

Sometimes known as Surname Referral Index.

MEMORIAL INSCRIPTION see Monumental Inscription.

MERCER A mercer was a dealer in silk, cotton, woollen and linen goods. The Mercers' Company was regarded first in order of precedence of all the London Livery Companies. Richard (Dick) Whittington was one of the Masters of the Company as was Lord Baden-Powell. The Mercers' Hall is in Ironmonger Lane, London EC2V 8HE. Enquiries as to records can be made there.

MERCHANT The term tended to be used for those who carried on trade on a large scale, especially with foreign countries, but an ordinary shopkeeper might describe himself as a merchant. An interesting list of those trading with New England in 1710 appeared in Gen. Mag. Vol.8 No.2(June 1938) but refers only to London merchants and traders.

MERCHANT NAVY see Seamen.

MERCHANT TAYLORS Their Livery Company was an influential one and founded the Merchant Taylors' Public School in 1561. The foundation exists to this day. See *Memorials of the Guild of Merchant Taylors* by C.M. Clode, 1875 and 1888.

MESNE LORD see also Manorial Records. A middle lord of the manor who himself held under a superior lord.

MESSUAGE A term often found in wills. It meant a house with its outbuildings and yard and sometimes also included the garden.

METHODIST The Movement was founded by John Wesley in 1740. It tended to split into factions. These included the Methodist New Connexion, 1797, the Primitive Methodists, 1811, the Bible Christians, 1815, the Protestant Methodists, 1828, and the United Methodists Free Churches, 1857.

Registers of Baptisms and Burials to 1837 were deposited with the Registrar General and are in the PRO. The Methodist Archives address is Miss A. Peacock, c/o The John Rylands Library, Deansgate, Manchester, M3 3EH. Only national and District records are preserved in that library; circuit and chapel records are kept locally in county record offices and similar repositories. There are no genealogical records in the Methodist Archives, no baptismal, marriage or burial records, nor is it possible for any member of the staff to undertake any form of research as the Centre is not financed for this purpose.

The Library does hold official obituaries of Methodist ministers, but these are largely concerned with the spiritual life of ministers, and not with their temporal affairs. There is little information in the archives on Methodist local preachers and lay persons, the only regularly used source being their index to the obituaries in the major Methodist periodicals.

The Keeper of Printed Books, Mr D.W. Riley FLA, is prepared to supply details of the stationing of Methodist ministers, and supply photocopies of the official obituaries. He can be contacted at The John Rylands University Library.

Each of the 32 Methodist Districts in the country has its own honorary archivist who should be able to direct enquirers to the appropriate repository. Should further difficulty be experienced the Methodist Connexional Archives Liaison Officer, Dr E. Dorothy Graham, 34 Spiceland Road, Northfield, Birmingham B31 1NJ should be contacted. Dr Graham is also secretary of the Wesley Historical Society.

The Methodist Church Archives and History Committee, Methodist Church Property Division, Central Buildings, Oldham Street, Manchester M1 1JQ holds a lot of printed material, including Methodist Magazines and obituaries.

Mr J. Lenton, 21 Vineyard Road, Wellington, Telford, Shropshire TF1 1HB is secretary of the Methodist Historical Society. A magazine 'The Arminian' was first issued in 1778, and there followed several changes of title. An index covering the years 1778 to 1839 was published in the *Proceedings of the Wesley Historical Society, Volume 7 (1909-10)*. In later magazines there are many references to members as well as to preachers.

The 'Local Preachers' Magazine' 1851 to 1930 contains useful obituary notices and has been indexed. A copy of the Index is held by Rev.William Leary, 4 Calder Green, Messingham, Lincolnshire. A copy of his *Ministers & Circuits in the Primitive Methodist Church* is in the library of the SOG.

Minutes of local Methodist Meetings are sometimes found deposited in CROs. These often name individuals, either because they acted in some official capacity or were given financial assistance or for some other reason.

There was a Methodist Metropolitan Registry for the registration of baptisms begun in 1818 and surrendered to the Registrar General with other registers in 1840.

See *My Ancestors Were Methodists how can I find out more about them?* by William Leary, reprinted 1993, SOG, price £4.45 inc. p&p. The subject has also been dealt with in some detail in Vol.II of the *National Index of Parish Registers* by D.J. Steel (q.v.). See also *Methodists*, by Cyril D. Blount, FTM Vol.4 No.3. (Jan 1988).

M.I. These abbreviations can mean either Memorial Inscription, Monumental Inscription or Marriage Index so beware!

MICHAELMAS The Feast of St Michael, 29th Sept. One of the Quarter Days (q.v.).

MICROFORM/MICROFICHE/MICROFILM Modern technical way of presenting records. See IGI for example. The FFHSs leaflet *Publishing On Microfiche* is obtainable from the Administrator of the FFHS in exchange for sae plus one first class stamp or 3 IRCs.

Whilst microfiching may not be a preferred alternative to traditional methods of publishing it *is* a very economical method, and is particularly useful for indexes or for reproducing large projects or publications. For obvious reasons FHSs in particular are taking advantage of this technique. See *Current Publications on Microfiche* by John Perkins, obtainable from the FFHS, and published every 12-18 months.

MIGRANTS The term is used to describe people moving from one place to another *within* a country, as opposed to immigrants and emigrants who move from one country to another. See *My Ancestors Moved in England or Wales: How can I trace where they came from?* by Anthony J. Camp, SOG, 2nd revised ed. 1994, price £5.60 inc. p&p.

Poor Law Migrants from Agricultural to Manufacturing Districts, 1835-1837 is an index of 4,500 pauper migrants, mainly from agricultural districts (in particular Norfolk and Suffolk) to manufacturing districts in the north. List taken from Parliamentary Papers 1843, supplemented by details of migrants from Poor Law Commissioners' first three Annual Reports (1835-1837) and 1841-1871 censuses in some receiving areas (e.g. Cheshire). Details in exchange for sae or 2 IRCs from Mr A. Benton, 46 Waldegrave Gardens, Upminster, Essex RM14 1UX.

MILITARY see Army, Navy, Royal Air Force, Royal Marines, Nursing etc.

MILITIA From the Anglo-Saxon period, able-bodied men between the ages of 16 and 60 were liable to perform military service for local defence and occasionally further afield.

Formal inspections were known as 'musters'. Militia Muster Rolls from 1522 to 1640 are in the PRO. See PRO Records Information leaflet 46 *Militia Muster Rolls 1522-1640* and PRO Readers' Guide No.3 *Records of the Militia from 1757* by Garth Thomas, PRO Publications, 1993, obtainable from the FFHS price £4.60 inc. p&p. Later Muster Rolls may be found in Quarter Sessions records deposited in CROs. An enlightening book on the subject is *The English Militia in the Eighteenth Century: The Story of a Political Issue 1660-1802* by J.R. Western, Routledge and Kegan Paul, 1965.

Tudor and Stuart Muster Rolls by Jeremy Gibson and Alan Dell and *Militia Lists and Musters 1757-1876* by Jeremy Gibson and Mervyn Medlycott give further locations of these documents where extant. The Introductions are most informative. Both booklets published by and obtainable from the FFHS.

See also *Some Georgian 'Censuses': The Militia Lists and 'Defence' Lists* by Mervyn Medlycott, Gen. Mag. Vol.23 No.2 (June 1989).

Muster Roll of Prince Charles Edward Stuart's Army 1745-46 ed. Alistair Livingstone, Christine Aikman and Betty Hart. Published by Aberdeen University Press, 1984, it contains some 4,800 names culled from almost 50 written sources.

MILLINERS see also Haberdasher. Maker or seller of women's hats.

MINING see also Industrial Archaeology. You are advised to read *Coal Mining Records in the PRO*, PRO Records Information leaflet 82, and 83 *Sources for the History of Mines and Quarries*.

Annual Reports of H.M. Inspectors of Mines contain information often of help to researchers (e.g. persons killed or injured in a mining accident). Check with the relevant CRO to ascertain what deposits they have.

The British Coal Open Cast Executive Headquarters & Archive Centre, 200 Lichfield Lane, Berry Hill, Mansfield, Notts NG18 4RG has records of the coal industry, other than those of pre-nationalised companies which are held by CROs.

Further information can be obtained from the National Association of Mining History Organisations, 38 Main Street, Sutton in Craven, Keighley, West Yorks. BD20 7HD.

There are many books in reference libraries on such subjects but below are a few titles of interest.

Discovering Lost Mines by Peter Naylor, Shire Publication No.265.

The Collier by A.R. Griffin, Shire Album No.82; has short bibliography.

Lead and Lead Mining by Lynn Willies, Shire Album No.85 with bibliography.

The Cornish Miner by A.K.Hamilton Jenkin, 3rd edition David & Charles.

Slate Mines and Quarries: Guide to North Wales Quarrying Museum, HMSO.

Mr Ian Winstanley, 83 Greenfields Cres, Ashton-in-Makerfield, Wigan Lancs WN4 8QY is compiling an index of persons killed in mining accidents (coal, tin, ironstone etc.) throughout the British Isles, 1850 to c.1920. Send sae or 2 IRC's for details of charges.

MINISTER (of Religion) Clergyman (especially in Presbyterian and Nonconformist Churches).

MISSING PERSONS Tracing a relative or erstwhile friend or acquaintance can sometimes prove more difficult than tracing your ancestors! If you have tried the obvious sources such as a mutual contact, telephone directory, letter to newspaper to no avail read *Tracing Missing Persons: An introduction to agencies, methods and sources in England and Wales* by Colin D. Rogers, Manchester University Press, 1986, which suggests new lines of approach in unravelling problems early in the present century.

The Missing Live Persons Index, originally started by the SOG, is now with The National Missing Persons Helpline. This is a charity which seeks to locate people who have gone missing for whatever reason and which offers support to those left behind. In the event of the missing person being located, a confidential link between the two will be provided. Queries should be addressed to the NMPH, Roebuck House, 284-286 Upper Richmond Road West, East Sheen, London SW14 7JE enclosing sae or 2 IRCs. The service is free but donations would be greatly appreciated.

Your relative may have died. You can try searching the Death Indexes at St Catherine's House, in the hope of finding an entry — remember recent entries give date of birth, earlier ones age at death — and if you can find an entry the death certificate will have an address and possibly the name of a relative who registered the death.

At one time The Department of Social Security, Special Section 'A', (now The Contributions Agency) would attempt to contact a missing person by forwarding a letter on submission of certain information. This service is no longer available for genealogical research purposes.

The Salvation Army Family Tracing Service will assist in tracing a living relative for the *purpose of reconciliation* only. They will give advice on procedures to adopted persons. There is a modest Registration Fee. Enquiries should be directed to the above section at 105-109 Judd Street, Kings Cross, London WC1H 9TS.

The Salvation Army International Heritage Centre, 117-121 Judd Street, Kings Cross, London WC1H 9NN, has some sketchy records of its soldiers, better ones of its full time officers and they will search these if there is a possibility that your ancestor may have been a member of the Salvation Army. Please enclose sae or 2 IRCs. The Heritage Centre houses a small museum which is open to the public Mon-Fri 9.30am-3.30pm, Sat 9.30am-12.30pm.

Mrs Wyn Burkhill, Brentfield, Burton Row, Brent Knoll, Somerset TA9 4BW operates a service called "In-Touch". This is a national register acting as a central contact point for family and friends who are anxious to find each other. In-Touch offers to register your details and that of the person you are hoping to contact. These details are cross-referenced and checked against every new enquiry, with a view to a match. The fee for inclusion in the register is £3.50 UK, £5.00 overseas. Whilst Mrs Burkhill does all she can to help this is *not* a tracing or search agency merely a cross-referencing system as outlined above.

MISSIONARIES Usually persons sent overseas or into urban areas by a religious community to spread its gospel; they often worked in hospitals or schools. The choice of which Missionary Society a missionary worked for depended on a person's denomination.

Some of the largest Missionary Societies were:

London Missionary Society (Congregational) Archives are deposited in the library of the School of Oriental and African Studies, University of London, Malet Street, London WC1. As well as the printed *History of the London Missionary Society* there is a published Register of Missionaries, edited by James Sibree, 1923, which gives basic details of them.

Methodist Missionary Society: its archives are also deposited in the School of Oriental and African Studies.

The Baptists's Missionary Society's archives are still at their headquarters, 93 Gloucester Place, London W1H 4AA.

United Society for the Propagation of the Gospel (Anglican), archives are deposited in Rhodes House Library, University of Oxford, South Parks Road, Oxford OX1 3RG.

The Society for Promoting Christian Knowledge; archives at Holy Trinity Church, Marylebone Road, London NW1.

The Church Missionary Society (Anglican), Partnership House, 157 Waterloo Road, London SE1 8XA. Initial enquiries should be specific and brief and sent to the archivist at this address. If a classification reference as used by the society is located in the index an appointment may be made to consult the archives. These are deposited in Special Collections at Birmingham University Library.

The British and Foreign Bible Society, publisher and distributor of bibles in all languages around the world, deposited its archives in Cambridge University Library, West Road, Cambridge CB3 9DR, but they contain very little biographical information.

MONUMENTAL BRASSES The Monumental Brass Society, c/o Hon. Sec. W. Mendelsson, 57 Leeside Cres, London NW11 0HA, has done much work on the study, preservation and recording of monumental brasses. *Discovering Brasses and Brass Rubbing* by Malcolm Cook is a Shire Publication.

MONUMENTAL INSCRIPTIONS In recent years, encouraged by the FFHS, many County FHSs have organised groups of members to record the inscriptions on tombstones in churchyards and in the older parts of cemeteries.

These transcripts are then usually deposited in local record offices, libraries and in the Library of the SOG. The Monumental Inscriptions Co-ordinator or Projects Co-ordinator of your local society will advise you as to what has so far been accomplished. Their names and addresses can be found in the FFHS *Handbook*. Local Women's Institutes in some counties have recorded large numbers of MIs.

If you are contemplating helping with, or organising, such a project then you would do well to read *Rayment's Notes on Recording Monumental Inscriptions: 4th Edition Revised by Penelope Pattinson* again available from the FFHS. It gives guidelines on recording, and includes useful advice on safety, organisation and publicity.

Many older transcripts are already with repositories, and they can be extremely valuable since they may contain copies of inscriptions now illegible, or of stones which have been removed. For example see *Monumental Inscriptions in the Library of the Society of Genealogists*: Part 1, Southern England (1984) and Part 2, Northern England, Wales, Scotland, Ireland and Overseas (1987). Price £2.80 and £3.40 respectively inc. p&p.

Anyone involved with, or who has an interest in, Monumental Inscriptions, should enjoy reading *English Churchyard Memorials* by Frederick Burgess, SPCK, London, 1979. Paperback ed. Originally published by Lutterworth in 1963; in this re-issue the text has been retained in its entirety with the diagrams faithfully reproduced. There are chapters on the origins and developments of churchyards and cemeteries, on the types and designs of monuments and the techniques of the masons. A useful glossary of terms associated with memorials and a list of some monumental stone carvers may give another source in that search for an elusive ancestor!

Memorial inscriptions to people connected with the sea (including shipowners, shipwrights, merchant seamen as well as naval men) are being collected by the National Maritime Museum. The Manuscripts Section, National Maritime Museum, Greenwich, London SE10 9NF, would be pleased to receive any inscriptions you discover and will look in their index for you.

Church Monuments Brian Kemp, Shire Album 149 is a basic introduction to the subject which gives suggestions for further reading. An enormous number of monuments dating from the 12th to the 20th centuries can be seen in cathedrals and churches throughout the country. As well as being part of our historical and cultural heritage, many bear inscriptions of interest and should not be overlooked in the course of research. The address of the Church Monuments Society is c/o The Armouries, HM Tower of London, London EC3N 4AB.

MORAVIANS The Moravian Church developed as a revival of the 'Bohemian Brethren' founded by followers of John Huss in 1457. Their beliefs were spread all over the world by missionaries, and churches were set up in this country in the mid-18th century. Their registers were deposited with the Registrar General in 1840. John Wesley was much influenced by their chief belief which was that faith is directly inspired by God. Their established settlements, some of which still survive, hold useful records; Mirfield, Fulneck and Pudsey, in Yorkshire, Dukinfield, Cheshire and Fairfield, Lancs among them.

MORMONS see Church of Jesus Christ of Latter-Day Saints.

MUNIMENTS These are documents which provide evidence of rights and privileges. Family muniments — mainly those of landed families — may still be in private possession, but many have been deposited in Record Offices. You might get advice as to the location of such collections from the Historical Manuscripts Commission.

MUSEUMS These provide hours of endless fascination, education, entertainment and background information on a host of subjects. They are to be found in abundance throughout the world — many of a specialised nature. *The Good Museums Guide* lists most of the best museums to be found in this country and *Museums and Galleries of Great Britain and Ireland* provides details of the collections, contents and opening hours of hundreds of British Museums.

A list of the Principal General Museums and comprehensive list of Specialist Museums is given in *The Local Historian's Encyclopedia* (q.v.).

National Heritage is an organisation launched in 1971 to support, encourage and protect all the museums and galleries in Britain. It combines individual members, affiliated museums and friends of museums all over the country. Further details can be obtained from National Heritage, 9a North Street, London SW4 OHN.

MUSIC HALL see Theatre.

MUSICIAN There was a London Livery Company of Musicians. See *A Short History of the Worshipful Company of Musicians* by H.A.M. Crewdson.

Well-known musicians will be found in *The New Grove Dictionary of Music and Musicians*, edited by Stanley Sadie, 20 vols, Macmillan, 1980, 6th (and latest) edition. Also *Organists of the City of London, 1666-1850* by Donovan Dawe, 1983. Copy at SOG.

Dr Andrew Ashbee is editing *Biographical Dictionary of English Court Musicians, 1485-1714*, projected date of publication 1996. Meanwhile volumes of his *Records of English Court Music* (1485-1714), Scolar Press, 1986-in progress, can be found at the SOG and possibly other libraries. Eventually there will be a cumulative index volume to include extracts from the Court records at PRO and elsewhere.

MUSTERS see Militia.

NAILMAKING A thriving industry in the Midlands in the 19th century. An 'Occasional Paper' published by the Northfield (Birmingham) Conservation Group entitled *The Nailmakers of Northfield* includes interviews with residents who remember the last of the nailmakers, and sketches by a local artist. Copies in local libraries. *Nailmaking*, a Shire Publication, gives a further insight into the industry.

NAMES see Christian names, also Surnames.

NAPOLEONIC PRISONERS see Prisoners of War.

NATIONAL ARMY MUSEUM see also Army. The Museum was established in 1960 to collect, preserve and exhibit objects and records relating to the regular and auxiliary forces of the British Army. It is the only museum in Great Britain dealing with the army in general during the five centuries of its existence and includes the story of the Indian Army to independence in 1947 and of the colonial forces.

In 1971 the Museum moved from the Royal Military Academy, Sandhurst to its present home at Royal Hospital Road, Chelsea, London SW3 4HT, next to Wren's Royal Hospital.

The Museum is also a major national archive. The collection includes the papers of such famous soldiers as the 1st Marquess of Anglesey, Lord Raglan and Lord Roberts, but equally important are the hundreds of letters, journals and memoirs of lesser-known men and women of all ranks. The reference library contains over 30,000 books, many of them extremely rare, on British military history. All aspects of army life can be studied from a collection of prints and drawings and photographs. The Reading Room is open Tues-Sat from 10am-4.30pm, by appointment. The new viewing galleries are open 10am-5.30pm seven days a week. Further information about all the services and publications available and the NAM Society of Friends, from the above address.

NATIONAL ASSOCIATION OF DECORATIVE AND FINE ARTS SOCIETIES (NADFAS) This Association was formed in 1968 and consists of Member Societies throughout the country whose aim is to increase enjoyment, knowledge and care of the arts and to stimulate interest in the preservation of our cultural heritage.

Events are arranged in different parts of the country in association with museum exhibitions and historic houses and gardens; study groups are arranged for those interested in extending their knowledge. The Voluntary Conservation Corps was started in 1970 and became National in 1973. Under guidance they undertake refurbishing books in a library, repairing textiles or acting as guides for the National Trust. Church Recording is another aspect of NADFAS. They photograph and record the history and details of Church Furnishings, MIs, Stained Glass etc. For further details write to NADFAS, 38 Ebury Street, London SW1W OLU.

NATIONAL BUILDINGS REGISTER see Royal Commission on the Historical Monuments of England.

NATIONAL HERITAGE see Museums.

NATIONAL INDEX OF PARISH REGISTERS see Parish Registers.

NATIONAL MARITIME MUSEUM see also Monumental Inscriptions. Located at Greenwich, London SE10 9NF, and housed in several separate buildings, entailing a walk of about three miles in order to cover all the galleries, which are arranged in chronological order. Probably the world's most comprehensive Maritime Museum it has over three million maritime-related artefacts in its collection: more than 3,000 oil paintings from the 17th to the 20th centuries, 50,000 prints and drawings, 300,000 historic photographs, 750,000 plans of ships built in the UK since the beginning of the 18th century, 3,000 ship models, rare maps and charts, navigational instruments, manuscripts, weapons and uniforms. 70,000 of these across the whole range of the collection are now photographed and together with the historic photographs are the basis of the Maritime Picture Library. Anyone wanting to locate a picture or photograph of an ancestor's ship has a good chance of finding it here.

The Library holds a complete set of Lloyds List, Lloyds Register and the Mercantile Navy List. There is a large collection of books and pamphlets on all aspects of shipping in addition to the Museum's own publications. The newscutting collection of Frank C. Bowen covering the period 1880-1940 is of particular importance.

Amongst the manuscript collections it has Lloyds Ships' Surveys, Applications for Masters/Mates Certificates, Agreements and Crew Lists for specific years and the Wreck Registers. Many shipping companies have deposited their archives with the Museum.

The Marine Society, founded in 1757, indentured some 16,000 boys into the Merchant Navy between 1815 and 1854; it kept detailed records of the boys and their parents or guardians. These Registers of Boys Placed by Private Subscription by The Marine Society are at the Museum, along with other archives of the Marine Society.

Charitable institutions such as The Marine Society and the Maritime Society endeavoured to train poor and orphaned boys and a book recommended by them is *Seamen in the Making* by E.C. Millington. The Metropolitan Asylums Board established ships for a similar purpose and boys were required to serve two and a half years training. For background of life on board see *Reformatory and Industrial School Ships* by Commander E.P. Statham, published in *Army Illustrated* 28 Jan 1899, and also another article on the same topic which appeared in *Maritime Wales*, No.8, 1984. Copies are available in the Maritime Museum library.

The Museum library is undertaking various indexing projects. There is such a wealth of material here that the best advice is, if in doubt, ask.

The staff are happy to deal with *reasonable* enquiries; the Reading Room of the library is open to visitors with a Reader's Ticket. Details from the above address.

See also *Maritime Information: A Guide to Libraries and sources of Information in the United Kingdom* by Rita V. and Terence N. Byron, Maritime Information Association (address as above), 3rd ed. 1994, £25 inc. p & p.

NATIONAL PEDIGREE INDEX Originally compiled for the purpose of putting genealogists working on the same families in touch with each other; a pioneer of its time when it began in 1976. See Gen. Mag. Vol.17 No.18 (June 1976).

It has now been superseded by the various National and International and computer-based members' interests directories. Consequently the contents of the National Pedigree Index have been passed to the SOG (q.v.) for inclusion in their Index of Members' Interests.

NATIONAL REGISTER OF ARCHIVES see Archives.

NATIONAL TRUST A booklet published by the National Trust, and written by Barry Williamson, entitled *Using Archives at National Trust Properties* might contain useful leads for the family historian though it was compiled primarily for the use of teachers planning coursework on Social and Economic History.

It lists the 'stately homes' for which archives exist, a brief summary of them and their location (many in CROs). Obtainable from The National Trust, 8 Church Street, Lacock, Chippenham, Wilts SN15 2LB, price £1.00 inc. p&p.

NATURALISATION see also Aliens, Emigration and Immigration. Naturalisation is the means by which a person of foreign birth obtains citizenship of another (adopted) country. The majority of aliens settling in Britain did not go through the legal formalities of an Act of Naturalisation as it was expensive and only the rich could afford it.

It was less expensive to become a denizen by Letters Patent. This gave the status of a British subject, without the full rights of a natural-born subject (i.e. unable to hold public office, could hold land but not inherit it).

Records are kept at the PRO. See Records Information leaflet 70 *Immigrants: Documents in the PRO*.

NAVVY see also Railways. This term was applied to a labourer digging canals and later constructing railways.

NAVY see Royal Navy.

NEATHERD A cowherd.

NEEDLEMAKER There is an article in the Journal of the BMSGH No.34 August 1974 entitled *Family History in the Needle District*, by Eric H. Whittleton. Although it refers specifically to needlemaking areas in Warwickshire and Worcestershire, there is much of general interest in the article especially concerning the various specialised skills used.

The leading centre for needlemaking was, and still is, in the Redditch/Studley area of Worcestershire — some 15 miles south of Birmingham. Needlemaking began in this area in the early 17th century, with production peaking at some 70 million needles per week in the late 19th century!

A fascinating insight into needle manufacture and the people who made them can be found in the Forge Mill Needle Museum, Riverside, Redditch. The museum is housed in an 18th century restored water-powered needle scouring (polishing) mill.

The museum welcomes enquiries related to the needle industry and families involved. Please contact the Keeper of Collections, Forge Mill Needle Museum, Riverside, Redditch, Worcestershire B97 6RR (Tel 01527 62509). In addition to the museum's archives, Redditch Library also has a considerable amount of information (Tel 01527 63291).

The Needle Museum and Library also have information on the town's other local industries, in particular fishing tackle and Royal Enfield.

Mr B. Wright, 66 Illshaw Close, Winyates Green, Redditch, Worcs B98 0QZ is compiling an index of Needle and Fish Hook Makers, mostly covering Warwickshire and Worcestershire. Contributions are welcome and he will search the index in exchange for sae or 2 IRCs.

The novel by Roy Clews entitled *Young Jethro*, Heinemann, 1975, gives a vivid picture of the conditions of the workers in industry at the time when England was at war with Napoleon; the Shire Publication *Needlemaking* gives more practical information on the trade.

The Worshipful Company of Needlemakers of the City of London was one of the Livery Companies.

NELSON The Nelson Society is seeking information on men who served with Horatio Nelson throughout any part of his career. Any details about the lives of these men are required but, most importantly, where they now rest. There were 17,000 sailors of all nationalities in the British Fleet alone at Trafalgar. Where are the final berths of these and other crews?

Contributions should be sent to the Project Officer, Mr G. Dean, 8 Wrenfield Grove, Liverpool, L17 9QD. He is able to respond to *brief* enquiries in exchange for sae or 2 IRCs.

More specifically, Mr & Mrs D. Ayshford, 52 Perry Street, Wendover, Aylesbury, HP22 6DJ are compiling an index to the Seamen at the Battle of Trafalgar, 1805; also a list of Marines at the Battle of Trafalgar. Details in exchange for sae or 2 IRCs.

NETHERLANDS A booklet about genealogical research and records in the Netherlands can be purchased from the Central Bureau voor Genealogie, PO Box 11755, 2502 AT The Hague, Netherlands. See*Researching Ancestors from the Netherlands* in Families, Vol.22 No.3 (1983), Journal of the Ontario Gen.Soc. and *Research in Holland* by Dr R.Kirk, FTM Vol.4 No.12 (Oct 1988).

A list of family history societies in the Netherlands is available from the Administrator of the FFHS in exchange for sae or 3 IRCs.

NEW POOR LAW see Board of Guardians.

NEWGATE CALENDAR Printed lists of prisoners to be tried at Newgate (with MS additions). There are 60 volumes in the PRO (class HO 77) covering the period 1782 to 1853. After 1822 the results of trials are included.

NEWSPAPERS see also Local History, London Gazette and Scotland. Newspapers can be an invaluable source of information about people and events in the locality in which your ancestors lived. For example a single issue of Jackson's *Oxford Journal* for 21st April 1810 contained the names of some 300 people. A list was published in Gen. Mag. Vol.9 Nos.6 & 7 (Mar and Sep 1942).

Recommended reading is *Using Newspapers and Periodicals* by Colin R. Chapman, published by the FFHS, 1993, in its *An introduction to...* series.

See also *Family History From Newspapers* by Eve McLaughlin. Obtainable through FTM price £1.55 inc. p&p. Since the two subjects have great relevance to each other don't pass over *Newspapers and Local History: The Local Historian at Work* No.5 by Michael Murphy, Phillimore for BALH, 1991, price £2.95 plus p&p.

We are fortunate in this country to have at our disposal a remarkable collection of newspapers of the world at the British Library Newspaper Library situated at Colindale Avenue, London NW9 5HE (very near to Colindale Underground station). London newspapers earlier than 1801, however, are stored in the British Library, Gt. Russell Street, London WC1B 3DG. Known as the Burney Collection, this is particularly useful since the arrangement is in chronological order, and not as separate newspapers. A microfilm set of the Burney Collection is available at Colindale.

If you know the precise date and location of an event that might have been reported in a local or national newspaper, the Colindale Library will try to locate it for you and you can order a photocopy. You can, of course, visit it yourself and do your own searches. If you write do not expect an early reply, they are inundated with such requests.

The BLNL has reading rooms with 102 places, 70 for users of original newspapers and 32 for users of microfilm. They are open to readers from 10.00am-4.45pm, Mon-Sat except for Bank Holidays and a week at the end of October. Persons under 21 are not normally admitted. For further details telephone 0171 323 7353 or send for leaflet entitled *Newspaper Library: An Introduction to the Collections and Services*.

Newspapers by John Westmancoat, The British Library, 1985, is not a guide to sources but an illustrated record to the background and development of newspapers and an introduction to the collections in the BLNL. Obtainable from the Colindale address at a modest cost.

You may be able to find what you need a little nearer home by consulting *Local Newspapers 1750-1920, England and Wales; Channel Islands; Isle of Man: A Select Location List* by Jeremy Gibson, FFHS. It tells you just what papers are available in local libraries, CROs and other repositories.

There are two useful printed volumes you may wish to consult — *Handlist of English and Welsh Newspapers 1620 to 1920*, arranged chronologically and published by *The Times* in 1920, and a geographically arranged *Handlist of English Provincial Newspapers and Periodicals 1700 to 1760* by G.A. Cranfield.

A very informative section of *The National Index of Parish Registers, Vol.I* by D.J. Steel deals with the value of newspapers as a source for family history. An article in Gen. Mag. Vol.19 No.3 (Sep 1977) by I.R. Harrison deals with Provincial Newspapers as a genealogical source, as does Chapter 10 of *Town Records* by John West, Phillimore,1983. Entitled *Provincial Newspapers 1690* the chapter concludes with a Gazetteer of English and Welsh newspapers 1690 to 1981 which runs to 34 pages!

Many large Reference Libraries have copies of *The Times* on microfilm, and there are bound volumes of indexes. See Gen. Mag. Vol.21 No.4 (Dec 1983) for article by John Gurnett on *Newspaper Indexes for the Family Historian* dealing mainly with *The Times*.

The British Library Newspaper Library Newsletter is distributed twice yearly free of charge. Its purpose is to encourage an exchange of information about all aspects of newspaper collections. Copies should be found in Reference Libraries.

Marriages, Deaths and Obituary notices from *The Times* 1875 to 1894 are to be found in the Library of the SOG. Mention should be made of *The London Gazette* where such notices as changes of name, naturalisation, service promotions etc. can be found. Mr R.D. Dawson, 327 Judge Ave, Waukegan, IL 60085, USA, is a historian indexing this publication. He has indexed 1665 to the mid 18th century, advertisements, bankruptcies, deaths etc. For further information contact Mr Dawson enclosing return postage. Search fees may be costly.

An article on 18th Century Irish Newspapers to be found in the Newspaper Library appeared in Gen. Mag. Vol.7 No.8 (Dec 1936). The Bodleian Library in Oxford also has a fine collection of early newspapers. There is a *Catalogue of English Newspapers and Periodicals in the Bodleian Library, 1622 to 1800* by R.T. Milford and D.M. Sutherland, 1936.

Two basic sources for modern newspapers are *Willing's Press Guide* and *Benn's Media Directory*. Both have a regional index and provide a quick and easy method of identifying particular newspapers.

NEW YEAR RESOLUTIONS FOR FAMILY HISTORIANS The following appeared in the 'Essex Family Historian'and was reprinted with their permission in TMA.:

I will not be a bore about my ancestors.

I will always send sae (self-addressed, stamped envelope) when writing to individuals or organisations for information.

When I write for information, I will always give a full outline of the ground I have already covered and what I have found out.

If I have information about particular families, I will register this with the Surname Referral Index and will reply to the inquiries I receive as a result.

I will sort out the information I have gathered and will stop writing things down on the backs of envelopes.

I will always write down the full and correct reference for the documents from which I take information and I will also note the period within that document that I have examined so that I don't assume, years later, that I have looked at the whole when really I have read only part.

I will use the cassette recorder I was given at Christmas to record conversations with relatives, particularly at family gatherings when the truth about Aunt Em's goings-on may be hammered out. I will then try to heal the family feud that results from the discussion.

I will try to contribute to family history by joining in one of the many transcribing and indexing projects that so badly need helpers.

I will try to persuade elderly relatives to write or record their life stories and to annotate the family photographs. I will also write down my own life story, remembering that I will be the legitimate prey of a future family historian who will enjoy the quaintness and olde-worlde charm of my way of life.

NEW ZEALAND see also Army. An article on genealogical research in New Zealand by Lucy Marshall and Verna Mossong appeared in Gen. Mag. Vol.20 No.2 (June 1980); the SOG have published *Genealogical Research in New Zealand*, Leaflet No.11.

For more expansive textbooks see *Tracing Family History in New Zealand* revised edition 1991 and *Tracing Family History Overseas from New Zealand* 1991, both by Anne Bromell, GP Publications Ltd, Petone, Wellington, New Zealand. Price $NZ30.00 each plus postage and available from New Zealand Society of Genealogists if all else fails. Anne Bromell has been President of the New Zealand Society of Genealogists and has written numerous papers and articles. The first-listed book contains sections on all the usual headings for sources plus one on Maori genealogy and records of arrivals in New Zealand.

For names being researched within New Zealand (no overseas content) the *New Zealand Society of Genealogists Family Research Directory* might prove useful. Obtainable from the society at PO Box 8795, Symonds Street, Auckland 1035, NZ; price around $NZ25.00 plus postage.

See under Australia for details of *Searching Overseas: A Guide to Family History Sources for Australians and New Zealanders* by Susan Pedersen.

Archives New Zealand 4 — a Directory of Archives in New Zealand, and the Cook Islands, Fiji, Niue, Tokelau, Tonga and Western Samoa compiled by Frank Rogers, Archives Press, Plimmerton, New Zealand, 1992, price $NZ30.00. A comprehensive coverage of archives and libraries listing small collections as well as the national archives; supplemented by a classified list of art galleries, religious institutions plus index of subjects. Clear details of how to get to the various archives and notes on opening times.

Genealogical Research in Fiji by Lawrence Burness, Gen. Mag. Vol.24 No.6 (June 1993) is a first-hand account of the author's experience of using these archives and contains helpful facts and figures on this little known source.

NONCONFORMIST see also under names of various denominations and Cemeteries. Before 1640 the only nonconformist registers were those of foreign churches because only they were allowed some measure of toleration. The Walloon Congregation of Southampton's register dates from 1567, Quaker registrations begin in 1650 and those of Presbyterians from 1662.

The Non Parochial Register Act of 1840 required that all such registers should be surrendered to the Registrar General. Sometimes registers were contained in the same book as minutes of chapel meetings, lists of members, expulsions etc. and these may not have been surrendered. In this way a few have found their way to CROs. A list of surrendered registers was published in 1841 and a revised list in 1859 — these are likely to be available in Reference Libraries.

Prior to the Toleration Act of 1689 it was often thought too risky to keep a register. In general the Presbyterians were the most conscientious in keeping registers and the Baptists least so.

Chapels often changed their allegiance. Presbyterians often became 'Independent'. One chapel became in succession Presbyterian, Unitarian, Independent and then Baptist. A single nonconformist register might contain entries for several congregations where the minister travelled a 'circuit' and carried the book around with him. It is thus desirable to know which churches were cared for by the same minister and during which years. Early baptisms might be in the register of a minister who preached, virtually as a missionary, in an area before a congregation was organised there, and whose church was some distance away.

See Vol. II of *The National Index of Parish Registers* which is sub-titled *Sources for Nonconformist Genealogy and Family History*, Phillimore, 1973, and *Understanding the History and Records of Nonconformity* by Patrick Palgrave-Moore, Elvery Dowers Publications, FFHS.

Some nonconformists had their own burial grounds; the most famous of these is Bunhill Fields in London where burials took place between 1713 and 1852. The burial registers have been deposited in the PRO.

There is a series of black and white illustrated books by the Royal Commission on The Historical Monuments of England: *Nonconformist Chapels and Meeting Houses*. The entries are extracted from An Inventory of Nonconformist Chapels and Meeting Houses in Central England. They cover the following counties in volumes:
Buckinghamshire; Gloucestershire; Herefordshire, Worcestershire & Warwickshire; Derbyshire; Staffordshire & Shropshire; Northamptonshire & Oxfordshire; Leicestershire, Nottinghamshire & Rutland. Prices vary according to thickness of volume between £1.95 and £2.50. Obtainable from HMSO.

NORWAY Some years ago the Royal Norwegian Ministry of Foreign Affairs, Oslo, Norway, issued a free pamphlet entitled *How To Trace Your Ancestors in Norway* by Jan H. Olstad & Gunvald BOC. If you discover Norwegian ancestry in the course of your research it might be worth writing to enquire if this useful pamphlet is still available. You could also read *Research in Norway* in 'The New Zealand Genealogist' Vol.15 p.145 (1983).

NOTES & QUERIES see Bibliography.

NUMERALS See also Roman Numerals. Arabic ones are those used as standard in the Western World.

NUNCUPATIVE WILL A will made orally, normally by a testator on his deathbed, written down and sworn to by witnesses, but not signed by the deceased.

NUNS see Roman Catholics.

NURSE CHILDREN A term common in burial registers of the home counties, mainly because many thousands of infants sent out of London to spend the first few years of their life in the country, died in the nurse's parish.
    Contrary to popular belief, many of these children were not unwanted or illegitimate, but were from a wide spectrum of middle-class homes and were often sent to parishes with which their parents had some connection.
    A study of the population of nurses and nurse children is being made with the support of the Wellcome Trust; an index is being compiled. See *Nurse Children* by Gillian Clark, Gen. Mag. Vol.21 No.9 (March 1985).

NURSING see also Hospitals, Medals and South Africa. The Library of the Royal College of Nursing, 20 Cavendish Square, London W1M OAB, will advise what records are held by them and which are available to the public.
    Burdett's *Official Nursing Directory* is of interest. There is a copy for 1898 in the Library of the SOG. More general reading is *The Story of the Growth of Nursing* by Agnes Pavey, revised ed. 1959; *A History of the Queen's Nursing Institute* by Monica Baly, Groom Helm, 1987 and *A Hundred Years of District Nursing* by Mary Stocks, George Allen & Unwin, 1960.
    See also PRO Records Information leaflets 113 and 120 *Civilian Nurses and Nursing Services: Record Sources in the PRO* and *Military Nurses and Nursing Services* and *Tracing your nurse ancestors* by Janet Rose, FTM, Vol.9 No.1 (Nov 1992).
    The Florence Nightingale Museum is on the site of St Thomas's Hospital, 2 Lambeth Palace Road, London SE1 7EW, open Tues-Sun 10.00am-4.00pm.

OATH OF ALLEGIANCE The Act of 1722 made it necessary for all persons in England over 18 years of age to swear an oath of Allegiance to the Crown at Quarter Sessions. Where these lists survive they will be found in CROs. Those for Cheshire have been published both as a book and on microfiche.

OBITUARIES see also Newspapers. It is worth enquiring when magazines were first issued by the church in your ancestors' parish. Obituary notices are often found in them and they can contain interesting details.

OCCUPATIONS see also Trades and Shire Publications. Many occupational names have long since ceased to be used. If you trace your ancestry back to early registers you may be confronted with the occupation being given in Latin. In *A Latin Glossary for Family and Local Historians* by Janet Morris, FFHS, there is a long list of Latin names; though you can guess some of them, you would probably be puzzled if you found your ancestor was an aromatarius (a grocer) or a burriarius (a dairyman), unless, of course, you are well-versed in Latin.

The Unknown Mayhew eds. E.P. Thompson and Eileen Yeo, Pelican Books, 1973 has very detailed descriptions of the work, living conditions and pay of a number of occupations. It covers in great detail silk weavers, needlewomen, tailors, boot and shoe makers, toy makers, merchant seamen, sawyers, joiners, coopers, dressmakers and milliners, hatters and tanners. *Made in England* by Dorothy Hartley is a fascinating guide to some of the age-old jobs and skills practised in England. First published in 1939 by Methuen & Co.Ltd, 2nd ed. 1987, Century in Association with The National Trust.

A series covering a wide variety of Old Occupations is ongoing in FTM commencing with Vol.3 No.2 (Dec 1986). See also *Occupations: A Preliminary List* by Joyce Culling, and more specifically *Londoners' Occupations: A Genealogical Guide* by Stuart A. Raymond, both published by FFHS.

The Registrar General's *Classification of Occupations* is the basis of classifications used in census and other OPCS publications. It has been revised and published approximately every decade since the late 19th century. A copy may be in your local library.

ONE-NAME STUDIES Many people who have unusual surnames are intrigued by them and tend to widen the scope of their research and record all instances of the name, attempting to arrange them in family groups.

It is a temptation to think that all must be related, but this is seldom the case, largely because of variations in spelling over the centuries. Two names which in the 16th century were quite evidently different in both pronunciation and spelling finish up alike by the end of the 18th century.

However, pursuing a one-name study can be quite fascinating. Often this leads to the formation of a One-Name Family History Society. There are a number of long established ones in this country and many thousands in the USA although the latter often concentrate only on the descendants of one couple. If you are tempted to form such a group there is a booklet to help you, *Forming A One-Name Group* by Derek Palgrave, FFHS.

A Register of persons researching a particular surname was started by the late Frank Higenbottam. From this beginning The Guild of One-Name Studies was formed in 1979, and the *Register of One-Name Studies* was subsequently compiled and is regularly updated. Members of the Guild receive a quarterly journal. For further details write to: The Registrar, Box G, 14 Charterhouse Buildings, Goswell Road, London EC1M 7BA.

Other publications are *Sources for One-Name Studies*, *Surname Periodicals* (a worldwide listing), *Organising a One Name Gathering* and *Record Keeping for a One-Name Study*. Obtainable from the FFHS.

Even if you are not tempted into this fascinating byway, you should certainly consult their Register to see if your surname has been subjected to extensive study. If it has, you may be in luck for a great deal of information could be obtained from the specialist, saving you much time and effort. Most enthusiasts, for example, have copied out all the entries for the name from St Catherine's House indexes, and culled information from Calendars of Wills, and lists of all sorts!

See also SOG Leaflet No.25 *Guide to Sources for One-Name Studies in the Library (with information about the Guild of One-Name Studies)*.

ORAL EVIDENCE This is a term used by family historians for information handed down in the family by word of mouth. It is surprising how far back this can take us. If you ask an elderly relative what she can remember being told as a child by her grandmother, you are listening to stories about the family relating probably to the beginning of the last century, or even earlier.

Gen. Mag. once quoted James Agate's 'EGO' Vol.2 in which the following anecdote appears: '. . . E.M. Kellett recalls an old lady who, in 1884, said to somebody "I am astonished you cannot make up your mind about Oliver Cromwell. My dear husband's first wife's first husband knew him well and liked him very much". This is just possible . . .'

To perpetuate 'oral evidence' modern technology, in the form of a tape recorder, might be put to use and these memories of the past preserved exactly as they are related. In any case, recordings of the voices of our parents and if possible of grandparents or aunts and uncles would be a precious addition to the family records. *Interviewing Elderly Relatives* by Eve McLaughlin is an excellent guide to the 'whys and wherefores' of doing this. Obtainable from FTM price £1.55 inc. p&p.

There is a Centre for English Cultural Tradition and Language at the University of Sheffield, Weston Bank, Sheffield S10 2TN.

ORDNANCE SURVEY see Maps.

ORGANIST There is a book entitled *Organists of the City of London 1660 to 1850* published by the author, Donovan Dawe, 1983. It is a hardback book costing £18 (inc. p&p) obtainable from Quill Printing Services Ltd., 6 Cross Street, Padstow, Cornwall, PL28 8AT. It lists the succession of organists for each City of London Church, followed by biographical notes.

ORIENTAL AND INDIA OFFICE COLLECTIONS See also Cemeteries in South Asia. Records of those who served in India either as servants of the East India Company, or in the services, are kept in the British Library, Oriental and India Office Collections, 197 Blackfriars Road, London SE1 8NG.

The Library contains a remarkable collection of documents and is a rich source of biographical information. They have published *A Brief Guide to Biographical Sources* by Ian A. Baxter, 2nd ed. 1990. You should find this in most Reference Libraries, or you can obtain a copy from Turpin Distribution Services Ltd, Blackhorse Road, Letchworth, Herts SG6 1HN, price £5.95 plus p&p; it will save time if you study this before visiting the Library. It gives a description of the records with the relevant reference numbers. Although described as 'Brief' the Guide covers 53 pages.

A General Guide to the India Office Records by Martin Moir, published by the British Library in 1988 costs £35. Again obtainable from Turpin Distribution Services Ltd and possibly some local libraries may have a copy.

See also *Sources for Anglo-Indian Genealogy in the Library of the Society of Genealogists,* by Neville C. Taylor, 1990. Price £1.90 inc. p&p.

Many of the records in the Oriental and India Office Collections are on open shelves. Some records deal with countries other than India — Aden, Afghanistan, Central Asia, China and the Persian Gulf States being just a few examples.

Cloakroom facilities and a drinks vending machine are available.

There are over 1,000 volumes of returns (births, marriages and deaths) c.1698 to 1947. There is a somewhat inadequate index but this is in the process of being completely revised.

The Army in India For most of the time the British were in India there were two armies there — the Indian Army and the British Army in India. The latter was made up of British Regiments serving in India but controlled from the War Office in London. The first Indian troops to serve under the British were recruited by the Honourable East India Company to guard their trading posts; under the command of their own Indian officers they wore native dress and used their own weapons. As the company expanded and its military commitments increased, these grew into fully fledged battalions. India was divided by the Company into three great administrative areas called Presidencies — Bombay, Madras and Bengal. The huge size of India and the difficult terrain, coupled with the almost total lack of communications meant that there was very little contact between them at first so each developed its own entirely separate army and these continued until after the Mutiny in 1857.

In 1748 all three armies of the Presidencies were put under one Commander-in Chief, Major Stringer Lawrence. Nine years later, in the Bengal Presidency, Robert Clive organised the first battalions of Indian troops to be equipped and trained on the same lines as the British Army; to be commanded by a small core of British officers with subordinate Indian officers. Madras followed in 1759 and Bombay in 1767. This set the pattern for nearly 200 years although many attempts were made to improve the organisation. One of the changes to take place was the introduction of the 2-battalion regimental system in 1796 but with its attendant problems it was not wholly a success.

Units were formed to police particular areas such as the Punjab Frontier Force and the Hyderabad Contingent but these were under the control of the Civil Power not the military. Some cavalry regiments were raised as irregular regiments for use in emergency and commanded by the local ruler or landowner with a minimum of British officers to provide training and organisation. In 1784 some regular cavalry regiments were raised but all except three were disbanded after the Mutiny, when all the troops of the East India Company that were not disbanded were transferred to the Crown and in

SEASON, 182

To the Honourable Court of Directors of the United East-India Company.

The humble Petition of *Stephen Prescott*

SHEWETH,

    That your Petitioner is desirous of entering the Military Service of the Company, as a Cadet for the *Madras Infantry* to which he has been nominated by *John Huddleston* Esq. at the recommendation of *Colo. Marshall* Esq., and should he be so fortunate as to appear to your Honours eligible for that station, promises to conduct himself with fidelity and honour.

    That your Petitioner has been furnished with the Articles of War, has read the Terms, and also the Resolution of the Court of the 9th August 1809, to which he promises faithfully to conform; as also to all the Rules, Orders, and Regulations, which have been, or may be established by the Honourable Court, or the Governor and Council at the Presidency to which he is appointed.

    And your Petitioner, as in duty bound, will ever pray.

         Stephen Prescott.

DIRECTOR'S NOMINATION.

    I, *John Huddleston* Esq., being one of the Directors of the East-India Company, beg leave to present the Petitioner as a Cadet for the *Madras Inftry* on one of my Nominations of the season *1621* provided he shall appear to you eligible for that station: and I do declare, that I have inquired into the character, connexions, and qualifications of *Mr Stephen Prescott* and that in my opinion he is a fit person to petition the East-India Company for the appointment he now herein solicits.

    Recommended to me *be.*

Colo Joseph Marshall ~~Esq.~~

    East-India House,

    24th Octr 1825

I hereby transfer my right of Nomination to the above appointment to

     Esq., in exchange for

       East-India House,

Entry from a Cadet Book, Oriental and India Office Collection.

1861 the whole Army in India was reorganised. The Presidency Armies remained until 1895 when they were replaced by area commands which still, however, operated quite separately.

In 1866 a further re-organisation took place; the Punjab Frontier Force was transferred to the Commander-in Chief and all battalions were grouped, usually in pairs. A voluntary reserve was created at the same time. This still proved unwieldy and it was left to Lord Kitchener as Commander-in-Chief in 1902 to properly unify the army. He renumbered all the regiments in order of seniority so that all traces of the three Presidency Armies disappeared completely except in the historic names of the regiments. The Frontier Force was abolished on the premis that all regiments were to serve there in turn. Most of his ideas had been put into force by the outbreak of World War I in 1914.

In 1921 further changes took place, included the disbanding of all part-time cavalry units. Indianisation, the replacement of all British officers with native Indians, commenced in 1923 and the Indian Military Academy for training Indian officers was established in 1931. An Indian Territorial Force was founded in 1920 and there were also the Auxiliary Forces consisting of Europeans or persons of mixed race who volunteered to serve for home defence. British Officers and NCOs were known by the same ranks in the Indian Army as in the British Army but Indians had their own rank names.

When India was granted independence in 1947 the old Indian Army was disbanded and split between India and Pakistan (with the exception of the four 2-battalion Gurkha Regiments who were transferred to the British Army) and many of those famous old names with which we were so familiar – Hodson's Horse, Sam Browne's Cavalry – disappeared for ever.

Information relating to the army in India and other sources in the Oriental and India Office Collections is referred to in the articles listed below:

Some families with long East Indian connections, Major V.C.P.Hodson, Gen. Mag. Vol.6 No.1 (March 1932) – continued in subsequent numbers – *'India Office Records',* same author, Gen. Mag. Vol.6 No.5 (March 1933).

List of Indian Monumental Inscriptions, 3 volumes published by the Indian Government, Gen. Mag. Vol.7 No.1 (March 1935).

East India Company Ancestry by T.V.H. FitzHugh, Gen. Mag. Vol.21 No.5 with letter in Vol.21 No.6 (March/June 1984).

Family History Material in registers of deeds by G.Hamilton-Edwards, Gen. Mag. Vol.16 Nos.8, 9 & 10 though less Indian material in the later numbers (Dec 1970 to June 1971).

Anglo-Indian Family History by Brigadier H. Bullock, 'The Amateur Historian', Vol.1 No.4 (Feb/March 1953).

East India Company Families by T.V.H. FitzHugh, 'Family History', New series 69/70, (IHGS.) (Nov.1982).

East Indiamen – The East India Company's Maritime Service by Sir Evan Cotton, ed. Sir Charles Fawcett, London 1949. Reviewed Gen. Mag. Vol.11 No.1 (March 1951).

As an example of the research done on these records see *Lists of Officers in the Bengal Army, 1758 to 1834* by Major V.C.P. Hodson. There are 4 volumes, with an index. It is packed with biographical and genealogical information about thousands of people, from all levels of society – sons of plumbers and glaziers, mariners, hairdressers, builders' assistants and clergymen.

Another valuable source of information is *The Makers of Indian Colonial Silver: A Register of European Goldsmiths, Silversmiths, Jewellers, Watch-makers and Clockmakers in India and their marks 1760-1860* by Wynyard R.T. Wilkinson, 1987. Many names are cross-referenced to other non-trade names. Illustrated and indexed, this publication is available from the compiler at 99D Talbot Road, London W11 2AT. At £97.50 it could prove too costly for all but the specialist; a copy may be available in your local library or that of the SOG.

ORPHANS AND ORPHANAGES see Children's Societies.

OSTLER sometimes 'hostler'. A stableman at an inn. In recent times a hostler was the name given to a person in charge of locomotives etc when not in use.

OUT-OF-AREA INDEX see Strays.

OUT PENSIONERS see Chelsea Royal Hospital.

OVERSEAS see Deaths Overseas and Worldwide Family History.

OVERSEERS OF HIGHWAYS & OVERSEERS OF THE POOR see Highways and Poor Law.

OXFORD UNIVERSITY Lists of names of graduates and some information about them appear in a publication in several volumes entitled *Alumni Oxonienses* by J.Foster (to 1886).

PALAEOGRAPHY Defined as the study of the handwritings, and often the manuscripts, of the past. Once you are back to the 17th century in your researches, you will certainly need a guide to decipher the handwriting. There are a number of these available. Before investing in a larger work try the McLaughlin Guide *Reading Old Handwriting*, obtainable from FTM price £1.55 inc. p&p.

Enjoying Archives (see 'Archives') has an excellent chapter on handwriting and reproduces various forms of the letters of the alphabet from the 10th to the 18th century.

Then there is *Examples of English Handwriting 1150 to 1750* by H.E.P. Grieve (5th impression 1981) and *Examples of Handwriting 1550 to 1650* by W.S. Buck, published by Phillimore. Much of Chapter I in *Genealogical Research in England and Wales, Vol.III* by Smith & Gardner, published Bookcraft Inc. 1966, is devoted to the subject. There is a delightful little book entitled *A Secretary Hand ABC Book* by Alf Ison, Berkshire Books, 1982. It is fully illustrated and costs £2.35 inc. p&p from Wheaton Publishers Ltd, Hennock Road, Exeter EX2 8RP.

Scottish handwriting is dealt with in Grant G. Simpson's *Scottish Handwriting 1150-1650* published by the Aberdeen University Press.

When Roman numerals are used the final figure 1 is often shown as a j; thus 3 is rendered as iij. Arabic numerals did not come into common usage until the 16th century.

An excellent article entitled *Handwriting 1550 to 1725* by Dr F.G. Emmison appeared in the Bedfordshire FHS magazine in 1978. The article is well illustrated.

PALLOT INDEX This index covers more than 98% of marriages in 101 of the 103 ancient parishes of the square mile of the City of London between 1780 and 1837. It also includes many thousands of other marriage entries. There is a baptismal section consisting of tens of thousands of slips, which suffered severe damage during the Second World War, from the Greater London area and even further afield such as Cornwall and Lancashire. Many of the entries are from records which have been destroyed since it was started in 1818. There is a high success rate for those with 'lost marriages' in London.

The index is owned by Achievements Ltd., 80 Northgate, Canterbury, Kent, CT1 1BA. Fees are charged — they consult the index for you. Write for further details. See also *The Pallot Marriage Index: circa 1780-1837*, FTM Vol.2 No.3 (Mar-Apr 1986).

PANNAGE This was the right to pasture swine, or the payment for the same right, in woodland.

PAPERMAKERS Mrs Jean Stirk, Shode House, Ightham, Kent TN15 9HP has an extensive index of paper makers and their families in the British Isles, including details of master papermakers, journeymen, apprentices, employers and employees. Records of first trade union, Original Society of Papermakers, being sought and searched. Searches for specific names will be undertaken in exchange for sae or 3 IRCs.

An additional modest charge may be made for any photocopies supplied.

Mrs Stirk would welcome contributions to the index. See also her series of articles in FTM Vol.6 Nos.6,7 & 8 (Apr-Jun 1990).

PAPIER MACHE see Japanning.

PARISH Subdivision of a diocese, having its own church and a clergyman; the area within the responsibility of a parson, to whom tithes and other ecclesiastical dues were paid.

In the 16th and 17th centuries, secular administration passed from the manorial courts to the parish except in matters regarding land transfers. Two important matters of administration which the parish had to contend with were the relief of the poor (q.v.) and the maintenance of the highways (q.v.). By the end of the 19th century, most of these secular matters had become the responsibility of the municipal or county boroughs.

See *Discovering Parish Boundaries* by Angus Winchester, Shire Publications, 1990. Price £2.50. (Number 282 in the Discovering series.) An excellent introduction to a subject which features predominantly in both local and family history. Indexed; detailed bibliography.

PARISH CHEST The poor law of 1552 directed the parishioners in every parish to provide a strong chest, having three keys, for holding the alms for the poor. From the early 16th century separate legislation required that every parish should have a locking chest to contain the Parish Registers and all other documents pertaining to the parish. Often one chest was provided, or adapted, to serve both purposes!

The standard work on this subject is *The Parish Chest* by W.E. Tate, first published by the Cambridge University Press in 1946. A third ed. appeared in 1969 and in 1983 it was reprinted by Phillimore with the kind permission of CUP. Its sub-title is *A Study of the Records of Parochial Administration in England*.

In addition to PRs the contents of the Parish Chest should have included: Churchwardens Accounts, Charity Accounts, Glebe Terriers, Tithe Records, Vestry Minutes and Agreements, Petty Constables' Accounts, Records of Poor Law Administration, Highway Maintenance, Open-Field Agriculture Enclosure, other Ecclesiastical and miscellaneous Civil Records. Where any of these documents survive they should be accessible in some form at the relevant CRO or DRO.

PARISH CLERK He normally held this position for life; his duties included the arrangement of baptisms and communions; he rang the church bell and led the responses at services. Parish register entries were often written by the Parish Clerk. For further information read *The Parish Clerk* by P.H. Ditchfield, Methuen & Co. 1907.

PARISH MAGAZINES These date mainly from the 19th century. They often contain details of Christenings, Marriages and Burials and Obituaries. Sometimes extracts from early Parish Registers are reprinted in them.

A two-part article *Parish Magazines: their availability and usefulness to Family Historians* appeared in Vol.2 Nos.4 and 5 of FTM (May-June/July-Aug 1986). The article cites interesting examples of the contents of parish magazines.

PARISH MAPS Measuring 17" x 13" these have been prepared by the IHGS (q.v.). Maps are available for each county of England, Wales and Scotland.

Please note, Yorkshire is in four maps: North Riding, East Riding, West Riding − (A) Rural area north of Bradford and Leeds, (B) Industrial area including Bradford, Leeds, Huddersfield, Halifax and Sheffield.

Lincolnshire is in two maps: (A) Kesteven and Holland (B) Lindsey.

Wales is in three maps: North Wales (Anglesey, Caernarvon, Denbigh, Flint); Central Wales (Monmouth, Montgomery, Cardigan, Radnor); South Wales (Pembroke, Carmarthen, Brecon, Glamorgan).

The City of London is overprinted with streets.

The Scottish counties are divided into the following maps:

1. Orkney & Shetland
2. Sutherland & Caithness
3. Ross & Cromarty
4. Inverness: mainland & Harris
5. N.E.Scotland: Nairn, Elgin, Banff, Aberdeen, Kincardine
6. W.Inverness & N.Argyll
7. Perthshire & adjoining counties: Perth, Forfar, Clackmannan, Kinross & Fife
8. S.Argyll & adjoining counties: greater part of Argyll with Stirling, Dunbarton & Renfrew
9. S.W.Scotland: Wigtown, Ayr, Kirkcudbright, Bute & Lanark
10. The Lothians & S.E.Lowlands: Dumfries, Peebles, Selkirk, Roxburgh, Linlithgow, Edinburgh, Haddington, Berwick

The maps show parochial boundaries and dates of commencement of existing registers. Coloured outlines show the jurisdiction of ecclesiastical courts which administered probate and licences. They can be purchased individually at a cost of £4.00 each inc. p&p but also available is the *Phillimore Atlas and Index of Parish Registers.*

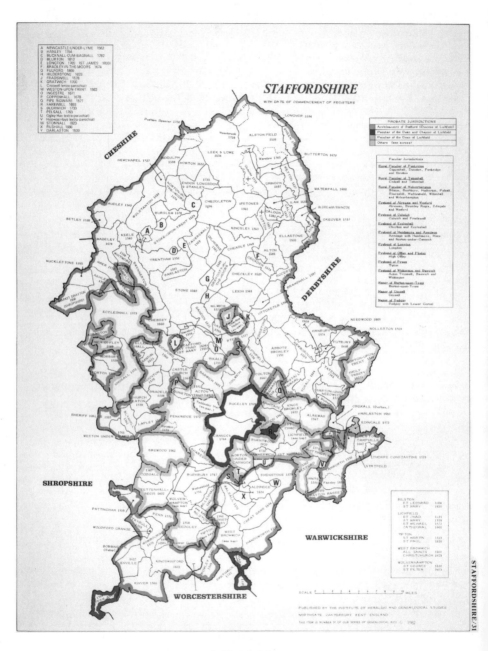

A Parish Map

Compiled by the IHGS and edited by Cecil R.Humphery-Smith, it contains the parish maps of all the counties of England and Wales (second edition to include Scotland) which existed before the boundary changes of 1974. The maps show the ancient parishes which existed before 1832, the ecclesiastical court jurisdictions, the situation of churches and chapels where appropriate and the date of commencement of the surviving registers of the parish.

Alongside each parish map in the Atlas there is a reproduction of a topographical map from James Bell's *A New and Comprehensive Gazetteer of England and Wales 1834* which should help the researcher to pin-point the whereabouts of a parish and the routes by which an ancestor might have travelled from one place to another. Together with the maps there is a large index which lists the parishes for each county and gives a grid reference enabling the user to find each place quickly. A further feature is a reference to deposited parish registers and parish register copies and their coverage in the variety of local and national genealogical indexes which are available, namely the IGI, local marriage indexes, Boyd's and Pallot's marriage indexes (q.v.). There is also a listing of non-conformist chapels situated in a particular parish whose records are at the PRO. Bear in mind however, that many of the names and addresses it contains may be out of date. It is advisable to check with the IHGS if in doubt. New edition due in 1995. Price in the region of £50.

It must be noted that the Index is a consolidated *guide* to the coverage of these indexes. It will list the earliest and latest dates available but will *not* state what gaps exist in the series nor will it distinguish between baptismal, marriage and burial registers.

PARISH RECORDS see Parish Chest.

PARISH REGISTERS (PRs) see also Marriages and Parish Maps. The publication *Parish Registers* by Eve McLaughlin provides good background information to this subject, especially for the newcomer to research. Obtainable from FTM price £1.83 inc. p&p.

See also *The Parish Registers of England*, J.C. Cox, 1910 and *Parish Registers: their uses and limitations* by Joe Bagley, Gen. Mag. Vol.22 No.8. Dec 1987.

Below we give a summary of the various stages of development in the keeping of parish registers:

1538: Thomas Cromwell ordered that each parish should keep a register of baptisms, marriages and burials. The entries were to be made after each Sunday service.

1598: The Provincial Constitution of Canterbury required that the registers should be of parchment. All previous entries — which had usually been written on paper — had first to be copied up — particularly those since the accession of Queen Elizabeth. This is the reason so many registers commence in 1558, the previous registers having become unreadable through damp and decay. Up to about 1732 it was common to record the entries in Latin with the Latin forms of Christian names.

1644/5 An Ordinance stated that the date of birth should be given when a child was baptised and dates of death were also to be given (this was not effective).

1653 This was the period of the Commonwealth, and the Government took over the custody of registers and appointed officers called 'Parish Registers' to be responsible for the entries. These have become known as Civil Registers, but unfortunately not many have survived.

1667 & 1678 Legislation was passed requiring that all burials should be in a woollen shroud, and an affidavit made at each burial that this had been done otherwise a fine was payable. The Act gradually became ignored and was repealed in 1814. Its purpose had been to help the wool trade. Some parishes kept separate Registers of 'Burials in Woollen'.

1694 A tax of 2/- was levied on each birth, 2/6 for a marriage and 4/- for a burial. Births were to be notified to the incumbent within 5 days, and he was to receive a fee of 6d for recording them. This tax was short-lived.

1711 An Act stated that proper register books with ruled lines and numbered pages were to be used (largely ignored).

1754 Hardwicke's Marriage Act, limited to England and Wales, took effect from 25th March. This Act declared that a marriage could be solemnised only in a parish church or public chapel after the publication of banns or by a licence issued by the bishop of the diocese. Banns books and marriage register books were required to be kept separate from those for baptisms and burials. The marriage had to be performed by a clergyman of the Church of England. Jews and Quakers were exempt. Minors (under 21) needed the consent of parents or guardians. Some Catholics were married in the Church of England, as well as in their own churches, to ensure legality. (see Alias.)

1783 A Stamp Act was passed. This decreed that a duty of 3d had to be paid for every entry of a birth or christening, marriage or burial. The duty was collected by the incumbent who was allowed to retain 10% as a commission. This came into force on 1st October but was repealed 10 years later. It had several interesting consequences. There was a great increase in the number of baptisms in the last few days of September 1783, many of the children being of several years of age and a similar 'bulge' after its repeal in 1793. Those in receipt of parish relief were exempt from the tax, no payment being required for any person buried from 'any Workhouse or Hospital or at the sole expense of any Charity'.

The letter 'P' appears after numerous entries for the duration of the Act. It is likely that this meant 'Pauper', but the theory has been advanced that it might mean the incumbent had obtained a licence whereby he need not stamp his registers, and the 'P' in fact stands for 'Paid' when he did his accounts for the Tax Commissioners.

1813 George Rose's Act came into effect requiring that specially printed registers should be used, with separate books for baptisms, marriages and burials. Baptismal entries were to include the names, address and occupation or status (e.g.'gent') of the parents. Burial entries were to include age, and place of residence of the deceased. The form of marriage registers was again changed in 1837.

176

Banbury Old Church.

Most registers have been deposited in CROs the majority of which have published a Handlist of their holdings. These are usually available on request at a modest price. In some cases they are still in the care of the incumbent who will certainly have current registers and, in a small rural parish, these may have commenced many years ago.

You may have to write to the incumbent to ask him to search his registers for you. The Parochial Fees Order in operation from January 1994 stipulates that the incumbent may charge a flat rate of £9 for the first hour or part thereof for searching the registers, and £7 for each subsequent hour and part thereof. This is for consultation only. The incumbent can charge extra for his or his official's time — you are advised to obtain fees stated *in writing* beforehand. See *A guide to Church of England Fees* and *Table of Parochial Fees* obtainable from The Church Commissioners' Office, Pastoral Dept. (General Section), 1 Millbank, London SW1P 3JZ.

The National Index of Parish Registers was an ambitious project which has yet to be completed. Those volumes which have been printed are very useful works of reference, though they are out of date as to the location of registers, so many of which have now been deposited in Record Offices or Libraries. The following volumes have been published though some are presently out of print.

Vol I *Sources of Births, Marriages and Deaths before 1837*. It deals with parish registers and how they were kept, Marriage Licences, Monumental Inscriptions, Clandestine Marriages, Divorce, Mediaeval Sources and other records. There is a general bibliography.

Vol II *Sources for Nonconformist Genealogy and Family History*.

Vol III *Sources for Roman Catholic and Jewish Genealogy and Family History*.
(includes index to Vols 1-3)

Vol IV Part 1 *Surrey*.

Vol V *Gloucestershire, Herefordshire, Oxfordshire, Shropshire, Warwickshire and Worcestershire*.

Vol VI Part 1 *Staffordshire.* Part 2. *Nottinghamshire*

Vol VII *Cambridgeshire, Norfolk, Suffolk.*

Vol VIII Part 1 *Berkshire.*

Vol VIII Part 2 *Wiltshire*

Vol IX Part 1 *Bedfordshire, Huntingdonshire* Part 2 *Northamptonshire* Part 3 *Buckinghamshire* Part 4 *Essex*

Vol XI Part 1 *Durham and Northumberland.*

Vol XII *Sources for Scottish Genealogy and Family History*. This volume gives a historical background, deals with parish registers, ancillary sources and nonconformists. Again there is a useful bibliography.

Vol XIII *Parish Registers of Wales* (does not include Nonconformist material).

Work on most of the earlier volumes was done by D.J. Steel.

PARISH REGISTERS IN IRELAND see also Irish Ancestry. About two thirds of Irish Parish Registers were destroyed in the Civil War of 1922, but Catholic registers dating from c.1820 had not been deposited and thus survived. Registers can be consulted at the Office of The Registrar General, 8/11 Lombard Street East, Dublin 2.

Three articles, by Paul Gorry, which have appeared in FTM, enlarge upon these records. *Roman Catholic Parish Registers*, Vol.3 No.7 (May 1987), *Church of Ireland Parish Registers*, Vol.3 No.11 (Sep 1987) and *Presbyterian Church Records*, Vol.4 No.5 (March 1988).

PARISH REGISTERS IN SCOTLAND see also Scottish Ancestry. Registers of the Church of Scotland (Presbyterian) commenced in 1558, earliest surviving is 1560 deaths at Aberdeen and 1561 baptisms at Perth & Dunfermline. The original registers are at New Register House, Princes Street, Edinburgh EH1 3YT. Most Public Libraries throughout Scotland have microfilm copies for their area.

The "English" Church in Scotland is known as the Scottish Episcopal Church. Each local Diocese keeps its own records but those for the Diocese of Aberdeen and Orkney are on microfilm at The Family History Shop, 164 King Street, Aberdeen, AB2 3BD.

Scottish Old Parochial Registers which relate to the Established Church of Scotland (Presbyterian) have more omissions than English Parish Registers but baptismal entries are more detailed, nearly always with the maiden surname of the mother.

The Register Indexes (commonly called Scottish OPR Indexes) are available on microfiche and comprise the most comprehensive collection of indexed Scottish births and marriages covering the 300 years prior to the commencement in 1855 of Scottish statutory Civil Registration. The indexes are available at New Register House, SOG, LDS FHCs and similar institutions worldwide.

PARISH REGISTER TRANSCRIPTS Many have been published by various County Record Societies, and in more recent years these have been augmented by publications of regional FHSs. Some are manuscript, or typescript, copies. Various County PR Societies still publish volumes – notably Lancs., Staffs., Yorks., and they hold large collections of unpublished transcripts. Check with relevant CRO.

It is worth noting that some ROs (the Borthwick Institute for one) use 'PRT' to mean 'Bishop's Transcripts'.

The SOG has published *Parish Register Copies in the Possession of the Society of Genealogists*, 1992, price £5.65 inc. p&p.

PARLIAMENTARY RECORDS see also House of Lords Record Office. The House of Lords has many useful records. Parliamentary Debates are reported in detail from 1804 (Cobbett's Parliamentary Debates which, from 1811, was produced by Thomas Hansard . This is now an official parliamentary record). Newspapers also reported parliamentary debates in detail.

The standard reference work is *Guide to the Records of Parliament* by Maurice F. Bond, HMSO 1971. Two shorter works also by Bond, who was the Clerk of the Records, are: *The Records of Parliament – A Guide for Genealogists and Local Historians*, published by Phillimore, 1964 and *A Short Guide to the Records of Parliament*, 3rd ed. from the House of Lords Record Office, 1980.

See also *Parliamentary Records in Guildhall Library: a lesser known source for Family Historians* by Richard Harvey, Gen. Mag. Vol.24 No.7 (Sep 1993).

PAROCHIAL CHAPELRY Chapelry within parish which generally had the right to maintain its own Registers. Some Parochial Chapelries retained the right to marry after 1754 and it is advisable always to check this. In some cases duplicate entries were made in the PR of the mother (parish) church, in other cases in the BTs only, in other cases Registers were maintained separately. Note that not all chapelries were Parochial Chapelries.

PAROCHIAL REGISTERS AND RECORDS MEASURE 1978 This Act of Parliament came into force on 1st January 1979 with subsequent amendments which came into effect 1st January 1993. Briefly this requires parishes to deposit in a diocesan record office all records completed more than one hundred years ago. If, however, the church opts to keep them in the parish (subject to the consent of the bishop) they must be kept in a fire-proof and rust-proof cupboard, and certain conditions relating to humidity and temperature must be observed.

Where they are retained by the parish, those wishing to see the registers must be given access 'at all reasonable hours'. However, no right of access is given to other records in parochial custody.

The Measure contains a clause concerning the fees which may be charged for searches to be made in baptism or burial registers. The scale of fees is set out in the Ecclesiastical Fees Order which may be changed from time to time. Marriage registers are not covered by the Measure, but in practice fees are required for searches in those registers also. (For details see under 'Parish Registers'.)

Fees are not charged in DROs except in the case of those offices run by private bodies rather than local authorities (e.g. Canterbury Cathedral Library, and the Bodleian Library, Oxford).

Fuller details are noted in *Parochial Registers and Records Measure 1978, A Record Users' Guide*. price £4.10 inc. p&p from The Bookshop, Church House Record Centre, Dean's Yard, London SW1P 3NZ. The guide takes into account the 1993 amendments.

PARSON A parish priest in the Church of England; any clergyman.

PARTNERSHIPS The partnership was governed in former times by principles decided on case law. In 1890 the Partnership Act was passed to declare and amend the law by statute and rules determined whether a partnership existed or not and what were its legal effects. Before that time differences between partners over distribution of profit, nature of business, scope and private arrangements as well as the bankruptcy of individual partners led to all sorts of difficulties and litigation. Dissolutions of partnerships in London and abroad were announced in the *London Gazette* (q.v.).

An Index to names of partners from notices of dissolutions of partnership for London and abroad but excluding country firms, taken from the *London Gazette* for 1794-1826 inclusive (except for notices in the Gazette or the eight years 1798-1800, 1802, 1806, 1808, 1811 and 1815), belonging to Cecil R. Humphery-Smith is held at the IHGS. Other such manuscript indexes possibly exist elsewhere. Typical examples include Samuel Abbott of St Swithin's Lane, London, and Oporto (Portugal) 1821; Ralph Montigue of Bristol, West India merchant 1818; William Moody of Wapping, sail maker 1809; Richard and Joseph Rankin of Change Alley (London) draper 1810.

Partnerships were the usual form of business arrangements before the Companies' Acts and many of these entries probably relate to insolvency. As they are chiefly concerned with the City of London and occupations are described, the entries may lead to notices in the records of the city livery companies.

There are over 15,000 entries in the index which can be searched in exchange for a modest donation to the IHGS and sae or 2 IRCs. See also *Something to think about* by Cecil R. Humphery-Smith, FTM Vol. 7 No.11 (Sep 1991).

PASSENGER LISTS see Emigration and United States of America.

PASSPORTS Their date of origin is not known; in England the equivalent of a passport was probably a 'Safe Conduct' certificate which is mentioned in an Act of 1414 in the reign of Henry V. The Privy Council appears to have granted passports from at least 1540 to 1683. During the Commonwealth, however, they were granted to foreign subjects by the two Houses of Parliament. A fee came to be charged. Up to 1794 passports were signed by the King himself and countersigned by the Secretary of State. From 1794 two forms of passport were in existence, the Royal Passport, as above, and one issued in the name of the Sovereign but signed by the Secretary of State alone. A record exists of all passports issued between 1794 and 1898.

These appear in the Passport Registers (FO 610) — 114 volumes — in the PRO. They show the intended destination of the applicant and are in chronological order.

There is an index of names (FO 611) 1851 to 1862 and 1874 to 1898 in 18 volumes. Correspondence (FO 612) 1815 to 1905 fills 71 volumes, and there are Registers of Correspondence (FO 613) 1868 to 1893 and 1898 to 1905 (4 volumes). The second volume has been much used also as a passport register for the period March to May 1915. There is also Correspondence with H.M.Embassies (FO 614) 1886, 1897 to 1900 in 2 volumes.

This relates to the issue of passports by consuls and the passport requirements of foreign countries. There are other records, 1809 to 1954, Reference Numbers FO 737 and FO 655. See also PRO Records Information leaflet 69 *Passport Records*.

PATENT OFFICE Although Patents were granted by the Crown as early as the 14th century, the Statute of Monopolies which was enacted by Parliament in 1623 laid the foundation for modern Patent Law. In principle, anyone can petition for a Patent so a search of Patent literature can be of assistance to the family historian as inventors' names are given in full, usually with their place of residence. A comprehensive collection of British and Foreign Patents is held at the Patent Office Library, 25 Southampton Buildings, Chancery Lane, London, WC2A 1AY. A number of public libraries in other parts of the country have collections of both specifications and abridgements.

In the Patent Office Library there is a name index of Patentees covering the period from 1617 to 1981, with one volume for the period 1617-1852 and then one volume for each year. The patent number and date the patent was applied for is given and from this information one can discover the full name and address.

See PRO Records Information leaflet 17 *Patents and Specifications for Inventions, and Patent Policy: Sources in the PRO*. At the PRO, is a book entitled *Reference Index to Patents and Inventions* by Bennett Woodcroft, 1855. This lists Patent Numbers 1-14359 covering the period from 2 March 1617 to 1 October 1852 and refers to any relevant books, journals or law reports in which a particular patent is mentioned.

A number of articles have been written on this subject: *The Patent Office* by B. Christmas, Journal of One-Name Studies, Vol.1 No.12 (Autumn 1984): *Researching Registered Designs, Registered Trade Marks and Patents* by Peter Hammond in the journal of the Nottinghamshire FHS, Vol.5 No.5, Oct.1986, and Grant John Harrison contributed one to the previous issue Vol.5 No.4.

PATENT ROLLS see Letters Patent.

PATRONYMICS This term is used to account for one of the ways in which surnames evolved, by taking the father's name, e.g. Johnson = John's son which might become Johns, or even by just using the Christian name John. 'Mac' or 'O' before a name, e.g. MacDonald or O'Connell also means 'son of'. Patronymics are especially common in Wales. Welsh 'ap' is a shortened form of Mab meaning 'son of'.

PATTENMAKERS Makers of wooden shoes with high heels (of wood or metal) designed to raise the feet above the level of mud in the streets. There was a London Livery Company – see *History of the Worshipful Company of Pattenmakers of the City of London* , Charles, revised by Lt.Col. D.A. Davies, 1962.

PAVIORS A pavior was appointed by a town or village to see to the repair of paving stones etc.

PECULIAR see also Inhibition. A parish or group of parishes, not necessarily adjacent or even in the same district or county, which were usually exempt from the testamentary jurisdiction of the archdeaconry and often the consistory court. Ecclesiastical peculiars were often subject to a dean or dean and chapter, though they might be administered by a locally appointed official; a bishop's peculiar might be administered by the consistory court; a number were royal or archbishop's peculiars, usually locally administered; and there were some lay, manorial or collegiate peculiars. Many Peculiars issued their own Marriage Licences and granted probate within their jurisdiction. If you know an area was in a Peculiar, check for separate indexes for these — for example the Borthwick Institute has some 50 separate Peculiar Probate Indexes for Yorkshire.

PEDIGREE see also Recording Data. The word, pedigree, is derived from *pied de grue,* crane's foot, used as a sign rather like an arrowhead to indicate genealogical descent. Normally the term, pedigree, refers to a formal record of ancestry showing several generations linked together in sequence. Such a record may be in the form of a detailed narrative, often with indents to distinguish the generations, or it may be presented as a chart more familiarly known as a "family tree".

Traditional pedigree charts, often found in published family histories, set out the generations in horizontal lines with the earliest at the top of the page and most recent at the bottom. Parents and their children, in the next generation, are linked by vertical lines. This method, among others, is described in some detail by Patrick Palgrave-Moore in his book, *How to Record Your Family Tree,* obtainable from FFHS. Charts based on this method can become very large but if this is inconvenient it is possible to split up the pedigree by drawing several smaller charts which may be suitably cross-referenced.

A very popular method of presentation is the birth-brief chart (see *Family History Record Sheets*). Generations are set out in columns with the youngest on the left. It is customary to enter one individual in the left hand column, his or her two parents in the next, the four grandparents in the next and so on. The column on the extreme right may provide for 16 or 32 or even more ancestors depending on the physical size of the sheet. Such charts are usually numbered to assist cross referencing.

Other options include the circular chart in which the descendant is placed at the centre and all earlier generations are represented as concentric rings, the earliest ancestors being entered on the outer ring. There are further possibilities based on specially designed pictorial charts, computerised systems or record books such as those available from the SOG, IHGS, etc. (q.v.).

During the early stages of pedigree compilation, standard formats may be useful but for final presentation one may need a greater measure of flexibility. For instance it is important to be able to accommodate individuals who cohabit or marry several times through death or divorce of spouse(s). Furthermore it may be necessary to be able to show the marriage of close cousins who ordinarily would appear elsewhere on the chart. There is probably no single method of setting out a chart which is universally applicable so it is very much a matter of making a selection on the basis of personal preference.

PEDLAR see Badger. Derived from the word Ped — a pannier or basket for carrying goods.

PEERAGE G.E. Cokayne has edited the *Complete Peerage* in 13 volumes, with a brief biography of every holder of a peerage since records began. However, this does not deal with ancestors or children. Collin's *Peerage of England* will give you ancestry and descendants, and Volume 9 contains a full index.

Burke's Peerage and *Debrett's Peerage* are the standard works of reference. The former is the more useful to the genealogist since the pedigrees given are more extensive. Both include extinct and dormant peerages.

Burke's *The History of the Commoners* in 4 volumes appeared in 1836 and deals with titled people; the name was changed for the 2nd ed. (1846 to 1849) and is called *The Landed Gentry of Great Britain and Ireland* (3 volumes). It has an index extending to 311 pages in which there are at least 100,000 names. For Scotland, James Balfour Paul's *The Scots Peerage* should be consulted.

Such books as these — there are others — will be found in most Reference Libraries. *A Directory of British Peerages* by Francis L.Leeson, SOG, 1984 lists British titles of nobility and the surnames of families or individuals who bear, or who have borne, them; it is arranged in one continuous alphabetical run. A most useful quick reference book. Price £6.00 inc. p&p.

PENSION see Annuity, Army, Royal Marines and Royal Navy. Pensions were paid to certain state employees. Records are at the PRO.

PERAMBULATIONS This refers to a custom of walking round the parish boundary. These perambulations are sometimes recorded in parish records, and sometimes name those who took part.

In 1861 the Vicar of Lillington, Warwickshire, explained to the 18 parishioners who accompanied him (8 being schoolboys) the purpose of the exercise thus:

'The object, for which it is done, is to prevent our neighbours encroaching upon us, and that we may not encroach upon them, and to save us from the expense of strife and ill-feeling, which future disputes might occasion, if the limits of the parish were not ascertained and kept up. Even God himself thought this such an important question, that he pronounced a curse upon anyone who should remove his neighbour's landmark'.

PERPETUAL CURATE A clerk/minister in a parish or chapelry where there was no regularly endowed vicarage and where tithes were held in whole or in part by a layman: also an incumbent of a parochial chapelry with some rights of baptism, burial etc.

PETTY SESSIONS These were meetings of local justices to deal with minor offences.

PEW RENTS These were a source of 'extra-legal' revenue for the church whereby pews were leased to parishioners in order of social precedence — sometimes the cause of difficulties! For further information see Chapter II of *The Parish Chest* by W.E. Tate.

PEWTERER There was a London Livery Company — see *History of the Worshipful Company of Pewterers* by Charles Welch, 1902.

PHARMACIST see Apothecaries.

PHILLIMORE & CO. LTD. These publishers specialise in books relating to genealogy and allied studies. You will find their catalogue useful. Write to them for a copy at Shopwyke Hall, Chichester, Sussex PO20 6BQ. See *W.P.W. Phillimore — the local historian* by John Astolat, 'Local History' No.17 (March 1988).

PHOTOGRAPHS Many family photograph albums have survived, but rarely has the name of the person portrayed been written on the back, though you will usually find a lot of information about the photographer!

Dating Old Photographs by Robert Pols, FFHS, looks at the early history of photography and considers the identification of the photographs we have inherited and the possibilities of dating them. There is a useful bibliography.

A study of fashion also helps to date a photograph. There is a useful guide to fashions for this purpose in the book entitled *Tracing Your Ancestors* by M. Mander, Paperback-Mayflower Books 1977. *Wedding Fashions 1860-1980*, 1983 and *Fashion A La Carte 1860-1900*, 1985, both by Avril Lansdell, Shire Publications, are another unusual aid to dating photographs.

Family History in Focus ed. by Don Steel and Lawrence Taylor, Lutterworth Press, 1984 is an excellent work. It seeks to help family historians with four main areas in which photography impinges upon their work: building up a photographic archive, identifying and dating the pictures, exploring sources of photographs other than family ones and making a photographic record.

The photographic process used also helps to date it, as does the photographer's 'backdrop' — balustrades, columns and curtains were popular in the 1880s. A good reference library will have useful books on early photography, and the Shire Publication *The Victorian Professional Photographer* will add to your knowledge. The Kodak Company has transferred to Bradford the display of the history of photography previously on view at their Harrow works. It is now housed at the National Museum of Photography, Film & Television, Princes View, Little Horton Lane, Bradford BD5 0TR, W. Yorks.

There is much to be said for plundering your family album for identified photographs for inclusion in your family history, but make a pencilled note in the space of what you have removed, since the order of the photographs may have a significance. You may well consider having your old photographs copied — often a faded brown photo can be improved in the process. Most reputable photographers will undertake to do this at a reasonable cost.

A very useful addition to your Family History is a photographic record of the places with which your family was associated. You should enquire at the appropriate Library or Record Office. Many of them do have photographic collections and you can obtain photocopies.

The Francis Frith Collection is a remarkable record of Victorian England. Francis Frith was for almost 40 years the most prolific of English photographers and the collection has more than 60,000 of his original glass negatives illustrating over 2000 towns and villages in Britain. Prints produced from these plates are outstanding for their quality. Details of membership of The Frith Collectors Guild or a list of prints available can be obtained from The Francis Frith Collection, Charlton Road, Andover, Hampshire SP10 3LE. Send a *stamp* or 3 IRCs but no envelope.

However, Birmingham Public Library have purchased the Francis Frith negative archive (which includes those of the prints at Andover); contact The Librarian, History and Geography Dept, Birmingham Reference Library, Chamberlain Square, Birmingham B3 3HQ if you have a specific enquiry.

The Royal Photographic Society's Historical Group, 38 Sutton Road, Watford, Herts WD1 2QF has lists of photographers who worked in various towns. Details from secretary on receipt of sae or 3 IRCs. *Directory of London Photographers 1841-1908* by Michael Pritchard, 2nd ed. 1994, PhotoResearch, price £14.95 plus £1.50 p&p from ALLM Systems and Marketing, 21 Beechcroft Road, Bushey, Hertfordshire, WD2 2JU.

Having assembled and identified your photographs some thought should be given to their future. Good advice is given in *Caring for your family photographs at home* by A. Linkman, Documenting Photography Archive, 1991. Price £4.75 inc. p&p from SOG.

If you wish to create your own photographic archives, useful tips may be gained from *Recording The Past – A Photographer's Handbook* by Eric Houlder, published by Local History, 3 Devonshire Promenade, Nottingham NG7 2DS, 1988, price £5.45 inc. p&p. This publication is a revised and enlarged version of the eight articles written for *Local History* and which appeared in issues 6 to 13.

Photographs and Local History by George Oliver, Batsford, 1990. Price £12.95. The chapter on interpretation and identification of photographs is of particular value but for the family historian who may not want to purchase this book see the author's article *Using old photographs* 'Local History' Nos. 20 and 21 (Dec 1988/April 1989).

PHYSICIAN see Medical Profession.

PINFOLD Also known as a Pound, this was an area in which stray animals were put. They were released on payment of a fine by the owner. The parish officer in charge was known as a Pinder, a Pinfold, a Poundkeeper or a Punder.

PINHORN'S see Indexes.

PIPE ROLLS Basically they were accounts rendered by the sheriffs to the Exchequer with details of Crown revenues from rents etc. They survive as a continuous series from 1155 to the 1830s although there are some for the period 1120-30. The Rolls are in the PRO.

PLACE NAMES If you discover there is a place corresponding to a surname in which you are interested, do not make the mistake of thinking it was named after one of your ancestors. This was rarely if ever the case. Place names usually date back to a period well before surnames were in use. It is more likely that one of your ancestors originally came from that place.

There is an English Place Name Society, headquarters at the School of English Studies, The University, Nottingham, NG7 2RD. The Society has published a series of volumes on English County Place-Names which will be found in most Reference Libraries. Counties so far not dealt with are Durham, Hampshire, Herefordshire, Kent, Lancashire, Norfolk, Northumberland, Rutland, Shropshire and Suffolk. Yorkshire has separate volumes for each of the Ridings. There are also several volumes dealing with aspects of the subject, and a booklet on Field-Names in the Borough of Ealing.

Discovering Place Names is one of the Shire Publications (q.v.) series and a general introduction to the subject. For the more serious student *A Reader's Guide to the Place*

Names of the United Kingdom by Jeffrey Spittal and John Field, 1990. Price £30.00 from Local History Bookshop, 37 Crookes Lane, Carlton, Nr. Barnsley, South Yorkshire S71 3JR. Each country, and county, is treated separately with three detailed appendices. Cross referenced and indexed.

PLANTATION INDENTURES Justices of the Peace were responsible after 1682 for issuing indentures for work on plantations in America or the West Indies.

PLEA ROLLS see Court of Common Pleas.

PLEDGEHOUSE A prison where debtors were kept.

PLUMBER A well established Guild existed as early as 1365, and there was a London Livery Company. See *Short History of the Worshipful Company of Plumbers*, 1965 (Privately printed).

POLAND The Polish Interest Group within the Catholic FHS collects and indexes records of Poles in the UK and helps those with Polish ancestry research. Details from the Co-ordinator, Mr Antoni W. Szachnowski, Woodcote, Laurel Grove, Penge, London SE20 8QJ.

Kazimierz Ameryk is secretary of Towarzystwo Genealogiczno-Heraldyczne Societas Genealogica Ac Heraldica, Wodna 27, Palac Gorkow 61-781 Poznan, Poland.

The Society is not able to answer specific research enquiries but all correspondence is available to members so that individual contacts can be established. General enquiries as to availability of sources etc. will be dealt with. Its journal contains English language summaries of articles.

Some Sources for Polish Genealogy by B. Klec-Pilewski appeared in Gen. Mag. Vol.16 No.4 (Dec 1969), and *Look for your Polish Forefathers* by Dr J. Szczepanski in North West Kent FHS journal Vol.5 No.1 (March 1989).

POLICE RECORDS The Metropolitan Police Force was formed in 1829. In 1835 the Municipal Corporations Act was passed allowing cities and boroughs to form police forces. The County Police Act was passed in 1839 allowing counties to form forces. In 1856 the County and Borough Police Act was passed compelling all cities and boroughs and counties in England and Wales to have police forces.

Sources of information are such publications as the *Police Almanac*, the *Police Review*, the (now defunct) *Police Chronicle* and various local police histories, the latter most probably available for consultation at the local Reference Library.

Police Forces themselves can supply information, in varying degrees, as can local record offices. The City of London Police have registers of the force since 1832; write to City of London Police Record Office, 26 Old Jewry, London EC2R 8OJ.

See also PRO Records Information leaflets 53 *Metropolitan Police Records of Service*; 11 *Records of the Royal Irish Constabulary* and Family Fact Sheet 8 *Tracing an Ancestor in the Metropolitan Police*.

For particulars of memorabilia, uniforms, weapons, headgear and such like write to the Metropolitan Police Historical Museum, c/o Room 1334, New Scotland Yard, London SW1V OBG.

The Royal Military Police, Roussillon Barracks, Chichester, Sussex PO19 4BL, keep their own records and there do not appear to be any records in the PRO for the police of the various railway companies. There are, however, some records for the South African Constabulary under Colonial Office.

A comprehensive list of approximate dates of formation of county police forces can be found in *The Local Historian's Encyclopedia* (q.v.).

The Police History Society has published *Notes for Family Historians*, by Les Waters, 1987, £2.50 inc. p&p obtainable from the Secretary Mr M. Stallion, 18 Corner Chase, Leigh on Sea, Essex: and *A Guide to archives of police forces of England and Wales*, now out of print but can be seen in some libraries and record offices.

See *Like a skeleton?* by Joy Lodey, FTM Vol.4 No.6 (April 1988) and *The Policeman* by Susan Pearl, FTM Vol.6 No.12 (Oct 1990). The former article is especially interesting and useful for its many references to *The Police Gazette and Hue and Cry* (published every three weeks from the late 18th century).

Brewin Books, Doric House, Church Street, Studley, Warwickshire B80 7LG, publish a series of County Police Histories. Those to date deal with West Mercia, Metropolitan Police, Shropshire, Northamptonshire, Mons to Messines & Beyond (Military history). Details from the publisher but prices range from £6 to £12.

For general information on the history of policing in England and Wales see *A history of police in England and Wales* by T.A. Critchley, Constable, 2nd ed. 1978 and *The English police: a political and social history*, by Clive Emsley, Harvester Wheatsheaf, 1991.

It is worth noting that police were at times empowered to issue licences which could yield useful information (e.g. Chimney Sweepers Act, 1875).

In Scotland an Act of 1857 established county forces in a similar way to those outlined in the legislation for England and Wales in 1856. The Scottish Police College Library, Tulliallan Castle, Kincardine, Alloa, Scotland can be used by the public. Scottish police records are held either at the Scottish Record Office or by Regional Councils.

POLL BOOKS see also Electoral Registers. These are lists of those who voted in Parliamentary elections. They are arranged by county. There is a great deal of variation in their arrangement i.e. they could be arranged alphabetically by parishes, by hundreds, by polling booths, by wards etc.

An excellent aid to using these records is *Poll Books c1696-1872: A Directory to Holdings in Great Britain* by Jeremy Gibson and Colin Rogers, FFHS.

It is as well to know which hundred a parish is in before starting to search Poll Books. Lewis's *Topographical Dictionary* will give you this information.

You will find copies of these Poll Books in large reference libraries and CROs; the SOG has a fine collection and has published *Directories and Poll Books in the library of The Society of Genealogists*, 1989, price £3.25 inc. p&p..

Brian Brooks and Michael Davies, partners in the firm of Brooks, Davies & Co., Genealogists, Cambria House, 37 Pembroke Avenue, Hove, Sussex BN3 5DB, are publishing on microfiche their large collection of directories and poll books. In excess of 112 publications have been produced so far. Send sae or 2 IRCs for details.

POLL TAX This is a tax which can list not just the head of the household but also his family and servants. It was raised in 1660, 1667, 1678, 1689, 1691, 1694 and 1697. Not many of the records survive but those that do are mainly in CROs though the PRO has a few lists, and, more frequently, lists of defaulters, which, though only relating to a very few people, give interesting evidence of mobility.

See Jeremy Gibson's *The Hearth Tax, Other Later Stuart Tax Lists etc.*, FFHS.

POOR LAW (OLD) see also Apprentices and Boards of Guardians. Administered by the Parish after the Act of 1597 which authorised them to levy a rate to be paid by those who could afford to do so. The collection of the rate was the duty of an 'Overseer' who also gave relief to those in need, either in money or in kind. Poor Law Documents and Overseers' Accounts can be a very useful record of people living in the parish since they encompass a wide range of subjects such as Settlement Certificates and Examinations, Removal Orders, Apprenticeship Indentures, Quarter Sessions Books and Church-wardens Accounts.

In the FFHSs series *An introduction to . . .* the subject is dealt with most thoroughly in *Poor Law Documents Before 1834* by Anne Cole. The author quite rightly cautions that, "It should not be assumed that these records are only of use to researchers with proven pauper ancestors. Those involved with local administration of the Poor Law were certainly not paupers, a very large number of families lived from hand to mouth – an accident could cause the family to become dependent upon poor relief, if only temporarily".

Anne Cole's publication cites further reading but see also *Annals of the Poor* by Eve McLaughlin, obtainable from FTM price £1.55 inc. p & p and the useful reference book *The English Poor Law* by Michael E.Rose, published by David & Charles in the *Sources for Social and Economic History* series.

The duties of Overseers passed to the Boards of Guardians set up in 1834, the Overseers then becoming assessors and collectors. The Rating and Valuation Act of 1925 finally abolished the office of Overseer.

POPULATION The population of England and Wales in 1801 was about 9 million. Prior to this there are no reliable statistics to guide us, but it is likely that the population was considerably smaller than this. Between 1800 and 1850 the population doubled. As a result of the Industrial Revolution there was a great shift of population from the countryside to the towns. Between 1770 and 1831 Liverpool multiplied its population five times, and towns such as Manchester, Birmingham and Bristol saw similar increases.

Prior to the Industrial Revolution, however, there was much more mobility of population than was originally believed. In pre-industrial England almost half of the population were servants of one kind or another (if we regard a labourer as a servant). Labourers were hired annually at the hiring fairs and moved to their employer's area.

You are advised to read *Sources for Internal and External Migration,* transcript of a paper delivered by Anthony J. Camp to the XIIIth International Congress of Genealogical & Heraldic Sciences, London 1976: 'Family History', Vol.12 No.93/94 (Nov 1982).

There is a thriving Local Population Studies Society; its journal carries excellent articles and statistical data, the results of many of its researches. Details from Col. Sir David Cooke Bt., 8 Royal Crescent, Harrogate, HG2 8AB. Please send sae or 2 IRCs.

PORTRAITS The National Portrait Gallery's Heinz Archive and Library was opened in 1993. The Archive dates back to 1856 and can assist research on the Gallery's collection of portraits. There are extensive files of engravings, photographs and reproductions of portraits in collections world-wide, arranged by sitter and artist. The Archive also houses most of the Gallery's portrait photograph collection of more than 150,000 original prints and negatives.

The Library contains some 30,000 books and a number of special collections.

The Archive and Library is open by appointment Tue to Sat 10.00am-5.00pm. The Gallery is open Mon to Sat 10.00am-6.00pm, Sun 12.00-6.00pm (Tel; 0171 306 0055). A Curator is available to give opinions *not valuations* on British portraits on Wednesday afternoons 2.00pm-5.00pm. No appointment necessary.

Written enquiries should be sent to the Research Assistant, Heinz Archive and Library, National Portrait Gallery, St Martin's Place, London WC2H OHE.

Silhouette Portraits were popular in the early 19th century. A splendid collection can be seen in the National Portrait Gallery, London. There is a catalogue of 5200 named and dated English Silhouettes by August Edouart (1789-1861); the Victoria and Albert Museum has information on him.

POSTCARDS Early postcards will greatly enhance your family history. The first picture postcards in this country were delivered by the Post Office in September 1894 and were immediately popular, with more than two million sent every week. (Plain cards had been in circulation for 20 years.) One could wish that they had been introduced earlier. However, if you have an early 20th century postcard of, say, a village street, it is likely that the buildings were erected perhaps hundreds of years earlier, and that the scene has changed little from what it was in earlier centuries.

If you have an old postcard album in the family, examine the backs of the cards carefully. There may be family news on them, and even the addresses could be helpful.

Handle the cards carefully — some may be quite valuable. Certain sought- after cards could fetch up to £25 each at auction. Real photographic street scenes with plenty of animation i.e. people, vehicles etc. sell for up to £5. Pretty scenes are not much collected. It is unfortunate that the type we need for our family histories are usually the expensive ones!

Picture Postcard Monthly is published by Reflections of a Bygone Age (Brian & Mary Lund), 15 Debdale Lane, Keyworth, Nottingham NG12 5HT. It contains many adverts by dealers of postcards for sale, and there is a 'Postcards wanted' section in which you can advertise for cards of the area in which your ancestors lived.

The subscription to the magazine is modest and further details can be obtained from the above address. *Discovering Picture Postcards* is one of the Shire Publications series (q.v.) which will also add to your knowledge.

Postcards of views all over the world are held at the Valentine Archive, St Andrews University Library, North Street, St Andrews, Scotland KY16 9JR.

See also *Dictionary of Picture Postcards in Britain 1894-1939*, by A.W. Coysh, Antique Collectors Club Ltd, Woodbridge, Suffolk, 1984.

POST OFFICE see also Telephone Directories. Some records date back to the 17th century and cover every aspect of the Post Office's history and personnel. As well as information on former employees (beginning 1831), other records document the development of telecommunications and the provision of telegraph, telephone and related services in the United Kingdom and the Commonwealth. Some may be subject to the '30 year' rule. See *A Guide to Post Office Archives* compiled by Jean Farrugia, 1988.

The Post Office Archives and Records Centre is at Freeling House, Mount Pleasant Complex, London EC1A 1BB (Tel 0171 320 7443). The Centre is open 9.00am-4.15pm Mon-Fri; the entrance is in Phoenix Place, just off Mount Pleasant at the rear of the Sorting Office. No appointment necessary and there is no charge to use the search room; a large number of research aids, including subject indexes, are available.

POULTER A dealer in poultry and game. There was a London Livery Company, see *The Worshipful Company of Poulters of the City of London*, by P.E. Jones, 1965, and *The Poulters of London Booklet* by J.K. Melling, 1977.

POUND see Pinfold.

PREROGATIVE COURTS OF CANTERBURY AND YORK (PCC & PCY) see also Doctors' Commons. Prerogative Courts of the Archbishops of Canterbury and York had superior jurisdiction over all diocesan courts and had to be used in cases where a will etc. involved property in 2 or more dioceses. They were sometimes used in preference to a diocesan court as a status symbol. Canterbury took precedence over York. PCC wills are in the PRO, PCY records in Borthwick Institute of Historical Research (York University), St Anthony's Hall, Peasholme Green, York YO1 2PW.

See *An Index to the Wills Proved in the Prerogative Court of Canterbury: 1750-1800* edited by Anthony J. Camp, published in 6 volumes by the SOG (q.v.). Further details on application to them.

Pinhorns hold an index to all wills and admons proved in the PCC for the period 1801-1809, inclusive, for surnames beginning with the letter B. Details of search charges in exchange for sae or 3 IRCs.

PRESBYTERIAN The Presbyterians followed the doctrines of the Reformation leader John Calvin, and it was John Knox, who had worked in Geneva with Calvin, who was largely responsible for the spread of Presbyterian ideas in Scotland, where it became the leading church. Churches were also set up in England and Wales.

In 1972 the Presbyterian and Congregational churches in England merged to form the United Reformed Church. This led to a merger of The Presbyterian Historical Society of England with the Congregational Historical Society, with the new name of The United Reformed Church Historical Society, with Headquarters at 86 Tavistock Place, London WC1H 9RT.

After 1840 English Presbyterian registers were deposited with the Registrar General and, with other nonconformist registers, are in the PRO.

The Catholic Apostolic Church was a little known branch of the Presbyterian movement. Information about records can be obtained from The Trustees, Catholic Apostolic Church, 2 The Cloisters, Gordon Square, London WC1H OAG.

See *Presbyterian Church Records (in Ireland)* by Paul Gorry, FTM Vol.4 No.5 (March 1988) and SOG publication *My Ancestors were English Presbyterians/ Unitarians: How can I find out more about them?* by Alan Ruston, 1993. £4.00 inc. p&p.

PRESENTMENTS see Churchwardens' Presentments.

PRIESTS see Roman Catholics.

PRINTERS The Seditious Societies Act of 1799 required printing presses to be licensed by Justices. Records give names and addresses and owners (to 1869) and will be found in Quarter Sessions Records (q.v.). Do not confuse Publishing Printers with Textile Printers.

PRISON HULK Body of dismantled ship used as a floating prison especially in the early 19th century. See *The English Prison Hulks*, W. Branch Johnson, revised 1970.

PRISONERS OF WAR With some exceptions, most records in the PRO about Prisoners of War before 1914 do not give lists of names or detailed information. See PRO Records Information leaflets 72 *Prisoners of War 1660-1919: Documents in the PRO* and 111 *Prisoners of War and Displaced Persons 1939-1953: Documents in the PRO*, both of which should be consulted.

The IWM Library, Lambeth Road, London SE1 6HZ has a great deal of material including a selection of books the Series title of which is *Tracing Individual Service Records and Medal Citations*; they are general guides to official documents held by themselves and elsewhere. Price £3 each, of particular interest might be 15F *Prisoners of War*

For the French Revolutionary and Napoleonic Wars (1793-1815) there are lists of British Prisoners in France and elsewhere forwarded by the agent for prisoners in Paris. Most prisoners were naval and civilian internees. There are registers of French prisoners in Britain and enemy prisoners on parole but there is no central index for these. In 1813 a register of American prisoners of war in Britain was compiled.

French and American prisoners of war were brought into Plymouth in the early 1800s and later transferred to the new prison at Princetown, Dartmoor. The Americans largely built the church of St Michael's, Princetown, which has a stained glass memorial window dedicated to them in 1910.

After his release Charles Andrews, an American prisoner, published a book entitled *The Prisoners's Memoirs of Dartmoor Prison*. A long list of prisoners who died in this prison 1813-1815 is included, with personal details. There is a copy of the book in Plymouth Local Studies Library, Tavistock Road, Plymouth. See *Prisoners of Dartmoor* by Pamela Magill, FTM Vol.5 No.10 (Aug 1989).

About 8% of the total of the seafaring manpower of the United States — approximately 7500 Navy and private seamen — were held as prisoners for at least part of the war 1812-14. In addition about 1000 United States Army or militia personnel were captured and held prisoner. The records relating to those taken prisoner by British Forces during the war are in the PRO and some entries in the relevant General Entry Books for American Prisoners of War are quite detailed.

A Napoleonic Prisoners' Index covering the period Sep 1803 to Nov 1814 was compiled by the late Madame Margaret Audin. The index includes 650 chronological entries from the births, marriages and deaths in Verdun, Meuse, during that period. It was to Verdun, a garrison town in Eastern France, that Napoleon sent British residents in France during the Continental Blockade.

There is also an alphabetical index covering prisoners of war, Army, Royal or Merchant Navy, mostly officers and a few civilians. The index includes wives of prisoners and mothers of prisoners' acknowledged children.

Mr Patrick Pontet, 31 Collingwood Walk, Admiral's Way, Andover, Hants SP10 1PU will advise on access to the Audin Index. Please enclose sae or 2 IRCs.

Some official material relating to Russian prisoners in British hands during the Crimean War (1854-1856) exists; records of the Russian Orthodox Church in London give lists of Russian prisoners (in Russian) who received money.

There are registers of Boer War (1899-1902) prisoners arranged by place of confinement (e.g. Natal) and correspondence concerning Dutch, German and French prisoners has survived.

The International Committee of the Red Cross in Geneva keeps lists of all known prisoners of war and internees of all nationalities in both the World Wars (1914-1918), (1939-1945). These are housed in the International Red Cross Library in Geneva and at time of publication there is no public access or enquiry service. Please send sae or 2 IRCs to the Administrator of the FFHS who will advise on current situation. See 'The Central Tracing Agency of the International Committee of the Red Cross' by C.R. Chapman. FTM Vol.10 No.7 (May 1994).

In 1990, J.B. Hayward & Son, The Old Rectory, Polstead, Colchester, Suffolk CO66 5AE, reprinted 3 volumes listing prisoners of war 1939-1945: Vol.1 British Army (£38), Vol.2 Naval & Air Forces of Great Britain and The Empire (£22), Vol.3 Armies and Other Land Forces of The Empire (£28). A set is available at the SOG (q.v.); alternatively try your local library.

During the First World War deaths of prisoners of war and internees, in military and non-military hospitals in enemy and occupied territory, were notified to the British authorities. These certificates can be consulted at the PRO.

Lists of British and Commonwealth servicemen who were prisoners of war in Korea (1950-1953) can also be consulted at the PRO.

PRISONS and PRISONERS see also Crime and Criminals and House of Correction. Up to the 19th century the main function of a prison was very different from what we understand today. They were not principally for punishment or the protection of society since so many offences were punishable by transportation or hanging The occupants were mainly prisoners awaiting trial or sentence or debtors waiting for their debts to be cleared by whatever means. Very early prisons were located in castles, large houses and fortified gateways. *The Local Historian's Encyclopaedia* (q.v.) has a list of locations of some, with more specific references to others and only general references to records.

Prison administration was transferred from the counties to the Home Office in 1877; whilst there should have been a corresponding transfer of archives some may still remain with the CROs.

Records of prisoners in many gaols in the period 1770-1894 are at the PRO but only those over 100 years old may be inspected.

In the PRO there are 207 large volumes classified as Quarterly Prison Returns, dated from Sep 1824 to March 1876. They contain the names of convicts with their offences, places and dates of conviction and periods of sentence. The returns are from Prison Hulks (q.v.) as well as from ordinary prisons. Unfortunately there is no index! However, the names of all prisons and hulks covered have been listed and a copy is in the PRO.

Calendars of prisoners awaiting trial exist in connection with the Assizes, and copies may be found in CROs.

Prisoners from the King's Bench, Marshalsea are in Class PRIS, PRO. The Corporation of London Record Office has a card index of people in London debtors' prisons from the mid-1700s.

A missing person in a family group in any of the Census returns could be explained by the fact that the person was in prison (assuming that no death has been traced) though it is equally likely that the person was working away from home.

An article by Colin J. Parry on *Prisons and Census Returns* appeared in Gen. Mag. Vol.20 No.4 (Dec 1980).

PROBATE (Grant of) see also Wills. The official proving of a will by the Probate Office. Procedure whereby the executor(s) is formally given the right to administer the estate of the deceased.

PROCTOR A person employed in civil or ecclesiastical causes, equivalent to a solicitor or attorney at Common Law. Also a University official at Oxford or Cambridge. Sometimes used to refer to a person licensed to collect alms for hospitals.

There is an index of Proctors (Ecclesiastical Lawyers) 1558-1910, comprising over 600 named proctors all of whom worked as attorneys in the Ecclesiastical Court at Doctors' Commons. Enquiries to Mr John Titford, Yew Tree Farm, Hallfieldgate, Higham, Derbys DE55 6AA, enclosing sae or 2 IRCs.

PROFESSIONAL RESEARCHER see also AGRA, Ireland and Scotland. There are times when it is convenient to employ a qualified researcher to consult records in some distant repository. There are two kinds of researchers – genealogists and record agents. The foreword to the List of Members of AGRA explains the difference as follows:

'Broadly speaking the genealogist directs research while the record agent undertakes it. The genealogist acts as a consultant, settling a line of enquiry, initiating, supervising and participating in the work it entails. He then reports and suggests possible lines of further research. The record agent's work lies in searching specified records for particular information which may be required by a genealogist, historian or biographer. Many members of the Association act in both these capacities as the need arises.'

The Foreword continues: 'Having chosen a genealogist or record agent from the list of members, the enquirer should send a preliminary letter setting out the problem and stating clearly the known facts, particularly dates and places of birth, marriage and death if known, together with some indication of occupation ...'

Members of the Association are subject to a rigid code of practice with which they undertake to comply when accepting membership. It stresses the need for a high standard of work and complete confidentiality. To obtain a copy, see under AGRA.

An article by the then Secretary of AGRA entitled *Employing a Professional Researcher: A practical Guide* appeared in Gen. Mag. Vol.20 No.7 (Sep 1981) (see also SOG Leaflet No.28 of the same name).

It was expanded upon in FTM Vol 1. Nos.3,4 & 5 (Mar-Apl/May- June/July-Aug 1985) and *The Professional Approach,* FTM Vol.9 No.5 (Mar 1993) was the report of a day seminar on the subject held at the IHGS (q.v.).

Anyone considering becoming a 'professional' is advised to read SOG Leaflet No.5 *Genealogy As A Career*.

PROJECTS see Federation of Family History Societies.

PROTESTATION RETURNS In 1641 Parliament organised a national protest against 'an arbitrary and tyrannical government' – aimed at Charles I. All males of 18 years of age or over were required to sign a declaration of belief in the Protestant Religion, Allegiance to the King and support for the Rights and Privileges of Parliament.

These Protestation Returns have been described in an article by L.W. Lawson Edwards in Gen. Mag. Vol.19 No.3 (Sep 1977) as 'the nearest we have for England, to a male adult census prior to 1841'. The places for which Returns survive are listed in *Protestation Returns 1641-42 and Other Contemporary Listings* by Jeremy Gibson and Alan Dell, FFHS. This gives details of all published and other transcripts. Most of the Returns are in the House of Lords Record Office (q.v.), arranged within county by hundred. Survival is sporadic, some counties having good collections, some just a few and some none at all. The (Collection for) Distressed Protestants in Ireland 1642 (q.v.) complements the Returns and is listed in the same Guide.

PROVINCE The diocese over which an archbishop has authority, i.e. before 1858, in England and Wales, the provinces of Canterbury and York and, in Ireland, the province of Armagh. The prerogative courts of archbishops had superior jurisdiction to all others, and Canterbury was superior to York.

PUBLICATIONS see also Family Tree Magazine and Local History. Most family historians, in the course of their researches, find it useful to build up a collection of reference books relating to family history and genealogy – ranging from general books on how to trace ancestors to specialised publications dealing with particular aspects of research or with certain geographical areas.

As any researcher soon discovers, buying books can be very expensive! The FFHS, to assist researchers throughout the world, commissions or approves publications covering many aspects of family history research and the whereabouts of relevant records. Most of these booklets cost less than £5 including postage even if sent overseas airmail.

Many of these publications have been referred to throughout this book, and a comprehensive list complete with prices can be obtained from the Publications Manager of the FFHS, 2-4 Killer St, Ramsbottom, Bury, Lancs BL0 9BZ in exchange for sae or 3 IRCs. A current list of publications can also be seen in the twice-yearly editions of *Family History News and Digest*.

In addition, most of the member societies of the FFHS produce their own publications. As well as a regular (usually quarterly) journal, these frequently include members' interests directories, surname indexes to the 1851 census for all or part of the area covered by the society, transcripts of Parish Registers, copies of Monumental Inscriptions and so on. Most of these are available for purchase by interested family historians and further details and contact addresses can be found in *Current Publications By Member Societies* and *Current Publications on Microfiche*, compiled by John Perkins and obtainable from the FFHS.

PUBLIC RECORD OFFICE Throughout this book there are constant references to the amazing collection of national records held by this institution. There is a free full colour introductory leaflet about the office available from the Press and Public Relations Department, PRO, Chancery Lane, London WC2A 1LR (Tel 0181 876 3444).

We make frequent mention of the many helpful leaflets published by the PRO. These are available without charge from the PRO Shop. Each leaflet fills on average about 4 A4 sized sheets; some are considerably longer.

See PRO General Information leaflets 1 *The Public Record Office*, 14 *Access to Public Records*, 27 *Rules of the Reading Room* and 31 *Information for Readers*. Appendix II gives a complete listing of leaflets available in the Records, General and Census Information Series plus Family Fact Sheets.

One leaflet you should certainly obtain is PRO Records Information 14, *Family History in England and Wales: Guidance for Beginners*; Programme/Outings Secretaries should consult General Information Series 21 *Family History Parties Visiting Kew* and teachers might find useful General Information 20 *Teachers and the PRO*.

The PRO does not undertake genealogical research. Readers must either visit the search rooms or employ a record agent. Photocopies can be ordered by post if *specific* reference to a document is quoted. See PRO General Information leaflet 19 *Reprographic Copies of Records in the PRO*.

Tracing Your Ancestors in the Public Record Office by Amanda Bevan and Andrea Duncan, HMSO, 4th ed. 1990. Price £6.95 (£8.40 inc. p&p from FFHS). This book is excellent value for money, you should certainly invest in a copy. Not only will it save you valuable time in locating source material, it gives a summary of the subject matter with an account of the composition of the documents.

Never Been Here Before: a first time guide for family historians at the Public Record Office by Jane Cox, 1993. Written with the complete novice in mind this is a delightful book, wonderfully (and wittily) illustrated and should be on every family historian's bookshelf. This is PRO Readers' Guide No.4, £4.95 counter price or obtainable from the FFHS at £6.15 inc. p&p. (Jane Cox also edited *The Nations' Memory: A Pictorial Guide to the Public Record Office* HMSO, 1988.)

The PRO have launched a series of basic guides to their records. Already published are:

Making Use of the Census by Susan Lumas, 2nd ed. 1993, £4.75.
Army Records for Family Historians by Simon Fowler, 2nd ed. 1993, £4.75.
Records of the Militia from 1757 by Garth Thomas, 1993, £3.95.
Tudor Taxation Records by Richard Hoyle, 1994, £5.95.
Using Manorial Records by Mary Ellis in conjunction with the Royal Commission for Historical Manuscripts, 1994, £6.95.

Forthcoming titles in this series include *Maps for Family History*, *Records of the Royal Air Force*, *Education Records Explained*, *Guide to Railway Records in the PRO*, *'Never Complain, Never Explain': a guide to the State Papers Foreign and the records of the Foreign Office 1500-1960*, *How To Find Prerogative Court of Canterbury Wills and Administrations* and *Sources for the History of Nonconformity*.

The *Guide to the Contents of the Public Record Office*, in 3 volumes, is somewhat out of date but still the major source for some of the earlier records. It should be available in most reference libraries. The *Current Guide* briefly describes all the holdings of the PRO. Its three parts consist of: administrative histories of each government department, a description of each class of record, their content and location, and an index to parts 1 and 2. Copies are available in the Reading Rooms. It is also available on microfiche in larger libraries elsewhere. Much of the information in the

Current Guide of interest to family historians has been gathered together in Stella Colwell's *Dictionary of Genealogical Sources in the PRO*, 1992, price £20. See also by Stella Colwell *Family Roots: discovering the past in the PRO*, 1991, Weidenfeld & Nicolson. Obtainable from the SOG price £16.80 inc. p&p.

The records were originally held at the PRO Building in Chancery Lane, London WC2A 1LR. Most, but by no means all, were transferred to a new specially designed building in Ruskin Avenue, Kew, Richmond, Surrey TW9 4DU, which was opened in October 1977. See Appendix I: Division of Record Groups Between Kew and Chancery Lane (PRO General Information leaflet 22 *Division of Records*).

Also, PRO General Information leaflet 23 *Are You in the Right Place?*, 29 *How to order documents using the computer*, 5 *How to use the Reading Rooms at Chancery Lane*, 10 *Ordering Documents at Chancery Lane by computer* 2 *How to use the Reading Rooms at Kew* and 3 *Means of Reference at Kew*, and Family Fact Sheet 1 *How to Obtain a Document Reference*.

It is very **important to note**, however, that **Chancery Lane will be closing during 1996** and the records are gradually being transferred to a new extension at Kew. Only the census will remain in London where there will be a central microfilm reading room, the site of which is still to be decided. Between 1994 and 1996 there is likely to be considerable disruption to services at Kew as building work on the new extension progresses. Car parking space in particular may be limited. It would be worthwhile in advance of a visit to ring the office to check on the current position.

A radical new computerised document ordering system was introduced in 1993 – the Records Information System or RIS. Reader's Tickets are now bar coded and are essential for access to the reading rooms through the security barriers and for ordering documents. Obtaining a ticket is relatively simple! They are issued in the PRO shop, *not by post*. British visitors must take some form of identity; overseas visitors need to present their passport.

And to think it seems no time at all since we were reading an account of a visit to the new PRO soon after it opened in 1978! (See F.L. Leeson in Gen. Mag. Vol.19 No.5 (March 1978) & Vol.19 No.7 (Sep 1978).)

The PRO shops sell a wide range of family history books and other items. The Office produces an informative, illustrated quarterly *Readers' Bulletin*, which keeps users fully up to date with what is happening at the PRO. Copies are free.

PRO-phile is the journal of The Friends of the Public Record Office who hold regular meetings and undertake voluntary work on indexing. New members are welcomed and the subscription is modest. Details from The Secretary, Friends of the PRO, c/o Public Record Office, Chancery Lane etc.

The Census Room has instituted a family historians' Contact Book – an indexed ledger in which you can write the surnames in which you are interested, along with your own name and address. A member of staff will advise you where to find the book if it is not available at the entrance.

The List and Index Society (formed in 1966) publishes Lists and Indexes to records in the PRO; available in most large Reference Libraries; there is a full set of volumes in the Greater London Record Office.

The Records of the Nation: The Public Record Office 1838 to 1988: The British Record Society 1888 to 1982, edited by G.H. Martin and Peter Spufford, Boydell Press and the British Record Society, 1982, price £35. In four sections of essays this is an historical account of two of the most important organisations concerned with the material of the nation's history.

It should also be remembered that a number of British National Archives — or at least summaries of them — have been printed. Most are of early records. They are listed in Sectional List 24 issued by HMSO. Major libraries such as those in large cities have these printed records. Birmingham has virtually a complete collection. They are enormously expensive. The Calendar of State Papers Domestic for the reign of Charles I alone in 23 volumes cost £280 — and that was in 1974.

Having discovered for yourself what a wealth of material is available to the researcher you would do well to heed John Titford in FTM Vol.7 Nos.7&8 (May & June 1991) *The public records: Don't take them for granted!*.

PUBLIC SCHOOLS see Education.

QUAKERS Founded by George Fox, there were meetings of 'The Friends' as they were called in the 1650s.

Before handing over their registers to the Registrar General in 1840 as required by the Royal Commission of 1837, the Quakers indexed all their entries (over 500,000). This index is now on microfilm at the Religious Society of Friends, Friends' House, Euston Road, London NW1 2BJ. (Many CROs have copies of this 'Digest' for their areas.) Generally Quaker records are more detailed than those of Anglicans at that time and the Digests might reveal much more information than you would expect. Quakers did not believe in the baptism of children but they did record births and continued to perform marriages after 1754; their records often contain the names of almost all those present at the ceremony. Much Quaker material appears in Quarter Sessions because Quakers refused to pay Tithes.

Information leaflets on genealogical sources available at Friends' House will be sent on request to the librarian at the above address. Opening times are 10.00am-5.00pm, Tues-Fri and it is advisable to make an appointment to use a microfilm reader.

The Friends' Historical Society has published a Journal for many years, and this is worth consulting by anyone with Quaker connections. Minutes of Quaker meetings often contain references to individuals including 'sufferings', assistance given to emigrate, or movements to other parts of the country. Their archives are well described in an article by R.S. Mortimer in the 'Amateur Historian' Vol.3 page 55 (Winter 1956/7).

The SOG have published *My Ancestors were Quakers* by Edward H. Milligan & Malcolm J. Thomas, 1983, price £3.10 inc. p&p.

See also Vol. II of National Index of Parish Registers *Sources for Nonconformist Genealogy and Family History*.

The Quaker Family History Society was formed in 1993; for further details contact Mr Richard Moore, 1 Cambridge Close, Lawn, Swindon, Wilts SN3 1JQ.

QUARRYING see Mining.

QUARTER DAYS Days on which quarterly payments are due, tenancies begin and end etc. In England — Lady Day (25 March), Midsummer Day (24 June), Michaelmas (29 September), and Christmas Day (25 December): in Scotland — Candlemas (2 February), Whit Sunday (15 May), Lammas (1 August), Martinmas (11 November).

QUARTER SESSIONS The county justices met four times a year and dealt with such crimes as theft, assault, riot, poaching and even murder but not with civil cases, treason or forgery.

A great many aspects of local administration were dealt with by the Quarter Sessions, and many records relating to these can be of help to family historians and provide useful clues. You are advised to see what has been deposited in your CRO. Below are just some of the documents you may find. Most of them date from the 18th and early 19th centuries.

Constabulary Pay Lists and Crime Returns (lists of charges).
Lists of Deputy Coroners.
Enrolments of deeds and wills and of papists' estates.
Gamekeepers' Certificates.
Hair Powder Tax Certificates.
Woolwinders' Oaths.
Declarations of allegiance by Roman Catholics and Protestant dissenters, declarations against transubstantiation etc.
Lists giving names of pauper lunatics in parishes.
Relief of the poor — paupers and removals of Irish and Scottish poor.
Calendars of prisoners with sentences.
Depositions in criminal cases.
Indictment books giving names of offenders, offences and dates of conviction.
Insolvent debtors.
Lists of prisoners and papers relating to their release.
Victuallers' Recognizances.
Bastardy Orders.
Recognizance Books(q.v.) (These were really bonds kept by the Clerk of the Peace which secured the appearance of defendants, prosecutors or witnesses. Failure to appear meant a heavy fine.)
Lists of properties and occupiers of land in various parishes in the county with lists of amounts assessed.
Flax Bounty (to encourage the growing of flax and hemp, provision was made for the distribution of a bounty for growers. Claims had to be sent to the Clerk of the Peace.)
Freemasons' Lodges — annual returns of members.
Returns of persons using weights and measures.
Registration of boats, barges and other vessels used on navigable rivers.
Court registers of Courts of Petty Session.
Coroners' reports.

A useful guide is *Quarter Sessions Records for Family Historians, a select list* ed. by Jeremy Gibson. It is obtainable from the FFHS. See also *County records: Quarter sessions, petty sessions, clerk of the peace and lieutenancy* by F.G. Emmison and V. Gray, Historical Association, 1987. Price £4.50 from SOG.

QUEEN ANNE'S BOUNTY A fund established by Queen Anne in 1704 to receive and use the annates and tenths previously confiscated by Henry VIII, generally used towards supplementing the income of the poorer clergy.

The Fund was made responsible by the Tithe Act 1925 for the collection of tithe rent charges; abolished by the Tithe Act 1936 and Government Stock received in compensation. In 1948 Queen Anne's Bounty and the Ecclesiastical Commission were formed into the Church Commission for England.

A rare but useful find would be a copy of *Queen Anne's Bounty* by C. Hodgson, 1826, which listed hundreds of names of benefactors, with the benefices to which they contributed.

QUITCLAIM This term, from Anglo-French, means a formal discharge or release of property. Enquire at your CRO as to their whereabouts. Here is a typical quitclaim entry:

'John Tollas of Warwick to William Tollas his son a house in Smith Street, Warwick 1425. William Tollas of Coleshill died before 1441'.

Further research revealed the following entry:

'No. 607. 22 Henry VI March 17th (1444) QUITCLAIM of William Tolas son and heir of William Tolas of Colshull in Arden, Co.Warwick, and Eleanor his wife to Thomas Burton and Agnes his wife and Walter Persyvale: All his right in a piece of land in Colshull, between the land late of Roger Ypstoke and the Highway in length, and in breadth between the tenement late of John Ambresely and the late of the same Roger; which said piece of land Thomas, Agnes and Walter lately had by gift and Feoffment of John ...yfield, vicar of Colshull, William Leycroft and John Couper, Park Keeper of Colshull. A549.'

From this you will see that there is family data for a period at least 100 years before the advent of parish registers.

QUIT RENT A fixed annual payment made by a manorial tenant to be released, or quit, from services to the Lord of the Manor. Abolished in 1922.

RAGGED SCHOOLS see Education.

RAILWAYS The majority of records are in the PRO, having been assembled by the British Transport Commission. See PRO Records Information leaflet 32 *Records Relating to Railways*. Two relevant reference books on the shelves at the PRO are:
The British Railways Pregrouping Atlas and Gazetteer
Chronology of the Construction of British Railways 1778-1885 by Leslie James, published by Ian Allen.

Staff records have survived from only a few railway companies, but there are a great many other records, the best being those of the Great Western Railway (GWR). In 1992 British Rail Archives presented 270 volumes of the GWR Stockholders Probate Registers 1835-1932 to the SOG.

The FFHS have published *Was Your Grandfather a Railwayman? A Directory of Railway Archive Sources for the Family Historian* by Tom Richards.

See also *Finding Ancestors Who Were Railway Employees* by M.G. Walcot which appeared in the journal of the Liverpool FHS Vol.14 No.4 (Autumn 1982) and more recently *Railway Records for the Family Historian* by Frank Hardy, Gen. Mag. Vol.23 No.7 (Sep 1990).

For a fascinating insight into how the railways were originally built, read *The Railway Navvies* by Terry Coleman, first published by Hutchinson 1965, reprinted Pelican 1976. It might explain why some of your ancestors seem to have disappeared without trace!

There is a Railway and Canal Historical Society with headquarters at 64 Grove Ave, London W7 3ES and The National Railway Museum Library is at Leeman Road, York, YO2 4XJ. They have a very extensive collection of railway photographs which are predominantly views of locomotives, carriages, wagons and stations , together with general railway scenes of moving trains and railway-related subjects such as shipping and road vehicles.

There is no catalogue of the collection but if you have any specific subject in mind they will try to advise what is available.

RAPE Term used in Sussex for a grouping of several Hundreds.

RATE BOOKS These may survive for your area from the mid 18th century onwards. They generally give the occupants of houses. Where they survive you should be able to locate them in the CRO or local Reference Library.

RECOGNIZANCES These can be extremely useful to the family historian. They were bonds which ensured that defendants, prosecutors and witnesses required at the Quarter Sessions would appear when needed. They are found in Quarter Session records (q.v.) in CROs.

RECORD OFFICES see County Record Offices, Diocesan Record Offices, Public Record Office.

Most Record Offices make no charge to users, but in a few cases a charge is made for Search Room facilities, either per person per day or part of a day or by issue of a season ticket (valid for a certain number of months from date of issue).

Record Offices: How To Find Them by Jeremy Gibson and Pamela Peskett, gives major record repositories in England and Wales with addresses, telephone numbers and sketch maps showing their locations within the relevant towns or cities.

In and Around Record Repositories in Great Britain and Ireland compiled by Rosemary Church and Jean Cole, ed. Avril Cross, is more expansive in that it has notes on facilities for the disabled, procedures for document ordering etc. but it omits the useful sketch maps. Both these booklets are obtainable from the FFHS.

Record Repositories in Great Britain has been produced by the Royal Commission on Historical Manuscripts and published by HMSO. This is a geographical directory, now in its 8th ed. and costing £3.50. It lists all institutions in the UK which collect and preserve written records and also make provision for their public use. Addresses, telephone numbers and opening hours are given along with details as to whether microfilm facilities etc. are available. PRO Records Information leaflet 124 *Public Records outside the Public Record Office* gives a broad outline of what you may expect to find at these repositories.

Having located the RO, your visit will go more smoothly if you are fully prepared. *You and Your Record Office: a code of practice for family historians using County Record Offices* 2nd ed. 1990, is a pamphlet issued by the Association of County Archivists in conjunction with the FFHS. Obtainable from the Administrator of the FFHS in exchange for sae plus one first class stamp or 3 IRCs.

RECORDING DATA see also Computers in Genealogy, Family History Record Sheets and Pedigrees. As your study proceeds you will be collecting a mass of notes. The following are merely suggestions based on experience. Fellow enthusiasts may well have other and better ideas!

First read SOG Leaflet No.4 *Note Taking and Keeping for Genealogists*, then Leaflet No.3 *Family Records and Their Layout*. Having got the gist of things move on to *Basic Record Keeping For Family Historians: an antidote to chaos ... and no computers!* by Andrew Todd, Allen & Todd, 1991, obtainable from FTM price £3.98 inc. p&p.

It is a good idea to record all the stages of your research in the form of a diary. The essential items for inclusion would be the name and address of the place visited, notes on how you got there, telephone number, name of the archivist or assistant who helped you, details of the book or document consulted and especially its reference number. Often time runs out and you are unable to complete your study. You would note this in your diary thus − 'Parish register for Lesser Uppingham − consulted baptisms 1820 to 1852'.

Use A4 punched paper and file your notes in a loose-leaf binder. Be extravagant in your use of paper, leaving spaces here and there for future relevant observations. At the top of each entry make a note of the record from which the data was obtained, the place, its reference number (you may want to consult it again to check something) and the date it was consulted.

Your information may have come from a relative, in which case you might head it 'Information from Aunt Muriel in letter dated 4 July 82'. The letter itself can be filed following the digest of the information you have made. Later you may choose to insert the letter in your family history.

Many family historians maintain a card or slip index − one card for each relative located. A size 5" x 3" is convenient since it will fit most shoeboxes, and later you will probably treat yourself to a filing cabinet, most of which will take slips of this size. Slips of good quality paper take up less room than cards and are far cheaper. You might choose to have a colour coding system by using different shades of coloured paper, or put a coloured mark in the top right hand corner of the slip.

Your slips can be filed first by Surname and then chronologically by Christian name. Mathematically minded genealogists have devised all kinds of coding systems which indicate the location of a name on the family tree and the generation.

Three such articles have been published in TMA. The references are as follows:

Vol.4 No.7 Nov 1976; An article by Peter Bilbrough. A specimen family record sheet is illustrated.

Vol.4 No.9 May 1977; *Reference Numbers for Indexing* by Alan Kent.

Vol.4 No.10 August 1977; An article on a system of coding by K. Girdlestone.

More recently we have *A Binary Descent Code for Specifying Ancestors* by Anthony S. Velate, 'Family History' Vol.17 No.138 New Series No.114 (Jan 1994). (Journal of the IHGS (q.v.).)

You may also find of interest *Method of Family Reconstruction of large Victorian Families as an approach to the biography of the Father of the Family* by Dr R.J. Hetherington, in TMA, Vol.4 No.1 (May 1975).

With the coming of modern technology you may consider recording data by computer. There are as many trains of thought on this approach as there are with more conventional methods! However, *The Organisation of Genealogical Information: Some Computer Considerations* by A.Sandison, Gen. Mag. Vol.21 No.8 (Dec 1984) puts the facts clearly and might help to decide whether or not this is for you.

There comes a time when recording data is simply not enough — you **must** put it into a coherent form for posterity! John Titford explains how he did his and passes on a few tips in *Writing up your family history — you know you've always meant to get around to it!*, FTM Vol.3 No.12 (Oct 1987). Terrick V.H. FitzHugh goes into even greater detail in *How To Write A Family History*, Adam & Charles Black (Alphabooks), 1988, and Ken Morley discusses *Some problems and solutions* of doing so, in FTM Vol.9 Nos.4, 5 and 6 (Feb/Mar/Apr 1993).

Don't forget to deposit a copy of the finished work with either a member of your family, your regional family history society, the SOG or all three.

Having put everything in apple-pie order you might like to consider doing something else, slightly different, with all that material; in which case read *Presenting Family History — to Family and Friends* by Victor Williams, Feature Article FHN&D, Vol.8 No.3 (April 1992). (He compiled a very attractive calendar.)

RECTOR A clergyman who received all or part of the great tithes, that is one tenth of all crops grown in the parish. The tithe was also levied on farm animals. The rector also sometimes received the smaller or vicarial tithes.

RECUSANT ROLLS A Recusant was one who refused to comply with the rites and ceremonies of the Church of England. It was most commonly used of Roman Catholics and Nonconformist and other Protestant dissenters. In Elizabethan times fines were imposed by the Churchwardens for failure to attend Church on Sundays and Holy Days. In 1581 the offence became indictable and much more stringent fines were imposed by the Sheriffs. The details of such fines were recorded in the Pipe Rolls. Failure to pay fines led to seizure of the recusant's goods and much of his land. From 1592, the information was recorded in the *Rotuli Recusancium* on a county by county basis. The Rolls give the name of the Recusant, rent, description of land, date of seizure, payments or arrears of payment etc. These records which cover approximately a century are in PRO, Classes E 376 to 379.

RED CROSS (International) see Prisoners of War.

REDUNDANT CHURCHES FUND The Fund was set up in 1969 to preserve churches no longer needed for worship but which are of historic or architectural interest.

Most of the churches are in sparsely populated areas and need substantial repair when they come to the Fund. The Fund's main income is provided by Church and State equally and it relies heavily on volunteers for the maintenance of the churches.

Further information can be obtained from The Redundant Churches Fund, St Andrews-by-the-Wardrobe, Queen Victoria Street, London, EC4V 5DE.

REEVE He represented the tenants on a manor in negotiations with the lord of the manor or his steward, and arranged such things as the labour which tenants were required to provide for a stated number of days of the year.

REGISTER OFFICE Often inaccurately referred to as Registry Office. Certificates of births, marriages and deaths can be ordered from local Register Offices (address in telephone directory under Registration of BMD). See *District Register Offices in England and Wales*, published by E. Yorks FHS for details of Register Offices and addresses. £0.75 inc. p&p. Before doing so the following points should be borne in mind.

They do not have such detailed indexes as the General Register Office (St Catherine's House). Births and deaths are generally indexed by *sub* district and for marriages you need to know the church concerned as there is no central index. Some of the larger Register Offices are presently compiling composite indexes.

A local Register Office will usually search a five year period for the event – if you have an exact address it can be quicker and cheaper to order from here; remember that the reference number from the General Register Office Indexes is of no use to a local Register Office. If the required event cannot be found, the local Register Office will return your fee; the General Register Office makes a charge per entry for checking a reference from the indexes if it turns out not to be the correct event.

Remember to send sae or 3 IRCs, if ordering from a local Register Office.

Depending upon the availability of staff at the Register Office in question it may be possible for an applicant to conduct a search himself for a period of up to six hours. A fee is payable and such attendances must be by prior arrangement.

REGISTRATION DISTRICTS see also Civil Registration and Maps. Two maps produced by the IHGS (q.v.) show all the Registration Districts in England and Wales for the periods 1837-51 and 1852-1946. Price £4.50 each inc. p&p.

REGISTRATION TAX see also Parish Registers. From 1695 to 1706 a tax was levied on all births, marriages and deaths recorded in the parish registers. Also taxed were bachelors over 25 and childless widowers. The Act required a complete enumeration of the population as it stood in 1695.

Virtually none of the tax lists have survived except for the Cities of London and Bristol, a few other boroughs and 16 Wiltshire parishes. Returns for 80 of the 97 ancient parishes within the walls of the City of London and 13 outside have survived and are in the Corporation of London Record Office, with a published index to the City parishes and a card index to the others. The Bristol assessments have been published with an index. Full details of all known lists are given in Jeremy Gibson's *The Hearth Tax, Other Later Stuart Tax Lists,etc*, obtainable from the FFHS. In 1783 entries in the registers were again taxed, but the act was repealed 10 years later (1794 Act).

REGNAL YEARS This type of year starts with the date of accession of each sovereign. Thus 3 Henry VII would run from 22 August 1487 to 21 August 1488.

A full list of such years appears in *The Local Historian's Encyclopaedia* and *Dates and Calendars for the Genealogist* by Cliff Webb, SOG, 1994 – though you can work it out for yourself having first established the year of accession of each monarch. There are exceptions to this rule (George II being one, because of the change in the calendar!) Another useful source is *Handbook of Dates for Students of English History* ed. by C.R. Cheney, published by the Royal Historical Society, 1970, reprinted 1984.

RELATIONSHIPS The meaning of certain terms indicating relationships has changed over the years — see under the heading 'In-law'. The term 'cousin' was always rather loosely used, and should not be taken too literally.

How To Determine Relationship The chart illustrates the relationship between YOURSELF and a common ancestor. It could be extended indefinitely. Persons with a common GRANDPARENT are FIRST cousins. Persons with a common GREAT-GRANDPARENT are SECOND COUSINS etc. In order to determine your degree of relationship to any other descendant of a common ancestor:-

1. Determine the common ancestor, e.g. gt-grandparent, gt-gt. grandparent.
2. Determine how many generations you are from this ancestor (you are three generations from your great-grandparent).
3. Determine how many generations the other person is from the common ancestor. If he, too, is three generations from the common ancestor, he is your second cousin. If he is two generations from the common ancestor, he is your first cousin once removed (your father's or mother's first cousin). If he is four generations from the common ancestor he is your second cousin once removed (the child of your second cousin).

There is an ambiguity in that 'first cousin once removed' may be either your father's or mother's first cousin or your first cousin's child. These may be distinguished by 'ascending' or 'descending'.

The chart may also be used to determine the relationship between ANY TWO DESCENDANTS of a common ancestor.
1. Determine the common ancestor of the two persons.
2. Determine the generation number of the person nearest the ancestor, how many generation steps he is from the ancestor.
3. Determine the generation number of the second person in the same way.
4. SUBTRACT the smaller number from the larger number. This determines the number of generations one person is removed from the other e.g. 4−2 = 2. Go to row 2 in the Table.
5. Now ADD the two generation numbers. This determines the degree of relationship 2+4 = 6. Go to column No.6.
6. Find the point where the Row No. and the Column No. meet and read off the exact relationship — 1st cousin twice removed.

```
WIFE  =  HUSBAND         =        WIFE  =  HUSBAND
    └──────┘          └──────┘         └──────┘
  A        B         C        D       E        F
```

A and B are HALF brothers (or sisters) to C and D
E and F are also HALF brothers (or sisters) to C and D
A and B are STEP brothers (or sisters) to E and F

Since early records — including parish registers — were written in Latin the following list of Latin words for relationships may be of use:

HOW TO DETERMINE RELATIONSHIPS

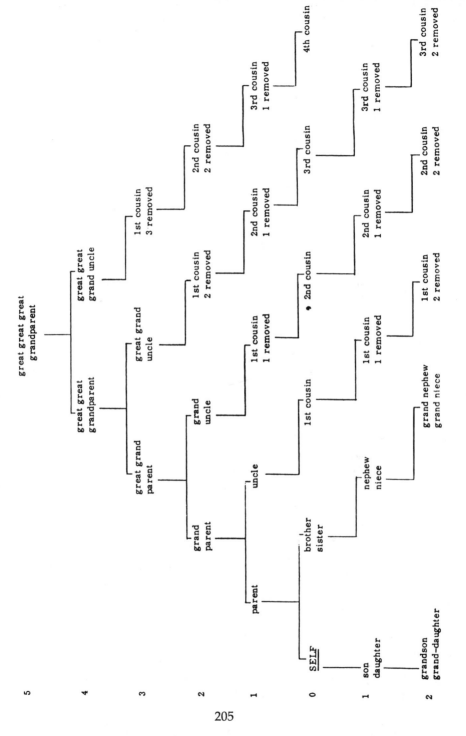

amita — aunt (paternal)	nurus — daughter-in-law
avunculus — uncle (maternal)	parens — parent, grandparent
avus — grandfather	pater — father
caelebs — single	patruus — uncle (paternal)
conjugata — married woman	priores — ancestors
conjures — married couple	proles — descendant
femina — woman, wife	propinquarius — relation
filia — daughter	relicta — widow
filiaster — son-in-law, stepson	relictus — widower
filius — son	soror — sister (or nun)
frater — brother (or monk)	sponsa — wife
gener — son-in-law, or grandson-in-law	sponsus — husband
ignoti parentis — of unknown parents	successio — descendants
majores — ancestors	uxor — wife
mariti — married couple	uxoratus — married
marita — wife	vevodus — widower
mater — mother	vidua — widow
matertera — aunt (maternal)	viduus — widower
nepos, nepus — grandson, nephew	vir — man, husband
nepta — granddaughter, niece	

REMOVAL ORDERS see also Examinations and Settlements. A pauper was considered to be the responsibility of his parish of legal settlement when in need of parish relief. An order would be made for him to be 'removed' to his last parish of legal settlement to which he would be escorted by the Constable (being passed from parish to parish and handed over at the boundary). These documents are often found in the Parish Chest (q.v.) or mentioned in Quarter Sessions(q.v.).

RENUNCIATION When an executor declines to apply for probate.

REQUESTS, COURT OF see Court of Requests.

RESEARCH SERVICE see AGRA and Federation of Family History Societies.

ROADS see Highways.

ROGUE MONEY Parishes were obliged to contribute up to 8d a week for the relief of poor prisoners in the County Gaol. This was collected by the parish constable.

ROMAN CATHOLIC see also Scotland and Strays. Some Roman Catholic Registers date from 1778 when the Roman Catholic Relief Bill was passed but very few were kept before then. Not many were surrendered to the Registrar General in 1840 and those deposited at the PRO are almost all from Yorkshire, Durham and Northumberland with only a very few registers from the whole of the rest of the country. After the reformation Catholics are most strongly grouped in these counties plus Lancashire and Staffordshire. Some early registers have been published by the Catholic Record Society but for an analysis of registers see *Catholic Missions and Registers 1700-1880* compiled by Michael Gandy; six volumes and an Atlas of parishes.

1. London and the Home Counties
2. The Midlands and East Anglia
3. Wales and the West of England
4. North East England
5. North West England
6. Scotland

Obtainable from the SOG (q.v.) at £6.70 each inc. p&p; Atlas £3.00 inc. p&p.

The National Index of Parish Registers (q.v.) Vol.III deals with Roman Catholic entries in Anglican registers. A list of these sources printed up to 1958 can also be found in *Texts and Calendars* by E.L.C. Mullins.

Quarter Sessions Records (q.v.) contain lists of recusants and details of catholic estates. Catholic archives reveal much information about charities, education and the poor. The archives of the Catholic landed gentry may contain details about their tenantry. Catholics appear in a great many State and Anglican records and these are thoroughly described in the Williams' book mentioned below. The address of the Catholic Record Society is The Secretary, 114 Mount Street, London W1X 6AX. In 1983 they published *Recusant History: Sources for Recusant History (1559 to 1791) in English Official Archives* by J. Anthony Williams. This valuable work was reviewed in FHN&D Vol.4 No.3 (April 1984).

See also *Catholic Ancestors* by Michael Gandy, Feature Article in FHN&D Vol.8 No.1 (April 1991).

The Catholic Family History Society, formerly English Catholic Ancestor, publishes a thrice-yearly journal. Further details from the Secretary; Mrs B. Murray, 2 Winscombe Crescent, Ealing, London W5 1AZ.

The Catholic Central Library is at 47 Francis Street, London SW1P 1QR.

A Catholic Marriage Index of over 30,000 entries covering mainly the period 1837-1880 is held by the IHGS (q.v.). Further details direct from them.

In the 18th century many prosperous Catholics who died in London were buried at St Pancras Churchyard. It is alleged that this was the last church in London to celebrate Mass. Many refugees from the French Revolution are buried here.

Records of priests and nuns are excellent and often give a great deal of information about their parents and even their brothers and sisters (with 19th century Irish nuns this can be the best or only source to determine from whence in Ireland the family had come). Also nuns were prominent in teaching, nursing and social work so their biographies are often very interesting.

The Catholic FHS has an index of over 14,000 19th century nuns (estimated at half the total number). All known priests have been listed in *English and Welsh Priests 1558-1800* by Dom Aidan Bellenger OSB, Downside, 1984, and *English and Welsh Priests 1801-1914* by Dom Charles Fitzgerald-Lombard OSB, Downside, 1993. There are detailed biographies of all secular priests 1558-1800, Jesuits, Benedictines, Franciscans, and Carmelites as well as many smaller Orders (see the Bibliographies in the books referred to above).

An enormous number of biographies will be found in *A Bibliographical Dictionary of the English Catholics* by J. Gillow, 5 vols. 1887-1902. *Biographies of English Catholics* was compiled by Rev. John Kirk, (1760-1851) and is very strong on the 18th century. Both the above are available in modern reprints — Gillow by Franklin, New York, and Kirk by Gregg, Farnborough.

ROMAN NUMERALS AND LATIN NUMBERS In the course of your research you are almost bound to encounter roman numerals at some point. The following may help you to work out that vital date! See also PRO Records Information leaflet 55 *How To Read Roman Numerals*.

I	= 1	XI	= 11	XXX	= 30	CCCC or	
II	= 2	XII	= 12	XL	= 40	CD	= 400
III	= 3	XIII	= 13	L	= 50	D	= 500
IV	= 4	XIV	= 14	LX	= 60	DC	= 600
V	= 5	XV	= 15	LXX	= 70	DCC	= 700
VI	= 6	XVI	= 16	LXXX	= 80	DCCC	= 800
VII	= 7	XVII	= 17	XC	= 90	CM	= 900
VIII	= 8	XVIII	= 18	C	= 100	M	= 1000
IX	= 9	XIX	= 19	CC	= 200	MM	= 2000
X	= 10	XX	= 20	CCC	= 300		

L (libra = pound £), S (solidus = shilling), D (denarius = penny.)

C (centum) = 100
D (dimidium, half) = 500
M (mille) = 1000

Summa totalis or in toto – the whole sum, total.
1 = unus, 2 = duo, 3 = tres, 4 = quattuor, 5 = quinque, 6 = sex, 7 = septem, 8 = octo, 9 = novem, 10 = decem.

ROYAL AIR FORCE The Royal Air Force was formed on 1 April 1918 by the amalgamation of the Royal Flying Corps (previously Army) and the Royal Naval Air Service. Service records prior to this date will be either Army or Navy.

For early enlistment in the ranks of the Royal Flying Corps, between May 1912 and August 1914, with Service Numbers 1-1400, consult *A Contemptible Little Flying Corps* by I. McInnes and J.V. Webb, London Stamp Exchange, 1991, which contains potted biographies of the men who served.

A Muster Roll listing all NCOs and men who were serving in the Royal Air Force on 1st April 1918 was compiled. It is arranged in service number order, listing date of joining, rank and trade. (It does not give first names, only initials and does not identify the Squadron or unit the airman was serving with.) Officers who served are listed in the Air Force List, the date of commission and branch of service can be identified, and an officer's career can be traced through these listings. Both the Muster Roll for April 1918 and a complete set of Air Force Lists are available in the PRO.

Where they survive, service records of the officers and men of the Royal Air Force, Royal Flying Corps and Royal Naval Air Service are in the custody of the Ministry of Defence, **not** at the PRO.

See PRO Records Information leaflets:

13 *Air Records as Sources for Biography and Family History*.

The PRO is due to publish *Records of the Royal Air Force* (1995) as one of its Readers' Guide series.

In the IWM (q.v.) Series *Tracing Individual Service Records and Medal Citations*; of particular interest might be:

See Civil Registration (q.v.) for notes on relevant indexes at St Catherine's House for servicemen and their families.

Relatives may obtain details of the service of officers from: Royal Air Force, PMC PM (AR1b), Eastern Avenue, Barnwood, Gloucestershire GL4 7PN, and of other ranks from Royal Air Force, P Man 3e (2), Innsworth, Gloucestershire GL3 1EZ.

The Royal Air Force Museum, Department of Aviation Records (Archives), Hendon Aerodrome, London NW9 5LL, has a card index of every aircraft that flew in the RAF. The Archives also contain air log books, photographs, and a large collection of privately-deposited officers' records. See also the series of leaflets issued by the Museum's Research and Information Services:

Medals awarded to personnel of the predecessors of the RAF – the Royal Flying Corps and the Royal Naval Air Service – for service in the First World War, are recorded on rolls in WO 329 and ADM 171 respectively. No later rolls are available.

With the creation of the RAF in 1918 four gallantry awards were instituted for the new service. Regulations governing the award of medals in the RAF are in Air Ministry Orders AIR 72. For the First World War surviving recommendations are in AIR 1; from 1918 AIR 2,"B", code 30 and AIR 30. During the Second World War awards were of two types: immediate (for single acts of bravery) and non-immediate (given at conclusion of a tour of duty between 25 and 30 operations). See PRO Records Information leaflet 108 *Records of Medals*.

A Biographical Register of all those who served in the Royal Flying Corps, Royal Naval Air Service and Royal Air Force during the First World War is currently being compiled. This covers both Officers and Other Ranks, aircrew and groundcrew, and part of the project involves re-arranging the Royal Air Force Muster Roll of April 1918 into alphabetical name order rather than the compiled service number order. Details of Casualties are also included in the register. The information is being collated by David J. Barnes, 21 Bury New Road, Ramsbottom via Bury, Lancs BLO OBT. Any contributions welcome. Enquiries should be accompanied by sae or 3 IRCs. Mr Barnes has also written *The Military Medal Winners of the RFC, RAF and AFC 1916-1920*, Ray Westlake Books, 1993 and *The Roll of Honour of the Royal Naval Air Service*.

In The Cross of Sacrifice Series *Officers who Died in the Service of The Royal Navy, Royal Naval Reserve, Royal Naval Volunteer Reserve, Royal Marines, Royal Naval Air Service and Royal Air Force 1914-1919* and *Officers of the Commonwealth and Colonial Regiments and Corps 1914-1919*. Alphabetical listing. Published by Roberts Medals Ltd, price in the region of £25.

The Royal Air Force Index is being compiled and already contains several thousand names. Ground staff are more difficult to locate than aircrew. References to WAAFs where located are included; they are obviously more difficult to trace as they may since have changed their surname by marriage. For details about the index send sae and 2 extra 1st class stamps, or 3 IRCs to Miss Eunice Wilson, 143 Harbord Street, London SW6 6PN. Contributions to the index welcomed, personal and otherwise.

Eunice Wilson has written *Finding The Few: Records of the Royal Air Force*, FFHS.

See also series of articles in FTM Vol.1 Nos.3,4 & 5 (Mar-Apl/May-June/July-Aug 1985), Vol.3 Nos.3 & 5 (Jan/March 1987).

Not quite ancestors, but already in the grandfather age group, are 'The Few' (aircrew who flew in the Battle of Britain, June 1940). Aircrew records of these are held in the Operation Record Books of each Squadron, Unit or Station at the PRO. Some squadrons have a long history dating back to the RAF's creation out of the Royal Flying Corps in 1918, but most were formed just before or during World War II. Eunice Wilson will be pleased to offer further advice on how to research these records, or will consult her extensive library and source material for a modest fee. Supply as much information as possible: squadron, unit or station, rank and full name, date of death or award, or when and where thought to be serving.

Airmail the magazine of the Royal Air Forces Association contains a section for those wishing to trace former fellow servicemen. Write to Royal Air Forces Association, 43 Grove Park Road, London W4 3RU.

Details of the Royal Air Force Historical Society can be obtained from the Hon.Sec., Group Capt. H. Neubroch, 19 Ivinghoe Road, Bushey Heath, Watford WD2 3SW.

ROYAL ARCHIVES These are particularly useful in relation to persons in the direct employ of the sovereign. The archivist at Windsor Castle, Windsor, Berkshire SL4 1NJ, could be helpful in dealing with enquiries.

See also PRO Records Information leaflet 29 *Royal Warrant Holders and Household Servants: An Introduction to the Records of the Lord Chamberlain's and Lord Steward's Departments*. The documents described in this leaflet are available at the PRO.

ROYAL BRITISH LEGION The Royal British Legion is a Charitable organisation offering assistance for the ex-Service community and dependents. Their War Graves Pilgrimages Department specialises in arranging group visits to War Cemeteries worldwide and will advise on individual visits. Further details from The Pilgrimage Department, The Royal British Legion, The Royal British Legion Village, Maidstone, Kent, ME20 7NX.

ROYAL COMMISSION ON HISTORICAL MANUSCRIPTS Acts as a clearing-house for information about the nature and location of historical manuscripts and papers outside the PRO. The National Register of Archives, the Manorial Documents Register and the Tithe Documents Register are available for public use in its searchroom. Its publications, which include an annual list of *Accessions to Repositories and Reports added to the National Register of Archives* are listed in HMSO *History in Print Sectional List, 60, 1990*. Open Mon-Fri 9.30am-5.00pm.

ROYAL COMMISSION ON HISTORICAL MONUMENTS OF ENGLAND The RCHME maintains The National Monuments Record, the collection of photographs, drawings and written records of archaeological sites and historic buildings in England. The National Buildings Record (NBR) comprises one section of this and contains more than one and a half million photographs, dating from the earliest days of photography to the present day, plus written records of all types of historic buildings, ecclesiastical, domestic, civic, commercial and industrial with details of their architectural fittings. Some photographs have been copies from family albums. The resources of the NBR are an invaluable source of visual material.

No appointment is necessary to consult the NBR index in the public search room which is open 10.00am-5.30pm Mon-Fri. The address is RCHME (NBR), Fortress House, 23 Savile Row, London W1X 2JQ.

Letters should state the purpose of your enquiry, giving concise details of what you hope to find.

ROYAL DESCENT Descents from members of the Royal Family were at one time greatly prized but they are far from uncommon and today there is much less interest in them. The fluid nature of English society and intermarriage through different social classes over a long period has brought a fine trickle of royal blood to many an ordinary person quite unaware of the fact. By 1911 King Edward III had about a hundred thousand descendants. The number must be much greater now. In 1903 the living descendants of Mary, Queen of Scots, numbered 1,440; now it is over 10,000. Beyond Edward III the royal blood flows out in England through Edmund Crouchback the son of Henry III, through Thomas of Brotherton and Edmund of Woodstock the younger sons of Edward I and their sisters Joan and Elizabeth, through Eleanor the daughter of King John, and through illegitimate lines like those from Robert, Earl of Gloucester, the bastard of Henry I. Sir Anthony Wagner has shown in *English Genealogy* (2nd ed. 1972, pp.233-240) how descendants of these have acted as gateways to royal ancestry in particular areas of the country. Nineteen settlers in New England before 1650 were descended from Edward I. In Europe it has been calculated that Charlemagne, Emperor of the West, who died in 814, probably has twenty million living descendants.

All the known legitimate descendants of James I were listed in A.C.Addington, *The Royal House of Stuart*, 3 vols. London, 1969-76. There are numerous descents from the illegitimate children of Charles II. Details of the British royal families may be found in *Burke's Guide to the Royal Family*, London, 1973 and most other royal families can be found in *Burke's Royal Families of the World*, 2 vols.London, 1977-80. Greater details of some appear in Marlene A. Eilers, *Queen Victoria's Descendants*, Baltimore, USA, 1987. The most detailed account of the ancestry of the British Royal Family in all its lines is Gerald Paget, *The lineage and ancestry of HRH Prince Charles, Prince of Wales*, 2 vols. Edinburgh, 1977.

ROYAL HOSPITAL CHELSEA see Chelsea Royal Hospital

ROYAL HUMANE SOCIETY Founded in 1774 by Dr William Hawes and Dr Thomas Cogan as "Humane Society instituted for the recovery of persons apparently drowned". The Royal was added in 1787. First mention of the well-known Grace Darling medal is in 1838. By 1989 approximately 127 Gold, 1,328 Silver and 11,143 Bronze Medals had been awarded. The criteria for an award is that it can only be made to a person who "at risk to his own life saves or attempts to save the life of a fellow citizen". The degree of bravery is reflected in the award of Medals, Testimonials and Certificates of Commendation. In addition, an 'In Memoriam' Testimonial is presented to the relatives of those who lose their lives in attempting to rescue others.

The RHS has no museum but the original Casebooks, Minutes and Annual Reports from 1774 to present date are open to research by appointment and for a search fee of £5.00. Enquiries to The Secretary, RHS, Brettenham House, Lancaster Place, London WC2E 7EP.

ROYAL LIFE SAVING SOCIETY Founded in 1891 as the Swimmers' Life Saving Society to combat a rising toll of over 2,000 deaths a year. The Society does not appear to keep any records of interest to family historians as anything over four years old is destroyed. Awards are made to volunteer lifesavers in recognition of achievement on attaining certain standards. However, *Lifesaving: the story of the Royal Life Saving Society, The First 100 Years* by Ronald Pearsall is indexed and a considerable number of names are listed. Appendix 2 gives names of Mountbatten Medal Winners (Worldwide) 1951-1988. Published by David & Charles, 1991, price £15.99. RLSS UK, Mountbatten House, Studley, Warwickshire, B80 7NN.

ROYAL MARINES see also Nelson. Whilst soldiers had been part of the complement of ships of war from early times the first British military unit raised especially for sea service was the Duke of York and Albany's Maritime Regiment of Foot, 1664. This later became part of the Army establishment and is the direct ancestor of the Buffs. From 1690 extra Marine Regiments were raised in wartime for sea service; at the end of the war these were disbanded, soldiers discharged and the officers put on half pay.

Though these early Marine Regiments were employed for sea service they were part of the Army and were organised like other foot regiments, the exception being that parties serving at sea came under naval discipline and were shown on their ships books (listed separately) for wages and victuals.

In 1749 these Marine Regiments were disbanded for the last time. In 1755 a new Corps of Marines was formed under Admiralty authority; it was not part of the Army. Though it continued to use Army ranks and uniform it had no regimental structure. The fifty companies were divided between three divisions, based at Portsmouth, Plymouth and Chatham. From 1805 to 1869 a fourth division was based at Woolwich. If serving under military command (i.e ashore, as landing parties) the Marines came under military discipline, otherwise they were responsible solely to the Admiralty.

Until the outbreak of war in 1939 the main role of the Royal Marines was to provide detachments in HM ships and to provide detachments ashore. There have always been other calls on their manpower to meet commitments as the situation demanded such as providing a brigade for the 63rd Royal Naval Division in the 1914-19 war, and the nucleus of a Mobile Naval Base Defence Organisation in the 1930s. During the 1939-45 war they continued to man HM ships, but even more personnel were deployed in landing craft and commandos under the auspices of Combined Operations.

Many books have been and continue to be written about the history of the Royal Marines and its units and formations over the years. The official history has been well documented and is contained in four books: *Britain's Sea Soldiers Volumes 1 and 2* by Colonel Cyril Field RMLI (up to 1914), and Volume 3 (1914-19), by General H.E. Blomberg, KCB, and *The Royal Marines 1919-1980* by James D. Ladd. The latter history is to be brought up to date to include the Falklands campaign, the Gulf War, and the many United Nations operations in which the Corps has been involved. The Royal Marines Historical Society has recently published two books of deaths in the two World Wars that contain the names, details, units and burials. These books are *With Full and Grateful Hearts, A Register of Royal Marines Deaths 1914-1919* and *Bid Them Rest in Peace, A Register of Royal Marines Deaths 1939-45*, both by J.A. Good. All these books, and many others, can be found in the library of The Royal Marines Museum, Eastney, Southsea, Hampshire PO4 9PX, which is well worth a visit. They have published *The Royal Marines: a Short Bibliography*, Southsea, 1978.

Other troops serving afloat were artillerymen. In 1804 the Admiralty formed companies of marine artillery to man the bombs; in 1859 there was a formal division between the Royal Marine Artillery (stationed at Eastney, Southsea and known as the Blue Marines) and the Royal Marine Light Infantry (known as the Red Marines). The two branches were amalgamated in 1923.

No records of Officers' services for men appointed before 1793 have survived. For officers commissioned after 1793 a search should first be made in the Records of Officers' Services. Only from about 1837 are these records complete. The *Navy List* published annually, also includes Royal Marine officers. The Corps Historical Records Officer, DRORM, Centurion Building, Grange Road, Gosport, Hants PO13 9XA holds the records of officers and other ranks who joined the Corps after 1918. All other records are held at the PRO. See PRO Records Information leaflet 74 *Royal Marines Records in the Public Record Office.*

There are numerous records of service for other ranks but individuals are hard to trace unless their Company or Division is known. Until 1884 there was no system of numbering individuals. However, a card index to the attestation forms is available, which will help considerably.

Each division of the Royal Marines kept its own registers of births, marriages and deaths, of children and wives borne on the strength. They give the Marine's rank and some information on posting. Registers for Chatham cover 1830-1913; Plymouth 1862-1920; Woolwich (marriage rolls only) 1822-1869 and for the Royal Marine Artillery 1810-1853 and 1866-1921. No registers survive for Portsmouth Division.

Records survive for Royal Marine wills and administrations, and pensions. The Royal Greenwich Hospital catered for the Marines as well as the Navy.

Campaign/War Medals awarded to Marines are recorded in Admiralty Medal Rolls ADM 171 and 171/89-134 (mostly on microfilm). Gallantry Medals are in ADM 1 (code 85) and ADM 116 (code 85). During the First World War, many Royal Marines were given army gallantry medals.

See PRO Records Information leaflets:

108 *Records of Medals*

101 *Service Medals and Award Rolls: War of 1914-1918 WO 329*
105 *First World War: Indexes to Medal Entitlement*.

In The Cross of Sacrifice Series *Officers who Died in the Service of The Royal Navy, Royal Naval Reserve, Royal Naval Volunteer Reserve, Royal Marines, Royal Naval Air Service and Royal Air Force 1914-1919* and *Non-commissioned Officers and Men of all Allied Navies 1914-1919*. Alphabetical listing. Published by Roberts Medals Ltd, price in the region of £25.

Mrs M. Catty, 4 Alexandra Close, Chadwell St Mary, Grays, Essex RM16 4TT, has for sale microfiche publication index of Royal Navy Officers, 1846-65: certificates and declarations for placing widows on the Pension List, index of officers from pension forms. Price £1.50 UK inc. p&p.

ROYAL NATIONAL LIFEBOAT INSTITUTION The RNLI was founded in 1824, as the 'National Institution for the Preservation of Life from Shipwreck' and early records are sparse. With the introduction of the Institution's Journal *The Lifeboat* in 1852, records became much better but still not comprehensive.

People looking for ancestors by name might be lucky if the relative was (a) A Lifeboat's officer e.g. Coxswain or (b) he had been awarded some form of RNLI gallantry award such as the Gold, Silver or Bronze Medal. In early days the men who went to sea in the lifeboat were simply local fishermen or gentlemen, their names are not usually recorded. It is only in very recent years that all lifeboatmen have been formally enrolled and today there is a Station Personnel Department.

Requests for information post-1960 should be addressed to the Station Personnel Manager, other enquiries to the Honorary Archivist, Royal National Lifeboat Institution, Headquarters: West Quay Road, Poole, Dorset BH15 1HZ. Enclose sae or 2 IRCs.

The RNLI Museum is housed at the same address and is open Mon to Fri 9.00am-5.00pm. A General Information leaflet about the RNLI is available from the same address. Voluntary lifeboat services operate in other countries, including the Netherlands, Sweden, New Zealand and South Africa.

ROYAL NAVAL ASYLUM This was set up in Paddington in 1798 under the title 'British Endeavour', for the education and maintenance of orphans and destitute children of sailors and marines. By Acts of Parliament in 1806 and 1807 it came under royal patronage and transferred to new premises, which today house the National Maritime Museum at Greenwich. In 1825 it was amalgamated with the Greenwich Hospital School (q.v.). Records of the Royal Naval Asylum are at PRO (class ADM 73) and include applications, admission registers, disposal of children, lists of staff and servants.

ROYAL NAVY see also Greenwich Hospital and Greenwich Hospital Schools, Royal Naval Asylum, Seamen (Trinity House Petitions).

Much of what you need to know is contained in *Naval Records for Genealogists* by N.A.M. Rodger, HMSO, 1988. £4.95. A study of this book before visiting the PRO will ensure that optimum use is made of the time available.

That book recommends further reading but you might like to consult also the relevant chapter in *Tracing Your Ancestors in the Public Record Office* by Amanda

Bevan and Andrea Duncan, 4th ed. HMSO, 1990, counter price £6.95 or £8.40 by post from the FFHS: PRO Family Fact Sheet 4 *Tracing an Ancestor in the Royal Navy: Ratings*, and 5 *Tracing an Ancestor in the Royal Navy: Officers*. See also General Information leaflets:

2   *Admiralty Records as Sources for Biography and Genealogy*
3   *Operational Records of the Royal Navy 1660-1914*
43   *Operational Records of the Royal Navy in the Second World War, 1939-45*
49   *Operational Records of the Royal Navy in the First World War*
108   *Record of Medals*
101   *Service Medal and Award Rolls: War of 1914-1918 WO 329*
105   *First World War: Indexes to Medal Entitlement*
125   *Navy, Royal Air Force and Merchant Navy Pension Records*

These all give detailed information of the classes of records available and advise which are of use to the family historian.

The IWM (q.v.) Series *Tracing Individual Service Records and Medal Citations*; of particular interest would be:

15B   *Royal Navy*
15F   *Prisoners of War*

Gerald Hamilton-Edwards' book *In Search of Ancestry* has a chapter on Naval research.

Also helpful are Leaflet No.20 published by the SOG *Navy Research: selected bibliography*; *Printed sources of Naval Biography and History* by Norman Hurst, FTM Vol.4 No.11 (Sep 1988) and *The Royal Naval Museum, Portsmouth: genealogy at the King Alfred Library and Reading Room* by Andrew Trotman, Gen. Mag. Vol.24 No.5 (Mar 1993).

See Civil Registration (q.v.) for notes on relevant indexes at St Catherine's House for servicemen and their families.

There are no systematic records listing men serving in the Navy prior to the Restoration (1660). However, various classes of 17th century records survive and are in the PRO.

The printed *Navy Lists* (which began in 1782 as *Steel's Navy List*) are on open shelves in the PRO Reference Room; from these it is fairly easy to trace the career of a commissioned officer's career in the Royal Navy. Other printed sources are available in the Reference Room.

Chaplains can be traced through succession books though more recent records are still held by the Chaplain of the Fleet. See also *Chaplains of the Royal Navy 1626-1903* by A.G.Kealy.

The Guildhall Library (q.v.) has records of the issue of certificates by the Barber-Surgeons' company to those intending to serve as surgeons in the Royal Navy 1705-45. They relate to prospective naval surgeons from the provinces as well as London. After the formation of the new Company of Surgeons in 1745 such certificates were issued by them.

Where they have survived, copies or original wills made by officers and ratings are attached to many applications made after their death for their back pay; registers of these claims and wills can be helpful in tracing the names of next of kin.

Campaign and War medal rolls are in ADM 171 (mostly on microfilm). Medal rolls for the First World War are in records class ADM 171/89-134. Gallantry medal rolls are in ADM 1, code 85 and ADM 116, code 85. Registers of awards to naval officers during the First World War are in ADM 171/78-88.

Commissioned Sea Officers of the Royal Navy 1660-1815 published by the National Maritime Museum gives details of careers. Periodicals devoted to military interests can also be a fruitful source of information if you have ancestors in the services. The *United Service Journal and Naval and Military Magazine* was first published in 1829, later becoming *Colburn's United Service Magazine*; it contains notices of births, marriages and deaths, often with detailed obituary notices relating to officers. Unfortunately it is not indexed.

The *Naval Chronicle* was published monthly from 1799 to end of 1818; an index to its births, marriages and deaths announcements has been compiled and published by Norman Hurst, 1989. Price £8 from 25 Byron Avenue, Coulsdon, Surrey CR3 2JS. Brides are indexed as well as naval bridegrooms and notes are appended to entries where appropriate. Names of long-lived pensioners are included.

The London Stamp Exchange Ltd, 5 Buckingham Street, London WC2N 6BS publishes *The Naval and Military Book List*, 1990.

In The Cross of Sacrifice Series *Officers who Died in the Service of The Royal Navy, Royal Naval Reserve, Royal Naval Volunteer Reserve, Royal Marines, Royal Naval Air Service and Royal Air Force 1914-1919* and *Non-commissioned Officers and Men of all Allied Navies 1914-1919*. Alphabetical listing. Published by Roberts Medals Ltd; price in the region of £25.

The Navy Records Society will be pleased to send details of the society and its publications. Write to the secretary, Mr N.A.M. Rodger, c/o Public Record Office, Ruskin Avenue, Kew, Richmond, Surrey TW9 4DU.

There are several other societies which might be able to provide information or background material. They are as follows though in no specific order of priority.

Naval Historical Collectors and Research Association, Secretary, Mr J.T. Mock, 17 Woodhill Ave, Portishead, Bristol BS20 9EX; publishes in its quarterly journal *The Review* numerous lists which include medal rolls, casualty lists, ships rolls etc. many of which come from sources other than the PRO.

The Society for Nautical Research, National Maritime Museum, Romney Road, Greenwich, London SE10 9NF.
(Remember that the National Maritime Museum (q.v.) itself has magnificent records!)

The Britannia Royal Naval College Library, Dartmouth, Devon TQ6 OHJ, is open to the public for research.

The Naval History Library is within Plymouth Central Library, Drake Circus, Plymouth PL4 8AL.

The Liverpool Nautical Research Society, Merseyside County Museums, William Brown Street, Liverpool L3 8EN.

Naval Historical Library, Room 2502, Ministry of Defence, Empress State Building, Lillie Road, London SW6 1TR. The library contains principally **published** works dealing with all aspects of naval history; they do **not** hold Records of Service and can, at best, only supply very brief details about an Officer's career. It is necessary to make an appointment to visit.

Advice on obtaining specific information may be sought from: Head of Naval Pay, Pensions and Conditions of Service (for NPC 36), Ministry of Defence (Navy), Archway Block South, Old Admiralty Building, Spring Gardens, London SW1A 2BE.

First published in the 1970s *The Royal Navy Day by Day* has been brought completely up to date and reprinted (1994) in association with the National Maritime Museum (q.v.). A record of British Naval Heritage over 700 years, generously illustrated. Price £29.95 plus p&p.

The Captain of the restored Victorian ironclad *HMS Warrior* 1860 is seeking information about members of past Ships' Companies who have served in his ship, or in other vessels of the same name. A genealogical index has been created. Contact: The Captain, HMS Warrior 1860, Victory Gate, HM Naval Base, Portsmouth, Hampshire PO1 3QX.

ROYALIST ESTATES COMPOSITION PAPERS see also Interregnum. During the Interregnum the administration of the country was in the hands of Parliamentary Committees. At least two of these committees were involved with so-called *Delinquents* (q.v.). In many instances a *Delinquent*, after investigation, was deprived of most of his estate. However there were sometimes options to pay a fine based on a valuation of an estate and the extent of an individual's delinquency. Orders and correspondence were filed in the State Paper Office PRO Class SP 2, volumes G61 to 173 and depositions, given under oath by those who were permitted to compound, together with the amount of **compositions** at which assessments were made, appear in volumes G174 to 227. A Calendar of the papers of the Committee for Compounding with Delinquents 1643 to 1660 has been published in 5 parts, ed. by Mrs Everett Green.

See PRO Records Information leaflet 88 *Confiscations, Sales and Restoration of Crown and Royalist Land 1642-1660: sources in the PRO*.

RURAL DEAN see Dean.

RURAL LIFE The Museum of English Rural Life at the Institute of Agricultural History, University of Reading, PO Box 229, Whiteknights, Reading RG6 2AG, is a national centre for information on agricultural history and rural life. Their library records can be consulted by appointment.

See also PRO Records Information leaflet 129 *Records of The National Farm Surveys of England and Wales, 1940-1943* which points out that these records will provide a useful source for local and family historians but will be of greater value to the historical geographer as they present a database of land ownership and usage in mid-20th century Britain.

RUSSIA see also Prisoners of War. The Leeds Russian Archive was established in 1982 by the Brotherton Library and the Department of Russian Studies at the University of Leeds. It concentrates exclusively on Russian and Russian-related material and in particular on the history of the British in Russia.

Limited resources prohibit extended research being undertaken but enquiries about and information on families with Russian connections are welcomed. Write to The Archivist, Leeds Russian Archive, Brotherton Library, University of Leeds, W.Yorkshire LS2 9JT.

See *Leeds Russian Archive: The British in Russia* by Richard Davis, FTM, Vol.4 No.4 (Feb 1988). The article concludes with a most useful bibliography: *Guide to Documents and Manuscripts in the United Kingdom Relating to Russia and the Soviet Union*, Janet M. Hartley, London & New York: Mansell, 1987, and *The Study of Russian History from British Archival Sources*, (editor and publisher same) 1986, are considered to be of vital importance to students of the British community in Russia.

SACRAMENT CERTIFICATES From 1673 any person holding civil or military office had to produce a certificate signed by a minister, churchwardens and two witnesses that he had received the Sacrament i.e. that he was a practising member of the Church of England. These certificates, which frequently gave the occupation of the man and of his witnesses, were sent to the Clerk of the Quarter Sessions (q.v.). Whilst this law was not repealed until 1828 fewer certificates were issued after 1750.

SADDLER There is a book by J.W. Sherwell entitled *The History of the Guild of Saddlers*, 3rd ed. 1956.

S.A.E. In UK − a stamped, addressed envelope. In USA this means a self- addressed envelope − they use s.a.s.e. (self-addressed stamped envelope).

SAILORS see Royal Navy, Seamen.

ST CATHERINE'S HOUSE see Civil Registration. This is the repository of the Civil Registration Indexes formerly located in Somerset House. Open to the public 8.30am.-4.30pm. Mon-Fri.

SALE OF WIVES see Divorce.

SALTER Salt was of great importance in the past as the main food preservative. A salter was a maker of or dealer in salt. There was a London Livery Company, see *A History of the Salters' Company* by J.S. Watson, 1962.

Northwich, Nantwich and Middlewich, all in Cheshire, and Droitwich, Worcestershire, were well established as salt producing towns by the time of the Norman Conquest. A Salt Museum is housed at 162 London Road, Northwich, Cheshire CW9 8AB.

SALVATION ARMY see Missing Relatives.

SAMPLERS A sampler is an embroidered piece of material displaying stitching skills. Early samplers are believed to be ways of recording new patterns or stitches but from the 17th to the early 20th century it was customary for young girls to embroider a sampler. Usually included in the design was their name, a verse or quotation, and the date the work was completed.

An index of the genealogical details on such samplers was compiled by Mrs Charlotte Soares who has subsequently donated it to the FFHS. It is being edited and will eventually be published on microfiche. Contributions of details, especially of samplers still in private possession, would be gratefully received. Send them to the FFHS c/o the Administrator marking the envelope 'Samplers'.

Samplers gives an insight into their origins. Written by Jenny Mukerji it appeared in 'Root and Branch', journal of the West Surrey FHS, Vol.13 No.1, 1986.

See also *British Samplers, a Concise History*, by J. Toller, 1980, and Shire Album No.30 *Samplers* by Pamela Clabburn.

Care of your heritage fabrics by Althea Douglas FTM Vol.4 No.3 (Jan 1988) gives good advice on the treatment of these family treasures. The Royal School of Needlework, 25 Princes Gate, London SW7 1QE undertakes renovation and repair to a high standard. The Textile Conservation Centre, Hampton Court Palace, East Molesey, Surrey, will also answer enquiries.

SCHOOLS see Education. There is a Shire Publication entitled *Discovering Schools*.

SCILLY (ISLES OF) The Isles of Scilly Museum, Church Street, St Mary's, Isles of Scilly TR21 0JT, contains some material available to researchers. An appointment to view is necessary. During the summer season the library is open Tuesdays, Thursdays and Fridays but during winter strictly by arrangement with the librarian or Honorary Secretary of the Museum (Tel. 01720 22337).

Charges are modest: Life Membership £10, Annual Membership £2 or 75p per session.

Of particular interest to family historians are:

Blanchminster Family
Custom House Incident Book (1715-1735)
Custom House Letter Book (1771-1781)
Court Record Books (1786-1801 & 1835-1917)
Duchy Archives Extracts (1800-1835)
Duchy of Cornwall Rental Book (1710-1739)
Family Trees compiled by R.M.Baxter and others
Godolphins
Overseers of the Poor Parish Account
Overseers of the Poor, St Martins Account
Parish Registers from 1721
Parliamentary Survey of Scilly, 1652
School Log Books 19th and early 20th centuries
Scillonian Wills (1672-1772)
Complete run of Scillonian magazines 1926 to present
Soldiers of the Garrison (1695-1715)

Other sources of information relating to the Isles of Scilly may be found on the mainland at CRO Truro, Royal Institution of Cornwall, Truro, Penzance Library, Redruth Local Studies Library, or from the Cornwall FHS.

SCOTLAND see also Civil Registration in Scotland, Parish Registers in Scotland, Emigration, Family Histories and West Indies.

There are two principal establishments with which those searching Scottish ancestry are likely to be involved:

The first is The General Register Office for Scotland, New Register House, Edinburgh, EH1 3YT. This holds mainly old parish registers, statutory registers of births, marriages, deaths, still births, adoptions, divorces and census records. They will send a copy of their pamphlet (SU/1 786) on request.

A system by which the public is allowed to see the actual registers of births, marriages and deaths was radically changed early 1989 and waiting is reduced to a minimum.

Up to 3 registers at a time can be brought to your table and you can return a volume with an order for a replacement. It is necessary to reserve a place at least 2 weeks beforehand; if this is not possible you need to arrive well before the opening time of 9.30am and wait in a queue for a limited number of 'stand by' places.

There is a charge (Sep. 1994) of £15 per day for an 'inclusive' search which covers Registers, Censuses and Old Parochial Registers and even for looking at the Index to the registers. No reduction is given for a period shorter than a day.

The second is the Scottish Record Office, General Register House, Edinburgh, EH1 3YY. This office has a vast collection of material useful to the family historian; their Leaflet 9 *Family History* lists the records available together with general advice on tracing Scottish Ancestry.

Also available on receipt of sae or 3 IRCs are *Indexes in the Historical Search Room to Deeds, Sasines and Testamentary Records* (Leaflet No.19), and *Indexes in the Historical Search Room to Chancery and Privy Seal Records* (Leaflet No.21).

See *Tracing Your Scottish Ancestors: A Guide to Ancestry Research in the Scottish Record Office* by Cecil Sinclair, HMSO, 1990. Price £7.40 inc. p&p. Obtainable from FFHS. Essential reading if you plan to use this repository.

Also *Exploring Scottish History: A Directory of Resource Centres for Scottish Local and National History in Scotland* edited by Michael Cox, Scottish Library Association & Scottish Local History Forum, 1992. Obtainable from FFHS price £7.85 inc. p&p.

Probate records are in the Scottish Record Office (see above). There is no charge to consult these but you need to go through ticket issue formalities and be shown how to use the records which is not simple.

In Scotland there are records of land inheritance from 1500 to 1700, and a Register of Deeds 1554-1667.

The Association of Scottish Genealogists & Record Agents (ASGRA) issues a list of members who offer professional services. Obtainable by post in exchange for sae or 3 IRCs from the Secretary, PO Box No. 174, Edinburgh, EH3 5QZ.

There is also Scots Ancestry Research Society, 29b Albany Street, Edinburgh EH1 3QN. Details on request in return for exchange postage as above.

Scottish Catholic Archives are at 16 Drummond Place, Edinburgh, EH3 6PL and the Scottish Record Society, Department of Scottish History, University of Glasgow, G12 8QQ. Scottish Catholic history is well covered by *The Innes Review* published twice-yearly since 1951. There were substantial pockets of Catholicism in Aberdeen, Banff,

Inverness, the Outer Hebrides and Kirkcudbright. In the 19th century the growth was mostly in Glasgow, Lanarkshire and Renfrewshire.

Scottish Roman Catholic registers have been photocopied and microfilmed by the Scottish Record Office. *Scottish Catholic Secular Clergy 1879-1089* ed. Christie Johnson, published by John Donald, 1992, price £30: gives biographical notes for each priest, listed alphabetically within diocese.

The Scottish Association of Family History Societies has a list of Member Societies available from the Secretary Mr Alan J.L. MacLeod, 51/3 Mortonhall Road, Edinburgh, EH9 2HN. SAFHS Members now represent all the regions of Scotland. A more detailed booklet about the Societies, their holdings and publications is available from Miss S.M. Spiers, SAFHS Publications, 27 Woodend Drive, Aberdeen AB2 6YJ, price £1.50 plus p&p.

The Aberdeen Family History Shop, 164 King Street, Aberdeen, AB2 3BD has on microfiche a set of Old Parochial Registers indices (pre 1855) for Scotland, the 1988 World IGI and microfilm of various Registers and Census covering Shetland Isles, Orkney and the Counties of Caithness, Sutherland, Ross and Cromarty, Inverness, Nairn, Moray, Banff, Aberdeen and Kincardine. Note that the OPR indices are *not* the same as the IGI (q.v.). More information will be found in the OPR indices than is in the IGI. A search and print out service is offered and a publications list is available on request.

The Tay Valley Family History Centre, 179 Princes Street, Dundee, DD4 6DQ has several publications. One of the best is *Beginners Guide to Scottish Genealogy*, compiled by Ewen K. Collins, 1993, price £4.50 plus p&p. They also have the OPR indices for Scotland plus microfilm of the Registers and census for the Tay Valley area.

The Scottish Genealogy Society, 15 Victoria Terrace, Edinburgh has a range of books, microfilm and microfiche which covers not only the Edinburgh area but the whole of Scotland.

Sources for Scottish Genealogy and Family History the title of Vol.XII of *The National Index of Parish Registers* (q.v.) by D.J. Steel. Published by Phillimore in 1970.

Scottish Roots by Alwyn James, published by Macdonald, Edinburgh, 1984, £5.95 inc. p&p, obtainable from the FFHS.

Parishes, Registers and Registrars of Scotland, SAFHS, 27 Woodend Drive, Aberdeen, AB2 6YJ, price £3.75 plus p&p.

Scottish Ancestry Research: A Brief Guide, by Donald Whyte, published by Scotpress, Morgantown, WV, 1984.

The Scots Overseas: A Selected Bibliography by Donald Whyte, obtainable from the FFHS, suggests further sources for Scots in particular countries. By the same author in FTM Vol.4 No.8 (June 1988) *Published Sources on Scottish Family History*.

The Emigrant Scots by James Lawson, Aberdeen & North East Scotland FHS, price £3.75 plus p&p, detailing the whereabouts of Shipping and Emigrant records in Canada.

In Search of Scottish Ancestry by Gerald Hamilton-Edwards is a mine of information, published by Phillimore, 1971; there is also a useful chapter on the subject in the same author's book *In Search of Ancestry*.

See also *Scottish Research* FTM Vol.7 Nos.9-12 (July-Oct 1991).

The *Directory of Scottish Newspapers*, by Joan P.S. Ferguson, Edinburgh 1984, revised edition of 1956 *Scottish Newspapers held in Scottish Libraries*. Three times the size of the original edition, comprising the varied holdings and locations of some 1,178 individual newspapers including approximately 80% of the Scottish newspaper holdings of the BLNL, Colindale. Earliest reference is the Aberdeen Journal 1748. Price £10.00.

A rather more specialised publication which can probably be found in larger reference libraries is *The Register of the Great Seal of Scotland*. In 11 volumes it covers the period 1306-1668 and contains the charters granting land by the crown to its vassals. Volumes 1-9 are in Latin, Volumes 10 and 11 in English.

The address of the National Library of Scotland is George IV Bridge, Edinburgh EH1 1EW.

The Scottish National War Memorial, The Castle, Edinburgh EH2 2YT is administered by trustees as an independent body and employs only a small part-time staff who are unable to undertake genealogical research. Specific enquiries should be addressed to the secretary, T.C. Barker. Rolls of Honour for all Scottish regiments are available there for public inspection. (See also Army.)

Scottish local government reorganisation took place in 1975, a year later than in England. The former counties were disbanded and their functions divided between Regional and District Councils. However, the former counties are still used in addresses e.g. Dundee, Angus rather than Dundee, Tayside Region.

The Anglo-Scottish Family History Society was formed as a branch of the Manchester and Lancashire FHS in 1982 to promote the study of Scottish migrant families and assist with tracing their ancestors back to Scotland. Further details from the Secretary, Mrs D. Ramsbottom, c/o Clayton House, 59 Piccadilly, Manchester M1 2AQ.

SCOTTISH EMIGRANTS *A Dictionary of Scottish Emigrants into England and Wales* edited by J.D. Beckett, Vol.1 1984, Vol.2 1988, Vol.3 1989. These publications have been issued by the Anglo-Scottish FHS section of Manchester and Lancashire FHS. A number of reference sources have been indexed recording families of which little is known. The introduction gives a guide to variants of Scottish names.

For those with Scottish ancestry trying to locate the origins of their migrant ancestor who was born before 1855, this series could be a useful aid. Details from Mr J.D. Beckett, 34 Eastwood Avenue, Droylsden, Manchester, M35 6BJ.

See also *The Emigrant Scots* by James Lawson, Aberdeen & North East Scotland FHS, price £3.75 plus p&p.

SCRIVENER He was a clerk who specialised in drawing up bonds etc. At a time when many people were illiterate, he offered an important service to the community. The Scriveners have their own London Livery Company.

SEAMEN see also Nelson and Royal Navy. The records of the Registrar General of Shipping and Seamen 1835 to 1857 could be a useful source of information for an ancestor who was in the merchant navy, for place of birth is given. These are at the PRO. See PRO Records Information leaflet 5 *Records of the Registrar General of Shipping and Seamen*, 125 *Navy, Royal Air Force and Merchant Navy Pension Records* and Family Fact Sheet 6, *Tracing an Ancestor in the Merchant Navy: Seamen*; and 7 *Tracing* *an Ancestor in the Merchant Navy: Masters and Mates*.

For earlier records, such as lists of the crews of ships and each voyage made, you need to know the names of the ships and their ports of registration.

Apart from the Register of Seamen, there are other registers such as:

1. Certificates of competence and service of masters and mates.
2. Certificates of competence and service of engineers.
3. Certificates of competence of skippers and mates: fishing boats.
4. Registers of the wages and effects of deceased seamen.
5. Index of apprentices and apprentices' indentures.
6. Registers of births, marriages and deaths of passengers at sea compiled from official ships' logs.
7. Registers of births and deaths of British Nationals at sea.

In the IWM (q.v.) series *Tracing Individual Service Records and Medal Citations* those of interest might be:

15C *Merchant Navy*
15F *Prisoners of War*

You may find it helpful to read *Certificates of British registry of vessels* by Dr Reginald Davies, FTM Vol.9 No.11 (Sep 1993). *My Ancestor Was A Merchant Seaman: How can I find out more about him?*, 2nd ed. 1991 by Christopher and Michael Watts, price £4.40 inc. p&p from the SOG.

Lloyd's Marine Collection, deposited at the Guildhall Library (q.v.), includes Lloyd's Captains' Registers 1868 to 1947 listing all holders of masters certificates with full name, place and date of birth and a complete service history.

The Information Centre, Lloyd's Register of Shipping, 71 Fenchurch Street, London, EC3M 4BS holds some records which may be useful and can be consulted without prior appointment between 9.00am-4.30pm Mon-Fri. A set of six Information Sheets is available on request.

They have Registers of Ships from 1764 which name the owners and builders of the ships; Registers of Shipyards just prior to 1800 through to 1980 and some Casualty Returns. They *do not* hold crew or passenger lists or records of naval ships.

See *Dictionary of Disasters During the Age of Steam (including sailing ships and ships of war lost in action) 1824-1962* (2 vols.), by Charles Hocking, Lloyd's Register of Shipping, 1969.

Registers of births and deaths of Merchant Navy personnel 1837 to 1890 are at St Catherine's House. From 1891 they are held by the Registrar-General for Shipping and Seamen, Block 2, Government Buildings, St Agnes Road, Gabalfa, Cardiff CF4 4YA.

Requests by dependents of seamen, naval men etc. for assistance were made to Trinity House (founded in 1529 to deal with matters related to safety at sea etc.) in the form of a 'petition' from which we can glean interesting family history data. They span the years 1780 to 1854 and are to be found, arranged alphabetically, in the Library of the SOG. See *Trinity House Petitions* by Anthony J. Camp, FTM Vol.2 No.4 (May-June 1986) and *Trinity House Petitions. A Calendar of the records of the Corporation of Trinity House, London in the Library of the Society of Genealogists*, 1988, a publication of the index. Price £10.00 inc. p&p.

A very large collection of Crew Lists, Agreements and Official Logs 1861- 1938 are in the custody of the Memorial University of Newfoundland. The University has a research and photocopying service. A fee is payable. Enquiries to: Chairman, Maritime History Group, Memorial University of Newfoundland, St John's, Newfoundland, A1C 5S7 Canada. These were originally at the PRO and it is believed that only about 10% of this class of record now remain there. An index to the records on microfiche is available on request in the Reference Room.

See Feature Article *The Maritime History Archive: sources for research* by Roberta Thomas, FHN&D, Vol.9 No.3 (April 1994).

SECOND FLEET see Convicts, Emigration and Transportation.

SEE Often used as a synonym for diocese, though technically the seat of the bishop or the diocesan centre.

SELF-ACTER MINDER A person who looked after a self-acting 'mule' in a spinning machine.

SERGEANTRY/SERJEANTRY see also Manorial Records. A form of English feudal tenure where dues were rendered to the Sovereign, not a mesne lord (q.v.). It was divided into Grand and Petty, the former a special service to the crown, the latter the renderings of an implement of war to the Sovereign.

SERVANTS TAX (Male) Between 1777 and 1852 a tax was levied on households employing male servants (which would include gamekeepers and gardeners). Female servants were taxed in 1785, a guinea being payable in each case. The SOG holds returns for the year 1780.

SERVICEMEN'S WILLS see also Army. Servicemen (including minors) in actual military service and mariners or seamen at sea could make nuncupative Wills, i.e. Wills verbally declared in the presence of witnesses. When on active service, or under orders for this, they could make holograph Wills, i.e. Wills in their own handwriting without witnesses. Servicemen of Scottish or Channel Islands domicile could make handwritten Wills without witnesses at any time. Servicemen's Pay Books carried forms for both types of Will.

SESSIONS BOOKS Virtually minutes of the proceedings of the Quarter Sessions kept by the Clerks of the Peace. Details of those present, the indictments, verdicts and sentences were included.

SETTLEMENT see also Examination. From 1691 a settlement could be gained by birth in a parish, by various rent/rate qualifications, by being apprenticed to a parishioner or by serving a year in service in the parish. Anyone from the working class wishing to move from one parish to another had to obtain a certificate saying that his parish of settlement would be responsible if he needed poor relief. The system lapsed early in the 19th century. The transcribing and indexing of these certificates is progressing for various counties; your county FHS should be able to inform you of any such indexes being prepared.

SEXTON He was appointed by the Vestry, the Incumbent or the Churchwarden. He was sometimes responsible for grave-digging and generally acted as caretaker, cleaner and carried out simple repairs in the church.

SHERIFF He was the Crown's representative in the County, but there was some overlapping with the duties of Lord-Lieutenant. His duties gradually passed to the Justices and Coroners and the Lord-Lieutenant became the Crown's Representative.

SHIP MONEY A tax first levied by Charles I in 1634 to finance the Navy and protect English ships against pirate attacks and impending threats from the Dutch and the French. Initially it was applied to citizens in maritime areas but later on to those in other areas. It became one of the chief issues between King and Parliament and was declared illegal in 1641. Many lists of those paying the tax survive; documents may be found among the State Papers-Domestic at the PRO.

SHIPWRIGHTS England, as a maritime nation, had great need of these 'makers of ships'. There was a London Livery Company, see *Records of the Shipwrights' Company* by C.H. Ridge and A.C. Wright, 1939.
　　Their records have been published by Phillimore – Vol.1 1428 to 1780 (1939) and Vol.2 1728 to 1858 (1946). These Guild records contain 241 pages of alphabetically arranged names of all known members of the Company with references to the volumes in which they are found with some details of what may be discovered.

SHIRE PUBLICATIONS Shire Publications, Cromwell House, Church Street, Princes Risborough, Aylesbury, Bucks, HP17 9AJ publish a series of booklets known as Shire Albums some of which provide brief introductions to particular trades and occupations. There is also a 'Discovering' series by the same publisher and details have been given under the appropriate headings (e.g. Picture Postcards). A comprehensive list of these modestly priced, most useful, books can be obtained on request to the above address. Out of print titles can often be found in second-hand bookshops.

SHOEMAKER The index to shoemakers compiled by Miss Eunice Wilson has now been handed over to Northampton Museum and will eventually be amalgamated with the one they have been compiling over the last 25 years. A bibliography and list of publications on Shoemaking can be obtained from the Keeper of the Boot and Shoe Collection, Central Museum, Guildhall Road, Northampton NN1 1DP. Please send one 2nd class stamp plus sae, or 3 IRCs. The Museum would welcome information set out on 5" x 3" index cards giving details of Shoemaker, Bootmaker, Cordwainer etc. and contributor's name and address.

SILHOUETTES see Portraits.

SILVERSMITH see Goldsmith.

SIX CLERKS (The) The senior clerical officials of the Court of Chancery. In the 17th century each of the Six Clerks began to file cases separately in their respective divisions under their own names e.g. Bridges, Collins, Hamilton. The complexities of the system are very well described in the *Guide to the Contents of the Public Record Office* Vol.1 pp 32-33.

SKINNER The early guild controlled the English fur trade. Furs were part of male attire and much favoured by royalty. See *A Brief Description of the Worshipful Company of Skinners* by Dr Adam Fox, 1968.

SLAUGHTER HOUSES After 1786 owners had to be licensed by the Justices. Application had to be supported by a certificate from the minister and churchwardens approving the application. The records are with those of the Quarter Sessions (q.v.). They can be useful in tracing butchers.

SMITH A worker in metal. Usually specified as Blacksmith (iron), Whitesmith (tin), Goldsmith, Silversmith etc.

SOCIAL STATUS There was great preoccupation with social status in the 18th and 19th centuries. One has only to read the novels of Jane Austen to be very conscious of this. The highest social status was accorded to those who were titled or connected with titled people and whose wealth lay in the possession of great estates. Those whose wealth came from 'trade' were not considered high in the social scale. However, success and fame could be achieved by those born of humble status – e.g. Ben Jonson, Josiah Wedgwood, Richard Arkwright, Robert Burns, and even Jane Austen herself. Cardinal Wolsey is reputed to have been the son of a butcher.

SOCIETY OF GENEALOGISTS The Society (at 14 Charterhouse Buildings, Goswell Road, London EC1M 7BA, Tel. 0171 251 8799) was founded in 1911 to promote and encourage the study of genealogy. There are over thirteen thousand members paying an annual subscription, fourteen hundred living outside the British Isles. It is a registered charity and completely self-supporting.

See *Society of Genealogists 1911-1986* by Anthony J. Camp, Gen. Mag. Vol.22 No.4 (Dec 1986).

Members and non-members have access to a library which is unique in this country and provides incomparable sources for students. There are over 70,000 volumes as well as much manuscript and microform material, arranged on three floors. The collection of copies of parish registers, monumental inscriptions, printed and typescript family histories, census indexes, directories, poll books, school registers, and the vast indexes of marriages, chancery proceedings etc. are justly famous. Most books and typescripts are on open shelves. Members in the British Isles may borrow printed books, microfilms and microfiche with certain exceptions. The material relates mainly to the British Isles but there are collections on British people living abroad, in the Commonwealth and in America.

An outline Guide *Using the Library of the Society of Genealogists*, is available and should be read in advance by all visitors. Catalogues of many parts of the Library (including the parish registers, monumental inscriptions and census indexes) have been published and are regularly updated.

The library is closed on Mondays, but open Tuesday, Friday and Saturday 10.00am-6.00pm, Wednesday and Thursday 10.00am-8.00pm. It is closed for stocktaking in the week of the first Monday in February and on Friday afternoons and Saturdays prior to bank holidays. No appointment is necessary. If you wish to stay all day there is a common room with tea and coffee making facilities etc for those bringing sandwiches.

Non-members may use the library on payment of fees (Aug 1994): £3 for an hour, £7.50 for four hours, £10 for a day and evening.

All members pay an Entrance Fee of £7.50 when first joining the Society. The annual subscription for those living within 25 miles of Trafalgar Square is £30. For those outside that limit or abroad the rate is £21. There are reduced rates for married couples and registered full-time students under the age of 25. Members receive the quarterly *Genealogists' Magazine* which is available to non-members at £12 a year. (All prices as at Sep 1994.)

The Society also publishes the quarterly periodical *Computers in Genealogy*. The subscription is £6 to members or £7 to non-members. Meetings and conferences on the subject are held regularly.

Open lectures take place at the Society throughout the year. Courses for beginners are run twice a year and a variety of other courses, meetings and conferences are held. A programme may be had on request. The lecture room is also used for London meetings of a number of family history societies and is available for hire at reasonable rates.

The Society maintains a bookshop which is open Tuesday, Friday and Saturday 10.00am-5.45pm, Wednesday and Thursday 10.00am-7.45pm. It publishes and sells a wide variety of books of interest to genealogists. Members receive a 10% discount on the Society's own publications. A list may be had on request.

Members of five years standing may be elected to Fellowship of the Society by the Fellows for distinguished services to the Society or to genealogy. Honorary Fellows may be elected for very distinguished services to genealogy.

SOLICITOR see Legal Profession.

SOMERSET HOUSE see also Divorce and Wills. This was built on the site of the 16th century palace of Protector Somerset, the present building was specifically intended to house various public bodies. The principal present occupant is the Board of Inland Revenue.

The rooms facing onto The Strand housed the indexes of Births, Marriages, and Deaths until their removal to St Catherine's House.

Directly across the main courtyard from The Strand entrance is the Principal Registry of the Family Division of The High Court (Principal Probate Registry) where are available for public inspection the consolidated annual indexes, starting on 12th January 1858, of grants of probate (wills) and letters of administration (admons.), the latter being separately indexed up to and including 1870. Copies of wills and admons. may be examined on payment of a small fee; a photocopying service is available. Open to the public Mon-Fri 10.00am.-4.30pm.

Copies of divorce decrees absolute (England and Wales only) since 1858 are kept by the Record Keeper of the Divorce Registry; the index is not open to the general public but a search service is available for a fee. Permission to see closed files may be sought from the Principal Registry of the Family Division, Somerset House, Strand, London WC2R 1LP.

Somerset House Wills from 1858 by Eve McLaughlin, is a good introductory guide to those unfamiliar with Somerset House. It gives information on the indexes of wills and admons., intestacy, the Married Women's Property Act etc. Obtainable from FTM price £1.55 inc. p&p.

SOUTH AFRICA see also Emigration. A very detailed survey of the subject appears in *Handbook of Genealogical Research in South Africa* 2nd edition, by R.T.J. Lombard, published by the Institute of Historical Research. Obtainable from the Human Sciences Research Council, Private Bag X41, Pretoria 0001, South Africa.

The National Archives of South Africa was the subject of an article by Mark Tapping in FTM Vol.2 No.6 (Sep-Oct 1986). He subsequently wrote for the same journal *Human Sciences Research Council of South Africa* , Vol.3 No.4 (Feb 1987), *Marching On Pretoria* Vol.3 No.6 (April 1987), *Genealogy and the Albany Museum* Vol.4 No.4 (Feb 1988), *South African Death Notices* (FTM Year Book 1986).

Mark Tapping is Chairman of The West Rand FHS, PO Box 760, Florida 1710, South Africa. Information on the Genealogical Society of South Africa can be obtained from The Secretary, PO Box 1344, Kelvin, 2054, S.A.

The Human Sciences Research Council has published *South African Genealogies, Vol.1 A-C, Vol.2 D-G* compiled by J.A. Heese, ed. by R.T.J. Lombard. These are the first volumes in a series based on *Geschlacht-register der oude Kaapsche familien* by C.C. de Villiers, of 1894, tabling Dutch and Huguenot families who settled in the Cape Colony from 1652, and their descendants to 1810.

Another in a series of volumes to be published by the University of Natal Press is *British Settlers in Natal 1824-1857: A Biographical Register* .

The South African War 1899-1902: Service Records of British and Colonial Women. A Record of the Service in South Africa of Military and Civilian Nurses, Laywomen and Civilians compiled by Sheila Gray, published by the author, 1993, and available from her at 54a Towai Street, Auckland 5, New Zealand or try your local library. Taken from a wide variety of sources this comprehensive work has over 1,700 names

An article on obtaining information about Emigration to South Africa appeared in the Aberdeen & North East Scotland Newsletter No.15, June 1985. It was written by Diane Baptie and quoted contact addresses in that country. *Worldwide Family History* by Noel Currer-Briggs has a chapter dealing with the subject.

SOUTH PACIFIC ISLANDS see New Zealand.

SPELLING As the study of your ancestors takes you further back in time you will come up against the problems of spelling variations. It must be remembered that even in the mid 19th century many people could neither read nor write, nor were they certain how their surname was spelt.

When a baptism, marriage or burial took place, the incumbent or church official would enter the name in the register as it seemed to him it should be spelt, but the dialect of the informant might mislead him. The same applies to BMD entries made by Registrars after 1837.

It is an idea to study the sound of your name and then write down all the possible spellings which would produce the same sound when read. A name such as 'Wright' could be found as Rite, Right, Write etc. The more unusual your name is, the more strange variants you may find. David Iredale, in his book *Discovering Your Family Tree*, tells us that he has found his name in old records appearing as Yoredale, Uredale, Yoreval and even Jervaulx.

A useful tip is to hold your nose and say the name (some of our ancestors were very adenoidal) — it can produce remarkable results!

STAMP DUTY see Parish Registers.

STATE PAPERS (Domestic and Foreign) Originally informal reference collections of papers compiled by clerks to successive Secretaries of State. In 1610 an official Keeper was appointed to register and care for the growing collection.

Not every Secretary of State passed over all the papers accumulated during his tenure of office so many remain in private collections although their whereabouts are listed in the reports of the Royal Commission on Historical Manuscripts. State Papers in the official collection are now in the PRO.

STATIONERS HALL Copyright (q.v.) presented no problem until the development of printing; the need to sell multiple copies of a single printed work before the final profit was made raised the question.

From 1554 until 1924 copyright was normally secured by registration with the Stationers' Company in London. Throughout the period during which registration was necessary to establish copyright, there was widespread disregard of the procedure, partly because of the registration fee, but mainly to evade the obligation to provide complimentary copies for copyright libraries.

The Stationers' Company has copyright registers from 1554 to 1842; the entries up to 1709 have been published in *A Transcript of the Registers of the Company of Stationers of London 1554-1660* ed. E. Arber and *A Transcript of the Registers of the Worshipful Company of Stationers from 1640 to 1708 (1709) ed. Briscoe Eyre, London, 1913-14.* For entries from 1710 to 1842 the original registers need to be consulted; the absence of an index from 1700 makes knowledge of the date of publication essential.

Copyright records held at the PRO cover the years 1842 to 1924. Since 1911 the Stationers' Company has maintained a voluntary register. These and the pre-1842 records may be seen at Stationers' Hall, Stationers' Hall Court, London EC4.

The Stationery Office is responsible for copyright in government publications as well as for their printing, publication and sale.

See PRO Records Information leaflet 60 *Stationers' Hall Copyright Records* (includes detailed notes on the various Copyright Acts and a diagram showing the arrangement of the Registers).

The Stationers' Company — A History, 1403 to 1959 by Cyprian Blagdon, 1960.

'STEP' RELATIONSHIP see In-Law.

STEWARD He usually presided over the manorial courts, kept records and dealt with rents and land transfers. The bailiffs (q.v.) were under his supervision. He was accountable to the lord of the manor.

STOCKINNER/STOCKINGER see also F.W.K. One who worked at a stocking hand loom, a stocking weaver or framework knitter.

STRAYS (Out-of-Area-Index) see also Deaths Overseas, Migrants. A stray is a recorded event (baptism, marriage, burial,etc.) which takes place *outside the area in which the person normally lived*. Most family history societies interpret this as 'out-of-county' (e.g. in the case of a gentleman from Stafford marrying a lady from Warwick at Coventry, only the groom is a stray); some give a narrower interpretation particularly if they cover a city. Yorkshire sometimes uses a wider interpretation and defines strays by Riding. Census strays are rather different as they normally show people resident outside their county of birth.

Strays appear in all kinds of places! If extracted they can be of great value in locating that lost ancestor. The most frequent types are those found in marriage and census records. Many coastal parishes record numerous stray burials of sailors drowned at sea and washed up on the foreshore, and you will also find baptisms, gravestone inscriptions, settlement papers etc. If you find a stray whilst researching, record the entry carefully, using block capitals for all surnames and place names. Note both the county of origin of the person(s) concerned and the one where the event took place; make sure that you give enough information to take the researcher back to the source e.g. newspaper (giving title, full date and page number), Parish Register, Bishop's Transcript, gravestone (don't forget to identify the churchyard).

Make two copies of the entry on 5" x 3" slips, using carbon paper if necessary. Send them to the FFHSs Strays Clearing House, where they will be sorted and forwarded twice yearly — one slip to the relevant FHS, the other to the National Strays Index. See FFHS Leaflet *The Strays Clearing House and The National Strays Index*, obtainable from the Administrator of the FFHS. Please send sae and an extra first class stamp or 3 IRCs.

Most FHSs now have a 'strays index' for their county compiled from the slips forwarded to them; these can usually be consulted in exchange for sae or 3 IRCs (and sometimes a small donation to society funds). Some societies publish their strays in booklet form. Details of co-ordinators can be found in the FFHSs *Handbook*.

Generally speaking, 'Marriage strays' will be found in the appropriate County Marriage Index, likewise 'Census strays'. Addresses of those contacts will be found in *Marriage, Census and Other Indexes for the Family Historian* also published by the FFHS.

The National Index of Strays is not open to enquiries. Each collection is arranged alphabetically by surname and is periodically typed up, microfiched and distributed free of charge to member societies on request. Four Collections of these strays are now on fiche; copies are also deposited at the SOG and the IHGS (q.v.). Copies of these fiches can be purchased by individuals at a very modest price. Further details in FFHS leaflet referred to above.

Ms Eileen Crook and Mr Ken Turner are compiling an index of Strays from the Roman Catholic and Church of England records in Liverpool Record Office. The index contains thousands of entries including soldiers, militiamen and midshipmen, beginning in the early 1700s, and references to foreign or unusual names or addresses. For further information write to Ms Crook, 60 Leafield Road, Hunts Cross, Liverpool L25 OPZ, enclosing sae or 2 IRCs.

SUBSIDIES These had been the main means of raising money before the Civil War, and they occur again during the 1660s. Collection was by instalments so they are difficult to date precisely. Only the wealthier members of the community were affected, gentry, landowners, the more substantial tradesmen. Distinction was made between taxation on goods ('moveables') and land. The amounts paid had become stereotyped and did not relate closely to real wealth, but are still an indication of status.

Names are not given in the 14th and 15th century Rolls; the 'Great Subsidy' of 1524-27 is probably the most genealogically useful. The last subsidies to be levied were in Charles II's reign. Surviving records are in the PRO, often in poor repair. See Gibson's *Hearth Tax, Other Later Stuart Tax Lists etc.* FFHS, and *The Lay Subsidies* by M.W. Beresford, 'The Amateur Historian' Vol.3 No.8 (1958)

SUFFRAGETTES The Fawcett Library, Old Castle Street, London E1 7NT specialises in the history of this movement and the personalities involved. The Library is available to the public.

SUNDAY SCHOOL see Education.

SURGEON see Medical Profession.

SURNAMES see also Deed Poll and Spelling. It is doubtful whether knowing the origin of your surname will in any way help you trace your ancestry, but it is obviously of interest. Surnames came into use in the 12th and 13th centuries. See *The Relevance of Surnames in Genealogy* SOG Leaflet No.7 and *Surname Variants* by Derek Palgrave, Feature Article, FHN&D, Vol.8 No.4 (Sep 1992).

Your nearest Reference Library, or family history society to which you may belong, should have some of the following books which you can consult.

Sir William Addison *Understanding English Surnames*, B.T. Batsford, 1978.
H. Barber *British Family Names, their origin and meaning*, 1894 reprinted 1903 and 1968.
C.W. Bardsley *Dictionary of English and Welsh Surnames with special American instances*, 1901 reprinted 1967.
Basil Cottle, *The Penguin Dictionary of Surnames*.
E. Ekwall, *Concise Oxford Dictionary of English Place-Names*, Oxford, 1960.
C.L. L'Estrange Ewan *A History of the Surnames of the British Isles* reprinted 1968.
H.B. Guppy, *The Homes of Family Names in Great Britain*, reprinted Baltimore, 1968.
Patrick Hanks & Flavia Hodges *A Dictionary of Surnames,* OUP, 1988.
W.O. Hassall *History Through Surnames*, 1967.
G.W. Lasker & C.G.N. Mascie-Taylor *An Atlas of British Surnames*, published for the Guild of One-Name Studies (q.v.) by Wayne State University Press, 1990.
Padraig MacGiolla-Dhomnaigh *Ulster Surnames*, Dublin 1985.
R.A. McKinley *A History of British Surnames*, Longman, 1990.
L.G. Pine *The Story of Surnames*, 1965 reprinted 1969.
T.J. & Prys Morgan, *Welsh Surnames*, Cardiff, 1985.
P.H. Reaney, *The Origin of English Surnames*, London, 1967, 1980.

P.H. Reaney *Dictionary of British Surnames*, 1961.
E.C. Smith *The Story of Our Names*, 1950.
Shire Publications *Discovering Surnames*

Under 'Spelling' we have dealt with variations in the spelling of names. Another problem arises in records up to the end of the 18th century from the common practice in parish registers and elsewhere of abbreviating names by contraction e.g. Wmson would be written for Williamson, Hilt for Hilton etc. Usually a short wavy line was placed over the name where letters were omitted. It is easy to miss these marks.

There are specialist books on Irish and Scottish surnames.

Sir R.E. Matherson's *Irish Surnames* lists those surnames which have at least 5 entries in the national birth indexes for 1890 and gives information as to the distribution of the name and variant spellings.

E. McLysaght *The Surnames of Ireland*, Dublin 1985. This is an expanded version of an earlier *Guide to Irish Surnames*.

George F. Black *The Surnames of Scotland*, 1946, published by New York Public Library. This is a very thorough book of reference.

SURROGATE Appointed by a bishop to act on his behalf. Often empowered to issue Marriage Licences.

SURTEES SOCIETY Named after Robert Surtees, author of the *History of Durham*. The Society, founded in 1834, was one of the earliest publishing societies concentrating on the records of the counties of North Eastern England. Hon. Secretary: A.J. Piper, The Priors' Kitchen, The College, Durham, DH1 3EQ.

SURVEYOR OF HIGHWAYS see Highways.

SWEEPS From earliest times households possessed fires which over the centuries developed into the more sophisticated fireplaces and chimney stacks which we know today. Houses were frequently haphazardly enlarged by simply adding an extension to the back or side wall and as most rooms had a fireplace each flue went up to join another and possibly another, creating a maze which eventually opened to the sky. Irrespective of the number of fireplaces in a household or the type of fuel burnt in them, soot accumulated in these often very narrow flues which had to be swept, an unpleasant job. One of the most effective means of achieving this was to send someone up the flue with a scraper and brush and obviously the person had to be small; in the majority of cases very young boys were used though it was known for girls to be employed too. All too frequently these children were foundlings or orphans from the parish workhouse whose lives were held cheaply.

The job of a climbing boy was unpleasant to say the least and often fatal. Whilst there would have been exceptions to the rule most sweeps had little regard for their 'apprentices', indeed the job of a chimney sweep was itself not popular. An Act of 1788, largely brought about by the campaigning of Jonas Hanway, forbade the use of boys under eight for this purpose but it was widely disregarded. In 1803 a Society was founded to obtain the abolition of chimney sweeping by climbing boys and in 1817 a Select Committee was set up to examine the whole question. Further Acts were passed in 1834 and 1840 forbidding boys under the age of ten, then 21 respectively to sweep chimneys by climbing, but again these were largely disregarded by master sweeps. It took the publication of Charles Kingsley's *The Water Babies* in 1863 to arouse public awareness of the problem but it was not finally resolved until Lord Salisbury's Chimney Sweepers Bill of 1875, which provided for the registration of master sweeps with the local police. (Some of the licences issued to them may still be found amongst police records.)

See *Sweeps* by J.R. Goddard FTM Vol.7 No.7 (May 1991) which gives further bibliography.

SWING RIOTS Agricultural Riots 1830: a wave of rick-burnings and destruction of threshing machines in southern and eastern England resulting in 19 executions and 481 transportations. Threatening letters to farmers were signed 'Swing'. Although suppressed by the government better conditions were eventually won by the labourers.

See *Machine Breakers and Convicts,* Jill Chambers, FTM Vol.9 No.11 (Sep 1993). Considerable research into these Riots has enabled her to make contact with a number of descendants of those involved with the riots. She has published three books on the subject and from 1994 a Newsletter will appear twice a year as a means of putting people in touch with each other. There is a growing index of names open to search in exchange for a modest fee. Details of all these in exchange for sae or 2 IRCs to Jill Chambers, 54 Chagney Close, Letchworth, Herts SG6 4BY.

TAILORS see Merchant Taylors.

TAXATION see also Game Duty, Hearth, Income, Land, Poll, Queen Anne's Bounty, Registration, Servants, Ship Money, Subsidies and Window Tax.

We have expanded upon only those taxes most likely to be of value to family historians; for most of these, if records exist the location is given in Jeremy Gibson's *Hearth Tax, Other Later Stuart Tax Lists etc*, FFHS. See also PRO Records Information leaflet 56 *Tax Records as a Source for Local and Family History c.1198 to 1698*, and PRO Readers' Guide No.5 *Tudor Taxation Records: a Guide for Users* by Richard Hoyle, PRO Publications, 1994, price £5.95 plus p&p.

Numerous other taxes have been levied over the years and a comprehensive list of these National, Local and Ecclesiastical taxes, with dates, is given in *The Local Historian's Encyclopedia* (q.v.).

Additional information can be gained from *Local taxation: national legislation and the problems of enforcement* by J.V. Beckett, Standing Conference for Local History, 1980.

TEACHERS see Education.

TELEPHONE DIRECTORIES The earliest directory is dated April 1880 and contains entries for numerous subscribers. (Prior to this numbers were not published and a caller asked the operator for someone by name and address!)

The collection is held by British Telecom and can be viewed by prior appointment. Contact BT Archives, GO9, Telephone House, Temple Avenue, London EC4Y OHL (Tel. 0171 822 1002). Other BT archives control records outlining the history of tele-communications filling almost a mile of shelving in total. BT have plans to pass on to local record offices deeds which are no longer required by them, relating to many thousands of properties which date back to the 17th century.

The Guildhall Library (q.v.) also has an excellent collection of both London and Provincial directories.

Most public libraries hold a complete set of telephone directories so it is possible to build up distributions of specific surnames quite easily. Apart from the inevitable concentrations in large modern conurbations the results often reflect earlier settlement patterns which may lead a researcher to consider exploring source material in the areas concerned.

TENANT IN COMMON A person who has a specific share in a property with others. No one of them has exclusive possession of the property since each is entitled to occupy or use the property in common with the others. The interest *can* be left by will on the occasion of the death of one of the tenants in common. If it is not left by will it will pass under the rules of intestacy. The interest of a tenant in common will *not* necessarily pass therefore to the other tenant(s) in common (unlike joint tenancy (q.v.)).

Business property held by people in partnership *must* be held by them as tenants in common and can *not* be held by them as joint tenants. A joint tenancy can be 'severed' and converted into a tenancy in common but not vice versa.

TENANT IN TAIL see Entail.

TERRIERS see Glebe Terriers.

THEATRE The information given below is taken from an article *Family History and the Theatre* by Alan Ruston published in 'Hertfordshire People', No.35 (Winter 1988) the magazine of the Hertfordshire F & PHS.

The most useful source of information about actors, actresses, playwrights, producers, theatrical managers etc. is the Theatrical Press. In these, obituaries are often elaborate. Below are the main theatrical journals:

The Era (1838-1939), *Theatrical Journal* (1839-1873: weekly),
L'Entracte (1873 to 1906 **Annual**), *Illustrated Sporting and Dramatic News*
(1874-1945), *Era Almanac* (1868-1919 **Annual**),
The Theatre (1877-1897), *The Stage* (1881-date),
Theatre World (from 1925 to date).
Who's Who in The Theatre 20th century.

Of these *The Era* and *Theatrical Journal* are the most important. The latter is on microfilm at Westminster City Library, which specialises in the theatre. Although these publications concentrate on the London stage they do cover the theatre in the rest of the country, often for quite obscure places. Theatres in virtually every town are mentioned in detail, at one time or another. There is also coverage of the USA and what were termed 'the colonies'.

The main British historical journal *Theatre Notebook* has been published since 1946. It is fully indexed in separate volumes.

Accounts and reviews of plays can be found in *The Times*, *The Illustrated London News* and local newspapers. The latter are a mine of information for their area especially for pantomimes in December. Pantomimes pre-1870 were very different to those we know today; actors of all types took part in them.

Theatre programmes only came into regular use from the 1800s. Before that all advertisements and lists of players were announced on playbills. Collections of playbills can be found in large Reference Libraries, especially in London. Their location in London is given in Diana Howard's *London Theatres and Music Halls 1850 to 1950* published by the Library Association 1970. The Guildhall Library's (q.v.) collection goes well beyond London and there are extensive collections in the USA e.g. at the Harvard Theatre Collection.

A Dictionary of Actors by Edward Nungezer, 1929, and *The Organisation and Personnel of the Shakespeare Company* by T.W.Baldwin, 1927, contain hundreds of names; you should be able to see these books in your local Reference Library.

Also *A Biographical Dictionary of Actors etc 1660-1800* ed. Highfill, Burnim and Langhams Publications, Southern Illinois University Press: at least 7 vols.

English Theatrical Literature 1559-1900, by Lowe, Arnott and Robinson, London, 1970 is a guide to earlier books.

The Theatre Museum is at 1e Tavistock Street, London WC2E 7PA, public entrance in Russell Street. The Theatre Museum Library is open to readers by appointment Tuesday to Friday, admission is free. This is also the postal address of The Society for Theatre Research. Eventually the Museum's internationally-renowned Archive will be situated in premises at Blythe Road, London.

Collections are also held at the Royal Opera House in London and the Glasgow University Library, Hillhead Street, Glasgow G12 8QE.

There is also the University of Bristol Theatre Collection, Vandyke Building, Bristol BS1 5LP.

The British Music Hall Society can be contacted c/o Brodie & Middletone Ltd, 68 Drury Lane, London WC2B 5SP. *British Music Hall — Illustrated Who's Who from 1850 to the Present Day* by Roy Busby, Elec. Pub., 1976 and *British Music Hall* by Raymond Mander and Jo Mitchenson, Gentry Books, 1974 are just two of the books available on this particular section of the theatre.

See also *London Theatres and Concert Halls* by Debra Shipley and Mary Peplow, Shire Album No.203, 1987.

An Index of Entertainers of any nationality born before 1920 is being compiled by Mrs M. Dunn, 2 Summer Lane, Sheffield S17 4AJ. Contributions would be welcome from anyone who can provide details of entertainers, their career history with original and stage names, place of birth and parentage etc.

Enquiries should be accompanied by sae or 3 IRCs.

THIRD FLEET   see Convicts, Emigration and Transportation.

THORESBY SOCIETY   Named after the antiquary Ralph Thoresby; has published more than 70 volumes of material mainly concerned with Leeds, South Yorkshire and the surrounding neighbourhood. Holds regular meetings. Hon. Secretary: Claremont, 23 Clarendon Road, Leeds LS2 9NZ.

THOROTON SOCIETY Named after Robert Thoroton author of *Antiquities of Nottinghamshire* and specialising in the publishing of material of that county. Hon. Secretary: J.S. Childs, 20 Cransley Ave, Wollaton, Nottingham NG8 2QY.

TIDE WAITER Tide Waiters and their predecessors Tidesmen, were Customs officers of the 18th century whose duties were to board ships coming in on the tide with a view to preventing smuggling and the like. Other officers were known as Land Waiters and King's Waiters. For a more detailed history see *Ancient and Rightful Customs* by Edward Carson, Faber & Faber, 1972.

TINKERS see Gypsies.

TITHES see also Queen Anne's Bounty. A tenth part of the main produce of the land and of both stock and labour such as wool, pigs, milk etc. was paid to the local church.

Tithe accounts — where they have survived — are a useful source of information for the family historian, particularly as the tithes were paid by quite humble people.

The Tithe Commutation Act of 1836 allowed tithes to be commuted to a rent- charge based on the price of corn. Tithes were abolished in 1936. See PRO Records Information leaflet 41 *Tithe Records in the PRO*.

Tithe Maps and Apportionments (mostly drawn up in the 1840s) should be in CROs. They are very useful for pin-pointing the exact spot where an ancestor lived (see Maps).

The Tithe Documents Register is available for public use in the search room at The Royal Commission on Historical Manuscripts, Quality House, Quality Court, Chancery Lane, London WC2A 1HP.

See *Tithes, maps and apportionments and the 1836 Act* by E.J. Evans, Phillimore for BALH, 1993, price £5.50 inc. p&p from SOG.

TITLE DEEDS see also Entail, Ireland and Scotland. This is a general term for documents relating to the ownership of land and property. They are useful for filling in details of your family history, and particularly in tracking down just where they lived. Occupations are often mentioned and the dates are useful. A great many deeds are in collections of Estate Records many of which are deposited in CROs. See *Old Title Deeds* by N.W. Alcock, Phillimore, 1986, *Title Deeds* by A.A. Dibben, Historical Association Booklet No.H72, reprinted 1972, and an article entitled *Title Deeds* by Janet Smith, Liverpool Family Historian, Vol.7 No.1 (March 1985).

In England Local Deeds Registries were established early in the 18th century for Yorkshire and Middlesex but were not extended to other counties. The Registers which contain Abstracts of Deeds including names, addresses and property descriptions are now held in the appropriate record offices. For further information see Journal of the Society of Archivists Vol.6 (1979-81) pp 274-286 *The Deeds Registries of Yorkshire and Middlesex* by F. Sheppard and V. Belcher and *Reading Old Title Deeds* by Julian Cornwall in FFHS *An Introduction to...* series.

TOLL see also Turnpikes. The right to levy dues and later described the dues themselves. Tolls were levied at markets and for the upkeep of roads and bridges.

TONTINES see Annuity.

TOPOGRAPHICAL DICTIONARY These are descriptions of places arranged in alphabetical order.

Samuel Lewis compiled a series for England, Wales, Scotland and Ireland during the mid 19th century listing parishes and the larger administrative units into which they were grouped. F.A.Youngs has updated much of the content to include the 1974 local government reorganisation in his *Guide to the Local Administrative Units of England, Part I: Southern England*, published by the Royal Historical Society in 1979. *Part II: Northern England* published by the Royal Historical Society in 1991. It is important to be able to establish the jurisdiction, civil and ecclesiastical, for each hamlet/village/town in order to determine the likely whereabouts of archival material.

TOWN WAITER see Tide Waiter.

TRADE UNION Records relating to trade unions are held at Warwick University Modern Records Centre, University Library, Coventry, CV4 7AL (Tel. 01203 524210).

See *Trade Union and related records* by J. Bennett and A. Tough, Warwick University, revised ed. 1991, price £4.50 from SOG.

TRADES see also Occupations and Shire Publications. We have given under separate headings some of the important trades in which our ancestors were engaged, with references to books about the London Livery Companies. Although your ancestor may have lived elsewhere, these books could give useful background information about the trade for use in your family history.

See also *The Book of Trades or Library of Useful Arts*, in three volumes, edited by Beryl Hurley, illustrated. Originally published in 1811 and 1818 now issued by the Wiltshire FHS and obtainable from the FFHS.

The Tool and Trades History Society has published numerous articles in its Newsletters, and there are publications of use to family historians who are doing an in-depth study of their ancestors' occupations. Details of this Society can be obtained from TATHS, Winson Grange, Debenham, Stowmarket, Suffolk, IP14 6LE.

Pinhorns hold an index to a collection of mainly late 18th century and early 19th century trade cards. Largely covering London and Wiltshire but a number of other counties are included in the index. Details of search charges in exchange for sae or 3 IRCs.

TRADING COMPANIES see Companies.

TRAINING SHIPS see National Maritime Museum.

TRANSLATORS The FFHS maintains a list of volunteers who are able to help with translating the occasional correspondence to or from the following countries: Denmark, France, Germany, Greece, Hungary, Italy, Japan, Norway, Poland, Rumania, Russia, Spain, Sweden. One volunteer has regular contact with overseas students so, if in doubt, ask and we will see what can be done. Enquiries to the Administrator of the FFHS enclosing sae and an additional second class stamp or 2 IRCs.

Alternatively the relevant embassy might help or perhaps your local school where the language teacher could use the correspondence as a practical exercise!

TRANSPORTATION see also Convicts and Emigration. This was a very common form of punishment, often replacing the death sentence. Most were transported to the West Indies (until the 18th century) or to Australia (18th and 19th centuries). Arrangements for convicts to be transported were made by the Clerk of the Peace.

Records are to be found in those of Quarter Sessions and Assizes. Minor offenders were sent to American colonies as 'Indentured Servants', and lists of these can be found.

Various indexes of transportees are being compiled. See *Marriage, Census and Other Indexes for Family Historians* by Jeremy Gibson and Elizabeth Hampson, FFHS.

TRAVELLERS see Gypsies.

TRINITY HOUSE PETITIONS see Seamen.

TRONER He was an official in charge of weighing merchandise at the Tron (the scales or weighing machine).

TUITION see also Curation. Guardianship over orphaned minors, under 15 years (boys) or 13 (girls).

TURNPIKES In order to finance road maintenance from the late 17th century onwards, turnpikes were set up at intervals. Travellers would have to pay a toll at each turnpike so that in principle the roads requiring the most upkeep were appropriately funded.

The records of Turnpike Trusts which managed specific sections of roadway often survive in CROs. They include minute books, plans, maps, accounts, local regulations, and even day books of individual toll-house keepers (see p157 *Village Records* by John West, 1962, reprinted Phillimore 1982).

The records provide evidence relating to those employed by Turnpike Trusts and, in a less direct way, highlight the important lines of communication by means of which one's forebears may have migrated.

TYBURN TICKET This was a colloquial name for a certificate granted by the Clerk of the Peace to a person successfully prosecuting a felon. It exempted the person from holding a parish office; it was highly valued and saleable.

UNION see also Workhouse. A grouping of parishes sharing a common workhouse.

UNITARIAN This was a religious denomination which developed from Presbyterianism in the 17th century. Their churches were run by the congregation. Registers were deposited with the Registrar General in 1840.

See *My Ancestors were English Presbyterians/Unitarians: How can I find out more about them?* by Alan Ruston, SOG, 1993, price £4.00 inc. p&p.

UNITED REFORMED CHURCH HISTORY SOCIETY see also Presbyterians and Congregationalists. The United Reformed Church was formed by the joining together of the Congregationalists and the Presbyterians in 1972. The Historical Society of each denomination joined to form the United Reformed Church History Society with headquarters at 86 Tavistock Place, London WC1H 9RT.

UNITED STATES OF AMERICA see also Apprentices, Emigration and Prisoners of War. This is too vast a subject to deal with adequately in this book, but a few comments may be helpful.

Family Historians in Great Britain may have two reasons for wishing to do genealogical research in the U.S.A. It may be that one of their ancestors is of American birth; or they may wish to link up with present day Americans descended from an ancestor who emigrated.

If you are a member of a FHS, you will certainly find that some U.S.A. citizens are members also. By writing to them you may make contact with someone who would be willing to do some research for you, and in return you would do research in your area for them.

There are a great many Genealogical Societies throughout the U.S.A. and if you know the location of your ancestor you could write to the appropriate Society for advice.

In America there are no national indexes such as we have here for births, marriages or deaths. Vital records in America are not inter-state and vital record keeping was not adopted by most states until 1913. Prior to this date there were varying degrees of availability of records. You are advised to find out the location of the source material you need before writing away for information.

See *A County is not a State* by Leonard H. Smith Jr, FTM Vol.4 No.12 (Oct 1988) and *The Researcher's Guide to American Genealogy* by Val D. Greenwood, Genealogical Publishing Co.Inc., 2nd. ed. 1990, $US24.95 plus $US2.50 p&p.

The National Archives and Records Service, Constitution Ave.,Washington DC 20408, houses millions of documents which could assist in genealogical research, and a Guide to these has been published – probably available in our main Reference Libraries, if not then obtainable on request along with a list of accredited researchers. There are Regional Archives Branches in Boston, New York, Philadelphia, Fort Worth, Denver, Los Angeles, Atlanta, Chicago, Kansas City, and Seattle. Addresses from the Administrator of the FFHS in exchange for sae or 3 IRCs.

The American equivalent to our British Library is the Library of Congress, (Genealogical Room), Thomas Jefferson Annex, Washington DC 20540.

The largest genealogical library in the world is located in Salt Lake City. Details of the service they can provide and a list of accredited researchers will be sent on request to the Family History Library, Church of Jesus Christ of Latter Day Saints (q.v.).

The US Government has required a census of the population to be taken every ten years since 1790 though until 1850 these recorded only names of the head of the household. Some states have done likewise though they usually appeared five years later than the Federal ones. The state censuses often show more detail of use to the genealogist. There are many census indexes available for various states for various years. See *State Census Records* by Ann S. Lainhart, 1992, $US17.95 and *Map Guide to the Federal Censuses, 1790-1920* by William Thorndale and William Dollarhide, GPC, reprint 1992, $US39.95 ($US2.50 p&p for one copy). Both Genealogical Publishing Co. Inc.

Where they survive and can be located (not always easy), valuable records are passenger lists – the earliest for Philadelphia dates from 1800, but most start in 1820. Some passenger lists have been published, enquire at your local library. Otherwise the Genealogical Publishing Co., Inc., and the Gale Research Co. are just two of the publishers who have catalogues available.

Federal homestead land records date from the 1860s and may give the location, the man's age, address, date and place of birth, wife's name and size of family. In the case of an immigrant we get details of the country of origin, with port and date of arrival. The latter information may make it easier to find the relevant passenger list.

See also PRO Records Information leaflet 34 *Land Grants in America and American Loyalists' Claims*.

American Wills Proved in London 1611-1775 by Peter Wilson Coldham, Genealogical Publishing Co.Inc., 1992. Will abstracts from the Prerogative Court of Canterbury of testators who include any reference to America. Not just those who lived and died in the New World yet left assets in England, but Americans who died in Europe, British Mariners who died in the colonies and Englishmen who left bequests to people in America.

UNIVERSITIES Much research has gone into producing a record of graduates at the Universities of Oxford and Cambridge: *Alumni Oxonienses 1500 to 1886*, 8 volumes by J. Foster. *Alumni Cantabrigienses* 10 volumes by J.A. Venn should be available in most large Reference Libraries.

There are similar publications for other old-established universities. For a list see *Registers of Universities, Colleges and Schools of Great Britain and Ireland* by P.M. Jacobs.

VACCINATION The Vaccination Act 1871 required registrars to make a monthly return of births and infant deaths to the Vaccination Officer. These records are very similar to the registers of birth and where extant should be in the CRO. Vaccination Registers listing the children, their ages, parishes and dates of vaccination exist from 1862 to 1948 but are closed to public inspection for 50 years. For further information read *Were They In The Union? Workhouse Administration and Records* by Marion Joy Lodey, Gen. Mag. Vol.20 No.4 (Dec 1980).

VALUATION OFFICE (FIELD BOOKS) The Finance Act (1909-1910) required the Inland Revenue to survey all property in the UK and ascertain its site value. Each unit of property was assigned an hereditament number which was marked for reference purposes on a set of record maps in much the same way as Tithe Apportionments and Maps were cross-referenced. To discover the correct number for the house you want to research you need to look at the Valuation Office Record Maps (IR 121/1-1R 135/9). The final record of the survey was written up in standard form and bound in volumes called Field Books which are arranged by hereditament numbers.

The following information on each property is usually included:-

(*a*) Names of owner and tenant (but not the occupier) and whether freehold, leasehold etc.

(*b*) Details of term and rental of tenancy.

(*c*) Area of property, date of erection of buildings, number of rooms, state of repair, liability for rates, insurance and repairs, date(s) of previous sale(s).

(*d*) Value of the whole property and the market value of the site excluding structures and vegetation.

(*e*) Sometimes they include a sketch plan of the property.

There is also another set of books called Domesday Books which include the names of the occupiers as well as the owners and tenants. These are to be found in CROs which may also have duplicates of the Record Maps. The PRO, has the Domesday Books for the City of London and for Paddington (IR 91).

See PRO Records Information leaflet 68 *Valuation Office: Records created under the Finance (1909-1910) Act*.

VERDERER He was an officer responsible for the preservation of the King's forest and the post probably dates back to the 11th century; the office was held for life. There were four Verderers to each forest and they were elected by freeholders. It is a term used in the south west for a petty constable.

VESTRY This was the governing body of the parish. There were two main kinds: Select Vestries (or Close Vestries) and Open Vestries. The former were not elected by parishioners but perpetuated by the co-option of new members. The latter were virtually general meetings of all the parishioners; they often proved unsatisfactory and were replaced in some cases by an elected Parish Committee. These also were sometimes called Select Vestries, which gives rise to some confusion.

VETERINARY SURGEON The address of the Veterinary History Society is 32 Belgrave Square, London SW1X 8QP.

VICAR An incumbent in receipt of smaller or vicarial tithes.

VICAR GENERAL A deputy of an archbishop or bishop.

VICTORIA COUNTY HISTORY see County History.

VICTORIAN SOCIETY This was founded in 1958 and its aim is to preserve the best of Victorian and Edwardian architecture, and also to study the art and history of the period. It is particularly concerned to protect important 19th and early 20th century buildings, both public and private, industrial monuments and historical areas. Further details about activities and membership can be obtained from the Society Headquarters, The Victorian Society, 1 Priory Gardens, Bedford Park, London W4 1TT.

VICTUALLERS' Licences see Alehouses.

VISITATIONS (Ecclesiastical). Periodic Inspections by a Bishop or Archdeacon covering both spiritual and temporal matters. These generated a substantial volume of records including lists of clergy, churchwardens, schoolmasters, charities etc. BTs were commonly sent in for the visitation. (For a more detailed explanation see Dorothy M. Owen, *The Records of the Established Church in England*, published by the British Record Association, 1970.) See also Heralds' Visitations.

VISITORS' BOOKS Always check at least those in churches used by ancestors. Someone else may be hunting them too. It is surprising how many cousins are found in this way!

WAGES see also Inflation. It is very hard to appreciate the changes in the value of money which have taken place in the last 400 years and to realise that a man leaving £20 in the 17th century was not poor! It may help to know the average weekly wages of day labourers which were (converted to decimal currency):

Early C17 – about 15p   Late C17 – about 20p
Early C18 – about 25p   Early C19 – about 50p   Early C2O – about 75p

In 1938-39 the average minimum agricultural wage was about £1.75.

See *How Much Is That Worth* by Lionel Munby, Phillimore (for BALH), 1989. Price £4.35 inc. p&p from Phillimore (q.v.). Definitely worth the money!

WAIFS AND STRAYS SOCIETY see Children's Societies.

WALES Research into some Welsh families can be quite straightforward, since the basic sources for England and Wales are the same: civil registration, the census, parish registers and wills may present few problems. The main difficulties lie in the poverty of records in many areas, the relatively late development of surnames (and lack of variety in those names) and in problems connected with the high proportion of ancestors who were nonconformists by the nineteenth century. Nevertheless, many family historians with only Welsh ancestry find their research satisfying, and these problems are not necessarily insuperable.

Welsh Family History: a Guide to Research, edited by John Rowlands and others, FFHS, has articles by specialist authors on many aspects of Welsh research and its problems. In particular the book addresses the need to understand the background to Welsh research: the social and cultural differences (including a different language), and how to cope with them.

Six family history societies cover Wales, and are members of the Federation of Family History Societies. Their current addresses appear on the back cover of FHN&D. They are based chiefly on the post-1974 Welsh counties: Clwyd (covering the pre-1974 counties of Denbigh, Flint and part of Merioneth), Dyfed (Cardigan, Carmarthen and Pembroke), Glamorgan (Glamorgan), Gwent (Monmouthshire), Gwynedd (Anglesey, Caernarfon and Merioneth), and Powys (Brecon, Montgomery and Radnor). In common with other societies, they produce journals with specialist articles and are involved in projects and indexes which help researchers find their way around large numbers of common names.

These FHSs form the Association of Family History Societies of Wales (AFHSW), the main purpose of which is to act as a forum for the exchange of ideas between the societies. The AFHSW cannot assist with individual research enquiries but will direct you to the most appropriate county society. Letters should be addressed c/o The AFHSW, The Benson Room, Birmingham and Midland Institute, Margaret Street, Birmingham B3 3BS. Please enclose sae or 3 IRCs when writing.

Many Welsh records will be found at the National Library of Wales, Aberystwyth, Dyfed SY23 3BU: these include wills, estate records, census microfilms, about fifty per cent of parish registers, bishops transcripts, many nonconformist records, maps, manuscript and printed pedigrees. NLW has copies of the OPCS (civil registration) indexes on microfiche, as well as the IGI for England and Wales. County Record Offices,

Welsh Ancestry

listed in *Welsh Family History,* cover each post-1974 county, with branches in the pre-1974 counties, and most hold parish registers, (including, in many cases, films of NLW holdings), parochial records, nonconformist registers and estate records, together with other genealogical sources. Useful and inexpensive leaflets are published describing the holdings of both NLW and CROs (in which there is a measure of overlap) and it is very important to find out what records are available for the area of research and, most important before a long journey, where they are kept.

A particularly useful book for locating parish registers is *Cofrestri Plwyf Cymru/ The Parish Registers of Wales* by C. J. Williams and J. Watts-Williams. It is the result of collaboration by the staffs of the National Library of Wales and the County Record Offices together with the SOG and is Volume 13 of the National Index of Parish Registers (q.v.). It is obtainable from the National Library of Wales, from any Welsh CRO, or from the SOG, price £6.95 plus p&p. A volume covering the nonconformist registers of Wales is in the late stages of preparation (details obtainable from NLW).

The Gibson Guides for Genealogists and Family Historians cover Wales and are invaluable for locating less common sources, both in Wales and in London.

Welsh Surnames by T. J. Morgan and Prys Morgan (University of Wales Press, 1985, price £9.95 paperback, £25 hardback, plus p&p) is an historical survey of Welsh surnames and includes surnames of Welsh origin found not only in Wales but beyond its borders, often in disguised or corrupted forms.

A bonus in Welsh research is that quite ordinary families today can often be connected to noble families in the past, recorded in the large number of Welsh pedigrees in manuscript and printed form. Michael Powell Siddons in *Printed and Manuscript*

Pedigrees in Welsh Family History provides the best guide to locating these. The same author has written *The Development of Welsh Heraldry* (NLW, Vol. I, 1991; Vols. II and III in preparation). Still valuable for these families is an article by Major Francis Jones, Wales Herald Extraordinary, *An Approach to Welsh Genealogy* (Transactions of the Honourable Society of Cymmrodorion, 1948).

See also *Researching Welsh Ancestry* by Sheila Rowlands, Feature Article, FHN&D, Vol.9 No.1 (April 1993).

WAPENTAKE Equivalent of a Hundred (q.v.) in some Midland and Northern Counties.

WAR MEMORIALS A general term used for the many ways in which those who fought and/or died during various conflicts are commemorated. The type of memorial varies from a simple tablet to a whole building and can be at national, local or individual level. Schools, places of work and of worship and special groups frequently made a commemoration of their members in some way. The most usual war memorials are to those who served and died in the two World Wars but there are also those to casualties of the Indian Mutiny, the South African wars, the Korean war etc. Some memorials are considered works of art in their own right (e.g. Sandham Memorial Chapel at Burghclere, now in the possession of the National Trust, with its 19 paintings by Stanley Spencer). The details of names on war memorials can vary from a simple list of initials and surname to full details of name, rank, number, regiment and place and date of death.

See *Monuments of War: How To Read a War Memorial* by Colin McIntyre, Robert Hale, 1990; and by the same author *War Memorials: A magnificent primary source,* FTM Vol.9 No.1 (Nov 1992). *At the Going Down of the Sun: British First World War Memorials* by Derek Boorman, William Sessions (York) Ltd, 1988. *On Boer War Memorials*, Anglo-Boer War Memorial Project, c/o 21 Bassano Street, East Dulwich, London SE22 8RU.

WAR MEMORIALS: NATIONAL INVENTORY OF A national project administered by the IWM to record the location and other details of all war memorials in the United Kingdom (including Channel Islands and the Isle of Man). Although names are not being comprehensively indexed they are being recorded for each memorial and a search can be made of a specific memorial if requested. Write to NIWM Co-ordinator, IWM, enclosing sae or 3 IRCs. The Co-ordinator will also be pleased to send details of how you can help with the project.

See *The National Inventory of War Memorials* by Catherine Moriarty, FTM Vol.7 No.1 (Nov 1990).

WARD Equivalent of a Hundred in parts of Northern England.

WARRIOR see Royal Navy.

WATCH AND WARD Men were appointed to 'police' the area under the supervision of the Constable. 'Watch' referred to night duty, and 'Ward' to daytime duties. Wrongdoers were arrested and placed in the care of the Constable.

WATER-GAVIL A rent paid for fishing in the lord's river.

WATERMEN AND LIGHTERMEN (COMPANY OF) Until the mid eighteenth century London Bridge or boat were the only means by which to cross the Thames.

Because of the potential difficulties this posed the Corporation of London was appointed Conservator of the Thames in 1193, its duties including the licensing of boat operators on the river. The Company of Watermen was formed in the latter half of the sixteenth century and they were joined by the Lightermen in 1700. Lightermen unloaded cargo from ships and carried it into port by lighter; they were formerly members of the Woodmongers' Company.

The company's influence on the Thames stretched from Gravesend to Windsor so that its members were often drawn from areas of some considerable distance from the City of London; since 1857 the western limit of jurisdiction has been Teddington Lock. The company has no livery – possibly because the freedom of the City that the liveried would enjoy would exempt them from impressment into the Navy.

The records of the company are at the Guildhall Library (q.v.) and contain a wealth of information. The trades of waterman and lighterman frequently continued through several generations of a family and so records can often be traced through a long span of years. Those admitted to the freedom of the company did so, until the late nineteenth century, exclusively through apprenticeship so it is best to begin a search for a freeman in those records.

The leaflet *Records of The Company of Watermen and Lightermen at Guildhall Library* gives detailed information on this company with a listing of the records available. The Library holds a number of published works on the company. Also of interest is Henry Mayhew's *London Labour and the London Poor*, which includes 19th century interviews with watermen and lightermen.

Any enquiries concerning records not held at the Guildhall should be addressed to The Clerk, Watermen's Hall, 16 St Mary at Hill, London EC2R 8EE.

Mr R. Cottrell, 19 Bellevue Road, Bexleyheath, Kent DA6 8ND, is compiling an index to the records held at the Guildhall Library; 1692-1908, comprising well in excess of 50,000 entries. Send sae or 2 IRCs for details and charges.

WEALD A term used mainly in Kent, Surrey and Sussex to describe wooded country.

WEAVER There was a London Livery Company. See *The London Weavers' Company, 1600 to 1970* by Alfred Plummer.

WESLEYAN METHODISTS see Methodists.

WEST INDIES see also Emigration. Microfilm copies of many West Indian parish and civil registers can be ordered through the LDS FHCs. See PRO Records Information leaflet 23 *Records of The American and West Indian Colonies before 1782*.

It is worth looking in the six volumes of *Directory of Scottish Settlers* by Dobson; a good percentage of these emigrants went to the West Indies.

Some of the following sources could be helpful with West Indies research. They were summarised in an article *West Indian Sources in England* by Anthony J. Camp in FTM Vol.4 No.1 (Nov 1987).

The Smith Collection at the SOG, 43 volumes, indexed and presented to the Society in 1913.

Jamaica: Material for family history – Gen. Mag. Vol.15 No.7 (Sep 1966) p.239. MI's (Review) Gen. Mag. Vol.15 No.11 (Sep 1967).

Sketch pedigrees of some early settlers in Jamaica , by Noel Livingstone, 1909.

MI's of Jamaica , Philip Wright, SOG, 1966.

See also *Jamaican research in Britain* by Charlotte Soares, FTM Vol.7 No.6 (April 1991)

Barbados: Genealogical sources in Gen. Mag. Vol.17 No.9 (March 1974). Jewish MI's in Barbados (Review) Gen. Mag. Vol.13 No.1 (March 1959).

Bahamas: Family History in Gen. Mag. Vol.18 No.4 (Dec 1975).

MI's of British West Indies, with historical and genealogical notes by J.B. Lawrence Archer, 1875.

MI's of the British West Indies , V.L. Oliver, 1927.

W.H. see Workhouse. A common abbreviation for 'Workhouse' on birth and death certificates.

WHEELWRIGHT *The Worshipful Company of Wheelwrights of the City of London, 1670 to 1970* by Eric Bennett, 1970 has very useful appendices which include lists of all the Masters and Clerks from 1670. See also Shire Publication *Village Wheelwright and Carpenter* .

WHITESMITH A maker of tin utensils – especially those used in dairying operations.

WILLS see also Bank, Emigration, Estate Duty, Kin, Probate, Servicemen's Wills, Somerset House and United States of America. Early in your researches, you should seek out copies of wills of your ancestors. They might well be described as a 'best buy' for the family historian, and can often contain a great deal of information to help you to piece together your family history, though it should be borne in mind that the majority of ordinary people did not leave wills.

An excellent introduction to the subject is *Affection Defying the Power of Death: Wills, Probate & Death Duty Records* by Jane Cox, FFHS, in *An Introduction to . . .* series.

Wills and Administrations in England and Wales from 1858 are at the Principal Probate Registry, Somerset House, The Strand, London WC2R 1LA. You may consult the Indexes without charge, and these are quite informative. We are given some facts about the deceased e.g. bachelor, with occupation, address, place of death, sometimes former place of residence, date of death, names of executors or administrators, their address and relationship (if any) to the deceased and value of estate. There is one set of volumes for each year. Sometimes the wills and administrations are in one alphabetical sequence, but they may be separated, with administrations at the end of the volumes. The District Probate Registries also have copies of these indexes which can be inspected by the public. Many have been deposited in local Reference Libraries or ROs.

For further reading see PRO Records Information leaflet 31 *Probate Records*, and *Somerset House Wills from 1858* by Eve McLaughlin, obtainable from FTM price £1.55 inc. p&p.

Wills may be viewed for 25p which is considerably cheaper than buying a death certificate; you can order photocopies of wills from 1858 from the Principal Probate Registry, at a modest cost. For postal enquiries Form RK1 can be obtained from Somerset House: a three year search costs £2. Once completed the form should be returned to York Probate Sub Registry, Duncombe Place, York YO1 2EA.

Prior to 1858, however, you do have to do some searching for wills. There are two excellent books to guide you. They are: *Wills and Their Whereabouts* by Anthony J. Camp and *Wills and Where to Find Them* by Jeremy Gibson. Most Reference Libraries will have copies of these. In 1980 the latter author published *A Simplified Guide to Probate Jurisdictions: Where to Look for Wills*. It is a condensation of his earlier book and quite inexpensive; obtainable from the FFHS. The McLaughlin Guide *Wills before 1858* is a very useful summary of the subject. Remember that you will rarely find a will of a married woman prior to the passing of the Married Women's Property Act of 1882. Prior to that all her possessions were legally the property of her husband. Widows and spinsters, however, may have left wills.

WINDOW TAX A tax imposed in 1696; replaced the Hearth Tax (q.v.). Each household paid a basic 2 shillings; those with between 10 and 20 windows paid a further 8 shillings. After 1747 households with between 10 and 14 windows paid 6 pence per window on top of the old basic 2 shillings and those with between 15 and 19 paid 9 pence; those above that paid one shilling per window. In 1825 all houses with fewer than 8 windows were exempted. The tax was abolished in 1851. Scotland was exempted altogether in 1707. To avoid payment of the tax some owners of property bricked up their windows. What records survive – and there are not many – will be found in local ROs but there are very few names listed.

See *The Window Tax: A survey of Holdings in Britain* by Mervyn Medlycott, Gen. Mag. Vol.24 No.5 (March 1993), *Land and Window Tax Assessments* by Jeremy Gibson, Mervyn Medlycott and Dennis Mills, FFHS, and *The Administration of the Window & Assessed Taxes 1696-1798* by W.R.Ward, Phillimore, 1963.

WOODWARD Keeper of wood or forest having charge of the growing timber.

WOOLLEN – Burials in, see Parish Registers.

WOOLMEN See *A History of the Woolmen's Company* by H.B.A.Bruyne, 1968.

WORKHOUSE Gilbert's Act, 1782, authorised parishes to combine for the purpose of setting up a 'proper' workhouse, but many parishes continued to act independently in dealing with their poor. Then, in 1834, the Poor Law Amendment Act compelled parishes to unite into groupings called 'Unions', whose responsibility it was to deal with the poor. Institutions to house the poor, known as workhouses, were set up. The administration was in the hands of Boards of Guardians.

Workhouse records, usually to be found in CROs or local Reference Libraries, are worth examination if one has 'lost' an ancestor as he may have ended his days in such a place. It should be remembered that many workhouses were used as hospitals until well into the 20th century and unexpected people died there. (Often seen abbreviated to 'WH' on birth or death certificates.)

An article entitled *Were They 'In The Union'?* by Marion Joy Lodey appeared in Gen. Mag. Vol.20 No.4 (Dec 1980). An extended version, re- titled *The Ins and Outs of the Workhouse* appeared as a series of articles in FTM Vol.2 Nos.2, 3 & 4 (Jan-Feb/Mar-Apl/May-June 1986).

See *The Workhouse System 1834-1929* by M.A. Crowther, Univ. of Georgia Press, 1982 (ITP 1983).

WORLD WAR I and WORLD WAR II see Army etc. HMSO have published *The Second World War: A Guide to Documents in the Public Record Office,* 1993, price £10.95.

WORLDWIDE FAMILY HISTORY Records of foreign ancestry in some countries has been dealt with under separate headings where relevant. Useful sources of information will be found in the following publications.

Worldwide Family History by Noel Currer-Briggs, published by Routledge & Kegan Paul, 1982. Price £9.95. This book deals with the problems of tracing ancestry of immigrants from countries overseas. In addition to European countries it covers Russia and the Balkans, Islam, China and Japan and South Africa. It sets out as succinctly as possible the way in which people of foreign descent can begin tracing their ancestors. In addition to source material and contact addresses history and background information is given in many instances.

In Search of Your European Roots: a complete guide to tracing your ancestors in every country in Europe by Angus Baxter, Genealogical Publishing Co. Inc., 1985, paperback, indexed. Price $US12.95. Not dissimilar in concept to *Worldwide Family History* it includes one or two countries (e.g. Malta and Cyprus) not covered by that publication. It also has chapters on the Mormon Records and European Jewish Records and a section on the Li-Ra-Ma Collection of 'Russian' consular records in the National Archives of Canada emphasising how useful these can be to Canadians and Americans with Armenian, Estonian, Finnish, Georgian, Jewish, Latvian, Lithuanian, Mennonite, Polish, Russian and Ukranian ancestors who came to Canada before 1922.

Genealogical Research Directory: National and International by Keith A.Johnson & Malcolm R. Sainty. Published annually (see Directories: Genealogical).

WRIGHT A constructor e.g. a millwright, wheelwright, cartwright etc. Hence the many surnames ending with this word.

YEOMAN Man holding (not necessarily owning) and cultivating small landed estate.

APPENDIX I

Public Record Office, Chancery Lane, London WC2A 1LR (Tel: 0181 876 3444)

Public Record Office, Ruskin Avenue, Kew, Richmond, Surrey TW9 4DU (Tel: as above)

The Chancery Lane building will cease functioning as the PRO at the end of 1996 and all the records will be transferred to Kew, but there will be a Central London Microfilm Reading Room.

RECORDS AT KEW

Admiralty	(ADM)
Advisory, Conciliation & Arbitration Service	(CW)
Agriculture, Fisheries & Food, Ministry of	(MAF)
Air Ministry	(AIR)
Aviation, Ministry of	(AVIA)
British Council	(BW)
British Railways Board	(AN)
British Transport Docks Board	(BR)
British Transport Historical Records	(RAIL) (ZLIB) (ZPER) (ZSPC)
Cabinet Office	(CAB)
Captured Enemy Documents	(GFM)
Central Midwives Board	(DV)
Certification Office for Trade Unions and Employers' Associations	(CL)
Civil Aviation Authority	(DR)
Civil Service Commission	(CSC)
Civil Service Department	(BA)
Civil Service Pay Research Unit	(CSPR)

Coal Industry Social Welfare Organisation	(BX)
Colonial Office	(CO)
Consumer Council	(AJ)
Copyright Office	(COPY)
Countryside Commission	(COU)
Crown Agents For Overseas Governments and Administrations	(CAOG)
Customs & Excise, Board of	(CUST)
Defence, Ministry of	(DEFE)
Defunct Temporary Bodies	(BS)
Development Commission	(D)
Dominions Office and Commonwealth Relations Office	(DO)
Education & Science, Department of	(ED)
Educational Technology Council for	(EA)
Energy, Department of	(EG)
Environment, Department of the	(AT)
Environmental Pollution, Royal Commission on	(CY)
Exchequer and Audit Department	(AO)
Exports Credits Guarantee Department	(ECG)
Foreign and Commonwealth Office	(FCO)
Foreign Office	(FO)
Forestry Commission	(F)
Forfeited Estates, Commissioners of	(FEC)
Friendly Societies, Registry of	(FS)
General Nursing Council	(DT)

General Register Office	(RG)
except Census Returns (RG 9-	
RG 12), Non-Parochial Registers	
and records (RG 4-RG 8) and	
certain other registers and	
associated papers (RG 18, 19 27, 30-37, 43)	
Government Actuary's Department	(ACT)
Health and Safety Commission	(EF)
and Executive	
Health & Social Security,	(BN)
Department of	
Health, Ministry of	(MH)
Health Visitors, Council for	(DW)
the Education and Training of	
Historical Manuscripts	(HMC)
Commission	
Home Office	(HO)
except Census Returns	
(HO 107)	
Housing & Local Government,	(HLG)
Ministry of	
Hudson's Bay Company	(BH)
Microfilm. Access by	
permission of the Company only	
Information, Central Office of	(INF)
Inland Revenue, Board of	(IR)
except Estate Duty Registers	
(IR 26 and IR 27)	
International Organisations	(DG)
records of International	
Whaling Commission and	
Western European Union	
Irish Sailors' and Soldiers'	(AP)
Land Trust	
Iron and Steel Board	(BE)
Joint Board of Clinical	(DY)
Nursing Studies	
Labour, Ministry of	(LAB)

Land Registry	(LAR)
Lands Tribunal	(LT)
Law Commission	(BC)
Local Government Boundary Commission for England	(AX)
Local Government Boundary Commission for Wales	(DD)
Location of Offices Bureau	(AH)
London Gazette	(ZJ)
Lord Chancellor's Office	(LCO)
Manpower Services Commission	(ET)
Meteorological Office	(BJ)
Metropolitan Police Office	(MEPO)
Monuments, Ancient & Historic in Wales and Monmouthshire, Royal Commission on	(MONW)
Monuments, Historic (England), Royal Commission on	(AE)
Munitions, Ministry of	(MUN)
National Academic Awards, Council for	(DB)
National Assistance Board	(AST)
National Coal Board	(COAL)
National Debt Office	(NDO)
National Dock Labour Board	(BK)
National Incomes Commission	(NICO)
National Insurance Audit Department	(NIA)
National Playing Fields Association	(CB)
National Ports Council	(DK)
National Savings, Department for	(NSC)
National Service, Ministry of	(NATS)

Northern Ireland Office	(CJ)
Occupational Pensions Board	(DM)
Ordnance Survey Department	(OS)
Overseas Development, Ministry of and Overseas Development Administration	(OD)
Parliamentary Boundary Commission	(AF)
Parliamentary Papers (ZHC)	(ZHL)
Parole Board	(BV)
Paymaster General's Office	(PMG)
Pensions & National Insurance, Ministry of	(PIN)
Pensions Appeal Tribunal	(BF)
Post Office Users National Council	(DJ)
Power, Ministry of	(POWE)
Price Commission	(CX)
Prime Minister's Office	(PREM)
Prison Commission	(PCOM)
Public Building & Works Ministry of	(WORK)
Public Health Laboratory Services Board	(DN)
Public Record Office all classes except transcripts (PRO 31) and certain classes of gifts and deposits (PRO 30)	(PRO)
Public Trustee Office	(PT)
Public Works Loan Board	(PWLB)
Racial Equality, Commission for	(CK)
Reconstruction, Ministry of	(RECO)

Remploy Ltd	(BM)
Research Institutes	(AY)
Royal Fine Art Commission	(BP)
Royal Mint	(MINT)
Scientific & Industrial Research, Department of	(DSIR)
Sessional Papers, House of Commons, House of Lords	(ZHC) (ZHL)
Social Security Commissioners	(CT)
Stationery Office	(STAT)
Supply, Ministry of	(SUPP)
Tithe Redemption Commission	(TITH)
Trade, Board of	(BT)
Transport, Ministry of	(MT)
Treasury	(T)
Tribunals, Council on	(BL)
United Kingdom Atomic Energy Authority	(AB)
University Grants Committee	(UGC)
Value Added Tax Tribunals	(CV)
Wallace Collection	(AR)
War Office	(WO)
Welsh Office	(BD)

RECORDS AT CHANCERY LANE

Admiralty, High Court of	(HCA)
Alienation Office	(A)
Assize, Clerks of	(ASSI)
Bankruptcy, Court of	(B)
Central Criminal Court	(CRIM)
Chancery	(C)
Chester, Palatinate of	(CHES)
Common Pleas, Court of	(CP)

County Courts	(AK)
Crown Estate Commissioners	(CRES)
Delegates, Court of	(DEL)
Durham, Palatinate of	(DURH)
Exchequer	(E)
Auditors of Land Revenue	(LR)
General Register Office Census Returns (RG 9- RG 12), Non-Parochial Registers and records (RG 4-RG 8) and certain other registers and associated papers (RG 18, 19, 27, 30-37, 43) only	(RG)
Home Office Census Returns 1841 and 1851 only	(HO 107)
Inland Revenue, Board of Estate Duty Registers only (IR 27)	(IR 26)
Judicature, Supreme Court of	(J)
Justices Itinerant	(JUST)
King's Bench, Court of	(KB)
King's Bench Prison	(PRIS)
Lancaster, Duchy of	(DL)
Lancaster, Palatinate of	(PL)
Land Revenue Record Office	(LRRO)
Law Officers' Department	(LO)
Lord Chamberlain's Department	(LC)
Lord Steward's Department	(LS)
Palace Court	(PALA)
Peveril, Court of the Honour of	(PEV)
Prerogative Court of Canterbury	(PROB)
Privy Council, Judicial Committee of the	(PCAP)

Privy Council Office	(PC)
Privy Purse Office	(PP)
Privy Seal Office	(PSO)
Public Prosecutions, Director of	(DPP)
Public Record Office Transcripts (PRO 31) and certain classes of gifts and deposits (PRO 30)	(PRO)
Queen Anne's Bounty	(QAB)
Requests, Court of	(REQ)
Signet Office	(SO)
Special Collections	(SC)
Star Chamber, Court of	(STAC)
State Paper Office	(SP)
Treasury Solicitor	(TS)
Wales, Principality of	(WALE)
Wards & Liveries, Court of	(WARD)

Some classes of records may require several days notice before production: please enquire beforehand.

APPENDIX II

PUBLIC RECORD OFFICE LEAFLETS

These leaflets give summaries of information on particular records or specific subjects, and are available on request from the PRO Chancery Lane or from the PRO Kew. See Appendix I for addresses.

They are being gradually divided and re-numbered into four series entitled Records Information, General Information, Census Information and Family Fact Sheet. As a result the numerical sequence of the listings does not necessarily follow through; where leaflets are quoted in the text every care has been taken to ensure accuracy and the numbers should correspond with this list. When requesting a leaflet quote full title as well as series and number.

Records Information Series

2. Admiralty Records as Sources for Biography and Genealogy
3. Operational Records of the Royal Navy, 1660-1914
4. Sources for the History of the Jacobite Risings of 1715 and 1745
5. Records of the Registrar General of Shipping and Seamen
6. Operational Records of the British Army in the First World War
7. Operational Records of the British Army in the Second World War
8. Records of HM Coastguards
11. Records of the Royal Irish Constabulary
12. Chancel Repairs
13. Air Records as Sources for Biography and Family History
14. Family History in England and Wales: Guidance for Beginners
15. Dockyard Employees: Documents in the PRO
16. Operational Records of the Royal Air Force
17. Patents and Specifications for Inventions, and Patent Policy: sources in the PRO
22. Records of the Foreign Office from 1782
23. Records of the American and West Indian Colonies before 1782
24. English Local History: A Note for Beginners
26. Assizes Records
28. Genealogy before the Parish Registers
29. Royal Warrant Holders and Household Servants: An Introduction to the records of the Lord Chamberlain's and Lord Steward's Departments
30. Chancery Proceedings (Equity Suits)
31. Probate Records
32. Records relating to Railways
33. The American Revolution: Guides and Lists to documents in the PRO
34. Land Grants in America and American Loyalists' Claims
38. Change of Name

General Information Series

Family Fact Sheet

Census Information

APPENDIX III

UNITS OF THE BRITISH ARMY

THE BRIGADE OF GUARDS

Raised		Became
1656	1st Foot Guards	The Grenadier Guards
1650	2nd Foot Guards	The Coldstream Guards
1660	3rd Foot Guards	The Scots Guards
1901		The Irish Guards
1915		The Welsh Guards

THE HOUSEHOLD CAVALRY

1660	1st Life Guards
1660	2nd Life Guards
*	Royal Horse Guards (The Blues)

* The only Cavalry Regiment to trace its descent from the Parliamentary Army of Cromwell.

THE ROYAL REGIMENT OF ARTILLERY

*	The Royal Garrison Artillery
1716	The Royal Field Artillery
1793	The Royal Horse Artillery

* Dates its foundation from the early years of the Hundred Years' War and established as a permanent force in 1716.

THE CAVALRY

1685	1st (Kings) Dragoon Guards
1727	2nd Dragoon Guards (Queen's Bays)
1746	3rd (Prince of Wales's) Dragoon Guards
1697	4th (Royal Irish) Dragoon Guards
1788	5th (Princess Charlotte of Wales's) Dragoon Guards
1685	6th Dragoon Guards (Carabiniers)
1688	7th (Princess Royal's) Dragoon Guards
1661	1st (Royal) Dragoons
1681	2nd Dragoons (Royal Scots Greys)
1685	3rd (King's Own) Hussars
1685	4th (Queen's Own) Hussars
1689	5th (Royal Irish) Lancers

1689	6th	(Inniskilling) Dragoons
1689	7th	Queen's Own) Hussars
1693	8th	(King's Royal Irish) Hussars
1697	9th	(Queen's Royal) Lancers
1697	10th	(Prince of Wales's Own Royal) Hussars
1697	11th	(Prince Albert's Own) Hussars
1697	12th	(Prince of Wales's Royal) Lancers
1697	13th	Hussars
1697	14th	(King's) Hussars
1759	15th	(The King's) Hussars
1759	16th	(The Queen's) Lancers
1759	17th	(Duke of Cambridge's Own) Lancers
1759	18th	(Queen Mary's Own) Hussars
1759	19th	(Queen Alexandra's Own Royal) Hussars
1759	20th	Hussars
1858	21st	(Empress of India's) Lancers

INFANTRY OF THE LINE

1633	1st	The Royal Scots (Lothian Regiment)
1661	2nd	The Queen's (Royal West Surrey Regiment)
1665	3rd	The Buffs (East Kent Regiment)
1680	4th	The King's Own (Royal Lancaster Regiment)
1674	5th	The Northumberland Fusiliers
1673	6th	The Royal Warwickshire Regiment
1685	7th	The Royal Fusiliers (City of London Regiment)
1685	8th	The King's (Liverpool Regiment)
1685	9th	The Norfolk Regiment
1685	10th	The Lincolnshire Regiment
1685	11th	The Devonshire Regiment
1685	12th	The Suffolk Regiment
1685	13th	Prince Albert's (Somerset Light Infantry)
1685	14th	The Prince of Wales's Own (The West Yorkshire Regiment)
1685	15th	The East Yorkshire Regiment
1688	16th	The Bedfordshire Regiment
1688	17th	The Leicestershire Regiment
1684	18th	The Royal Irish Regiment
1688	19th	Alexandra, Princess of Wales's Own (Yorkshire Regiment)
1688	20th	The Lancashire Fusiliers (was the East Devonshire Regiment)
1678	21st	The Royal Scots Fusiliers (was the Royal North British Regiment)
1689	22nd	The Cheshire Regiment
1689	23rd	The Royal Welch Fusiliers
1689	24th	The South Wales Borderers (was 2nd Warwickshire Regiment)
1689	25th	The King's Own Scottish Borderers

1688	26th	The Cameronians (Scottish Rifles)
1689	27th	The Royal Inniskilling Fusiliers
1694	28th	The Gloucestershire Regiment (was the North Gloucestershire Regiment)
1694	29th	The Worcestershire Regiment
1702	30th	The East Lancashire Regiment (was the Cambridgeshire Regiment)
1702	31st	The East Surrey Regiment (was the Huntingdonshire Regiment)
1702	32nd	The Duke of Cornwall's Light Infantry
1702	33rd	The Duke of Wellington's (West Riding Regiment)
1702	34th	The Border Regiment (was the Cumberland Regiment)
1701	35th	The Royal Sussex Regiment (was The Prince of Orange's Own)
1701	36th	2nd Battalion The Worcestershire Regiment (was the Herefordshire Regiment)
1702	37th	The Hampshire Regiment (was the North Hampshire Regiment)
1702	38th	The South Staffordshire Regiment (was 1st Staffordshire Regiment)
1702	39th	The Dorsetshire Regiment
1717	40th	The Prince of Wales's Volunteers (South Lancashire Regiment) (was 2nd Somersetshire Regiment)
1719	41st	The Welch Regiment
1739	42nd	The Black Watch (Royal Highlanders)
1741	43rd	The Oxfordshire & Buckinghamshire Light Infantry (was the Monmouthshire Light Infantry)
1741	44th	The Essex Regiment (was the East Essex Regiment)
1741	45th	The Sherwood Foresters(Nottinghamshire & Derbyshire Regiment) (was the Nottinghamshire Sherwood Foresters Regiment)
1741	46th	2nd Battalion Duke of Cornwall's Light Infantry (was the South Devonshire Regiment)
1741	47th	The Loyal North Lancashire Regiment (was the Lancashire Regiment)
1741	48th	The Northamptonshire Regiment
1743	49th	Princess Charlotte of Wales's (Royal Berkshire Regiment) (was the Hertfordshire Regiment)
1755	50th	The Queen's Own (Royal West Kent Regiment)
1755	51st	The King's Own (Yorkshire Light Infantry)
1755	52nd	2nd Battalion Oxfordshire & Buckinghamshire Light Infantry (was the Oxfordshire Light Infantry)
1755	53rd	The King's (Shropshire Light Infantry) (was the Shropshire Regiment)
1755	54th	2nd Battalion The Dorsetshire Regiment (was the West Norfolk Regiment)
1755	55th	2nd Battalion The Border Regiment (was the Westmorland Regiment)

1755	56th	2nd Battalion The Essex Regiment (was the West Essex Regiment)
1755	57th	The Duke of Cambridge's Own (Middlesex Regiment) (was the West Middlesex Regiment)
1755	58th	2nd Battalion The Northamptonshire Regiment (was the Rutlandshire Regiment)
1755	59th	2nd Battalion East Lancashire Regiment (was 2nd Nottinghamshire Regiment)
1755	60th	The King's Royal Rifle Corps (was the Royal American Regiment)
1758	61st	2nd Battalion Gloucestershire Regiment (was the South Gloucestershire Regiment)
1758	62nd	The Duke of Edinburgh's (Wiltshire Regiment)
1758	63rd	The Manchester Regiment (was the West Suffolk Regiment)
1758	64th	The Prince of Wales's (North Staffordshire Regiment)
1758	65th	The York and Lancaster Regiment (was the 2nd Yorkshire (North Riding) Regiment)
1758	66th	2nd Battalion The Royal Berkshire Regiment (was the Berkshire Regiment)
1758	67th	2nd Battalion The Hampshire Regiment (was the South Hampshire Regiment)
1758	68th	The Durham Light Infantry (was 2nd Royal Welch Fusiliers)
1758	69th	2nd Battalion The Welch Regiment (was the South Lincolnshire Regiment)
1758	70th	2nd Battalion The East Surrey Regiment (was the Surrey Regiment)
1777	71st	The Highland Light Infantry
1777	72nd	The Seaforth Highlanders (Ross-shire Buffs)
1780	73rd	2nd Battalion The Black Watch
1787	74th	2nd Battalion The Highland Light Infantry
1787	75th	The Gordon Highlanders (was the Stirlingshire Regiment)
1787	76th	2nd Battalion The Duke of Wellington's Regiment
1787	77th	2nd Battalion The Middlesex Regiment (was the East Middlesex Regiment)
1793	78th	2nd Battalion The Seaforth Highlanders (was the Ross-shire Buffs)
1793	79th	The Queen's Own Cameron Highlanders
1793	80th	2nd Battalion The South Staffordshire Regiment. (was the Staffordshire Volunteers)
1793	81st	2nd Battalion The North Lancashire Regiment (was the Loyal Lincolnshire Volunteers)
1793	82nd	2nd Battalion The South Lancashire Regiment(was the Prince of Wales's Volunteers)
1793	83rd	The Royal Irish Rifles (was the County of Dublin Regiment)
1793	84th	2nd Battalion York & Lancaster Regiment
1793	85th	2nd Battalion The Shropshire Light Infantry (was the Buckinghamshire Volunteers)

1793	86th	2nd Battalion The Royal Irish Rifles (was the Royal County Down Regiment)
1793	87th	Princess Victoria's (Royal Irish Fusiliers)
1793	88th	The Connaught Rangers
1793	89th	2nd Battalion The Royal Irish Fusiliers (was the Princess Victoria's)
1794	90th	2nd Battalion The Cameronians (was the Perthshire Volunteers Light Infantry)
1794	91st	Princess Louise's (Argyll and Sutherland Highlanders) (was the Argyllshire Regiment)
1794	92nd	2nd Battalion The Gordon Highlanders
1800	93rd	2nd Battalion The Argyll & Sutherland Highlanders (was the Sutherland Fencibles)
-	94th	2nd Battalion The Connaught Rangers
1832	95th	2nd Battalion Nottinghamshire & Derbyshire Regiment (was the Derbyshire Regiment)
1824	96th	2nd Battalion The Manchester Regiment
1824	97th	2nd Battalion Queen's Own (Royal West Kent Regiment) (was the Earl of Ulster's Regiment)
1824	98th	2nd Battalion The North Staffordshire Regiment
1824	99th	2nd Battalion The Wiltshire Regiment (was the Duke of Edinburgh's Lancashire Regiment)
1858	100th	The Prince of Wales Leinster Regiment (was the Royal Canadians)
1652*	101st	The Royal Munster Fusiliers (was the Royal Bengal Fusiliers)
1748*	102nd	The Royal Dublin Fusiliers (was the Royal Madras Fusiliers)
1661*	103rd	2nd Battalion The Royal Dublin Fusiliers (was the Royal Bombay Fusiliers)
1652*	104th	2nd Battalion The Royal Munster Fusiliers (was the Bengal Fusiliers)
1839*	105th	2nd Battalion The Yorkshire Light Infantry (was the Madras Light Infantry)
1839*	106th	2nd Battalion The Durham Light Infantry (was the Bombay Light Infantry)
1800		The Rifle Brigade (The Prince Consort's Own) (4 Battalions)

* Date when raised in India

1717	The Corps of Royal Engineers

THE SERVICES

1794	The Army Service Corps
1873	The Royal Army Medical Corps
1796	The Army Veterinary Corps
1858	The Army Chaplain's Department
(1455)	The Army Ordnance Department
1878	The Army Pay Department
1880	The Corps of Military Police
1644	The Royal Marines (originally raised as part of the Army but later transferred to the Royal Navy)

APPENDIX IV

CHAPMAN COUNTY CODES

Before 1974: 1975 for Scotland

England (ENG) before 1974:

BDF	Bedfordshire	YKS	Yorkshire
BRK	Berkshire	ERY	Yks East Riding
BKM	Buckinghamshire	NRY	Yks North Riding
CAM	Cambridgeshire	WRY	Yks West Riding
CHS	Cheshire	IOW	Isle of Wight
CON	Cornwall	IOM	Isle of Man
CUL	Cumberland		
DBY	Derbyshire		
DEV	Devonshire	**Wales (WLS):**	
DOR	Dorset		
DUR	Durham	AGY	Anglesey
ESS	Essex	BRE	Brecknockshire
GLS	Gloucestershire	CAE	Caernarvonshire
HAM	Hampshire	CGN	Cardiganshire
HEF	Herefordshire	CMN	Carmarthenshire
HRT	Hertfordshire	DEN	Denbighshire
HUN	Huntingdonshire	FLN	Flintshire
KEN	Kent	GLA	Glamorgan
LAN	Lancashire	MER	Merionethshire
LEI	Leicestershire	MON	Monmouthshire
LIN	Lincolnshire	MGY	Montgomeryshire
LND	London	PEM	Pembrokeshire
MDX	Middlesex	RAD	Radnorshire
NFK	Norfolk		
NTH	Northamptonshire	**Scotland (SCT):**	
NBL	Northumberland		
NTT	Nottinghamshire	ABD	Aberdeenshire
OXF	Oxfordshire	ANS	Angus
RUT	Rutland	ARL	Argyllshire
SAL	Shropshire	AYR	Ayrshire
SOM	Somerset	BAN	Banffshire
STS	Staffordshire	BEW	Berwickshire
SFK	Suffolk	BUT	Bute
SRY	Surrey	CAI	Caithness
SSX	Sussex	CLK	Clackmannanshire
WAR	Warwickshire	DFS	Dumfriesshire
WES	Westmorland	DNB	Dunbartonshire
WIL	Wiltshire	ELN	East Lothian
WOR	Worcestershire	FIF	Fife
			Forfarshire (see Angus)

INV	Inverness-shire		MEA	Meath
KCD	Kincardineshire		MOG	Monaghan
KRS	Kinross-shire		OFF	Offaly (Kings)
KKD	Kirkcudbrightshire			Queens (see Leix)
LKS	Lanarkshire		ROS	Roscommon
MLN	Midlothian		SLI	Sligo
MOR	Moray		TIP	Tipperary
NAI	Nairnshire		WAT	Waterford
OKI	Orkney Isles		WEM	Westmeath
PEE	Peebleshire		WEX	Wexford
PER	Perthshire		WIC	Wicklow
RFW	Renfrewshire			
ROC	Ross & Cromarty			
ROX	Roxburghshire			

N. Ireland (NIR):

ANT	Antrim
ARM	Armagh
DOW	Down
FER	Fermanagh
LDY	Londonderry
TYR	Tyrone

SEL	Selkirkshire
SHI	Shetland Isles
STI	Stirlingshire
SUT	Sutherland
WLN	West Lothian
WIG	Wigtownshire

Channel Islands (CHI):

ALD	Alderney
GSY	Guernsey
JSY	Jersey
SRK	Sark

Ireland (IRL):

CAR	Carlow
CAV	Cavan
CLA	Clare
COR	Cork
DON	Donegal
DUB	Dublin
GAL	Galway
KER	Kerry
KID	Kildare
KIK	Kilkenny
	Kings (see Offaly)
LET	Leitrim
LEX	Leix (Queens)
LIM	Limerick
LOG	Longford
LOU	Louth
MAY	Mayo

England (ENG) after 1974:

AVN	Avon
BDF	Bedfordshire
BRK	Berkshire
BKM	Buckinghamshire
CAM	Cambridgeshire
CHS	Cheshire
CLV	Cleveland
CMA	Cumbria
CON	Cornwall
DBY	Derbyshire
DEV	Devonshire
DOR	Dorset
DUR	Durham
ESS	Essex
GLS	Gloucestershire
GTM	Greater Manchester
HAM	Hampshire
HWR	Hereford & Worcester
HRT	Hertfordshire
HUM	Humberside
KEN	Kent
LAN	Lancashire
LEI	Leicestershire

LIN	Lincolnshire	
LND	London	
MSY	Merseyside	
NFK	Norfolk	
NTH	Northamptonshire	
NBL	Northumberland	
NTT	Nottinghamshire	
OXF	Oxfordshire	
SAL	Shropshire	
SOM	Somerset	
STS	Staffordshire	
SFK	Suffolk	
SRY	Surrey	
SXE	East Sussex	
SXW	West Sussex	
TWR	Tyne & Wear	
WAR	Warwickshire	
WMD	West Midlands	
WIL	Wiltshire	
NYK	North Yorkshire	
SYK	South Yorkshire	
WYK	West Yorkshire	
IOM	Isle of Man	
IOW	Isle of Wight	

Wales (WLS): after 1974

CWD	Clwyd
DFD	Dyfed
GNT	Gwent
GWN	Gwynedd
MGM	Mid Glamorgan
POW	Powys
SGM	South Glamorgan
WGM	West Glamorgan

Scotland (SCT): after 1975

BOR	Borders
CEN	Central Region
DGY	Dumfries & Galloway
FIF	Fife
GMP	Grampian
HLD	Highland
LTN	Lothian
OKI	Orkney Isles
SHI	Shetland Isles
STD	Strathclyde
TAY	Tayside
WIS	Western Isles

APPENDIX V

MAPS SHOWING COUNTIES AND THEIR BOUNDARIES
BEFORE AND AFTER 1974/1975

England and Wales
Scotland
Ireland

COUNTIES OF ENGLAND & WALES

(Before 1st April 1974)

COUNTIES OF ENGLAND & WALES

(After 1st April 1974)

NORTHUMBERLAND

TYNE & WEAR

DURHAM

CLEVELAND

CUMBRIA

NORTH YORKSHIRE

ISLE OF MAN

HUMBERSIDE

LANCASHIRE

WEST YORKSHIRE

GREATER MANCHESTER

SOUTH YORKSHIRE

MERSEYSIDE

LINCOLNSHIRE

CHESHIRE

DERBY

NOTTINGHAM

CLWYD

GWYNEDD

STAFFORD

LEICESTER

NORFOLK

SALOP (SHROPSHIRE)

WEST MIDLANDS

POWYS

WARWICK

NORTHAMPTON

CAMBRIDGE

SUFFOLK

HEREFORD AND WORCESTER

BEDFORD

DYFED

GLOUCESTER

OXFORD

BUCKINGHAM

HERTFORD

ESSEX

WEST GLAMORGAN

MID GLAMORGAN

GWENT

GREATER LONDON

SOUTH

AVON

BERKSHIRE

KENT

WILTSHIRE

SURREY

EAST SUSSEX

SOMERSET

HAMPSHIRE

WEST SUSSEX

DORSET

DEVON

CORNWALL

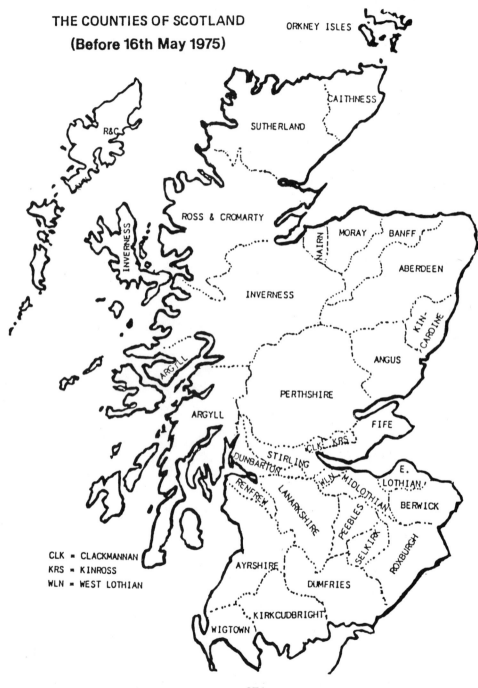

THE COUNTIES OF SCOTLAND
(Before 16th May 1975)

ORKNEY ISLES

CAITHNESS

SUTHERLAND

R&C

ROSS & CROMARTY

NAIRN
MORAY
BANFF

ABERDEEN

INVERNESS

INVERNESS

KIN-CARDINE

ARGYLL

ANGUS

PERTHSHIRE

ARGYLL

FIFE

STIRLING

CLK KRS

DUNBARTON

RENFREW

LANARKSHIRE

WLN MIDLOTHIAN

E. LOTHIAN

BERWICK

PEEBLES

SELKIRK

ROXBURGH

CLK = CLACKMANNAN
KRS = KINROSS
WLN = WEST LOTHIAN

AYRSHIRE

DUMFRIES

KIRKCUDBRIGHT

WIGTOWN

274

THE REGIONS, DISTRICTS &
ISLAND COUNCILS OF SCOTLAND

(After 16th May 1975)

ORKNEY ISLANDS

WESTERN ISLES

HIGHLANDS

GRAMPIAN

TAYSIDE

FIFE

CENTRAL

LOTHIAN

STRATHCLYDE

BORDERS

DUMFRIES AND
GALLOWAY

THE COUNTIES of IRELAND

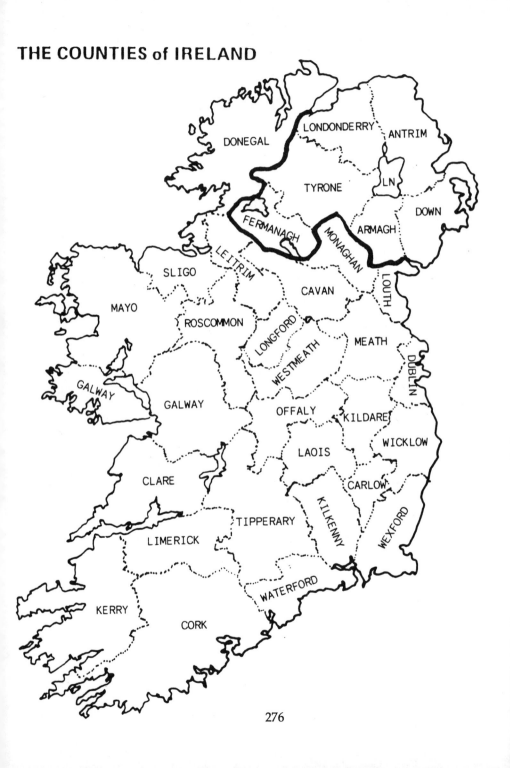

THE LOCAL GOVERNMENT ADMINISTRATIVE DISTRICTS of NORTHERN IRELAND
after 1974
(Note: The historic 6 Counties remained unchanged)

KEY

1. Carrickfergus
2. Newtown Abbey
3. Belfast
4. Castlereagh
5. N.Down

RECORD REPOSITORIES IN CENTRAL LONDON

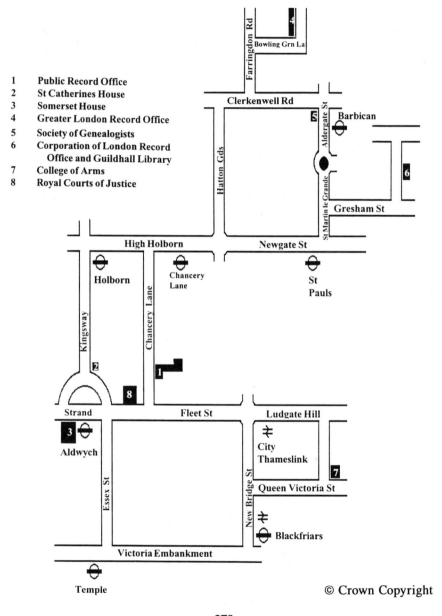

1 Public Record Office
2 St Catherines House
3 Somerset House
4 Greater London Record Office
5 Society of Genealogists
6 Corporation of London Record
   Office and Guildhall Library
7 College of Arms
8 Royal Courts of Justice

© Crown Copyright

INDEX